Conten

C000257782

OpenOffice.org

Greg Perry

SAMS
Teach
Yourself

Sams Publishing, 800 East 96th Street, Indianapolis, Indiana 46240 USA

Sams Teach Yourself OpenOffice.org All in One

International Standard Book Number: 0-672-32618-3

Library of Congress Catalog Card Number: 2003109346

Printed in the United States of America

First Printing: August 2004

07   06   05   04   4   3   2   1

Trademarks

All terms mentioned in this book that are known to be trademarks or service marks have been appropriately capitalized. Sams Publishing cannot attest to the accuracy of this information. Use of a term in this book should not be regarded as affecting the validity of any trademark or service mark.

Warning and Disclaimer

Every effort has been made to make this book as complete and as accurate as possible, but no warranty or fitness is implied. The information provided is on an "as is" basis. The author and the publisher shall have neither liability nor responsibility to any person or entity with respect to any loss or damages arising from the information contained in this book or from the use of the CD or programs accompanying it.

Bulk Sales

Sams Publishing offers excellent discounts on this book when ordered in quantity for bulk purchases or special sales. For more information, please contact

U.S. Corporate and Government Sales

1-800-382-3419

corpsales@pearsontechgroup.com

For sales outside of the U.S., please contact

International Sales

international@pearson.com

Acquisitions Editor
Betsy Brown

Development Editor
Jonathan Steever

Managing Editor
Charlotte Clapp

Project Editor
George Nedeff

Copy Editor
Bart Reed

Indexer
Heather McNeill

Proofreader
Jessica McCarty

Technical Editor
Jason Perkins

Publishing Coordinator
Vanessa Evans

Multimedia Developer
Dan Scherf

Designer
Gary Adair

Page Layout
Michelle Mitchell

Table of Contents

About the Author

Greg Perry is a speaker and a writer on both the programming and application sides of computing. He is known for his skills at bringing advanced computer topics to the novice's level. Perry has been a programmer and a trainer since the early 1980s. He received his first degree in computer science and a master's degree in corporate finance. Perry has sold more than 2 million computer books worldwide, including such titles as *Digital Video with Windows XP in a Snap, Sams Teach Yourself Windows XP in 24 Hours, Sams Teach Yourself Visual Basic 6 in 21 Days*, as well as the phenomenal bestseller *Sams Teach Yourself Office 2003 in 24 Hours*. He also writes about rental property management, social and political issues, creates and manages Web sites, loves to travel, and enjoys home life with his lovely wife Jayne and their two fluffy dogs Casper and Zucchi.

Dedication

Joseph Farah, a man I've admired for a long time, became my long-distance friend two years ago. I'll be forever grateful that our paths crossed. Joseph, a book dedication is the least I can do to express my gratitude for all you do for America.

Acknowledgments

I want to send special thanks to Betsy Brown for putting up with me on this project. She was the driving force behind the work, and I cannot express how glad I am that she wanted me to do this project.

Jason Perkins had to wade through all the problems I put into this book's first draft. Any problems that might be left are all mine. In addition, the other staff and editors on this project, namely Jon Steever, George Nedeff, and Bart Reed, made this book better than it otherwise could be.

Finally, I want to express massive thanks to readers who keep coming back to my titles. Teaching you how to do something is nothing but a pleasure for me.

I promise to keep you abreast of vital OpenOffice.org information you need to know even *after* you finish this book! How will I do that? Simple—I'll deliver myself to you past the last page.

To claim information that is rightfully yours as this book's reader, just send a blank email to me at Stuff@OOOGuy.com and—after a quick opt-in confirmation from you—I promise to do the following:

- Gift to you a wealth of free reports and tutorials worth hundreds of dollars elsewhere! These bonuses sent to you over a few weeks time walk you through tons of hands-on OpenOffice.org tips, traps, and techniques that show you how to make OpenOffice.org do even more work for you.

- Give OpenOffice.org newcomers, current users, and advanced gurus immediate solutions and sometimes even insider trade secrets throughout these reports and tutorials.

- Answer as many questions as possible about OpenOffice.org while sharing new suggestions, hot ideas, and sizzling ways to maximize OpenOffice.org.

You'll be able to cancel the further delivery of these tutorials, tip sheets, and other bonus gifts at any time. I'll *never* give away, rent, or sell your email to anybody or any other list for any reason. (If you don't receive something within a few minutes of sending the blank email to me at Stuff@OOOGuy.com, you may need to add that email to your incoming address book or ISP's whitelist when possible.)

Send that email now so you don't lose out on these bonus items available only through this book. Then turn the page to begin learning one of the most amazing software applications ever given away completely free!

—Greg Perry
  Stuff@OOOGuy.com

We Want to Hear from You!

As the reader of this book, *you* are our most important critic and commentator. We value your opinion and want to know what we're doing right, what we could do better, what areas you'd like to see us publish in, and any other words of wisdom you're willing to pass our way.

You can email or write me directly to let me know what you did or didn't like about this book—as well as what we can do to make our books stronger.

Please note that I cannot help you with technical problems related to the topic of this book, and that due to the high volume of mail I receive, I might not be able to reply to every message.

When you write, please be sure to include this book's title and author as well as your name and phone or email address. I will carefully review your comments and share them with the author and editors who worked on the book.

Email: consumer@samspublishing.com

Mail: Mark Taber
            Associate Publisher
            Sams Publishing
            800 East 96th Street
            Indianapolis, IN 46240 USA

Reader Services

For more information about this book or others from Sams Publishing, visit our Web site at www.samspublishing.com. Type the ISBN (excluding hyphens) or the title of the book in the Search box to find the book you're looking for.

1

✔ Start Here

Set your sights high because OpenOffice.org helps you work more efficiently and more effectively. OpenOffice.org offers an integrated set of tools that includes a word processor, a spreadsheet, a presentation program, and a drawing program. OpenOffice.org is a pleasure to use, and its price is stunning.

Did I mention that OpenOffice.org's price is stunning?

OpenOffice.org costs you nothing. It's free. Absolutely free. No strings attached. Free as in no money down and no payments afterwards. Free as in, if you bought 25 copies it wouldn't cost you any more than if you bought one.

When you hear OpenOffice.org's price, you'll probably say to yourself, "It must be worth what they charge for it." For most things, you'd be correct. You'd be wrong here. OpenOffice.org is jam-packed full of features that make even the most loyal Microsoft Office fan cringe when he or she pays hundreds of dollars every year or two for yet another Office upgrade.

NOTE

Wal-Mart became the nation's leading retailer based on price competition. But even Wal-Mart cannot compete with OpenOffice.org!

What OpenOffice.org Is and What OpenOffice.org Does

OpenOffice.org is a set of integrated programs maintained by the OpenOffice.org team that you download from the OpenOffice.org Web site. Talk about name branding!

NOTE

This book assumes you use a Windows operating system environment, although OpenOffice.org works uniformly on any supported operating system. So even if you work on a Solaris or Macintosh computer, you'll feel right at home here as you learn OpenOffice.org along with Windows readers.

NOTE

OpenOffice.org is often abbreviated *OOo*.

Originally, a German company named *StarDivision* created *StarOffice* in the mid-1980s. Sun Microsystems purchased StarOffice in 1999 and added features, lowered the price (to *free*), and changed the name to OpenOffice.org. OpenOffice.org works on the Windows, Linux, Macintosh, FreeBSD, and Solaris operating systems too. Current versions of OpenOffice.org share most features and an almost identical interface with Sun Microsystem's StarOffice package, a suite offered for sale as another alternative to Microsoft Office.

OpenOffice.org offers integrated software tools that are powerful yet easy to learn and use. Offices large and small can use OpenOffice.org–based applications for many of their day-to-day computer needs, as can families and home-based businesses that want simple but robust writing and analysis tools for their computers.

With each new revision, OpenOffice.org takes you to the next step with an improved user interface and more solid features that help you become more productive in the way you use the OpenOffice.org products. The OpenOffice.org Web site is loaded with information, technical support, white papers, forums, press information, upcoming events, and manuals that give you support and background information about OpenOffice.org.

With OpenOffice.org's help, you'll get your work done better and more quickly. OpenOffice.org automates many computing chores and provides tools that work in unison and share data between them.

There can be no hiding the fact that OpenOffice.org is a direct competitor to Microsoft Office. On a price/performance comparison, OpenOffice.org mangles Microsoft Office, even though Microsoft Office is more powerful than OpenOffice.org, at rare times more stable (depending on which Microsoft Office updates you've applied recently and how stable they are), and is better refined in certain tasks. For example, adjusting graphic images in a multicolumned document or on an Impress presentation isn't quite as simple as the same task in Word or PowerPoint. Yet, those fine-tuned advances in Microsoft Office come at a price, and the price is steep compared to the free OpenOffice.org system.

Lots of politics exist between those in the OpenOffice.org camp and those in the Microsoft Office camp. Throughout this book, I'll do my best to display my encouragement and strong support for OpenOffice.org, its concepts, and its power. At the same time, I don't want to enter the political debate between those on the OpenOffice.org side and those on the Microsoft Office side. I see no reason why both cannot coexist, especially given the ease with which OpenOffice.org works with Microsoft Office files.

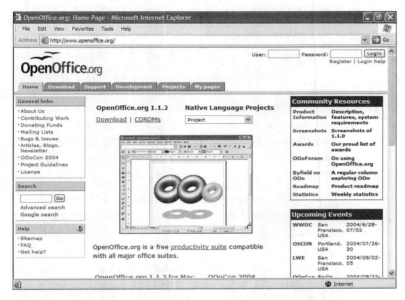

The OpenOffice.org Web site dedicates itself to helping you use OpenOffice.org better.

What's in OpenOffice.org?

OpenOffice.org contains the most needed applications—a word processor, a spreadsheet program, a presentation program, a drawing program—and more inside a single system. OpenOffice.org is designed so that its programs work well together, and although you might not need every program in OpenOffice.org, you can easily share information between any OpenOffice.org programs that you do want to use. Program collections such as OpenOffice.org are often called program *suites.*

NOTE

One of OpenOffice.org's primary strengths (in addition to its free price tag) is its strong support for Microsoft Office files. OpenOffice.org opens, converts, and lets you edit virtually any document that you or someone else created in Word, PowerPoint, or Excel. When you move to OpenOffice.org, you don't lose work created elsewhere.

KEY TERM

Suite—An application that contains multiple programs, each of which performing a separate function. These programs generally work well together, with each one easily reading the other programs' data.

NOTE

Calc includes database capabilities also, so you can easily organize, sort, analyze, collect, and report from a massive repository of data, such as your company's inventory.

The following is a quick overview of the primary OpenOffice.org programs:

- **Writer**—A word processor with which you can create notes, memos, letters, school papers, business documents, books, newsletters, and even Web pages.

- **Calc**—An electronic spreadsheet program with which you can create graphs and worksheets for financial and other numeric data. After you enter your financial data, you can analyze it for forecasts, generate numerous what-if scenarios, and publish worksheets on the Web.

- **Impress**—A presentation graphics program with which you can create presentations for seminars, schools, churches, Web pages, and business meetings. Not only can Impress create the presentation overheads, but it can also create the speaker's presentation notes and print compacted audience handouts.

- **Draw**—A powerful drawing program that you use to create drawings, utilize predesigned shapes, develop logos, and even design Web page graphics.

In addition to these four major programs, OpenOffice.org includes several other features, such as an HTML editor for Web page design and editing as well as a mathematical formula editor that you use to create complex math equations (see **30** **Use Mathematical Formulas in Documents**).

All the OpenOffice.org programs share common features and common menu choices. The next two figures show an Impress editing session and a Draw editing session. Even though the Impress screen shows a slide from a presentation and the Draw screen shows a flier being created, the surrounding interface elements are extremely similar. The menus, toolbars, and status bar buttons are almost identical for both programs. When you learn one OpenOffice.org program, you are well on your way to knowing quite a bit about all the other OpenOffice.org programs, too.

When you design and edit presentations with Impress, you'll recognize the interface because OpenOffice.org programs share a similar interface.

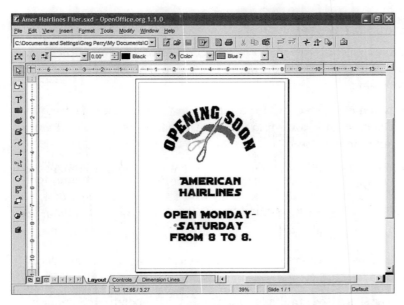

Draw's menu, toolbars, and status bar elements are virtually identical to those of other OpenOffice.org programs, especially those of Impress.

In addition to working with familiar interfaces in the OpenOffice.org products, you can insert data that you create in one program into another program within the OpenOffice.org suite. If you create a financial table with Calc, for instance, you can put the table in a Writer document that you send to your board of directors and embed the table in an Impress presentation to stockholders. Once you learn how to use any program in the OpenOffice.org suite, you will be far more comfortable using all the others because of the common interface.

OpenOffice.org Is Versatile

The OpenOffice.org products are general purpose, meaning that you can customize applications to suit your needs. You can use Calc as your household budgeting program, for example, and also as your company's interactive balance-sheet system.

You can integrate OpenOffice.org into your networked system. This way, OpenOffice.org provides useful features whether you are networked to an intranet, to the Internet, or to both. You can share OpenOffice.org information with others across the network. OpenOffice.org fits well within the online world by integrating Internet access throughout the OpenOffice.org suite.

Introducing Writer

When you need to write any text-based document, look no further than Writer. Writer is a word processor that supports many features, including the following:

- Automatic corrections for common mistakes as you type using special automatic-correcting tools that watch the way you work and adapt to your needs

- Templates and styles that make quick work of your document's formatting

- Advanced page layout and formatting capabilities

- Numbering, bulleting, bordering, and shading tools

- Integrated grammar and spelling tools to help ensure your document's accuracy

- Newsletter-style multiple columns, headers, footers, and endnotes in your publications

- Graphical tools that enable you to emphasize headers, draw lines and shapes around your text, and work with imported art files in your documents

The next figure shows a Writer editing session. Even though Writer is a word processor, you can see from the figure that it supports advanced formatting, layout, and graphics capabilities so that you can produce professional documents, covers, and title pages using Writer.

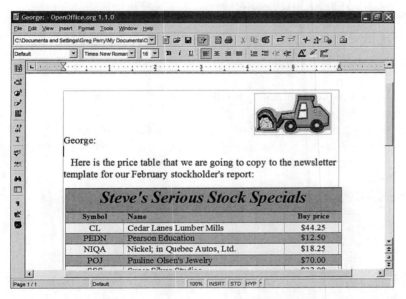

Writer easily handles text, graphics, and advanced formatted layout of any document you wish to create.

Introducing Calc

Calc's primary goal is to help you organize and manage financial information such as income statements, balance sheets, and forecasts. Calc is an electronic spreadsheet program that supports many features, including the following:

- Automatic cell formatting

- Automatic worksheet computations that enable you to generate a worksheet that automatically recalculates when you make a change to a portion of the worksheet

- Built-in functions, such as financial formulas, that automate common tasks

- Automatic row and column completion of value ranges with automatic completion of ranges of data

- Formatting tools that let you turn worksheets into professionally produced reports

- Powerful data sorting, searching, filtering, and analyzing tools that enable you to turn data into an organized collection of meaningful information

- Powerful charts and graphs that can analyze your numbers and turn them into simple trends

The following figure shows a Calc editing session. The user is entering income statement information. If you have worked with other worksheet programs, you might be surprised at how fancy Calc can get. Calc's automatic formatting capabilities make creating advanced worksheets easy.

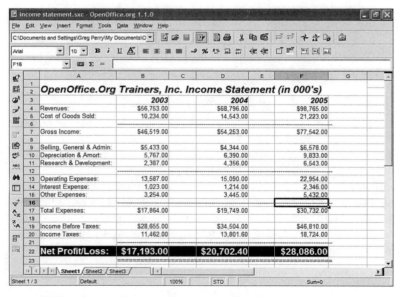

Calc helps you create, edit, and format numeric worksheets.

Introducing Impress

Have you ever presented a talk and longed for a better approach to messy overhead slides? Have you seen the pros wow their audiences with eye-catching, professional computerized presentations? With Impress, there is simply no reason why you shouldn't be wowing your audiences as well. Professional presentations are now within your reach.

Impress supports many features, including the following:

- The use of the AutoPilot feature to generate presentations automatically

- Sample design templates that provide you with a fill-in-the-blank presentation

- A screen display that imitates how a slide projector displays slides
- Complete color and font control of your presentation slides
- A collection of art files, icons, and sounds that you can embed to make your presentations more attention-getting
- Numerous transitions and fades between presentation slides to keep your audience's attention
- The capability to save presentations as Web pages that you can then present on the Internet

The next figure shows an Impress editing session. The user is getting ready for a presentation and has only a few minutes to prepare six color slides for the meeting. With Impress, a few minutes are more than enough time!

Introducing Draw

With Draw, you can generate drawings and graphics. Draw supports all popular graphics formats, both for importing images and for the drawings you want to save. You can create freeform drawings and you can use Draw's predesigned shapes to create more modern artwork, such as a commercial artist may require.

Here are just a few features that Draw supports:

- The use of predefined geometric shapes to include in your drawings

- The ability to create and use built-in three-dimensional shapes to add depth to your images

- The ability to adjust the perceived light source on the objects you draw to add realism

- The ability to convert two-dimensional text and graphics to three dimensions

- The ability to logically connect objects so that when you move or resize one, other objects adjust accordingly

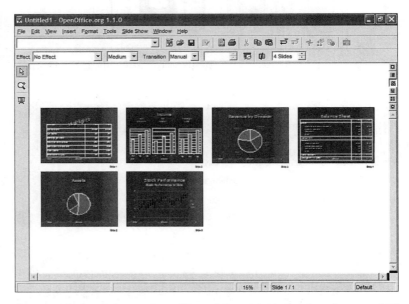

Impress helps you create, edit, and format professional presentations.

The next figure shows a Draw editing session. The drawing contains both text and graphics. Draw's ability to combine both text and graphics makes it great for businesses that need to design brochures, ads, fliers, logos, and other artwork necessary throughout the world.

No Database—Except There Is a Database!

Unlike Microsoft Office's Access database, OpenOffice.org doesn't offer a separate, standalone database management program. Nevertheless, Calc includes several built-in database features, and you will be able to use Calc for a surprising amount of database work.

With Draw, you can create impressive drawings and include text with them.

Calc's database capabilities include the following:

- The ability to store large amounts of data

- Filters that let you see only the data you need right now

- Groupings on subtotals, totals, and grand totals that enable you to see decision-making data such as company, division, and individual store totals

- The ability to import data from outside databases such as Microsoft Access

The next figure shows a Calc database session. As you can see, Calc can manage a lot of data. Although you see all the data here, the drop-down list boxes provide filters for you to limit the data you want to see, as well as other tools to sort and group the data in a more meaningful way, depending on your needs.

Click to Filter on Country Name

Let Calc manage your database.

Installing OpenOffice.org

TIP

As the owner of this book, you don't need to download OpenOffice.org because it's included with this book's CD-ROM!

For most users, installing OpenOffice.org takes little more than an Internet connection and some time (and more than some time if you don't have a high-speed broadband connection such as DSL or a cable modem). Basically, one needs only to go to the OpenOffice.org Web site, download OpenOffice.org, and install it onto a computer. Users will be creating Impress presentations and Draw drawings soon after that.

To download OpenOffice.org, you only need to surf to the OpenOffice.org Web site. One of the first and most prominent links on the page is the **Download** link. To download OpenOffice.org, you click this **Download** link to request OpenOffice.org.

Once the download completes, the user needs only click the **Open** button on the **Download complete** dialog box, and OpenOffice.org begins its installation. Even though you don't have to download OpenOffice.org, you'll need to remember where you read these instructions so when an updated version is released, you'll know where to get it. You download and install new versions the same way as you would download and install the very first installation.

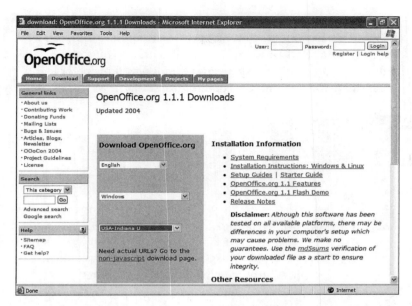

Once a user tells OpenOffice.org what the target computer system is, the download process begins.

To uninstall OpenOffice.org (why would you want to?), select **Add/Remove Programs** from the Windows **Control Panel** dialog box. Locate the entry for OpenOffice.org and click **Remove**.

Starting OpenOffice.org

Generally, you'll start one of the OpenOffice.org applications by clicking your Windows **Start** toolbar button and doing one of the following:

- Select **Open Document** from the **OpenOffice.org** menu option and select a file from the list that appears in the **Open** dialog box. The files will be compatible with the OpenOffice.org programs. If, for example, you select a Writer document, Writer automatically opens and loads that document so you can edit the contents. If you select a Calc spreadsheet, Calc starts and loads that spreadsheet file. Of course, you can also select a Microsoft Office Word, Excel, or PowerPoint file and either Writer, Calc, or Impress, respectively, will open that file. You then can save the file into a converted OpenOffice.org format if you wish.

NOTE

The installation routine may request that you restart your computer after the installation finishes to set up all the files properly.

NOTE

You can edit Microsoft Office data files without converting them to OpenOffice.org format because OpenOffice.org can read and write Office files.

- Select the **OpenOffice.org** menu from your Windows **Programs** menu and select from the list of OpenOffice.org programs. If, for example, you select **Drawing**, Draw will start and offer you a blank drawing area where you can begin a new drawing or load an existing drawing into the editing area.

You can start any OpenOffice.org program from your Windows menu.

 NOTE

As **132** Associating OpenOffice.org and Microsoft Office Files demonstrates, you can assign Microsoft Office data filename extensions to OpenOffice.org so that when you click on a DOC file inside a Windows Explorer window, Writer and not Word will automatically open the file.

- From any Windows Explorer–like window that displays a file listing, select any OpenOffice.org file and the appropriate OpenOffice.org program automatically launches with that file loaded.

- From any OpenOffice.org program, you can start any other OpenOffice.org program by selecting **File**, **Open** and selecting a file. If, for example, you are writing a letter inside Writer and remember that you have to update a spreadsheet, you don't need to start Calc. Instead, from Writer's **File**, **Open** menu, and select the spreadsheet to open. Calc will open and load that spreadsheet for you. Writer remains open with your document loaded for when you're ready to return to it.

Options for All

All of the OpenOffice.org programs provide their own set of options so that you can customize the program to suit the way you work. For example, if you are using Draw on an older computer, your drawing has to update when you add or change a shape on your screen. If you have one or more three-dimensional objects in the drawing, the screen update can be very slow. Therefore, Draw offers an option whereby you can display an image icon and frame, instead of the image itself, everywhere the image appears in your drawing. Once you've positioned all your images onto the drawing area, you can turn the graphic display back on to review the drawing.

 NOTE

The images always print even if you've chosen to suppress their display on the screen.

Throughout this book's tasks, you'll find descriptions of each OpenOffice.org program's options that you can modify. For example, **105** **Set Draw Options** explains all the Draw options and why you may want to change some of them.

From any individual OpenOffice.org program, you can change the overall OpenOffice.org options as well. These global options determine how all the OpenOffice.org programs behave and appear as you use OpenOffice.org. Because these general options are generic across all the OpenOffice.org programs, this would be a good time to review them. Doing so not only makes sense because these options are global in scope and the tasks in the chapters that follow are specific to individual OpenOffice.org programs, but also reading about the general OpenOffice.org options will give you an early feel of what OpenOffice.org is all about.

Table 1.1 describes the 12 general OpenOffice.org option categories from which you can select. From any OpenOffice.org program, you only need to select **Tools**, **Options** from the menu and click the plus sign to expand the **OpenOffice.org** entry to see the numerous global option categories.

Global OpenOffice.org Option Categories

Click to Expand

Review the OpenOffice.org option categories.

TABLE 1.1   OpenOffice.org Option Categories

OpenOffice.org Option Category	Explanation
OpenOffice.org	Describes general settings for all OpenOffice.org programs, such as your user information, path settings, and accessibility settings.
Load/Save	Describes how you want to load and save documents. For example, you can request that a backup copy of the previous version of any document is saved every time you save a file.
Language Settings	Defines the default language used by the OpenOffice.org programs as well as how you want writing aids to work, such as correcting the misuse of upper- and lowercase characters.
Internet	Describes how you want OpenOffice.org to interact with the Internet, such as which search engines you want OpenOffice.org to use.
Text Document	Describes Writer's primary options (see **1 Set Writer Options**]).
HTML Document	Describes how you want OpenOffice.org to interpret various HTML data, such as tables and background color defaults.
Spreadsheet	Describes Calc's primary options (see **38 Set Calc Options**).
Presentation	Describes Impress's primary options (see **80 Set Impress Options**).
Drawing	Describes Draw's primary options (see **105 Set Draw Options**).
Formula	Describes how OpenOffice.org prints and formats Math formulas (see **30 Use Mathematical Formulas in Documents**).
Chart	Describes basic chart color settings for charts you insert in documents.
Data Sources	Describes general settings for external data sources you use in OpenOffice.org documents and tables.

A New Kind of Mouse Click

OpenOffice.org supports a new kind of mouse click. In addition to the regular click with your left mouse button, the right-click, and the double-click, OpenOffice.org uses the *long click* for some selections. The **Main** toolbar (described in the next section) is where you'll use the long click the most to display toolbars that fly out from it.

Toolbar Eventually Appears

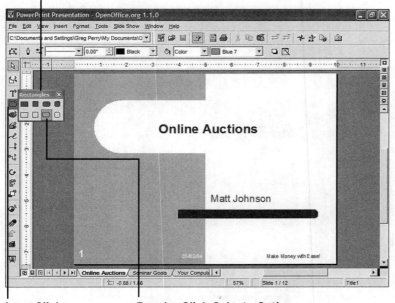

Long Click   **Regular Click Selects Option**

Sometimes OpenOffice.org requires a long click before an option or toolbar appears.

OpenOffice.org Toolbars

OpenOffice.org contains several toolbars, many of which are similar across all the OpenOffice.org programs. You'll use some more than others, however, and some change depending on the program you're using at the time.

TIP

Select from the **View**, **Toolbars** menu option to display and hide specific toolbars.

KEY TERM

Floating toolbar—A small toolbar that most often appears when you long-click a button on the **Main** toolbar.

In the previous section, you saw the **Main** toolbar in action when you learned about the long mouse click. The **Main** toolbar is a new kind of toolbar that doesn't have an equivalent in many other Windows programs. The **Main** tool (assuming you've chosen not to hide it) is the toolbar that resides on the left edge of your screen, left of the vertical ruler if the vertical ruler is showing. Often, when you long-click to select a button on the **Main** toolbar, another toolbar called a *floating toolbar* will appear at that location, and you then choose an option from the floating toolbar by clicking one of the buttons.

Floating Toolbar

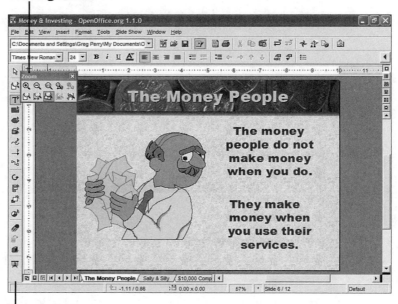

Main Toolbar

The Main toolbar is the toolbar you'll most likely select from as you use OpenOffice.org programs.

Table 1.2 describes the remaining toolbars available to you. The **Function** and **Object** toolbars are far more common and used throughout all the OpenOffice.org programs, whereas the "Formula" and **Hyperlink** toolbars are used only in specific instances. The "Formula" toolbar is generally only helpful when using Calc (see **52** **Enter Calc Functions**). The **Hyperlink** toolbar is most useful if you elect to work within OpenOffice.org's Web page editor (not covered in this book) to create, edit, and design Web pages.

TABLE 1.2 OpenOffice.org's Toolbars

Toolbar Name	Description
Function	Provides quick access to common functions, such as file opening, saving, printing, copying, cutting, pasting, undoing, and redoing. In addition, the **Function** toolbar provides one-click access to the **Navigator** and **Gallery** windows so you don't have to select from menus to show and hide these items.
Object	Offers formatting options, such as font name, font size, and bold, italics, and underlining. Depending on the program, the **Object** toolbar's buttons can change dramatically. For example, when you select a shape in Draw, the **Object** toolbar changes to show the edit points within that shape (see **110** **Draw from Scratch** for more information about edit points and how to use them).
Hyperlink	Enables you to type Web addresses and search the Internet using keywords.
Formula	Provides a way for you to enter formulas and functions in Calc spreadsheets and displays background formulas that produce values that show in the cells.

The following figure shows you where the most common toolbars—the **Function** bar, the **Object** bar, and the **Main** bar—are located.

NOTE

OpenOffice.org toolbars are also called *bars* in the online help. Therefore, the **Function** toolbar is also referred to as the **Function** bar.

TIP

You can turn any fixed toolbar into a floating toolbar, which you can drag elsewhere and resize. Hold **Ctrl** and double-click any blank spot within the toolbar to turn that toolbar into a floating toolbar. To return the floating toolbar back to its fixed position, hold **Ctrl** and double-click any blank spot within the toolbar once again.

Ctrl+Double-Clicking Makes the Toolbar Float **Function Toolbar**

Object Toolbar

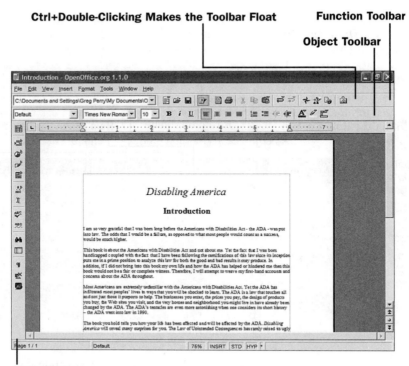

Main Toolbar

KEY TERM

Context-sensitive help—An automated system that looks at what you're currently doing and provides assistance for that particular menu, button, or command.

The Main toolbar is the toolbar you'll most likely select from as you use OpenOffice.org programs (the Hyperlink and Formula bars are not shown but are available from the View menu if you need them).

Getting Help

Any time you need help, press **F1** to produce a *context-sensitive help* screen.

KEY TERM

Hyperlinks—Text that's usually underlined in help screens (and Web pages, too) that you can click to navigate to other areas, such as when you want to learn more about the topic mentioned in the help text.

OpenOffice.org is surprisingly accurate at displaying the help you need when you need it. For example, suppose you're selecting from the **Tools** menu and you want to know what the **AutoCorrect** command does. Simply select **Tools** and move your mouse to the **AutoCorrect/ AutoFormat** option. Without clicking to trigger that option, press **F1** with the option still highlighted, and OpenOffice.org opens a help window that provides help on the **AutoCorrect** feature. Throughout most of OpenOffice.org's help screens, you'll find many *hyperlinks* that take you to other areas within the help system for more detailed assistance on topics related to the **AutoCorrect** menu option.

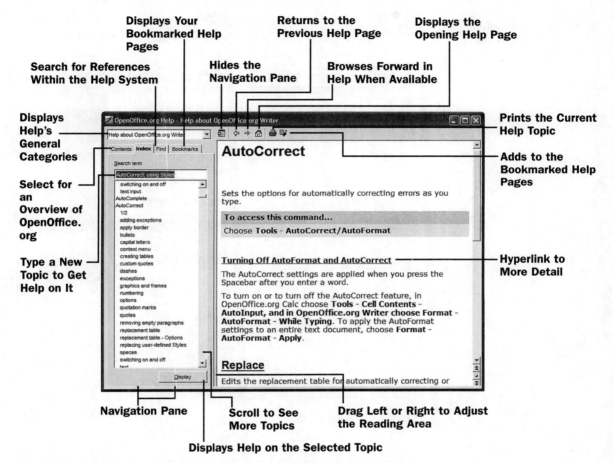

OpenOffice.org's help screens provide context-sensitive help for whatever topic you request.

In addition to the traditional help screens, OpenOffice.org provides three more kinds of help tools, described next. You can display or hide any of these help elements from the **Help** menu of any OpenOffice.org program:

NOTE

The Help Agent works a lot like Microsoft Office's animated *Clippit* assistant but is far less obtrusive and annoying!

- **Help Agent**—Displays a small window in the lower-right corner of your OpenOffice.org program when a task you're currently performing might be better done another way or when additional information about what you're doing may be of some assistance to you. If you click the Help Agent's window, the extra help appears in a window that you can read for more details.

- **Tips**—Also called *ToolTips* in Windows terminology, these are names that pop up in hovering description boxes over toolbar buttons and other areas of your screen that tell you the name or purpose for a particular object.

- **Extended Tips**—Display a description of menus and icons when you hover your mouse pointed over these objects.

Turns Help Agent On or Off

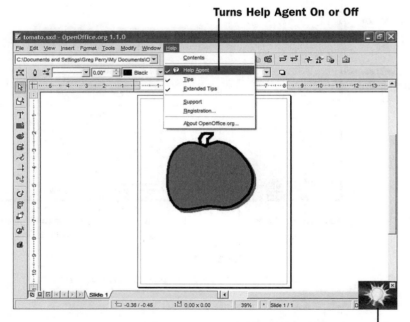

Click to See Help Agent's Advice

The Help Agent offers advice as you use OpenOffice.org programs.

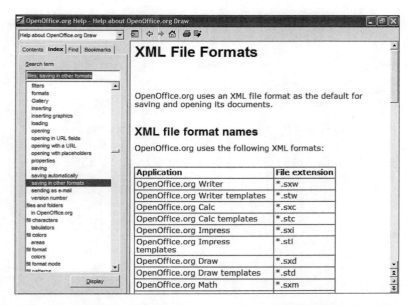

Help Agent produces this help screen when you click the Help Agent window while saving files; this help lets you know the file types available to you.

The help that OpenOffice.org provides is always customizable on your part. For example, not only can you turn off the entire Help Agent, if you leave the Help Agent on but ignore its offered advice three times in a row in a particular situation, the Help Agent stops offering that advice. You can always reset the Help Agent and restart this advice again by clicking the **Reset** button inside the OpenOffice.org **Option**'s **General** dialog box.

PART I

Writing Words with Writer

IN THIS PART:

2

Learning Writer's Basics

IN THIS CHAPTER:

1 Set Writer Options
2 Create a New Document
3 Open an Existing Document
4 Type Text into a Document
5 Edit Text
6 Move Around a Document
7 Find and Replace Text
8 Check a Document's Spelling
9 Print a Document

Writer is a full-featured word processor that you can use to produce notes, reports, newsletters, brochures, and just about anything that requires text and perhaps graphics as well. If you want to do something in Writer, Writer probably offers a way to do it.

In spite of all its bells and whistles, Writer's primary goal is to get text into a document. Hardly any word processor does that as easily as Writer (or as cheaply!). This chapter gets you started if you are new to Writer. You'll master the basic text-entering and document-navigation skills.

NOTE

Start Writer by selecting **Text Document** from the OpenOffice.org **Window** menu.

1 Set Writer Options

See Also

→ **2** Create a New Document

→ **4** Type Text into a Document

→ **5** Edit Text

NOTE

All options are available for all OpenOffice.org programs at all times. For example, you can control the display of a grid in Impress from Writer, and you can request that Draw print all drawings in black and white from within Calc.

Not everybody works the same way, so not every Writer user wants to use Writer the same way. By setting some of Writer's many options, you will make Writer conform to the way you like to do things. For example, you may want Writer to hide its horizontal scrollbar so you get more space on your screen for text. If so, Writer has an option to display or hide the horizontal scrollbar.

As a matter of fact, Writer has an option for just about anything! Table 2.1 describes Writer's options. You'll learn a lot about what Writer can do just by looking through the options available to you.

1 Request the Options

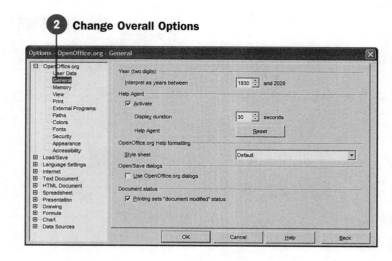

2 Change Overall Options

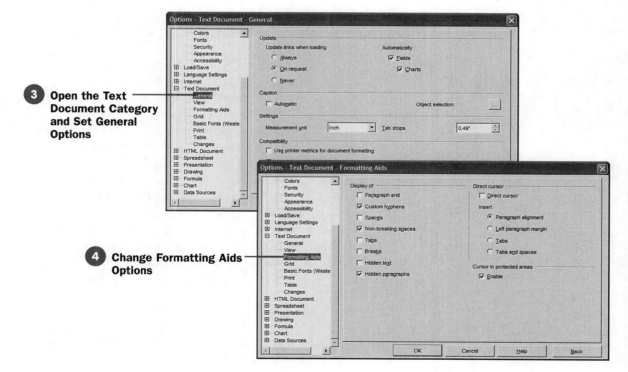

3 Open the Text Document Category and Set General Options

4 Change Formatting Aids Options

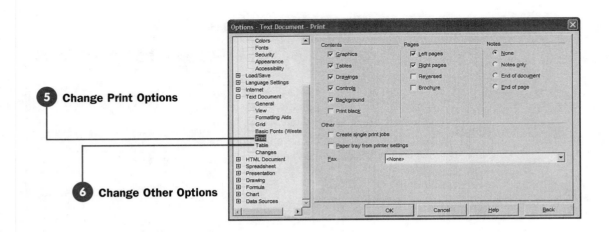

5 Change Print Options

6 Change Other Options

TABLE 2.1 Writer's Text Document Options

Writer Option Category	Explanation
General	Describes general Writer settings such as the default unit of measurements and the width of tab stops (see **11** **About Paragraph Breaks and Tabs**).
View	Describes how Writer appears on the screen and which Writer special elements, such as graphics and rulers, appear by default.
Formatting Aids	Describes how Writer displays formatting elements such as line breaks and paragraph alignment.
Grid	Describes how Writer's grid appears on the screen so you can align charts and other graphic elements with text in your documents.
Basic Fonts (Western)	Describes the default fonts you want Writer to begin with for regular text, headings (see **33** **About Headers and Footers**), lists (see **19** **Add a Bulleted List**), captions (see **27** **Insert Graphics in a Document**), and the index (see **22** **Create an Index**).

TABLE 2.1   Continued

Writer Option Category	Explanation
Print	Describes how Writer prints documents and enables you to determine which installed printer you want to print to (see **9** **Print a Document**).
Table	Describes how Writer formats tables and data within cells (see **23** **About Writer Tables**).
Changes	Describes how Writer displays revisions made in documents when multiple people perform group editing.

1 **Request the Options**

Select **Options** from Writer's **Tools** menu. The **Options** dialog box appears. From the **Options** dialog box, you can change any of Writer's options as well as the options from the other OpenOffice.org programs.

2 **Change Overall Options**

Select any option in the **OpenOffice.org** category to modify OpenOffice.org-wide settings such as pathnames. For example, if you don't like the pathname you see when you open or save a file, click the **Paths** option and change it to a different default file path.

If you're new to OpenOffice.org, consider leaving all the OpenOffice.org options "as is" until you familiarize yourself with how the OpenOffice.org programs work.

3 **Open the Text Document Category and Set General Options**

Click the plus sign next to the **Text Document** option to display the eight Writer-specific options listed in the table at the beginning of this task.

Click the **General** options category; the dialog box changes to show options you can select to make changes to the general Writer options. The **Update** section enables you to determine when Writer updates, or refreshes, linked data in a document such as an external worksheet that you link to your current document to use as a table.

 TIP

Often you'll work in one OpenOffice.org program and realize that you need to change an overall option. For example, if you want to print several kinds of OpenOffice.org documents to a file (instead of to your printer) to send to others via email, you can change the OpenOffice.org option labeled **Print**, from within Writer, to apply that setting to all OpenOffice.org programs.

The **Caption** section enables you to determine how a caption is to appear beneath graphics or charts you may want to include in a document. The **Settings** section enables you to determine how you want Writer to measure items. For example, you can click to open the **Measurement unit** drop-down list to change the default measurement from inches to centimeters if you work in, or travel to, a country that uses the metric system. Finally, the **Compatibility** section determines how Writer is to handle aspects of the current document's formatting, such as blank lines between paragraphs.

4 Change Formatting Aids Options

Click the **Formatting Aids** options category under the **Text Document** category; the dialog box changes to show options that modify the display of various Writer formatting characters such as spaces and line breaks.

Enable the check box for any formatting options you want to see in documents onscreen. For example, if you want to see the space format character (a horizontally centered dot in place of a space) every time you press the spacebar in a document, enable the **Spaces** check box.

5 Change Print Options

Click to select the **Print** category under the **Text Document** option category. View or set any print-related options you want to adjust. For example, if you want to print a draft of your current document's text, you could uncheck the **Graphics** and **Drawings** options so they don't print until you select them again.

6 Change Other Options

Continue viewing and changing the remaining options in the **Text Document** options category by first selecting the category and then looking at the individual options. You might find, for example, that you want to eliminate the scrollbars to give yourself more screen real estate to see the document. You could uncheck the scrollbar options on the **View** page of the **Text Document** options set.

When you're done specifying Writer options, click the **OK** button to close the **Options** dialog box.

TIP

Some users prefer to see all formatting characters, such as the space format character and the end-of-paragraph mark (¶). Such characters can make some editing chores easier. For example, you'll know you pressed the spacebar seven times if you see seven space formatting characters, whereas it's far more difficult to know how many spaces appear if there are no characters to "mark" the spaces.

NOTE

The more formatting characters you display, the more cluttered your screen will look; when you print the document that's onscreen, none of the formatting characters will be printed; the formatting characters are there to help you edit your document.

② Create a New Document

Writer gives you two ways to create new documents: You can create a new document from a completely blank document (if you choose this approach, you must decide what text to place in the document and where you want that information to go) or you can use *AutoPilot* to open a blank, preformatted document. If you use the AutoPilot approach to document creation, you can choose from several AutoPilot options that preformat your new document according to selections you make:

- **Letter**—This option formats a business or personal letter and can include an optional logo in various styles.

- **Fax**—This AutoPilot option formats a fax cover sheet and subsequent fax pages that you can fax directly from your computer if you have a fax modem.

- **Agenda**—This option formats an agenda template with which you can create meeting agendas and related notes.

- **Memo**—This options formats a memo document for short memos so that you can get right to the point and properly address the memo to the correct recipient.

In spite of the fact that AutoPilot provides a great starting point for the special documents you want to create, many times you'll begin with a blank document (that is, you'll bypass AutoPilot's guides). Starting with a blank document, without any preformatted logos, return addresses, and other items that appear with the AutoPilot guides, gives you the most flexibility in creating exactly the document you want to create.

Nevertheless, the AutoPilot guides are difficult to beat when you want to create special documents that fall into the AutoPilot guide categories. For example, it would probably take too much time to create a fax form from scratch, so you can select the AutoPilot **Fax** guide and have Writer do most of the hard formatting work for you. Of course, if you or your company requires a special fax form that differs dramatically from the ones AutoPilot generates, you'll need to create one from scratch or begin with the AutoPilot Fax guide and make major changes to it.

Before You Begin

✔ ① Set Writer Options

See Also

→ ④ Type Text into a Document

→ ⑨ Print a Document

→ ⑱ Use a Template

🔍KEY TERM

AutoPilot—Preformatted guides that help you create personal and business letters and forms more easily than if you began with a blank page.

📝 NOTES

Several AutoPilot guides appear when you view them from within Writer, but only the four described here are Writer documents. The others are for Calc (see ㊴ Create a New Spreadsheet) and Impress (see ㉛ Create a New Presentation).

If you've used Microsoft Word, you'll see strong similarities in Writer's AutoPilot guides and Word's wizards.

1 Request a New Document

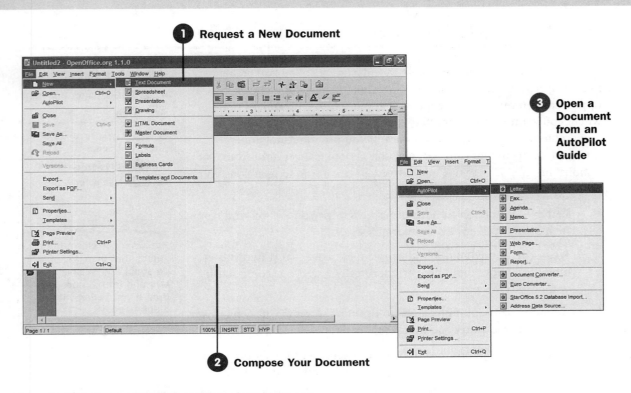

3 Open a Document from an AutoPilot Guide

2 Compose Your Document

4 Specify Letter Options

5 Select Logo Graphics Options

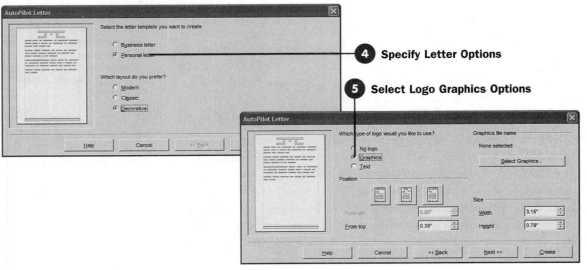

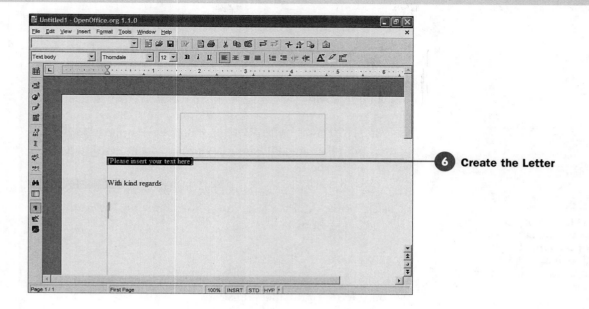

6 **Create the Letter**

1 Request a New Document

Select **Text Document** from the **File, New** menu option. Writer creates a completely blank document for you to work with. Alternatively, click the **New** toolbar button to open a new blank Writer document quickly.

2 Compose Your Document

Create your document using the blank work area Writer gives you. Start typing as you would in any word-processing document. Press **Enter** to end a block of text (be it a paragraph, an item you want to be part of a list of similar items, or a signature block). You can save your work (choose **File, Save**) and print your document (see **9** **Print a Document**) at any time.

3 Open a Document from an AutoPilot Guide

To create a document using an AutoPilot guide, choose **File**, **AutoPilot**. From the submenu that opens, you can select from a number of guides; choose the one that suites the kind of document you want to create. For example, if you want to create a fax, choose **Fax** from the **File**, **AutoPilot** submenu. A dialog box showing options for that particular kind of document appears; select options from the dialog box to fine-tune the document AutoPilot will create for you.

In this example, I'll use AutoPilot to create a letter. Consequently, I'll select **Letter** from the **File**, **AutoPilot** submenu. The **AutoPilot Letter** dialog box opens.

4 Specify Letter Options

Select the kind of letter you want to write by selecting either **Personal letter** or **Business letter**.

Select the style you want your letter to take by selecting **Modern** (for clean text using *non-serif* fonts), **Classic** (for *non-proportional* fonts), or **Decorative** (for *serif* fonts).

When you have selected the kind of letter and letter style, click the **Next** button to move to the next screen in the AutoPilot guide.

5 Select Logo Graphics Options

On the second screen of the **AutoPilot Letter** dialog box, select the **Graphics** option if you want Writer to reserve a space at the top of your letter for a logo. You can insert a graphic image of your company or personal logo after you begin adding your text to the letter (see **27** Insert Graphics in a Document).

If you elect to use a graphic logo, click the **Select Graphics** button to select the file that holds the graphic image. You may also select whether you want the logo centered, left-justified, or right-justified in the **Position** section. Finally, you can determine exactly where Writer places the logo by adjusting the **Size** options.

NOTE

AutoPilot actually creates a template you use to create your document. See **18** Use a Template to learn more about Writer's templates.

KEY TERMS

Non-serif—Also called *sans-serif*, a typeface that doesn't have finishing strokes on letters; rather, each letter is composed of smooth lines.

Non-proportional—Each letter, no matter how wide (such as *W*) or narrow (such as *i*) consumes the same amount of space on the line.

Serif—A typeface with finishing strokes (like small tails or stems that slightly protrude from parts of the letters). Serif fonts are often easier to read in print, whereas sans-serif fonts are often easier to read on computer screens.

---

6 ## Create the Letter

When you have selected the options appropriate to the type of letter you want to create, you have the choice to continue setting more options by clicking the **Next** button or you can click **Create** to create the letter with the options you've set so far. Many times you'll end an AutoPilot early by clicking **Create** before you've looked at all the options. This is because Writer puts the most critical options and the ones most subject to change at the beginning of the AutoPilot walkthrough.

For now, click the **Create** button to request that AutoPilot create your letter. By doing this, you bypass options such as specifying a sender's name and address box. The **AutoPilot Letter** dialog box closes, and AutoPilot creates a document that's preformatted according to the options you've selected.

In the preformatted letter that AutoPilot creates, you'll find notes telling you where to place certain parts of your document, such as opening text, a logo (if you chose to include one), the fax page count (if you had selected the AutoPilot Fax guide), and other hints that help you complete the document you requested through AutoPilot.

TIP

The preview area at the left of the dialog box updates as you select AutoPilot options so that you can see what your document layout looks like so far.

NOTE

Your screen may differ slightly from the one shown here depending on the options you selected as you went through the AutoPilot process. Also, you may see the **Stylelist** window floating on top of your document. You can close this window to give yourself more editing room (see **16** About Styles and Templates).

---

3 ## Open an Existing Document

Opening an existing document to edit with Writer is simple. You tell Writer you want to open a document file and then locate the file, and Writer loads the document in the editing area.

One important Writer feature is its capability to open documents you create in other word processing programs. Most notably, Writer opens Microsoft Word documents with ease. Although Writer might not fully support 100% of Microsoft Word's advanced features, Writer does a super job of loading Word documents into Writer's workspace so that you can edit the documents using Writer's interface.

Before You Begin

✔ **1** Set Writer Options

✔ **2** Create a New Document

See Also

→ **9** Print a Document

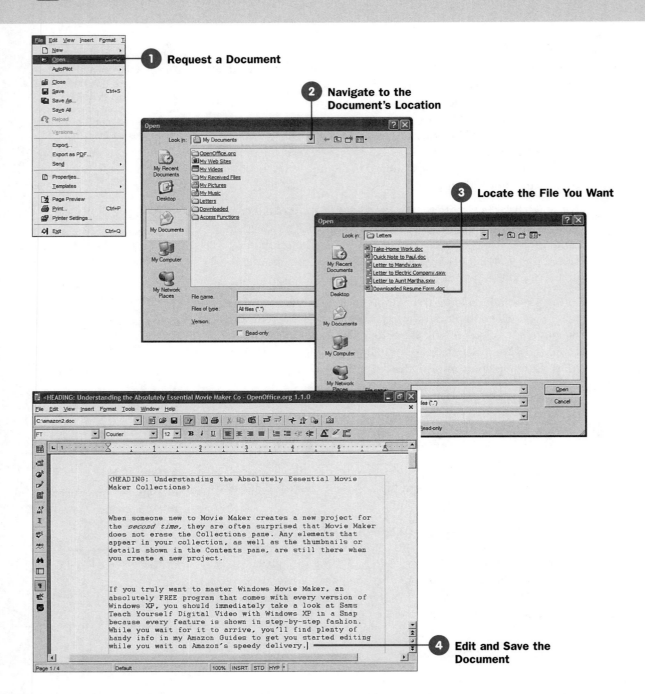

1 Request a Document

2 Navigate to the Document's Location

3 Locate the File You Want

4 Edit and Save the Document

① Request a Document

Select **Open** from Writer's **File** menu to display the **Open** dialog box.

Writer uses the document extension .sxw for its documents. Writer's file format is XML compatible. Microsoft Word uses the .doc file extension, and both types of files display when you want to locate files to open in Writer.

② Navigate to the Document's Location

The document you want to open might not appear at the default location shown in the **Open** dialog box, so navigate to the folder in which the document you're looking for resides using the **Look in** drop-down list.

③ Locate the File You Want

When you locate the folder that holds the document file, select the file you want to open. Then click the **Open** button to open the selected file in Writer's editing workspace.

If the default **Editing view** option on the OpenOffice.org **Options** page is set, Writer opens the document at the point where it last saved the document. For example, if the document is 35 pages long and you last edited page 20 before saving and closing the document last week, Writer will display that place on page 20 where you last quit editing. The **Editing view** option enables you to get right back to work where you left off.

④ Edit and Save the Document

After the file opens in the Writer workspace, you can edit the file. Navigate to where you wish to make edits (see **5** **Edit Text**) or move to the end of the document and add to it (see **4** **Type Text into a Document**).

Once you've made all the changes you wish to make, select **File**, **Save** to save your document. Your recent changes will be saved in the document file for your next editing session.

TIPS

You can open documents from your computer's disk or from elsewhere in the file system. If you want to open a document located on the Web, preface the filename with **http://** or **ftp://** to open document files from those sources.

Feel free to open more than one file by holding the **Ctrl** key while clicking multiple filenames. Writer opens each document you select in its own window. Use the **Window** menu to select an open document to edit.

4 Type Text into a Document

Before You Begin

✔ **2** Create a New Document

✔ **3** Open an Existing Document

See Also

→ **5** Edit Text

→ **9** Print a Document

🔍 KEY TERM

Main toolbar—A vertical toolbar that appears on the screen's left edge, giving you one-click access to spelling, grammar, chart, list, and other tools you'll commonly use.

If you've ever used any word processor before, even a simple one such as WordPad found in Windows, you'll have no trouble editing text in Writer. Writer's editing area remains fairly clear of clutter so you can concentrate on your work.

Writer has tools to help you make the most of your editing sessions. For example, you may want to see more of your document at one time, perhaps to help keep your current paragraph in context with the one before and after it. The **Full Screen** view removes all menus and toolbars from your editing area to give the maximum amount of space to your editing. Writer's various toolbars are there to provide one-click access to the editing tools you need. For example, Writer's *Main toolbar* is one of the handiest of all the available toolbars because it puts the common editing tasks just to the left of your editing area, where you can quickly access them. To select an item from the Main toolbar, you'll need to long-click your mouse on one of the buttons.

This task walks you through a short editing session, just to give you a feel for the kinds of movements and tools available to you. Many of the editing skills you acquire in one OpenOffice.org program, such as Writer, will apply to the other OpenOffice.org programs as well. For example, both Calc and Writer offer the capability to display or hide the Main toolbar. The Main toolbar changes slightly depending on which program you use, but most of its functions are similar across the OpenOffice.org programs.

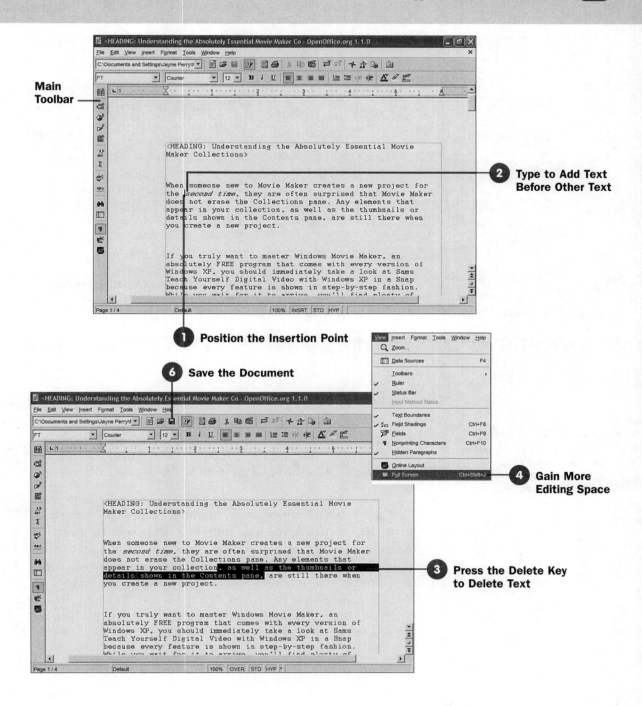

Main Toolbar

2 Type to Add Text Before Other Text

1 Position the Insertion Point

6 Save the Document

4 Gain More Editing Space

3 Press the Delete Key to Delete Text

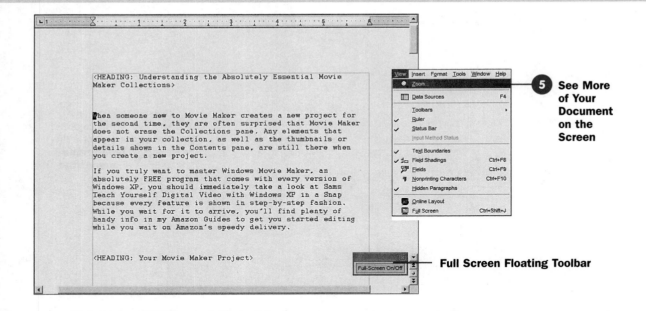

5 See More of Your Document on the Screen

Full Screen Floating Toolbar

① Position the Insertion Point

Press the arrow keys to see the text cursor move around your screen. The text cursor is called the *insertion point* and moves as you press any arrow key. You can also click your mouse within the document to place the insertion point where you next want to type.

Text that you type appears at the insertion point. If you make a mistake, press **Backspace** and Writer moves the insertion point backwards, erasing as you press **Backspace**. When you get to the right edge of a paragraph, Writer automatically wraps your paragraph onto the next line. Do not press **Enter** unless you want to end a paragraph and begin a new one. Writer may or may not insert a blank line between paragraphs, depending on how you set up your page (see **14** Set Up Page Formatting).

If you press **Shift+Enter** instead of **Enter**, Writer ends the current line and begins at the start of the line below without actually creating a new paragraph. You can easily see where paragraphs begin and end by displaying nonprinting characters (see **5** **Edit Text**). If you press **Ctrl+spacebar** instead of the normal **spacebar**, Writer inserts a *nonbreaking space* and will not end a line on that space but, if necessary, will move both the word before and after the nonbreaking space to the next line in a word wrap. If you press **Ctrl+Enter**, Writer begins a new page in the document, even if you had not yet filled up the previous page.

For more information about paragraph breaks and using tabs, see **11** **About Paragraph Breaks and Tabs**.

2 Type to Add Text Before Other Text

When you place the insertion point before existing text on a line, Writer normally inserts the text you type in front of the existing text and moves the existing text over to the right. This is called *insert mode* and is normal behavior for most editors and word processors. If your typing replaces text on the screen, you're in *overtype mode* instead of insert mode.

Press the **Insert** key to switch between overtype and insert modes. If you have a lot of text to replace, you'll find that it's easier to do so in overtype mode because you'll have less text to delete.

3 Press the Delete Key to Delete Text

Select text and press the **Delete** key to delete characters where the insertion point appears. Every time you press **Delete**, Writer removes one character (including a space, number, or even a blank line if that's where the insertion point is positioned).

4 Gain More Editing Space

Select **Full Screen** from the **View** menu to temporarily hide your toolbars, menu, and the status bar. You will be able to see more of your document at one time. Notice that even when all the other toolbars are hidden in **Full Screen** mode, the floating **Full Screen** toolbar appears in the editing area.

KEY TERMS

Nonbreaking space—A space that appears between words when you print the document but does not break at the end of a line. When you want to keep two words together without the end of a line causing them to separate (such as a person's title and name, as in Dr. Smith), use a nonbreaking space so that Writer will wrap them both to the next line if the end of the line would have otherwise separated them.

Insert mode—The state of Writer where new text you type is inserted before existing text. It is indicated by the **INSRT** message on the status bar.

Overtype mode—The state of Writer where new text replaces existing text as you type. It is indicated by the **OVER** message on the status bar.

TIP

Often you'll start typing a word, such as *following*, but before you type the fifth letter, Writer finishes the word for you with its word completion feature. Also, if you type a word incorrectly, such as *windoes*, Writer very well might correct it using its automatic spelling checker. You can turn off this AutoComplete feature from the **Tools**, **Options** dialog box.

Click the floating **Full Screen** toolbar's **Full-Screen On/Off** button to return to the normal editing workspace with full menus, toolbars, and the status bar.

5 See More of Your Document on the Screen

Select the **Zoom** option from the **View** menu to adjust how much of your document appears on the screen at any one time. In the **Zoom** dialog box that opens, select from the given list of percentages or click **Variable** and enter another percentage. The default zoom percentage is **100%**, which means that what you see on the screen is the same size as what appears when you print your document. If you change to a higher percentage, such as **200%**, you'll zoom more into your document, making the characters look larger on the screen. If you change to a lower percentage, such as **75%**, you'll zoom away from your document, seeing more of the page, although you won't see as much up-close detail.

Click **OK** to close the dialog box and see the result of your screen adjustment.

6 Save the Document

After you have edited the text in the document—and periodically while you are editing—you should save your changes to the hard disk. To save the document, choose **File**, **Save** or click the Save icon on the **Function** toolbar (the second icon from the left). Writer saves the current version of the file, overwriting the previous version of the file.

⚓ TIP

If you're not sure that you want the current version of the file to overwrite the existing version when you save, choose **File**, **Save As** instead. Writer asks you for a new filename for the current version of the document, saves it under that name, and doesn't touch the original version.

---

5 **Edit Text**

Before You Begin

✔ **2** Create a New Document

✔ **3** Open an Existing Document

See Also

→ **9** Print a Document

Writer makes it easy to edit your documents. Whether you want to edit a letter, add to your novel, or edit a report once more before sending it to clients, Writer provides quick and simple tools that help you get the job done right.

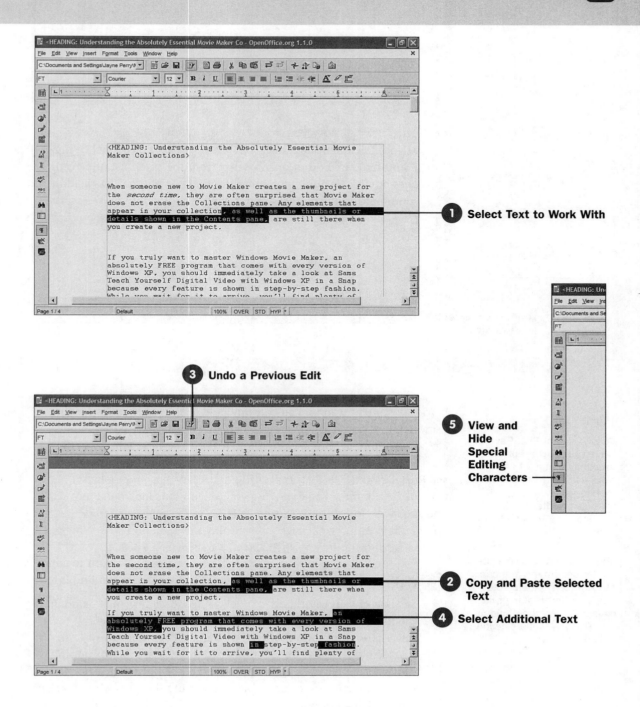

1 Select Text to Work With

3 Undo a Previous Edit

5 View and Hide Special Editing Characters

2 Copy and Paste Selected Text

4 Select Additional Text

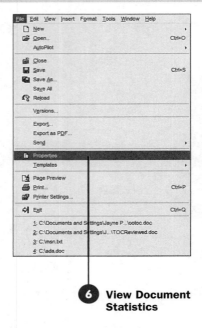

7 Save the Document

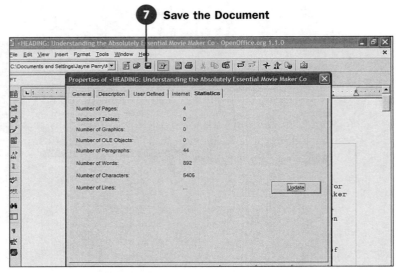

6 View Document Statistics

TIPS

Always select **File, Save** to save your document after making changes to it. If you attempt to exit Writer before you save your changes, Writer kindly reminds you to save the file.

Press **Ctrl+A** to select the entire document. You can also make multiple selections by first making one selection and then holding the **Ctrl** key while selecting additional text.

If your document is long, you can navigate to the place you want to edit using the keyboard (see **6** **Move Around a Document**). If you know of a key word or phrase that is close to the text you want to edit, you can search for that key word or phrase to move there quickly (see **7** **Find and Replace Text**). Writer's formatting and spell-checking tools will help you ensure accuracy while making your documents look good too. You'll find help with formatting starting in **12** **Apply Character Formatting**, and you'll learn how to check your document's spelling using Writer's built-in word dictionary in **8** **Check a Document's Spelling**.

1 Select Text to Work With

Select text using standard Windows selection tools (such as holding the **Ctrl** key as you press arrow keys to highlight a selection) to select more than one character at a time. You might want to select a large block of text for deletion or to apply a special format to that selected text (see **12** **Apply Character Formatting**). The selected text appears in "reverse video," meaning that it is white text on a black background.

2 **Copy and Paste Selected Text**

After you've selected text, you can press **Ctrl+C** to copy the selection to your Windows Clipboard. The original text remains unchanged in the document. After you've copied the selection to the Clipboard, move your insertion point to another place in your document (the text you originally selected is deselected) and press **Ctrl+V** to paste a copy of the text in the new location.

You can keep pressing **Ctrl+V** to paste the text as many times as you wish in your document. The normal Windows editing features work in Writer, so if you instead want to move the originally selected text to a new location, press **Ctrl+X** (for cut) instead of **Ctrl+C** (for copy) to delete the text from its original location; then reposition the insertion point and press **Ctrl+V** to paste the text in its new location.

Writer's **Edit** menu contains the typical **Cut**, **Copy**, and **Paste** options in case you don't want to use the keyboard shortcuts. In addition, the **Function** toolbar provides **Copy**, **Cut**, and **Paste** buttons for you to use.

3 **Undo a Previous Edit**

Writer's **Undo** feature undoes your previous edit—whatever that may have been. To invoke it, press **Ctrl+Z**, choose **Edit**, **Undo**, or click the **Undo** button on the **Function** toolbar. So if you accidentally erased a large block of text, press **Ctrl+Z** and Writer puts the text right back. You can undo just about any edit you make in Writer other than a style change.

4 **Select Additional Text**

Writer doesn't limit you to one selection at a time. You can select multiple blocks of text within your document at the same time. After you've selected the first block, hold the **Ctrl** key and select another block of text. You may keep doing this as often as needed to select all the text you need to select.

By selecting multiple items, you'll be able to work with them all as a group. For example, you may be writing about great works of literature and you realize you did not italicize each title. Instead of selecting the titles and italicizing them individually, you can select all the titles and apply italics to them in one step (see **12** **Apply Character Formatting**).

NOTE

You can paste selected text into another OpenOffice.org program or another Windows program that accepts text. The Windows Clipboard is handy for copying and moving data between programs.

 TIP

You can redo an Undo! Press **Ctrl+Y**, select **Edit**, **Redo**, or click the **Redo** button in the **Function** toolbar to reverse the previous Undo operation you performed.

5 **View and Hide Special Editing Characters**

Long-click the **Nonprinting Characters** button in the **Main** toolbar (or press **Ctrl+F10**) to turn on nonprinting characters, which show you where paragraph divisions, blank spaces, and other editing elements occur. These nonprinting characters don't print (unless you change the printing option to show them, as mentioned in **1** **Set Writer Options**) but can appear on the screen so that you'll know exactly what you're editing.

Long-click the **Nonprinting Characters** button on the **Main** toolbar button (or press **Ctrl+F10**) again to turn off the display of nonprinting characters.

6 **View Document Statistics**

As you type text into your document, you can maintain an accurate word count, along with other document statistics, by selecting the **Properties** option from the **File** menu.

Click the **Statistics** tab to view the **Statistics** page in the **Properties** dialog box. Here you see counts of various objects in your document, such as the number of paragraphs, words, characters, and lines. If you're writing for a magazine, for example, word count is an important statistic to track; if you're trying to fit all the text on a single page, you might want to keep track of the number of lines.

When you've viewed the statistics for your current document, click **OK** to close the **Properties** dialog box and return to the editing area.

7 **Save the Document**

After you have edited the text in the document—and periodically while you are editing—you should save your changes to the hard disk. To save the document, choose **File**, **Save** or click the **Save** icon in the **Function** toolbar (the third icon from the left). Writer saves the current version of the file, overwriting the previous version of the file.

NOTE

Click the **Statistic** page's **Update** button to force Writer to perform an update of the statistics before you fully rely on the numbers.

TIP

If you're not sure that you want the current version of the file to overwrite the existing version when you save, choose **File**, **Save As** instead. Writer asks you for a new filename for the current version of the document, saves it under that name, and doesn't touch the original version.

6 Move Around a Document

The faster you can move around a document, the faster you'll get your work done. If most documents consumed less than a screen of real estate, the ability to move around the document wouldn't be needed. Most documents, however, require far more than a single screen of room. Being able to navigate from place to place becomes second nature quickly because it's a skill needed before you can edit seriously.

One of the ways Writer and the other OpenOffice.org programs help you move from place to place is with the **Navigation** floating toolbar. In this task, you'll get a chance to use the **Navigation** toolbar and its cousin, the **Navigator** (which is a window but it's easy to confuse the **Navigation** toolbar and the **Navigator** window), to move from one graphic image in a document to the next with the click of your mouse. The true power of the Navigator really shows when your document is many pages long; the Navigator enables you to move from any element, such as a picture or footnote, to another element, no matter how far apart those elements might be in the document.

Table 2.2 lists several keystroke shortcuts that help you get from place to place quickly in Writer. The rest of this task shows you other ways available, such as the scrollbars and the **Navigation** toolbar, that get you where you want to go.

Before You Begin

✔ **2** Create a New Document

✔ **3** Open an Existing Document

See Also

→ **7** Find and Replace Text

→ **5** Edit Text

NOTE

Writer supports a wealth of additional keyboard short-cuts. Table 2.2 lists only the ones found to be among the most popular or useful for moving around a document.

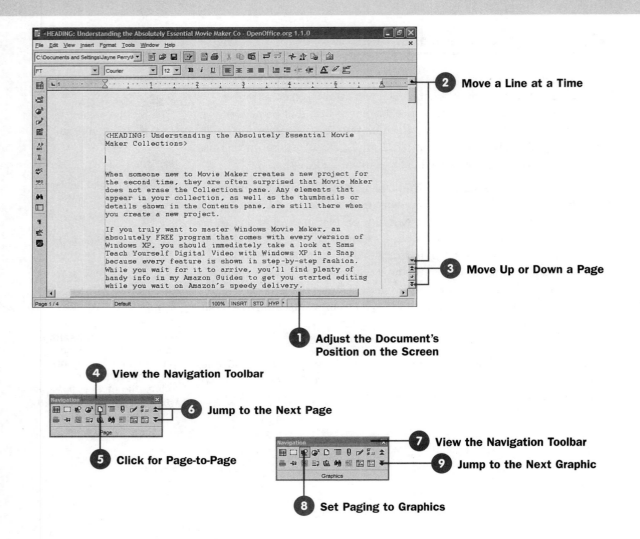

2 Move a Line at a Time

3 Move Up or Down a Page

1 Adjust the Document's Position on the Screen

4 View the Navigation Toolbar

6 Jump to the Next Page

5 Click for Page-to-Page

7 View the Navigation Toolbar

9 Jump to the Next Graphic

8 Set Paging to Graphics

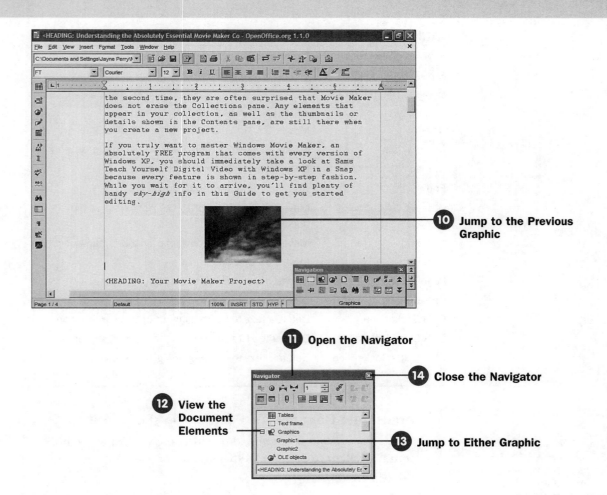

10 Jump to the Previous Graphic

11 Open the Navigator

14 Close the Navigator

12 View the Document Elements

13 Jump to Either Graphic

TABLE 2.2 Keyboard Navigation Shortcuts

Keyboard Shortcut	Description
F5	Toggles the Navigator toolbar on or off
Shift+Enter	Moves the text cursor to the next line but does not start a new paragraph or insert a paragraph mark
Ctrl+left arrow	Moves the text cursor to the beginning of the word
Ctrl+Shift+left arrow	Moves the text cursor to the left, word by word and extends the selection left

TABLE 2.2 Continued

Keyboard Shortcut	Description
Ctrl+right arrow	Moves the text cursor to the end of the word
Ctrl+Shift+right arrow	Moves the text cursor to the right, word by word and extends the selection right
Up arrow	Moves the text cursor up one line at a time
Down arrow	Moves the text cursor down one line at a time
Home	Goes to the beginning of the current line
End	Goes to the end of the current line
Ctrl+Home	Moves the text cursor to the beginning of the document
Ctrl+End	Moves text cursor to the end of the document
PageUp	Moves up one screen at a time
PageDown	Moves down one screen at a time
Ctrl+Delete	Deletes text to the end of the current word
Ctrl+Backspace	Deletes text to the beginning of the current word
Ctrl+Shift+Delete	Deletes text to the end of the current sentence
Ctrl+Shift+Backspace	Deletes text to the beginning of the current sentence

NOTES

Dragging the vertical scrollbar up and down the screen is much faster than paging through a very long document.

The **Previous Page** and **Next Page** scrollbar buttons may take on another function (such as paging to the next graphic or header or footer) if you've used the **Navigation** toolbar this session.

① Adjust the Document's Position on the Screen

When editing your document, drag either the vertical or the horizontal scrollbar to position a different part of your document on the screen.

② Move a Line at a Time

Click any scrollbar arrow to move one line up or down (or about five characters left or right if you click the horizontal scrollbar). You can hold down your mouse button to scroll rapidly up or down the screen.

③ Move Up or Down a Page

Click the Writer's **Previous Page** or **Next Page** button on the scrollbar to move up or down one page at a time. You can hold down your mouse button to scroll rapidly up or down the screen one page at a time.

4 ## View the Navigation Toolbar

Click the **Navigation** button on the vertical scrollbar to display the **Navigation** floating toolbar. With the Navigation toolbar, you can page through your document and move between different elements easily.

5 ## Click for Page-to-Page

Click the **Navigation** toolbar's **Page** button to set the vertical scrolling to move from page to page. If you've never used the **Navigation** toolbar before, the **Page** button will already be selected.

6 ## Jump to the Next Page

Click the vertical scrollbar's **Next Page** button to jump to the next page in the document.

At this point you may be wondering what good the **Navigation** toolbar did. After all, you clicked the **Next Page** button in the scrollbar in step 3 without having to display the **Navigation** toolbar first. That's because when you first use Writer, the **Navigation** toolbar mode is set to the **Page** button. The **Navigation** toolbar does not have to remain set to **Page**, however, as the next two steps show.

7 ## View the Navigation Toolbar

Click the scroll bar's **Navigation** button once again to display the **Navigation** toolbar once again.

8 ## Set Paging to Graphics

Click the **Navigation** toolbar's **Graphics** button to set the paging to graphics instead of a page of text.

9 ## Jump to the Next Graphic

Click the **Next Graphic** button that now appears on your vertical scrollbar to jump to the next graphic image in your document. Notice the floating ToolTip that describes the scrollbar has changed from **Next Page** to **Next Graphic**. That's because you just selected a graphic image when you used the **Navigation** toolbar in the previous step. As long as your document has a graphic image somewhere below your current position, Writer jumps to that image. If no graphic image appears in the document, Writer remains where it is.

TIP

Remember, if you can't see your scrollbars and you want to, or if you can see them and you'd rather hide them, you can decide which scrollbar (either one, both, or neither) you want to see from the Text Documents Options **View** page (see **Set Writer Options**).

⑩ Jump to the Previous Graphic

Click the **Previous Graphic** button to move back to the previous graphic image you viewed (assuming your document has multiple graphic images).

⑪ Open the Navigator

Press **F5** to open the **Navigator** floating window. The **Navigator** window differs from the Navigation floating toolbar, although their similar names never cease to confuse users. The **Navigation** toolbar is more directly linked to your vertical scrollbar, as the previous steps showed. The **Navigator** window provides a high-level look at your document's various elements (or possible elements, such as a header that you may not have yet added).

⑫ View the Document Elements

Scroll through the Navigator options to see various Writer-related elements that can appear in your document. If your document has multiple elements, such as the two graphic images found by Navigator here, Navigator shows both images so you can quickly jump to either one.

⑬ Jump to Either Graphic

Double-click either entry, **Graphic1** or **Graphic2**, in the Navigator to see either graphic image. When you click one, Writer scrolls directly to that item.

⑭ Close the Navigator

When you're finished using the Navigator to look for something, press **Esc** to hide the Navigator window or click the **Close** button.

7 Find and Replace Text

Long documents make locating what you need quickly important. Perhaps you need to make changes to some text in a table or perhaps a caption is wrong on a figure. Writer provides text-locating tools that will be familiar to you if you've done similar text-locating tasks in the past.

Of course, along with finding text, you'll need to replace the text you find sometimes. For example, you may have written a letter to Kim McDonald and learned that her name is Kim MacDonald before you mailed the letter. With Writer's Find and Replace tools, you can make quick work of changing all the McDonald references to MacDonald throughout the document. Whether the document is one page or 100 pages, you'll be able to find and replace text such as this just as quickly and easily.

1 Find Text

Select the **Find & Replace** option from the **Edit** menu to display the **Find & Replace** dialog box. You can also long-click the **Find Main** toolbar button or press **Ctrl+F** to display the **Find & Replace** dialog box.

2 Enter Search Text

Type the text you want to find in the **Search for** text box.

3 Start a Search

Click the **Find** button. Writer searches from the current text cursor's position in the document to the end of the file. If Writer finds the text, it highlights the text. You may be able to see the highlighted text, but if not you can move or close the **Find & Replace** dialog box to see the highlighted text. (If you had clicked the **Find All** button instead of **Find**, Writer would have highlighted all occurrences of any matching text in the document.)

4 Type Replacement Text

If you want Writer to replace found text with new text, type the new text into the **Replace with** text box.

Before You Begin

✔ **3** Open an Existing Document

✔ **5** Edit Text

✔ **6** Move Around a Document

See Also

→ **12** Apply Character Formatting

NOTE

The **Navigator** and **Navigation** floating toolbars are great for locating generic elements within your document, but use the **Find and Replace** tools, shown in this task, to locate specific text and editing marks within your document.

TIP

If you've searched for the same text before, you can click the down arrow to open the **Search for** drop-down list box and select the text to search for it once again.

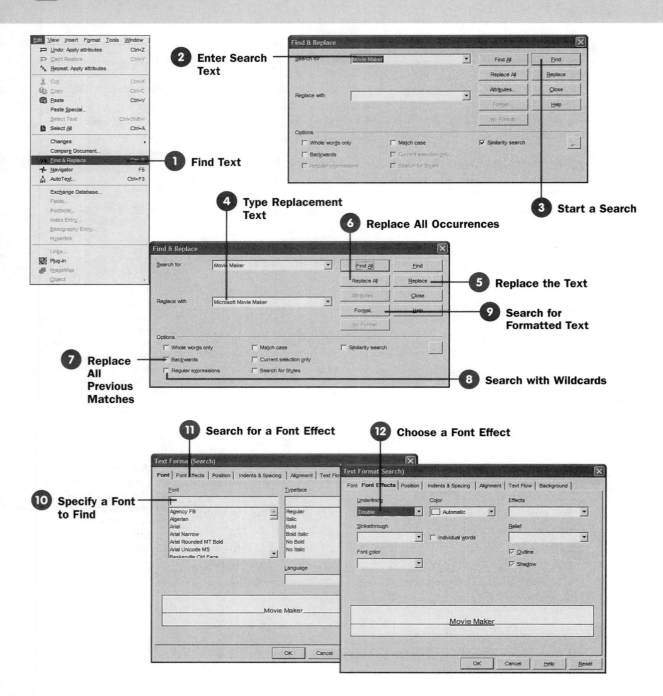

2 Enter Search Text

1 Find Text

3 Start a Search

4 Type Replacement Text

6 Replace All Occurrences

5 Replace the Text

9 Search for Formatted Text

7 Replace All Previous Matches

8 Search with Wildcards

11 Search for a Font Effect

12 Choose a Font Effect

10 Specify a Font to Find

PART I: Writing Words with Writer

5 Replace the Text

If the **Search for** text is found, Writer replaces that text with the text you entered in the **Replace with** text box.

6 Replace All Occurrences

Instead of **Replace** (or after you do a replacement), if you click the **Replace All** button, Writer replaces all the matches with your replacement text throughout the document. Such a change is more global and possibly riskier because you may replace text you didn't really want replaced. By clicking **Find** before each replace operation, you can be sure that the proper text is being replaced; however, such a single-occurrence find and replacement takes a lot of time in a long document.

7 Replace All Previous Matches

Click to select the **Backwards** option before doing a find or replacement if you want to find or replace from the current text cursor's position back to the start of the document.

8 Search with Wildcards

Click to select the **Regular expressions** option if you want to per-form a *wildcard search* using OpenOffice.org's *regular expressions*. Table 2.3 describes some of the more common regular expressions you may use in Writer and gives an example of each.

TABLE 2.3 Regular Expressions That Form Advanced Wildcard Searches

Regular Expression Character	How Used
.	Represents one and only one character in a search. Therefore, h.s matches *his* and *has* but not *hands* (similar to the question mark wildcard character in other programs).
^	Requests that a match be made only if the search term appears at the beginning of a paragraph. Therefore, ^The matches all occurrences of *The* that begin paragraphs, but it does not match any other *The* in the document.

KEY TERMS

Wildcard search—Allows you to use wildcard characters, such as *, to replace characters in a search.

Regular expressions—The name given to OpenOffice.org's extensive wildcard character support; OpenOffice.org supports far more wildcard characters than most Windows programs.

TABLE 2.3   Continued

Regular Expression Character	How Used
$	Requests that a match be made only if the search term appears at the end of a paragraph. Therefore, success$ matches all occurrences of *success* that fall at the end of paragraphs, but it does not match any other *success* in the document.
*	Represents zero, one, or more characters. Therefore, i*n matches *in*, *i123n*, and *ion*.
\>	Represents a search term located at the end of a word. Therefore, \>door matches *outdoor* and *indoor* but not *door-knob*.
\<	Represents a search term located at the beginning of a word. Therefore, \<door matches *doorknob* but not *outdoor* and *indoor*.
^$	Locates empty paragraphs.

9 Search for Formatted Text

If you want to search only for certain text values that are formatted in a particular way, such as all italicized instances of McDonald but not boldfaced instances of McDonald, you can do so by clicking the **Format** button to display the **Text Format (Search)** dialog box.

10 Specify a Font to Find

Select the font name, typeface, and size that the text much match before being considered found.

11 Search for a Font Effect

If you want to further refine your search to a specific font color or effect, click the **Font Effects** tab to display a page with those attributes you can look for.

⑫ Choose a Font Effect

Select the font effect you want to find. If the matching text also matches the font effects you select (as well as any font name and size you may have selected in step 10), Writer considers the match to be successful and highlights the found text.

When you finish finding and replacing all the text for this search session, click the **Find & Replace** dialog box's **Close** button to close the dialog box and return to the document's work area.

NOTE

Click the tabs on the other pages within the **Text Format (Search)** dialog box to see the other refinements you can make when searching and replacing text. You can even specify the background color that must appear behind any matching text before the text is to be considered a match.

⑧ Check a Document's Spelling

Writer can check your spelling in two ways:

- All at once after you've composed or opened a document

- As you type by highlighting your words with a red, wavy line beneath the misspelled ones

If Writer flags a word as misspelled but the word is spelled correctly, you can tell Writer to add that word to its spelling dictionary or to ignore the word for the rest of the editing session. Writer might flag some proper nouns and technical terms as misspelled that are not.

① Request a Spelling Check

Select the **Check** option from the **Tools**, **Spellcheck** menu to check the spelling of your current document. Writer begins checking the spelling of your document, from beginning to end. If Writer finds a misspelled word, Writer displays the **Spellcheck** dialog box and highlights the misspelled word in your document under the **Spellcheck** box.

Before You Begin

✔ ② Create a New Document

✔ ③ Open an Existing Document

See Also

→ ⑨ Print a Document

NOTE

Don't rely solely on Writer's spelling check capabilities. Writer's spelling checker does not replace the need for proofreading on your part. As a good example, consider that Writer will find absolutely no misspelled words in the following sentence: *Wee went two the fare too sea the bares.*

TIP

In addition to spellchecking, Writer can also offer synonyms from its online thesaurus. Don't type *confused* when *obfuscated* will baffle more people!

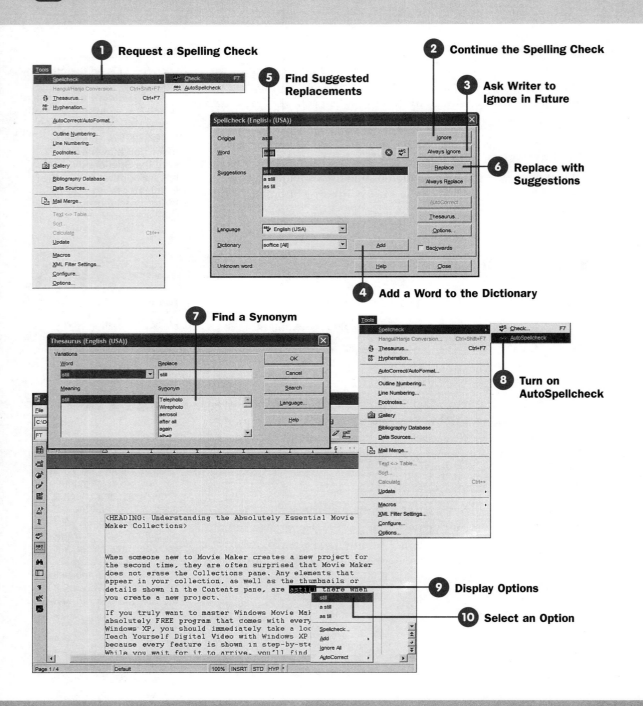

1 Request a Spelling Check

5 Find Suggested Replacements

2 Continue the Spelling Check

3 Ask Writer to Ignore in Future

6 Replace with Suggestions

4 Add a Word to the Dictionary

7 Find a Synonym

8 Turn on AutoSpellcheck

9 Display Options

10 Select an Option

② Continue the Spelling Check

If Writer finds a word that is not really misspelled (perhaps it's an abbreviation that you don't want to add to the Writer's spelling dictionary), click the **Ignore** button. Writer will ignore the word and continue checking the rest of your document.

③ Ask Writer to Ignore in Future

If you often type the abbreviation or other word found to be misspelled but really isn't, click the **Always Ignore** button and Writer will ignore that word in all subsequent spelling check sessions.

④ Add a Word to the Dictionary

If Writer finds a properly spelled word that it thinks isn't, such as a strange last name, you can add that word to Writer's spelling dictionary by clicking the **Add** button. Not only will Writer not flag the word as misspelled in the future, but Writer will offer the word as a possible correction for subsequent words found to be misspelled that are close to that one.

⑤ Find Suggested Replacements

If Writer finds a word that truly is misspelled, Writer tries to offer one or more suggestions in the **Suggestions** list box. Usually, the top word that is highlighted is the correct spelling for the misspelled word, but you may have to scroll down to locate the proper correction, depending on how many close matches Writer finds in its spelling dictionary.

⑥ Replace with Suggestions

If the top highlighted word is the word to replace the misspelled word with, click the **Replace** button and Writer will replace the misspelled word with the selected correction. If the correction is not the top word in the **Suggestions** list box but appears farther down the list, click the correct replacement word and then click the **Replace** button to make the replacement.

TIP

If you cannot see the highlighted misspelled word and you want to view it in the context of your document, you may have to drag the **Spellcheck** dialog box up or down to see the highlighted word that Writer considers to be misspelled.

7 Find a Synonym

TIP

The **Thesaurus** dialog box is also available via the **Tools, Thesaurus** menu or the **Ctrl+F7** keyboard shortcut.

7 Find a Synonym

If you want to see synonyms of any word, click to select that word from the **Suggestions** list and click the **Thesaurus** button to display the **Thesaurus** dialog box. If you find a better word than the one you selected, double-click that word to move it to the **Word** text box in the **Thesaurus** dialog box.

Click **OK** to close the **Thesaurus** dialog box. When you're done checking the spelling, click the **Close** button to close the **Spellcheck** dialog box.

8 Turn on AutoSpellcheck

To turn on the automatic spelling checker so that Writer checks your spelling as you type words into your document, select the **AutoSpellcheck** option from the **Tools, Spellcheck** menu. A check mark next to the **AutoSpellcheck** option indicates that Writer turned on the automatic spelling checker.

NOTE

You can turn off Writer's automatic spelling checker by once again selecting the **AutoSpellcheck** option from the **Tools, Spellcheck** menu.

9 Display Options

As you type, misspelled words appear with a red wavy line beneath them. Right-click over the misspelled word to see several options (including suggested replacement words) from which you can choose.

One of the options, **Spellcheck**, opens the Spellcheck dialog box, so just because you've turned on AutoSpellcheck doesn't mean you can't work within that dialog box as you did in step 1. You may also elect to add the word that Writer thinks is misspelled to the dictionary so future spelling checks of that word won't be flagged as incorrect. If you select the **Ignore All** option, Writer will not flag the word as incorrect for the rest of this session, but subsequent editing sessions will still view the word as incorrect because you didn't add it to the dictionary.

The **AutoCorrect** option tells Writer that if this word ever appears in the future, instead of marking it as misspelled, automatically correct the word with one of the options you suggest. If you find yourself mistyping the same word frequently, such as typing *mispell* for *misspell*, you could request that Writer automatically change *mispell* to *misspell* if and when you make that mistake in the future.

Writer corrects that misspelling as you type, and often you'll not notice the correction took place, but you will have a more accurate document. For more information on Writer's AutoCorrect feature, see **32** **Use AutoCorrect to Improve Your Typing**.

10 Select an Option

From the right-click menu, select the option you want to choose to handle the misspelled word. Although the **Spellcheck** dialog box offers more suggestions than this right-click menu, the right-click menu often brings up as many options as you will routinely need to ensure spelling accuracy when you type.

9 Print a Document

Once you're done creating your document, you'll want to print it to paper. Writer supports the standard printing options that most Windows programs support. If your document has color charts and you have a color printer, the charts will print just fine. Otherwise, the charts will print in shades of black and gray (and still look fine!).

Be sure to save your document before you print it. Actually, it's a good idea to select **File**, **Save** to save your document throughout the editing of that document. If your printer jams or the Windows print queue messes up during the printing process (rare but it can happen), you could lose changes you made to the document before you printed it.

If you select **File**, **Export as PDF**, Writer saves your document in the common PDF format, which you can send to any computer with *Adobe Acrobat Reader* and that user will be able to view or print your document with all the formatting preserved, even if he or she doesn't have Writer (see **36** **Save a Document as a PDF File**).

Before You Begin

✔ **2** Create a New Document

✔ **3** Open an Existing Document

✔ **4** Type Text into a Document

See Also

→ **10** About the Rulers

→ **14** Set Up Page Formatting

🔍 KEY TERM

Adobe Acrobat Reader—A free program, available from www.Adobe.com, that reads and prints PDF document files. All formatting of the document can be preserved, displayed, and printed by Adobe Acrobat Reader even if the user's computer is not Windows based.

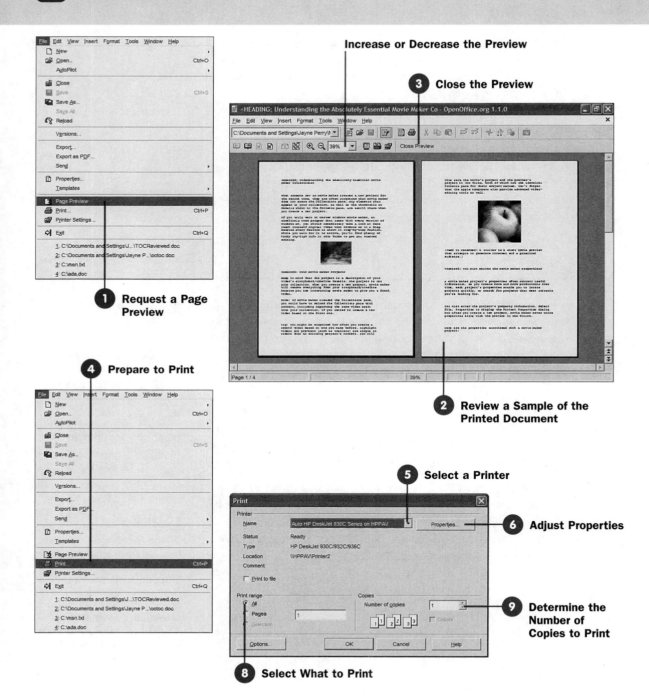

Increase or Decrease the Preview

3 Close the Preview

1 Request a Page Preview

4 Prepare to Print

2 Review a Sample of the Printed Document

5 Select a Printer

6 Adjust Properties

9 Determine the Number of Copies to Print

8 Select What to Print

Adjust Print Options

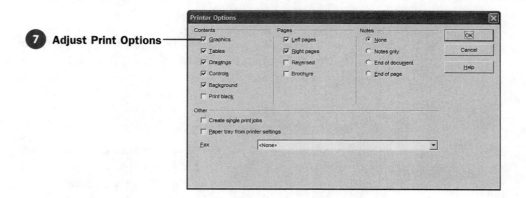

① Request a Page Preview

Select the **Page Preview** option from the **File** menu.

② Review a Sample of the Printed Document

Look over the preview of the document to see if it appears to be properly formatted.

③ Close the Preview

Once you've previewed what your document will look like printed, click the **Close Preview** button. If you need to make further edits to your document, do so now.

④ Prepare to Print

Once you're satisfied that the document is ready to print, select the **Print** option from the **File** menu. The **Print** dialog box appears.

⑤ Select a Printer

Select the printer you want to print to from the **Name** drop-down list.

TIPS

You can adjust the number of pages that Page Preview shows at one time by clicking to select the **Multiple Pages** toolbar button and designating the number of rows and columns of sample pages you want to view at one time.

If you have a fax modem, you can select your fax from the **Name** list to send your document to a fax recipient.

6 **Adjust Properties**

If you want to adjust any printer settings, click the **Properties** button. The dialog box that appears when you click **Properties** varies from printer to printer. Close the printer's **Properties** dialog box once you've made any needed changes.

7 **Adjust Print Options**

Click the **Options** button to display the **Printer Options** dialog box. From the **Printer Options** dialog box, you can adjust several print settings, such as whether you want graphics, tables, and drawings printed or omitted from the printed document.

Click the **OK** button to close the **Printer Options** dialog box.

8 **Select What to Print**

Click to select either **All** or **Pages** to designate that you want to print the entire document or only a portion of it. If you click **Pages**, type the page number or a range of page numbers (such as 2-5 or 1-10, 15-25) that you want to print.

9 **Determine the Number of Copies to Print**

Click the arrow box next to the **Number of Copies** option to determine how many copies you want to print.

Once you've determined how many pages and copies to print, click the **OK** button to print your document and close the **Print** dialog box.

NOTE

Although it's called *Printer Options*, the **Printer Options** dialog box is not printer specific but rather controls the way your document appears when printed. If, for instance, you want to print for a binder, you could click to select the **Left pages** and **Right pages** options to leave an extra middle margin on every other printed page.

3

Making Your Words Look Good

IN THIS CHAPTER:

Writer adds flair to your documents. Not only can Writer make your words read more accurately with its automatic correction tools, but Writer makes your writing look better too. Writer supports character, paragraph, and even complete document formatting.

When you begin learning Writer, don't worry with the formatting. Just type your text before formatting it so that you get your thoughts in the document while they are still fresh. After you type your document, you can format its text. Many writers follow this write-then-format plan throughout their entire careers.

10 About the Rulers

Before You Begin

✔ **1** Set Writer Options

✔ **4** Type Text into a Document

See Also

→ **11** About Paragraph Breaks and Tabs

→ **13** Apply Paragraph Formatting

→ **14** Set Up Page Formatting

KEY TERMS

Horizontal ruler—A guide you can display across the top of your document that shows the horizontal position of text and graphics on the page.

Vertical ruler—A guide you can display down the left side of your document that shows the vertical position of text and graphics on the page.

Writer has two rulers: the *horizontal ruler* and the *vertical ruler*. Both of these rulers are onscreen guides that display measurement values so you'll know where on the page your text will appear. For example, if your measurements are set to inches (see **1** Set Writer Options), the **2** on your horizontal ruler means that all text beneath that ruler's **2** is exactly 2 inches from the left margin.

If you do not see a vertical ruler, select the **View** option on the **Text Document** option list and click to check the **Vertical ruler** option.

The ruler measurements are relative to the left and right margins. For example, in this figure, the ruler's left edge is the left edge of the page, but the ruler's white area shows where the left and right margins appear.

In addition to showing margins and the page width, the horizontal ruler also shows this additional information:

- *Tab stop* (see **11** About Paragraph Breaks and Tabs)
- Paragraph *indent* (see **13** Apply Paragraph Formatting)
- Border (see **13** Apply Paragraph Formatting)
- Columns (see **15** Create a Multicolumn Newsletter)

Left Edge of Page   **Left Margin**   **Horizontal Ruler**

Top Edge of the Page

Top Margin

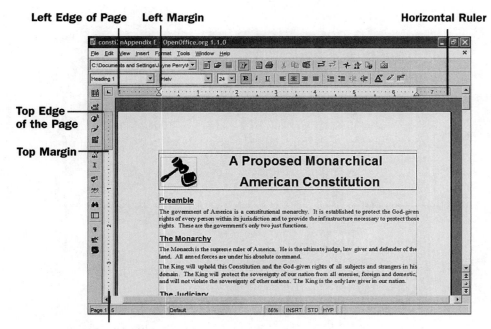

Vertical Ruler

Rulers show the position of text and graphics.

If you format different paragraphs in your document differently from one another, the ruler will change to reflect those differences. In other words, if the first paragraph has three tab stops and a first-line indent, when you click anywhere within that paragraph, the ruler changes to show those tab stops and the first-line indent, as shown in the following figure.

If a subsequent paragraph has a different set of indents, tab stops, and margins, the ruler will show those differences if you click within that paragraph, as shown in the next figure.

The horizontal ruler is so tied to paragraph formatting that if you double-click the ruler, the **Paragraph** formatting dialog box appears. **13** **Apply Paragraph Formatting** explains how to use the **Paragraph** dialog box.

 TIP

Right-click either ruler to change the measurement to a different setting, such as from inches to centimeters.

KEY TERMS

Tab stop—Controls the horizontal placement of text on a line.

Indent—The space between the left and right page margins and the current paragraph.

First-Line Indent

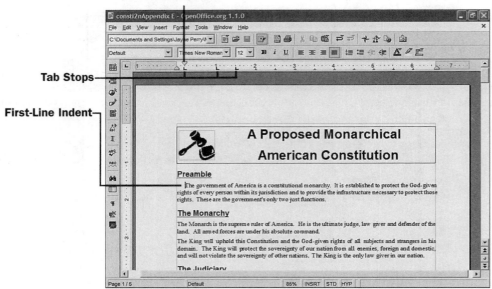

Tab Stops

First-Line Indent

A ruler showing three tab stops and a first-line indent.

Left-Margin Indent

A ruler showing no tab stops and a left-margin indent.

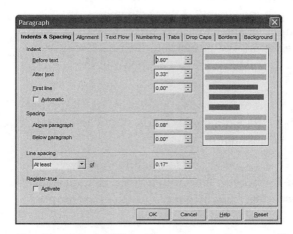

The Paragraph dialog box appears when you double-click the ruler.

Obviously, it's important that you keep in mind that the current horizontal ruler showing at any one time is only reflecting the current paragraph's tab and margin settings. A ruler can reflect each paragraph differently.

The ruler does more than update to reflect the current paragraph's settings. You can use the ruler to change tab, indent, and margin settings without using dialog boxes. Unless pinpoint precision is required, the ruler is actually the best place to make these changes.

For example, click anywhere on the ruler and a tab stop will appear at that location. You can drag that tab stop left or right to adjust its position. You can drag any tab stop left or right, even those you applied using the **Paragraph** formatting dialog box. To change the type of tab you place, first click the tab character box at the left of the ruler to change the next tab you place on the ruler.

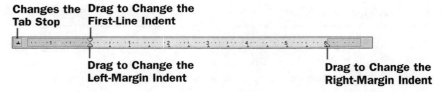

Changes the Tab Stop **Drag to Change the First-Line Indent**

Drag to Change the Left-Margin Indent   **Drag to Change the Right-Margin Indent**

Click the tab character box to change the kind of tab you want to place on the ruler.

If you want to increase a paragraph's *left-margin indent*, click in that paragraph to display its horizontal ruler. Then, drag the ruler's left-margin indent character to its new location. After you drag the ruler's left-margin indent character, the paragraph's actual left-margin indent changes to reflect the new setting. To change the *first-line indent*, drag the ruler's first-line indent character to a new location. To change the *right-margin indent*, drag the ruler's right-margin indent character to a new location.

Although the horizontal ruler is constantly linked to individual paragraphs, the page's overall left and right margins also appear on the horizontal ruler. The margins are set off of the gray areas on either end of the ruler. You can change the left or right margin by dragging the ruler's edge of either margin (the position between the gray and the white of the ruler's typing area) left or right.

NOTE

Don't confuse the ruler's half-inch placement marks with the centered tab stop. Both look the same, but the centered tab stop will be darker, when present, than the inch marks. See **11** About Paragraph Breaks and Tabs for more information on centered tabs.

KEY TERMS

Left-margin indent—An indention of the left edge of all lines in a paragraph, usually more so than in surrounding paragraphs, to set off the paragraph, as might be done for a quotation.

First-line indent—A right indent of the first line in a paragraph where subsequent lines in the same paragraph align closer to the left margin.

Right-margin indent—An indention of the right edge of all lines in a paragraph, usually more so than in surrounding paragraphs, to bring in the paragraph's right edge, as might be done for a quotation.

Be careful that you leave enough room for your printer's required margin. For example, many laser printers will not print less than one-half inch to the edge of the paper, no matter how wide you attempt to make your margins.

Select **Edit**, **Undo** (or **Ctrl+Z**) to undo changes you make to the left ruler.

You won't use the vertical ruler as much as the horizontal ruler, which is why Writer's default setting doesn't display this ruler. Nevertheless, the vertical ruler can be handy for showing the top and bottom margins on a page as well as the general position on a page where certain elements appear. For example, you can tell from the vertical ruler exactly how many inches down a page a graphic image will appear when printed.

One of the most common uses of the vertical ruler is to display it to show the top and bottom margin used by the document. You can drag these margins to a different location, and when you're satisfied with the new margin settings, you can once again hide the vertical ruler to give yourself more editing area on the screen.

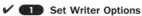

⑪ About Paragraph Breaks and Tabs

Before You Begin

✔ **①** Set Writer Options
✔ **⑩** About the Rulers

See Also

➔ **⑬** Apply Paragraph Formatting

The nonprinting characters enable you to see the hidden elements that Writer uses to determine where certain formatting should begin and end (see **④** Type Text into a Document).

Understanding exactly how Writer treats paragraphs is the first step in understanding Writer's formatting capabilities. Knowing exactly where a paragraph begins and ends is not always obvious. For example, in the next figure, it appears that the document has three paragraphs.

If you glance at the screen or print the document, three paragraphs certainly appear to be there. As far as your readers are concerned, the document does contain three paragraphs. Nevertheless, as far as Writer is concerned, this particular document contains only a single paragraph! Clicking the **Nonprinting characters** button on this particular document shows nonprinting characters that reveal this document contains only a single paragraph, as the following figure shows.

You can press **Shift+Enter** to start a new line without starting a new paragraph. The newline nonprinting character will appear when you turn on nonprinting characters. Without the nonprinting characters appearing, it looks as though the document will have multiple paragraphs.

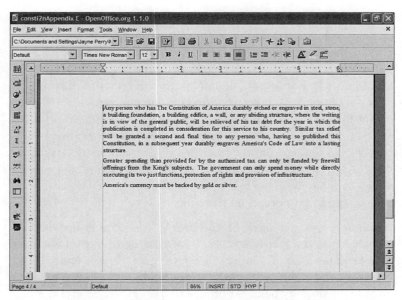

Seeing isn't always believing—how many paragraphs are in this document?

Nonprinting Characters Button

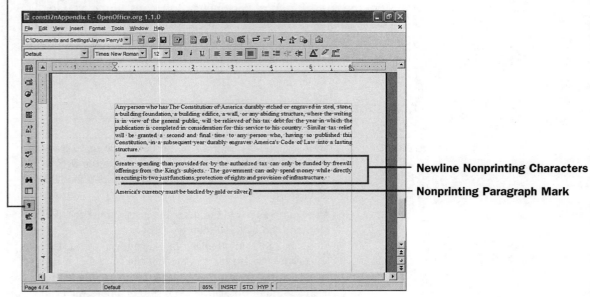

Newline Nonprinting Characters

Nonprinting Paragraph Mark

Only one paragraph mark appears, meaning that Writer views the entire document as one long paragraph.

TIP

Another advantage of keeping a section as one long paragraph is if you make a paragraph adjustment to the text later, your change applies to all the text and you won't have to apply the change multiple times over multiple paragraphs.

KEY TERM

Section—A block of document text that contains its own formatting, including possible headers and footers, that will differ from surrounding text.

You won't want to create an entire document this way. There are times, though, when you want to do this so that Writer formats all the lines uniformly as though they were different paragraphs. In other words, if you are typing a section of text that is more than one paragraph, and you want to format that section differently from the rest of the document, one way to do so is to keep the text all one paragraph. You'll press **Shift+Enter** to give the lines the look of multiple paragraphs, but Writer will see them as being only one. Then, any paragraph formatting you apply to the text—either from the ruler (see **10** About the Rulers) or from the **Paragraph** formatting dialog box (see **13** Apply Paragraph Formatting)—applies to all the text in that section. You won't have to format more than one paragraph individually.

This multiparagraph trick using **Shift+Enter** is wonderful to remember for the times when you have a couple or more paragraphs that you may need to adjust formatting for later. If, however, you have several paragraphs to format differently from surrounding text, or even a page or more of text, you may be better off creating a new *section* for that text. You can then easily change the formatting of all the paragraphs in that section without affecting the surrounding text. **14** Set Up Page Formatting discusses sections in more detail.

Tab stops are critical in most documents. Tab stops enable you to align values consistently across multiple lines. Also, when you use a tab stop, you don't have to press the **spacebar** many times to jump to the right on a line. Tab stops enable you to start paragraphs with an indented first line. Writer supports four kinds of tab stops, as detailed in Table 3.1.

TABLE 3.1 Writer's Four Tab Stops

Tab Stop	Description
Left tab	After you press **Tab**, the insertion point jumps to that tab stop and the text you then type appears to the right of the tab stop's position. A left tab is the tab most people are familiar with and use.
Right tab	After you press **Tab**, the insertion point jumps to that tab stop and the text you then type appears to the left of the tab stop's position. In other words, as you type the text moves left toward the left margin, against the tab stop. A right tab stop is useful for page or chapter numbers in a list because it ensures that the right edge of the numbers will align together.

TABLE 3.1   Continued

Tab Stop	Description
Decimal tab	After you press **Tab**, the insertion point jumps to that tab stop and the numeric values you then type will position themselves so that the decimal points all align on multiple lines.
Centered tab	After you press **Tab**, the insertion point jumps to that tab stop and the text you then type adjusts to remain centered around the tab stop.

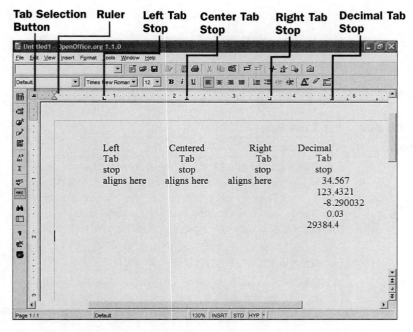

Use the ruler to set and change tab stops.

To set a tab stop, use either the ruler or the **Tab** dialog box. You can click the **Tab** selection button on the ruler to select which tab stop you want to place. Every time you click the **Tab** selection button, the symbol changes to a different kind of tab stop. When you then click anywhere on the ruler, that kind of tab appears on the ruler where you click.

To use the **Tab** dialog box, double-click the ruler or select **Format**, **Paragraph** to display the **Paragraph** dialog box. Click the **Tabs** tab to display the **Tabs** page.

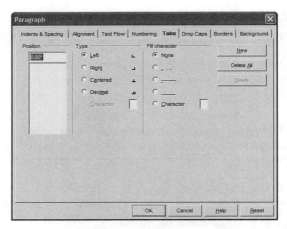

The Tabs page enables you to set tabs for the current paragraph.

Table 3.2 describes each of the options in the **Tabs** page.

TABLE 3.2   The Tabs Page Options

Option	Description
Position	Enables you to enter individual measurement values, such as **0.25"**, to represent one-fourth of an inch. After you type a value, click **New** to add that value to the list of tab settings. To clear an existing tab stop, select the value and click **Delete**. Click **Delete All** to clear the entire tab list.
Type	Determines the type of tab stop (such as a left tab stop) that you want to place.
Character	A character you want Writer to use as the decimal separator for decimal tab stops.
Fill Character	Leading characters that you want to appear, if any, between values and tab stops. The fill character forms a path for the eye to follow across the page within a tab stop. For example, a fill of dotted lines often connects goods to their corresponding prices in a price list.

12 Apply Character Formatting

When you want to make a point, you can format your text to modify the way it looks. Common character formatting styles are underline, boldface, and italicized text. Writer offers several additional character formats you can apply to your document's text.

One of the most common character formats you can apply is to change the *typeface* (loosely called a *font* in general discussions) in your document. The typeface determines the way your characters look, whether artsy or elegant. Fonts have names, such as **Courier** and **Times New Roman**. The size of a font is measured in *points*. As a standard rule of thumb, a 10- or 12-point size is standard and readable for most word-processed documents.

As you type and move the insertion point, Writer displays the current font name and size on the Object bar, as well as whether the current character is boldfaced, italicized, or underlined. Writer also enables you to change the color of your text.

When using character formatting, express but don't impress. Too many different kinds of characters make your documents look busy and distract the reader from your message.

1 Select Text

When you want to format characters, select the characters first. You can select a single character, an entire word, a sentence, a paragraph, or multiple paragraphs. However much text you select before applying a format is the text that will take on the character formatting you apply.

You can also apply a character format to text before you type it. Instead of selecting text first, pick a character format and then type the text. The text you type will have those character format attributes.

2 Choose a Format

Click either the **Boldface**, **Italics**, or **Underline** button on the **Function** toolbar to apply that format. You can click two or all three to combine the character styles.

Before You Begin

✔ **4** Type Text into a Document

✔ **5** Edit Text

See Also

→ **13** Apply Paragraph Formatting

 NOTE

Although they're called *character* formats, you can easily apply them to multiple characters, paragraphs, and even complete documents as easily as to single characters. Writer applies character formats to any text you select.

(K)EY TERMS

Typeface—A character design that determines the size and style of how your characters look.

Font—Loosely used as another name for typeface.

Point—Approximately 1/72nd of an inch.

TIP

Ctrl+B, Ctrl+I, and **Ctrl+U** are all shortcut keys to apply boldface, italics, and underlining.

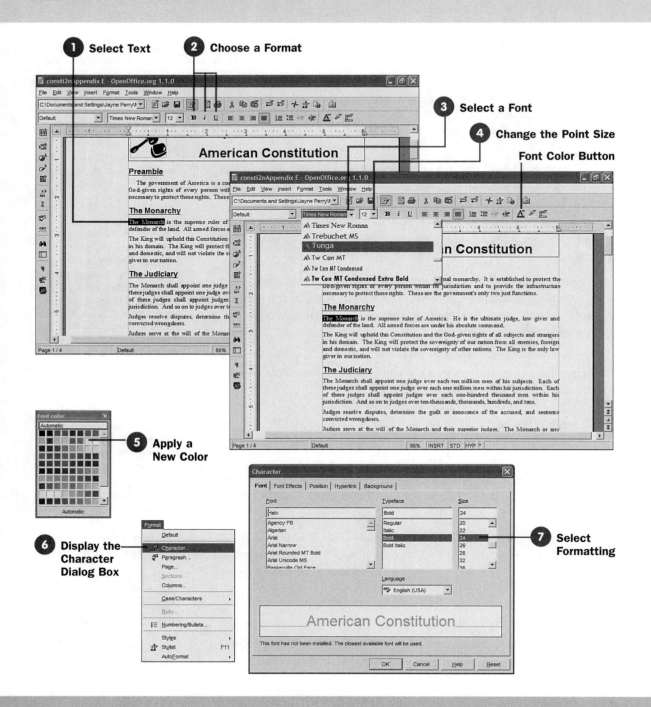

1 Select Text

2 Choose a Format

3 Select a Font

4 Change the Point Size

Font Color Button

5 Apply a New Color

6 Display the Character Dialog Box

7 Select Formatting

❸ Select a Font

To change a selected text's font (or text that you're about to type), click the drop-down arrow to the right of the **Font Name** box and select a new font. Each font name appears in its own font, so you'll know what your text will look like before you apply the format. After you select a new font, your selected text will change to that font.

❹ Change the Point Size

To choose a new point size for the selected text, click the drop-down arrow to the right of the **Point Size** list. When you click to select a size, your selected font will change to that size.

❺ Apply a New Color

To change the color of selected text (or text you're about the type), long-click the **Font Color** button on the **Function** toolbar. A **Font Color** *palette* appears. Click a color on the palette to change your selected text to that color.

KEY TERM

Palette—A collection of colors from which you can choose.

❻ Display the Character Dialog Box

Instead of using the **Function** toolbar to apply character formats, you can set such formats in the **Character** dialog box. Display the **Character** dialog box by selecting **Format**, **Character** from the menu bar.

❼ Select Formatting

The **Character** dialog box's **Font** page enables you to select common character formats such as the font name, bold, italics, and the size. The **Font Effects** page offers more options, including underlining, color selection, and special effects such as a shadow and blinking text. The **Position** page enables you to select a subscript or superscript version of your font as well as rotate your text so it travels up and down the page instead of across it.

TIP

Text rotated 90 degrees in the **Character** dialog box's **Position** page works well in some letterheads, for titles, or as a sidebar that travels down the length of your page.

The **Hyperlink** page enables you to add a link to a Web page or a filename to your text. Web pages often use such hyperlinks. The **Background** page enables you to set a background color for your text.

13 Apply Paragraph Formatting

Before You Begin

✔ **12** Apply Character Formatting

See Also

→ **14** Set Up Page Formatting

TIP

You can set up a paragraph format before typing a paragraph, and Writer applies the format to the newly typed paragraph.

KEY TERM

Justify—Determine the paragraph text's alignment in relation to the right and left margins. Many word processors use the term *justify* for any justification effect, such as right, center, and left justification.

You can change the format of entire paragraphs of text, such as the line spacing, justification, and indention of text. You can apply that format to selected paragraphs or to all the paragraphs in your document.

One of the most common ways to format a paragraph is to *justify* it. Writer supports these justification options:

- **Left justification**—Aligns (makes even) text with the left margin. Personal and business letters are often left-justified.

- **Center justification**—Centers text between the left and right margins. Titles and letterheads are often centered atop a document.

- **Right justification**—Aligns text with the right margin, and the left margin's text is not kept straight.

- **Full justification**—Aligns text with both the left and right margins. Newspaper and magazine columns are usually fully justified; the text aligns with the left and right margins evenly.

Writer provides many additional ways to format your paragraphs, such as the capability to put a border around them and indent the first lines.

❶ Select Text

Select the text you want to format. As **11** **About Paragraph Breaks and Tabs** explains, Writer considers all text up to the next non-printing paragraph symbol to be one paragraph. If you apply a paragraph format to any part of a paragraph, the entire paragraph changes to reflect the new format. You can format multiple paragraphs at once by selecting multiple paragraphs before changing the format.

❷ Change the Justification

Once you've selected the text you want to format, you may change the paragraph's justification by clicking the **Align Left**, **Centered**, **Align Right**, or **Justified** button on the **Function** toolbar. As soon as you click the button, Writer changes the selected paragraph's justification to reflect the change.

2 Change the Justification

1 Select Text

3 Change the Indention

4 Set a First-Line Indent

6 Add a Border

5 Display the Paragraph Dialog Box

7 Review the Border

TIP

You can make more precise paragraph indentions by dragging the ruler's **Indent** button left or right.

3 Change the Indention

If you want to indent the entire selected paragraph to the right, click the **Function** toolbar's **Increase Indent** button. For each click of the **Increase Indent** button, the paragraph shifts to the right one-half inch. Once you indent using the **Increase Indent** button, the **Decrease Indent** button appears so you can move the indention back half an inch. (Of course, **Ctrl+Z** undoes indentions you make also.)

4 Set a First-Line Indent

Drag the ruler's **First-Line Indent** button to the right to indent only the first line of the selected paragraphs. Adding a first-line indent ensures your paragraphs have their initial lines indented to the right without you having to press **Tab** manually each time you begin a new paragraph.

5 Display the Paragraph Dialog Box

All the paragraph-formatting commands are available from the **Paragraph** dialog box. Select **Format**, **Paragraph** to display the **Paragraph** dialog box.

The **Paragraph** dialog box's **Indents & Spacing** page enables you to set precise indents as well as specify a default number of blank lines to appear between your paragraphs. The **Alignment** page enables you to set the precise justification of your paragraphs.

The **Text Flow** page enables you to set automatic hyphenation so that Writer can insert hyphens as needed to make long words wrap better at the end of a line. The **Numbering** page enables you to number paragraphs as you might do for legal pleadings. The **Tabs** page enables you to set tab stops (see **11 About Paragraph Breaks and Tabs**).

The **Drop Caps** page lets you specify a *drop cap* letter format to start your paragraphs with. The **Borders** page enables you to create borders around paragraphs and color them. The **Background** page enables you to set a background color.

KEY TERM

Drop cap—A large starting letter or word, sometimes twice the size of the other letters in the same paragraph, that provides a visual starting point for paragraphs of text.

6 **Add a Border**

Click the **Borders** tab to display the **Borders** page. Click one of the line arrangements to determine whether you want to enclose all four sides of the paragraph with a border or only two opposing sides. The line style list determines how thick the border will appear. You can also adjust how far from the margins and text the border will appear by adjusting the **Left**, **Right**, **Top**, and **Bottom** settings. Special border effects, such as a shadowed effect, are also available here.

Your entire document can appear with a border around it, too. **14** **Set Up Page Formatting** explains how to create such a border.

7 **Review the Border**

Once you've set up a bordered paragraph, click **OK** to close the **Paragraph** dialog box and review the bordered paragraph to ensure you've got the right effect. Remember to reserve your use of borders, shadowing, and the other special effects for those times when you want to emphasize a title or a statement. Don't overdo the use of special formats. Your document can look too busy with too many formats, making it difficult to read.

 TIP

As you change values throughout the **Paragraph** dialog box, many of the box's pages display a thumbnail image that changes to show you what effect your new paragraph format will have on the selected paragraphs.

---

14 **Set Up Page Formatting**

You will often need to make format changes to your entire document. Perhaps you want to change the printed margins on the page. You may want to add a background color or even put a border around the document.

The **Page** dialog box contains all of Writer's options that enable you to modify your document's format. Any changes you make to the current page applies to all pages in your document.

If you want to start a new section, as you might do if you wanted to format several pages within a document differently from surrounding pages, select **Insert**, **Section** and click **Insert** to make Writer begin a new section. Any page formatting that you apply to the section stays in that section.

Before You Begin

✔ **5** Edit Text

✔ **12** Apply Character Formatting

✔ **13** Apply Paragraph Formatting

See Also

→ **15** Create a Multicolumn Newsletter

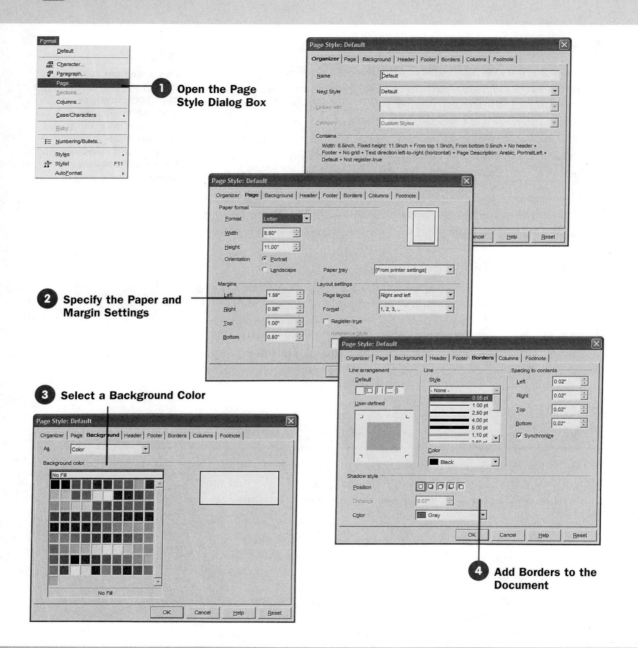

1 Open the Page Style Dialog Box

2 Specify the Paper and Margin Settings

3 Select a Background Color

4 Add Borders to the Document

1 **Open the Page Style Dialog Box**

Select **Page** from the **Format** menu to open the **Page Style** dialog box.

The **Page Style** dialog box contains several categories you can use to modify the pages in your document. Click each tab across the top of the dialog box to select different options. The **Organizer** page determines the default style currently used and enables you to select a different style. See **16** **About Styles and Templates** for help with understanding and using styles. The **Page** tab enables you to format your paper statistics, such as selecting a page length as well as margin settings. The **Background** page enables you to place a background color on the page.

The **Header, Footer,** and **Footnote** pages provide you the ability to place a header, footer, and footnotes on the pages of your documents. For example, you might want to place a company logo on the page header of your first page, and you'd do so inside a header. **33** **About Headers and Footers** explains how to use headers and footers. **35** **Add a Footnote or Endnote** explains how to add footnotes and endnotes to your document.

Use the **Columns** page to turn your document into a multicolumned document, as you might do for a newsletter. **15** **Create a Multicolumn Newsletter** explains how to work with multiple columns.

2 **Specify the Paper and Margin Settings**

Click the **Page** tab to show the page options. When you change the type of paper you use in your printer, such as going from letter size to legal, you'll need to select the proper option, such as **Legal**, from the **Format** list. If you use a nonstandard paper size, one that is not letter, legal, or one of the other options in the **Format** list, you can click to adjust the **Width** and **Height** settings to the unique settings of your paper.

You also may want to change the orientation of your printed page from *portrait* to *landscape*. In addition, you can give your margins more or less room by adjusting the **Left, Right, Top,** and **Bottom** measurements. If you have multiple paper trays in your

 TIP

If your document contains multiple sections, page formatting changes apply only to the current section unless you first select your entire document, with **Ctrl+A**, before modifying the page format.

 TIP

As with character formats, don't overuse background colors. You should use a colored stationary in your printer for best effect if you want to print on a colored background.

NOTE

You cannot undo many of the changes you make from the **Page Style** dialog box. If you apply a change and want to undo it, you'll have to display the **Page Style** dialog box again and change the incorrect setting back.

 TIP

The **Format** list contains common envelope sizes for when you want to print addresses and return addresses from your printer.

KEY TERMS

Portrait—Printed down the narrow edge, as you might do for a letter.

Landscape—Printed across the long edge, as you might do for a wide report.

printer, such as an envelope feeder, you may want to select a different tray from the **Paper tray** option. Finally, the **Layout settings** area enables you to control how the pages print in relation to one another; for example, if you plan to bind your output into a booklet, you may want the left and right margins to be mirrored to leave more room in the middle for the binding or hole punching.

③ Select a Background Color

Click the **Background** tab to add a background color to your page. Although you may want to use colored paper for extensive coloring, you might want to lightly highlight a report page that appears inside your document with a highlighted background color.

④ Add Borders to the Document

Click the **Borders** tab to display the border options. As with paragraph borders (see **13 Apply Paragraph Formatting**), you can specify which edges you want to use as a border (the sides, top and bottom, or all four sides) and the line thickness of the border (from the **Line Style** list). If you want to add an additional effect to your border, you can adjust the position and color of shading. Shading a border softens the border's look.

15 Create a Multicolumn Newsletter

Before You Begin

✔ **10** About the Rulers
✔ **13** Apply Paragraph Formatting

See Also

→ **16** About Styles and Templates

TIP

Generally, you should type your document's text before breaking the document into multiple columns.

When you want to create newspaper-style columns—such as those that appear in newsletters and brochures—configure Writer to format your text with multiple columns. You can assign multiple columns to the entire document or to only sections. By applying multiple columns to certain sections, you'll be able to span a headline across the top of two or three columns of text underneath.

① Type the Document

Create your initial document without worrying about column placement. Type your headline and other text using Writer's default styles and formats.

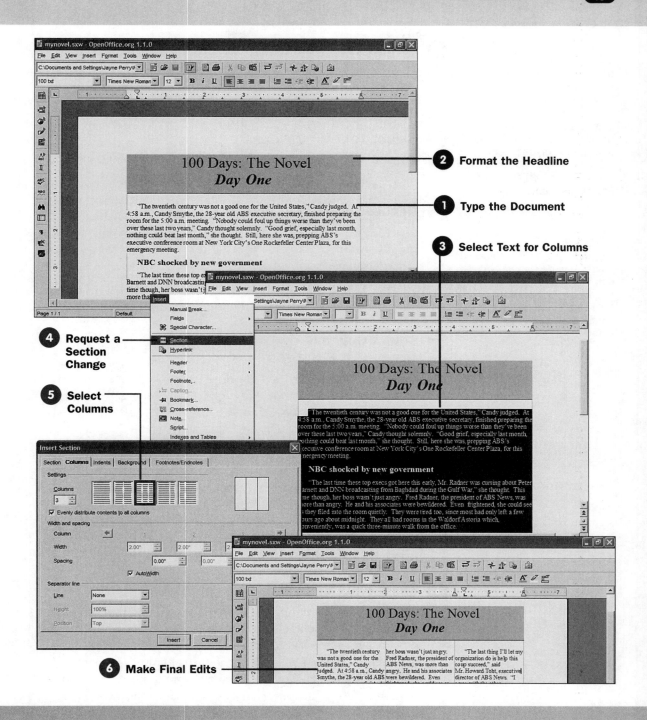

2 Format the Headline

1 Type the Document

3 Select Text for Columns

4 Request a Section Change

5 Select Columns

6 Make Final Edits

TIP

If you routinely write a newsletter or other multi-columned document, you may want to create a template that contains your headline and column layout and then apply that template to create each issue. For more, see **16** **About Styles and Templates**.

 TIP

Turn on nonprinting characters to ensure that you don't select any part of the headline. Start selecting following the headline's nonprinting paragraph character.

2 **Format the Headline**

Change your headline's format to match the style you want your newsletter to take on. Not all multicolumn documents have headlines across the top of the columns, but many do.

3 **Select Text for Columns**

Select all the text that will be converted to multiple columns. This generally begins immediately following your headline.

4 **Request a Section Change**

Select **Insert**, **Section** from the menu bar. This menu option is slightly misleading. You are actually converting the selected text to a new document section because you selected the text before selecting the **Section** option.

Click the **Columns** tab in the resulting dialog box.

5 **Select Columns**

You can select the number of columns you want by clicking to change the number in the **Columns** list. Generally, it's quicker to click the thumbnail image that displays the number of columns you want to convert to. The options beneath the **Settings** section enable you to precisely adjust each column's width and the space between them. Generally, Writer's default width and spacing values work well.

Feel free to select a separating line by selecting from the **Line** drop-down menu. Each option provides a different line width that will appear between your columns. You can also specify, from the **Height** option, if you want the line to run the entire column length (**100%**) or less.

6 **Make Final Edits**

Once your document appears in columns, you'll almost certainly need to make some final adjustments. For example, with three or more columns, the text becomes lumpy with too many spaces between the words if you've justified the columns. Newspapers often use full justification, but they suffer from this extra spacing at times. Most of the time, columns that you left-justify look the best with three or more columns. Also, subheadings that you formatted before converting to multiple columns may be too large in their columns, so you can decrease the font size of such subheadings (see **12** **Apply Character Formatting**).

16 About Styles and Templates

You can begin with a *template* to create a document that has a pre-arranged look. You can apply a *style* you've created previously to text within any document. By reusing templates and styles, you reduce the amount of work you have to do to create a document.

Suppose you find yourself typing a weekly report for your company and you often quote your corporate office's weekly sales records. If you format the sales record portion of your report differently from the rest of your report, perhaps putting it into a table with a heading and a lightly colored background with boldfaced numbers and titles, you can create a style for that section of text. In the future, when it's time to type that information, instead of formatting the corporate sales records, you only need to select the corporate sales records and apply your predefined style to that selection. By defining the style one time, you won't ever need to go through the motions of formatting of text that way again; instead, you just apply the style, and Writer formats the text according to the style.

Templates take styles further. Actually, a template is to an entire document what a style is to selected text. When creating a document that's to look like another that you often create, such as a fax letter that requires special formatting, you can elect to use a fax template you've already set up with the **To:**, **From:**, and **Cover Page Note** fields already placed where they belong and you only need to fill in the details.

Keep in mind that a template is a model for a document. A style is often a model for smaller blocks of text, usually paragraphs. A template may contain several styles. If you want to use a style that's available to your current document or template, you can easily select that style and apply it to existing paragraphs or text you're about to type.

The **Stylelist**, available from the **Format** menu or by pressing **F11**, is a dialog box that lists every style available in the current document. Each style has a name. If you create a new document using **File**, **New**, the

Before You Begin

✔ **5** Edit Text

See Also

→ **17** Use a Style
→ **18** Use a Template

🔍 KEY TERMS

Template—A predefined document with styles and other formatting, such as columns and tables, that forms a model for new documents.

Style—A set of character and paragraph formats you can apply to text to change that text's format details.

📝 NOTE

In reality, you always use a template when you create new Writer documents. Writer uses a default template named **Default** unless you specify another template. The font and margin settings offered when you create a new document come from this default template.

styles in the Stylelist will display the default template's styles. If you create a new document using a predefined template, the styles in the **Stylelist** dialog box come from the styles defined in that template.

— **Styles**

The Stylelist dialog box displays the current styles available to you.

You can also see the styles available to you in a different way. You can also display a catalog of styles that shows the styles in a format you may prefer over the **Stylelist** dialog box. Select **Format**, **Styles**, **Catalog** (or press **Ctrl+F11**) to see the **Style Catalog** dialog box. You can select paragraph styles, character styles, and other kinds of styles currently available to you.

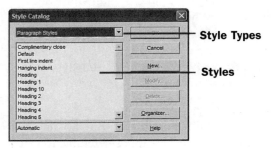

— **Style Types**

— **Styles**

The Style Catalog lists styles by paragraph style types, among other types.

When you want to use a template, you'll select **File**, **New**, **Templates and Documents** to choose the template you want to work from.

TIP

When you learn about styles and templates in Writer, you also learn about them in the other OpenOffice.org products, because they all use styles and templates in the same way.

17 Use a Style

Using a style is simple. You can apply a style to selected text to format that text with the style's character and paragraph formatting. Writer comes with several styles, and you can add your own.

Suppose that you routinely write résumés for other people. You might develop three separate sets of character and paragraph formats that work well, respectively, for the title of a résumé and an applicant's personal information and work history. Instead of defining each of these formats every time you create a résumé, you can format a paragraph with each style and store the styles under their own names (such as **Résumé Title**, **Résumé Personal**, and **Résumé Work**). The next time you write a résumé, you need only to select a style, such as Résumé Title, before typing the title. When you then type the title, the title looks the way you want it to look without your having to designate any character or paragraph format.

One of the easiest ways to apply a style is to keep the **Stylelist** dialog box showing at all times by pressing **F11** (or by selecting **Stylelist** from the Format menu). If you don't have the screen room to keep the **Stylelist** showing, you can display it when you want to apply a style and then click its **Close** button to hide the **Stylelist** once again.

1 Select Text for the Style

When you want to apply a predefined style to text, first select the text. Most of the time you'll select a paragraph to format with a style, so if nonprinting characters are showing, be sure to include the paragraph mark when you select the text if you want the style to apply to the entire paragraph. The format of the text will completely change depending on which style you apply, but the text itself will not change.

2 Display the Stylelist

Press **F11** to display the **Stylelist** dialog box. If you don't see paragraph styles (assuming you're adding a style to a paragraph), click the **Paragraph Styles** button in the dialog box's upper-left corner. The style names will then appear that you can apply to your selected paragraph text.

Before You Begin

✔ **5** Edit Text

See Also

→ **18** Use a Template

 TIP

The **Stylelist** provides existing styles, and you can define your own from text you select before displaying the **Stylelist**.

NOTE

The **Stylelist** provides styles for characters, frames, pages, and numbered lists in addition to paragraph styles.

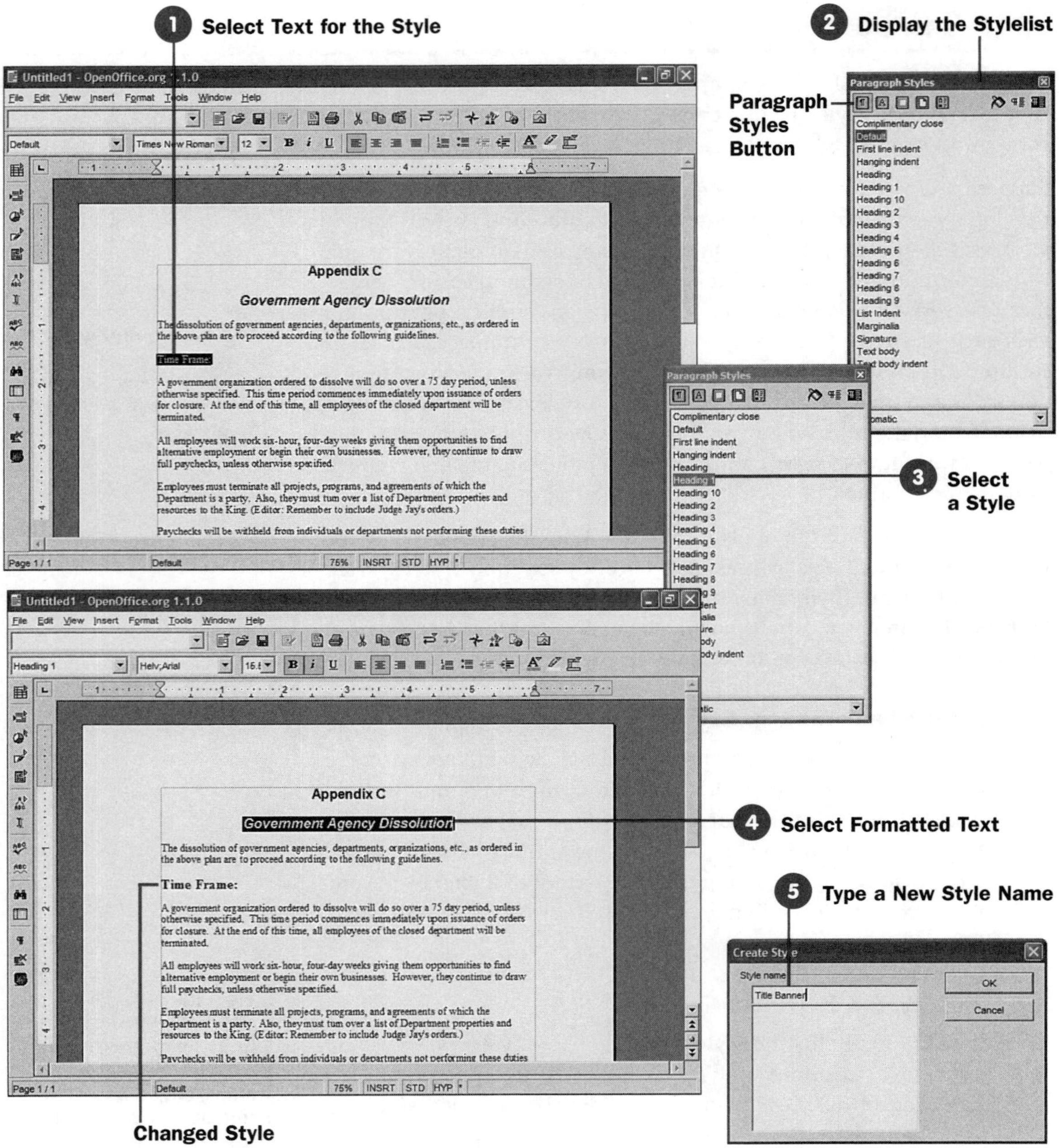

1 Select Text for the Style

2 Display the Stylelist

Paragraph
Styles
Button

3 Select
a Style

4 Select Formatted Text

5 Type a New Style Name

Changed Style

3 Select a Style

Double-click the style in the **Stylelist** that you want to apply.
Depending on the arrangement of your screen and windows, you
can usually see the style immediately applied to your selected text.
If you want to try a different style, double-click another in the list.
Feel free to keep the **Stylelist** dialog box showing or click **Close** to
hide it, depending on how much you plan to use the **Stylelist** during the rest of your editing session.

4 Select Formatted Text

You can easily add your own styles. You add styles to Writer's
Stylelist by example. In other words, you format text to match a
style you want to create and then tell Writer to create a new style
based on that formatted text.

To add a new paragraph style, for example, format and then select
an entire paragraph (including its paragraph symbol if nonprinting characters are showing). Press **F11** to display the **Stylelist** dialog box if it's not currently showing.

5 Type a New Style Name

Click the **New Style from Selection** button, the second button
from the right atop the **Stylelist** dialog box. Writer displays the
Create Style dialog box.

Type a name for your style (one that does not already exist in the
Stylelist, unless you want to replace one). When you click **OK**,
Writer creates the new style based on your selected text. The next
time you select that kind of text and select your new style, Writer
applies the new style's formatting to the text.

18 Use a Template

Before You Begin

✔ **2** Create a New Document

✔ **16** About Styles and Templates

See Also

→ **32** Use AutoCorrect to Improve Your Typing

(🔍)EY TERM

Template Management dialog box—An organizer of templates and styles that enables you to use and organize your templates.

🖎 NOTE

Writer organizes templates in folders. The name of the folder tells you the kind of templates that are inside. The **Default** folder may contain multiple templates, but a blank default template is used when you select **File, New** to create a new document.

💡 TIP

Click the **Preview** button atop the **Templates and Documents** dialog box to see a graphic thumbnail image of a blank document created with the selected template.

Templates contain formatting for complete documents. All the OpenOffice.org programs support templates. If you create a new document without specifying a template, Writer uses the **Default** template style to create the empty document and to set up initial font, margin, and other formatting-related details.

The *Template Management dialog box* lists all the templates available to you. You often work with templates, selecting and adding them, from the **Template Management** dialog box.

1 Request a Template

Select **File, New, Templates and Documents** to open the **Template Management** dialog box. Click the Templates icon to see folders of templates such as **Default** and **Presentations** (for Impress, see **85 Use an Impress Template**).

2 Choose a Template

Decide which template you want to work with. If you've recently installed Writer or have not added new templates, you may see only three templates: **Default**, **Presentation Backgrounds**, and **Presentations**. Only **Default** works well for Writer because the other two are for Impress.

Double-click the **Default** folder to display its contents. What you initially see will not be actual text but will be format instructions for text within any document you create using the template from the **Default** template folder. You may only see the **letter** template unless you or someone else has added templates to your **Default** template folder.

3 View the Letter Template

When you click **letter**, Writer displays the details of that template in the **Templates and Documents** dialog box's right pane.

Click **Open** to create a new document based on that template. Writer opens a new document based on the **letter** template. You'll find instructions for your letter body's text as well as for a logo.

PART I: Writing Words with Writer

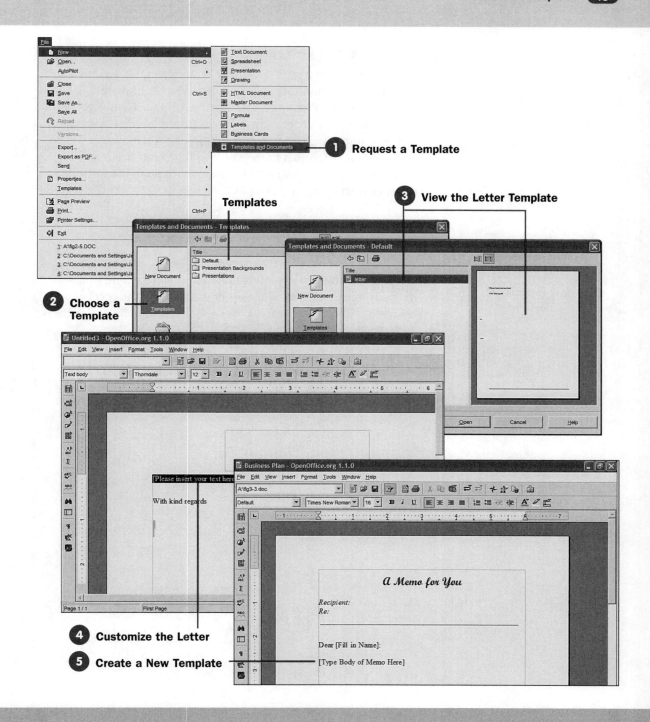

1 Request a Template

Templates

3 View the Letter Template

2 Choose a Template

4 Customize the Letter

5 Create a New Template

4 Customize the Letter

Add text to the template's document to complete the document. The template's formatting will remain in place, although you can always change any character, paragraph, or page format you wish to make the current document different from the foundation document you initially created from the template. A template is only a model of a new document, and you can base your document on the template you choose or make major changes to the initial document created by the template.

5 Create a New Template

Feel free to create your own templates! For example, you might write many memos, so you can create a memo template. Create the model for the template, including the title, recipient, and subject areas, but don't add memo-specific text. Keep the text general. Feel free to include instructions to the user of this template, such as [Type Body of Memo Here].

When you select **File**, **Templates**, **Save**, Writer opens the **Templates** dialog box, where you can assign a name and category folder for your template (such as **Default**). The next time you create a new document from a template, your new template will appear in the list.

4

Adding Lists, Tables, and Graphics

IN THIS CHAPTER:

- **19** Add a Bulleted List
- **20** Add a Numbered List
- **21** Create a Table of Contents
- **22** Create an Index
- **23** About Writer Tables
- **24** Create a Table
- **25** Format a Table
- **26** Manage a Table
- **27** Insert Graphics in a Document
- **28** Draw with Writer
- **29** Add a Chart or Spreadsheet to a Document

Writer provides the ability to add flair to your documents, such as bulleted lists and numbered lists, tables, charts, and graphics. With today's graphical technology, documents are far from text only, and you can easily add formatted graphic elements to get your point across to your audience.

So many of Writer's features, such as bulleted and numbered lists, work automatically. You just begin typing the list and Writer takes care of all the formatting and keeps track of the proper indention for you. When you want to return to regular text once again, Writer can easily return to regular paragraph mode.

19 Add a Bulleted List

OpenOffice.org supports 10 levels of bulleted lists. Therefore, as you might do in an outline, you can indent portions of a bulleted list to create sublists.

Writer makes bulleted lists easy to produce. You only need to type an asterisk or a hyphen before your list's first item, and when you press **Enter** at the end of the line, Writer recognizes the start of the list, converts the asterisk or hyphen to a bullet character, and automatically indents the next line and adds its bullet so you can quickly continue the list.

1 **Type the First Item**

Anytime you want to begin a new bulleted list, simply type an asterisk (*) or a hyphen (-), followed by a space, and then the first line of your list. Do this on a new line. So, to start your list, type an asterisk, a space, and then the text for the first item in your list.

Writer will recognize that you've begun a list when you press **Enter**.

2 **Continue the List**

You won't have to continue typing the asterisk once Writer recognizes that you're typing a list. Writer converts your asterisk to the bullet item on the first line and puts a bullet at the start of your next line so you can continue typing. You only need to worry about your list items, and Writer takes care of the bullets and the indention.

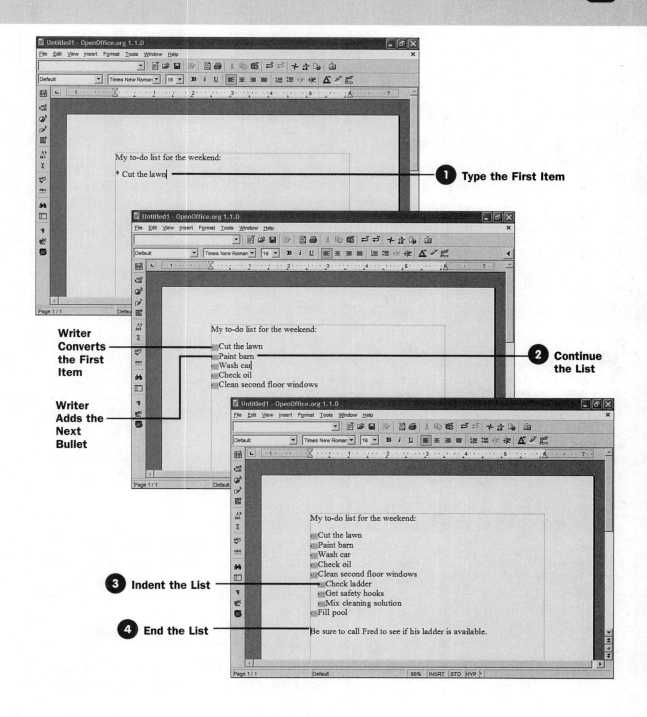

1 Type the First Item

Writer Converts the First Item

Writer Adds the Next Bullet

2 Continue the List

3 Indent the List

4 End the List

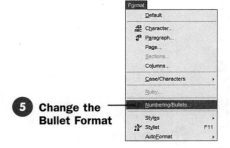

5 Change the
Bullet Format

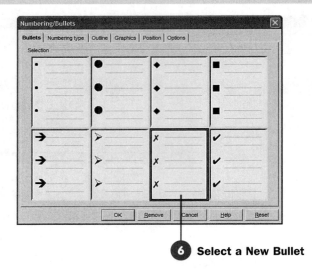

6 Select a New Bullet

3 Indent the List

When you want to create a sublist of bulleted items, press **Tab**
after the bullet. Writer indents the item to create the indented list.
Keep typing the list, and Writer keeps indenting the list, creating
the sublist.

When you want to return to the original indention to continue
your primary list items, press **Shift+Tab** to move back to the left
column.

4 End the List

To end your list, after the final item press **Enter** twice. The first
Enter keypress tells Writer that you don't want to indent anymore.
The second **Enter** keypress moves the cursor to the next line,
adding a blank line between the list's final item and your next regular line of text.

5 Change the Bullet Format

You don't have to settle for the default bullet symbol that Writer
uses. Highlight your bulleted list if you want to change the bullet
symbol used in the list.

Select **Numbering/Bullets** from the **Format** menu to show the **Numbering/Bullets** dialog box. Click the **Bullets** tab to show the **Bullets** page.

6 Select a New Bullet

Click any of the bullet formats to select a new bullet symbol. When you click **OK**, Writer converts your bulleted list so that the symbol you selected appears in your document.

 TIP

If you only want to change some of a list's bulleted symbols, such as the indented sublists, select only those portions of the list before opening the **Numbering/Bullets** dialog box.

---

20 Add a Numbered List

OpenOffice.org supports the use of numbered lists, indented lists with numbered items, in much the same way it supports bulleted lists (see **19 Add a Bulleted List**). Writer handles not only the formatting of your numbered list but also the renumbering if needed. Therefore, if you add items anywhere within or after a numbered list, Writer updates the numbers to reflect the new items. If you delete an item from a numbered list, Writer renumbers the remaining items so the numbers work properly.

As with bullets, OpenOffice.org supports 10 levels of numbered lists. Therefore, as you might do in an outline, you can indent portions of a numbered list to create sublists.

To start a numbered list, you only need to type **1.**, **i.**, or **I.** to signal to Writer that you're typing the first item in a numbered list.

After you type the first line in the numbered list and press **Enter**, Writer recognizes the start of the numbered list, continues the numbering using the same format you used in the first item, and automatically indents the next line and adds its number so you can quickly continue the list.

1 Type the First Item

When you want to begin a numbered list, simply type a number followed by a period or closing parenthesis, such as **1.** or **1**), followed by a space and then the first line of your list. Do this on a new line.

Writer recognizes that you've begun a numbered list when you press **Enter**.

Before You Begin

✔ **13** Apply Paragraph Formatting

✔ **19** Add a Bulleted List

See Also

→ **21** Create a Table of Contents

TIP

You can use a closing parenthesis after the number instead of a period when typing the first item in a numbered list. Therefore, you can type **1**) or **i**) or **I**) to start a numbered list.

TIP

Writer supports several numbering styles, including letters; a "numbered list" might begin with **A)**, **B)**, **C)**.

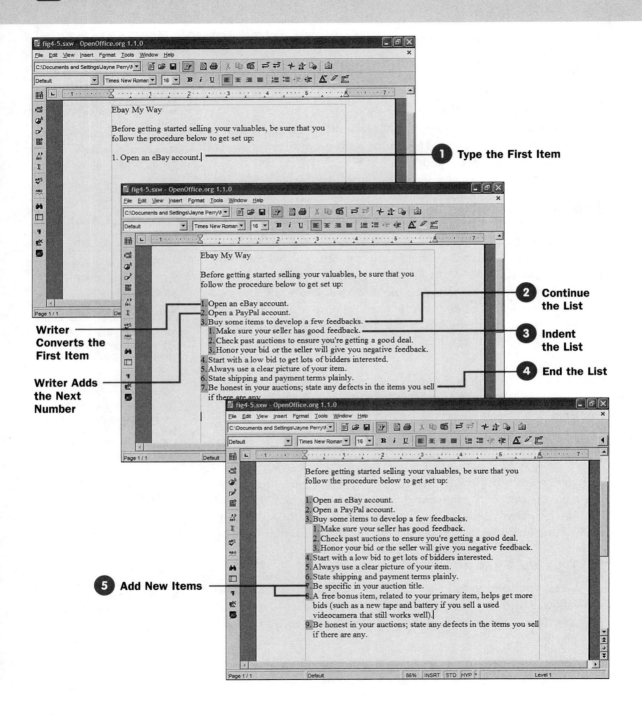

1 Type the First Item

Writer Converts the First Item

Writer Adds the Next Number

2 Continue the List

3 Indent the List

4 End the List

5 Add New Items

PART I: Writing Words with Writer

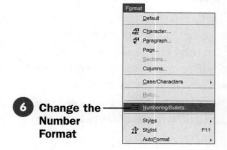

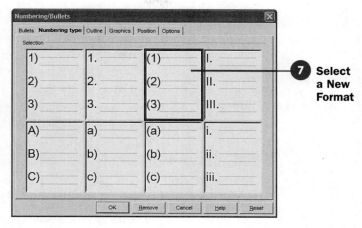

6 Change the Number Format

7 Select a New Format

2 Continue the List

You won't have to continue typing the number once Writer recognizes that you're creating a numbered list. Writer puts the second number at the start of your next line so you can continue typing. You only need to worry about your list items, and Writer takes care of the numbers and the indention.

3 Indent the List

When you want to create a sublist of numbered items, press **Tab** after the number. Writer indents the item and starts the numbering once again from 1. Keep typing the list, and Writer keeps indenting and creating the sublist.

When you want to return to the original indention to continue your primary list items, press **Shift+Tab** to move back to the left column and continue the numbering of the original list.

4 End the List

To end your list, after the final item press **Enter** twice. The first **Enter** keypress tells Writer that you don't want to indent anymore. The second **Enter** keypress moves the cursor to the next line, adding a blank line between the list's final item and your next regular line of text.

NOTE

Typically, a sublist should have more than one item. Writer supports up to ten levels of numbered lists, but three or four levels deep is often as far as you'll need to go.

TIP

If you only want to change some of a list's number style, such as an indented sublist, select only that portion of the list before opening the **Numbering/Bullets** dialog box.

5 **Add New Items**

The true power of Writer's numbered lists is Writer's capability to renumber the entire list when you add or remove list items. To insert new items, put your text cursor at the end of any item and press **Enter**. Writer inserts a new line with the next number and renumbers all subsequent items accordingly. You may keep inserting new items, and Writer handles all the renumbering for you.

If you delete a line, Writer renumbers the list to close the gap between the numbered items where you deleted the line.

6 **Change the Number Format**

You don't have to settle for the default number that Writer initially uses. Highlight your numbered list if you want to change the kind of number used in the list.

Select **Numbering/Bullets** from the **Format** menu to show the **Numbering/Bullets** dialog box. Click the **Numbering type** tab.

7 **Select a New Format**

Click any of the number formats to select a new number type. When you click **OK**, Writer converts your numbered list so that the new number format appears in your document.

21 Create a Table of Contents

Before You Begin

✔ **5** Edit Text

✔ **17** Use a Style

See Also

→ **22** Create an Index

KEY TERM

Table of contents—A table in the front of many books that typically tells on which page number a book's chapters and other elements appear.

When you write for others, a *table of contents* provides easy access for your readers. They can quickly go to whatever subject, or chapter, they want to go to. Making a table of contents used to be tedious, but with Writer, such a task is virtually work free. If you make changes to your document, such as adding new chapters, you can easily regenerate the table of contents to keep it fresh.

Generally, paragraphs that you apply the **Heading 1** style to will end up in your table of contents. With 10 heading styles, **Heading 1** through **Heading 10**, you have plenty of title, heading, and subheading styles with which to format your text. If any or all of these styles do not format paragraphs exactly the way you want them to, you can modify the styles. The important thing to note here is, if you do use the **Heading 1** style, whether or not you've modified the style, Writer considers each of those paragraphs to be part of the table of contents. All the contents should appear in the currently open document; otherwise, Writer won't be able to locate the entries. The only exception would be for a Master Document (see **129** **About Master Documents**).

You may request that Writer use paragraph styles other than the **Heading 1** style by clicking the **Additional Styles** option and selecting more styles by clicking the ... button.

❶ Find Text for the Table

Select one or more paragraphs that you want to include in your table of contents. If you're writing a book, generally such a paragraph will consist of the introduction, chapter titles, and appendixes (if any).

❷ Request the Heading 1 Style

If you've selected paragraphs to apply the **Heading 1** style to, select **Format**, **Styles**, **Catalog** from the menu to display the **Style Catalog**. You'll see a list of styles from which you can choose. (Click **Paragraph Styles** from the drop-down box if it's not already selected.)

❸ Select Heading 1

Select **Heading 1** from the style list and click **OK**. Continue applying the **Heading 1** style to all paragraphs in your document that you want to include in the table of contents. As you apply the **Heading 1** style, the format of those paragraphs typically change to become boldface.

❹ Determine the Style

Once you've applied the **Heading 1** style to all the paragraphs you want to include in your table of contents, you now can generate the table of contents. Move the text cursor to the beginning of your document (assuming you want the table of contents to appear there).

NOTE

Writer doesn't continually update a table of contents even when you use the **Heading 1** style. When you're ready for a table of contents, you'll request the **Insert Index/Table** dialog box, and at that point Writer generates the table.

NOTE

If you formatted your introduction, chapter titles, and appendixes with the **Heading 1** style, you don't need to reapply the style.

TIP

Add chapter numbers in front of chapter titles so the chapter numbers automatically appear in the table of contents.

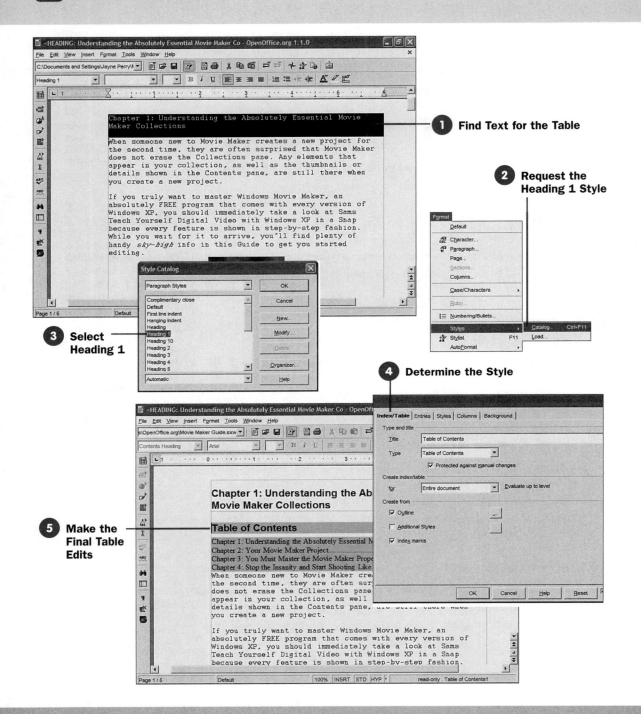

1 Find Text for the Table

2 Request the Heading 1 Style

3 Select Heading 1

4 Determine the Style

5 Make the Final Table Edits

PART I: Writing Words with Writer

Select **Insert, Indexes and Tables, Indexes and Tables** to display the **Insert Index/Table** dialog box. You can change various aspects of your table of contents, such as the title. As you change various options, the preview image of your table will update to the left of the dialog box. Deselect the option labeled **Protected against manual changes** if you want the ability to modify the actual table of contents after Writer generates it.

Once you're ready to generate the table of contents, click **OK**. Writer generates the table from your selected styles.

⑤ Make the Final Table Edits

You now must make final edits to the table of contents. You can format the table, put page breaks around it (using **Shift+Enter**), and add spacing between the lines if you wish. If you find that Writer doesn't let you change the table, you didn't uncheck **Protected against manual changes** when you generated the table in the **Insert Index/Table** dialog box. You can regenerate the table with the option unchecked so you then can make any edits you wish.

22 Create an Index

The longer your document, the more your audience will appreciate an *index*. As you write your document, or after you've written the document, you can mark any word in the document that you want to include in the index, and Writer can then generate the index showing the proper page numbers. If you make changes to the document, you can regenerate the index to keep it fresh.

You might wonder why you have to do all the work of marking every index entry. Writer is smart, but it's not *that* smart! Writer could never know which words you want to include in the index, so it's up to you to mark each of them. Unlike the days of old, however, once you mark which words go in the index, your job is over because Writer will search out the page numbers and generate the index.

Before You Begin

✔ **13** Apply Paragraph Formatting

✔ **21** Create a Table of Contents

See Also

→ **24** Create a Table

🔍 **KEY TERM**

Index—A table that appears in the back of some books that list the page numbers of certain key words, people, and terms in the book.

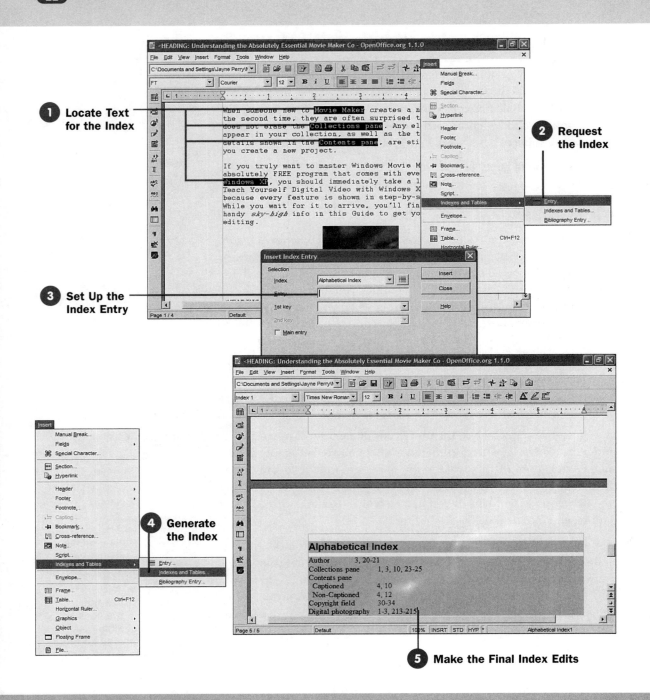

1 Locate Text for the Index

2 Request the Index

3 Set Up the Index Entry

4 Generate the Index

5 Make the Final Index Edits

PART I: Writing Words with Writer

1 Locate Text for the Index

Highlight a word or words and phrases that are to appear in your index. By using **Ctrl**, you can select many index entries at once or you can select them one at a time and then add each to the index individually.

Whatever you choose, make sure you've selected any word or phrase you want in the index before continuing.

2 Request the Index

With the text selected, choose **Insert**, **Indexes and Tables**, **Entry** from the menu. The **Insert Index Entry** dialog box appears, where you can define the entry.

3 Set Up the Index Entry

The typical index you'll be adding is an alphabetical index (click the **Index** list box to select **Alphabetical Index** if you don't currently see it), although you can define another kind of index, called a *user-defined index*, if you wish.

If you want to add a slightly different variant of the word to the index, use the **Entry** box. Here, you can reword the index entry (when you define one at a time). Instead, say, of using **micro**, if that's the word you highlighted for the index, you can type **microcomputer** in the **Entry** box. The entry in the index appears as **microcomputer**, although it refers to the text **micro**.

Use the **1st key** box if you want to create a *multilevel index*. You'd type the highest-level name in the **1st key** box and then Writer adds the selected entry to the next level. if you want a two-tiered entry, type a value in the **2nd key** box, and the selected entry will appear below that in the index.

Once you've defined the proper settings for the new entry, click **Insert** to add the entry to the index. Click **Close** to close the **Insert Index Entry** dialog box when you're done with it.

4 Generate the Index

Once you've defined all the entries, you make the request to Writer to generate the index. Writer will compile the index and place it at the cursor's current position. Therefore, place the text cursor at the

NOTE

A Writer document can support multiple indexes. When you define index entries, you can determine to which of multiple indexes the entries are to go. Most documents have only a single index, however.

NOTE

You don't have to select every index entry and add them all at once. You can add them individually. You can add some now, make additional edits, and add others later.

KEY TERM

User-defined index—An index that is secondary to the primary, alphabetical index, such as a figure index or a list of people index.

KEY TERM

Multilevel index—An index entry that contains a primary term such as *fruit* and two or more secondary entries, offset to the right under the primary term, such as *apple*, *banana*, and *pear*.

NOTE

The index does not generate when you close the **Insert Index Entry** dialog box. You generate the index once you've added all the entries.

NOTE

You use the same page of the **Insert Index/Table** dialog box to generate both the index and the table of contents.

end of the document and then select **Insert, Index and Tables, Index and Tables** to display the **Insert Index/Table** dialog box.

Click the **Type** list box to display a list of indexes and tables you can generate. Select **Alphabetical Index** for your index. A preview of your index then appears to the left of the dialog box. Click to uncheck the **Protected against manual changes** option if you want to make edits to the index later (which you almost always want to do, especially to format it to your liking).

Make additional edits to the index options in the **Options** area. For example, you can request that Writer combine index entries by checking the **Combine identical entries** box so that Writer doesn't duplicate the same index entry twice if you happen to select two of the same items for the index on the same page before generating the index.

Click **OK** to generate your document's index.

⑤ Make the Final Index Edits

Once your index appears, you can edit the index to adjust formatting, such as the font and spacing, if you need to so the index matches the format of the rest of the document. If you find that Writer doesn't let you change the index, you didn't uncheck **Protected against manual changes** when you generated the index in the **Insert Index/Table** dialog box. You can regenerate the index with this option unchecked so you then can make any edits you wish.

㉓ About Writer Tables

Before You Begin

✔ ⑤ Edit Text
✔ ⑬ Apply Paragraph Formatting

See Also

→ ㉔ Create a Table
→ ㉕ Format a Table

Writer's table-creation power shines when you see how easily you can compose customized *tables* of information in Writer documents. Tables might contain numbers, text, even graphics, or combinations of any of these. Each row and column intersection is called a *cell*. As you begin to use both Writer and Calc (see ㉟ **Create a New Spreadsheet**), you might want to embed part of a Calc spreadsheet into a Writer table. Such embedded spreadsheets enable you, for example, to report financial data from within a Writer report.

With Writer, you can easily create tables from your keyboard. You type a series of plus signs and hyphens, and Writer will interpret that as the start of your table. For example, suppose you type the following:

+--------+--------+--------+--------+--------+--------+

Writer then converts that to a one-row table with four columns. Once you fill in that column with values (pressing **Tab** and **Shift+Tab** to move between columns), Writer inserts a new row for you.

The ruler shows columns

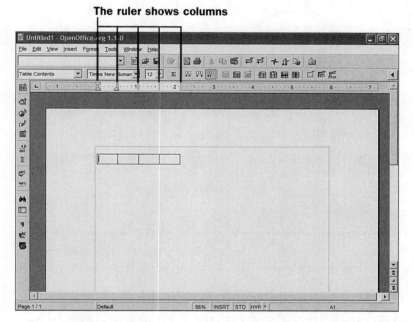

Writer generates a table with lines around rows and columns after you type a row of plus signs and hyphens.

You can also define a table before typing anything. For example, you can request a 12-row, 5-column table formatted a certain way by using the **Insert Table** dialog box.

Once you create a table, you then can easily adjust its height and width simply by dragging one of the edges with your mouse. You can add and delete rows and columns, too. In addition, you can apply formatting attributes to your table to add color, highlighting, special fonts, and other format attributes that make a dull table look good.

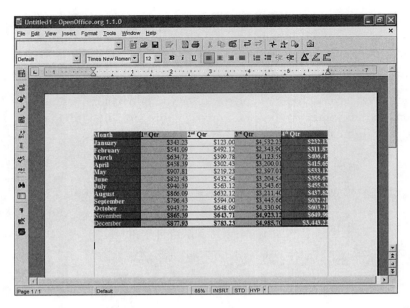

Writer can generate a fancy table with automatic formatting, including column shading and lines.

24 Create a Table

Before You Begin

✔ **23** About Writer Tables

See Also

→ **25** Format a Table

→ **26** Manage a Table

Writer gives you many ways to create, edit, and format tables. Not surprisingly, the simplest ways are usually the most preferred ways.

To add a new table to your document, you can

- Type an initial row of plus signs and hyphens to start your table

- Use the **Insert Table** dialog box to designate rows and columns and table formatting

NOTE

The minus sign is the same as a hyphen on your keyboard.

1 Start a Table

Open a new document to practice creating tables. Type a plus sign, followed by 10 hyphens. Type another plus sign and another 10 hyphens. Keep doing this until you type 6 sets and close with a plus sign. You can copy and paste these sets of hyphens instead of typing each one.

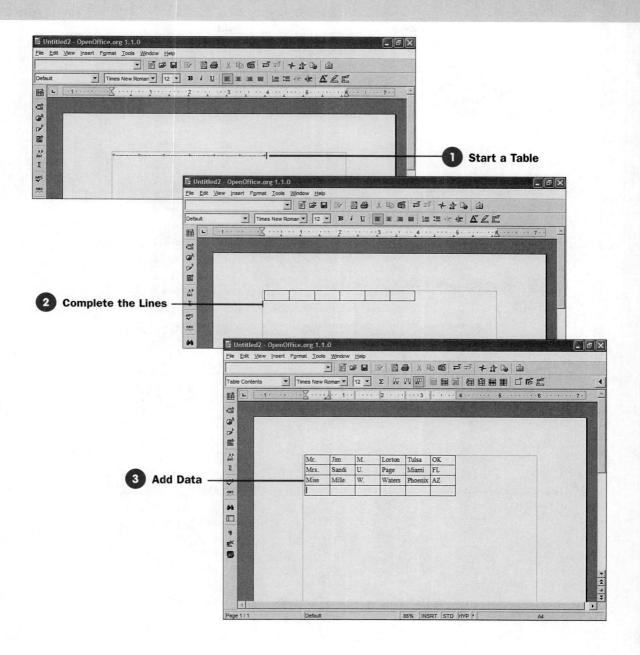

1 **Start a Table**

2 **Complete the Lines**

3 **Add Data**

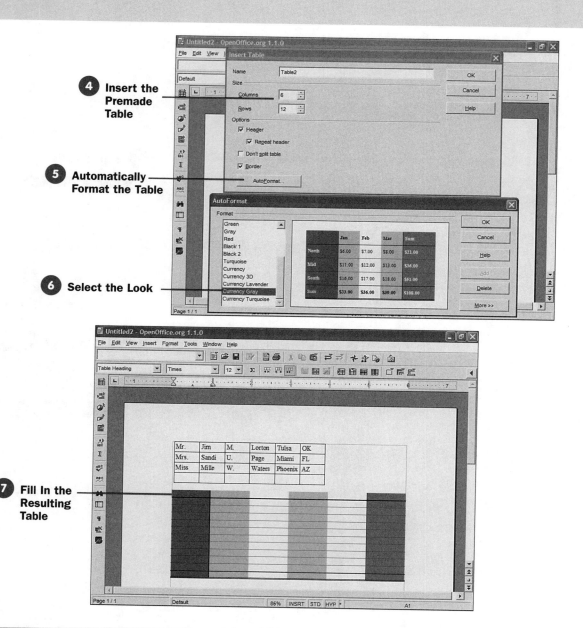

4 Insert the Premade Table

5 Automatically Format the Table

6 Select the Look

7 Fill In the Resulting Table

You have now typed what is needed to let Writer know you want to begin a new table.

2 Complete the Lines

Press **Enter** after the final plus sign. As soon as you do, Writer converts your line of plus signs and hyphens to one row of a table, designated by lines to form 6 columns.

3 Add Data

Once Writer creates the first row of the table, it places your text cursor in the leftmost cell so you can type the table's data. When you finish typing the data, press **Tab** to move to the next cell to the right. When you finish the row, press **Tab** again and Writer will create the next row for you. If you press **Enter** instead of **Tab** at the end of a row, Writer assumes you're through with the table and will not add an additional row.

4 Insert the Premade Table

Instead of creating your table by typing the plus signs and hyphens, you can request that Writer generate your entire table for you before you type anything.

On a blank line (not inside another table), select **Table** from the **Insert** menu to display the **Insert Table** dialog box. Select the number of columns and rows you want in your table. If you don't know exactly how many columns and rows you need, guess as closely as you can. (See **26** **Manage a Table** to learn how to add or remove extra rows and columns.)

Click the **Header** option if you want the first row of your table to be separated from the rest of the table with a bold line. You can use this row for your heading information, such as titles across the top of the table if you wish. Click the **Repeat header** option if you want the first row to be repeated on every page, assuming your table will span multiple pages. If you click **Don't split table**, Writer will not begin the table toward the bottom of the page if the page break would split the table; rather, Writer begins the table at the top of the next page.

5 Automatically Format the Table

Click the **AutoFormat** button to select an initial format for your table. You learn how to apply other kinds of formatting changes to

NOTE

If your cell is not wide enough to hold what you type, Writer increases the cell height to hold more data. Writer does not widen the cell. To widen the cell, see **26** **Manage a Table**.

NOTE

Some tables will be so long, the **Don't split table** option will not work. If a table is longer than one page, Writer has to split the table.

your table in **25** **Format a Table**, but you can select an initial format from the list you get when you click **AutoFormat**.

⑥ Select the Look

Select a format from the list, and when you do, Writer displays a preview of such a table at the right of the **AutoFormat** dialog box. You can keep selecting from the various formats until you find a format you want to use. Once you've selected a table format, click **OK** to close the **AutoFormat** dialog box. Then click **OK** to close the **Insert Table** dialog box as well.

⑦ Fill In the Resulting Table

Writer creates your table and displays its empty cells for you to fill in with data. Be sure to put titles in the first row if you chose an initial first-row heading for your table.

25 Format a Table

Before You Begin

✔ **23** About Writer Tables

✔ **24** Create a Table

See Also

→ **26** Manage a Table

 TIP

Always print a table onto paper to ensure that the formatting is not too distracting. Tables can look different when printed than when they appear on the screen.

If you're unhappy with the table format you chose with AutoFormat, you can change your table's look. A table's primary goal is to present information to its readers in a clear format. If the format detracts from that goal, you should change the format.

Some users initially create very fancy tables from the AutoFormat list that Writer provides. Often, the colors and format take away from the table's effectiveness more than they add to it. Give your table as much time in its formatting as you give other design elements of your documents, perhaps even more, to ensure that your tables clearly say what you want them to say to your readers.

① Select the Table

To change the overall format of your table, select the entire table. If you only want to change the format of some of your table, select just that portion of the table, such as the first heading row or perhaps all the data rows that fall below the heading row.

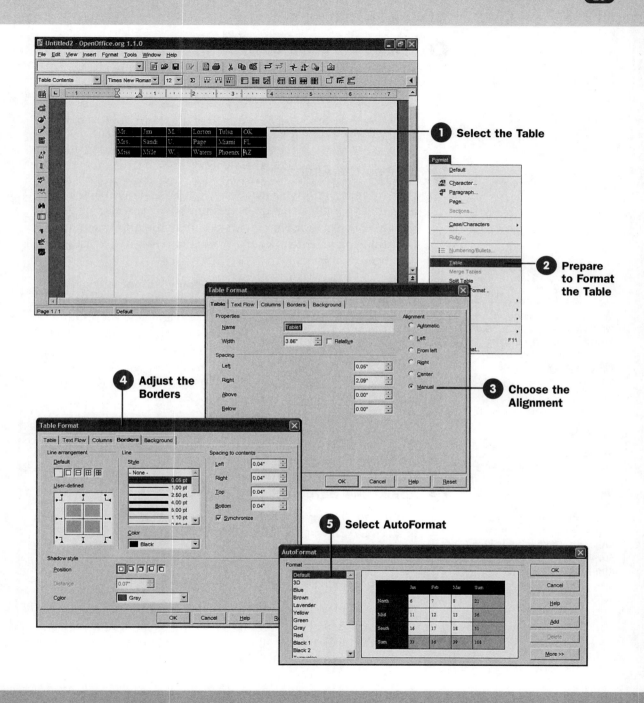

1 Select the Table

2 Prepare to Format the Table

3 Choose the Alignment

4 Adjust the Borders

5 Select AutoFormat

2 **Prepare to Format the Table**

Select **Insert**, **Table** from the menu. You don't want to insert a table but instead only format the selected table. Because you first selected your table before choosing **Insert**, **Table**, Writer displays the **Table Format** dialog box instead of the **Insert Table** dialog box (see **24** **Create a Table**).

3 **Choose the Alignment**

Click through the **Table Format** dialog box to change various aspects of your table's design. For example, you can change the way text aligns inside your table's cells from the **Alignment** area. Depending on your data, you may want to center or left-justify data beneath a heading.

Click the **Text Flow** tab to display the **Table Format** dialog box's **Text Flow** page. If you want a page break to appear before or after the table, click the **Break** option and designate how you want the page break to appear. You can change the table-splitting option for multipaged tables. The **Vertical Alignment** options enable you to specify where you want text to align to in a tall cell. For example, if your cells are large enough for three rows of text but you type only one row, you can specify whether the text is to appear at the top, center, or bottom of the cell.

Click the **Columns** tab to display the **Columns** page. You can enter new values for each column's width.

4 **Adjust the Borders**

If you want the borders (the dividing lines between your table cells) to take on a different appearance, click the **Borders** tab. You can elect to change the border thickness, add a shadow to the table's outline, and even determine how far from each cell's edges you want the cell contents to begin.

If you feel that you've changed too much of your table, click the **Table Format** dialog box's **Reset** button in the lower-right corner of the dialog box to reset all measurements back to their original state (before you began changing values inside the **Table Format** dialog box). Once you're happy with the changes you have made, click **OK** to apply those changes and to complete the table's format.

TIP

You can drag a column with your mouse instead of specifying exact column width measurements, as **26** Manage a Table shows.

NOTE

Writer's default table options handle things very efficiently. It's rare that you will need to adjust specific measurements such as text inside cell spacing because Writer generally creates appropriate spacing values for you when you create the table.

⑤ Select AutoFormat

Once you add data to your table's cells, if you don't care for the AutoFormat you chose previously (see **24** **Create a Table**), you can change to another AutoFormat scheme. Select **Format**, **AutoFormat** to display the **AutoFormat** dialog box and select another format to apply.

The **AutoFormat** dialog box shows a **More** button that, when you click it, produces several formatting options. You can elect to include or exclude all the following from the AutoFormat patterns: **Number format**, **Borders**, **Font**, **Pattern**, and **Alignment**. If, for example, you click to uncheck the **Borders** option, all the **AutoFormat** previews change to exclude a border around and between the table cells. Writer does not save your **AutoFormat** dialog box selections, so the next time you insert a table, you may have to select the same AutoFormat again if you want to reuse it.

26 Manage a Table

Once you're familiar with creating tables and formatting them, you'll still find yourself adjusting them as you work with them. Perhaps you need to add more rows or columns. Perhaps you want to make a quick adjustment to one of the column widths.

Formatting a table and getting data into it is most of the battle, but you also will find that traversing a table differs somewhat from traversing regular text. Table 4.1 shows the keystrokes needed to traverse tables efficiently.

Before You Begin

✔ **24** Create a Table

✔ **25** Format a Table

See Also

→ **29** Add a Chart or Spreadsheet to a Document

TABLE 4.1 **Writer's Table-Navigating Keystrokes**

Press This...	To Move the Table's Cursor Here
Shift+Tab and left arrow	The preceding cell
Tab and right arrow	The next cell
Up arrow	The cell above the current cell
Down arrow	The cell below the current cell
Ctrl+Home	The first cell in the table
Ctrl+End	The last cell in the table
Enter	Pressing **Enter** in the final cell ends the table you're creating

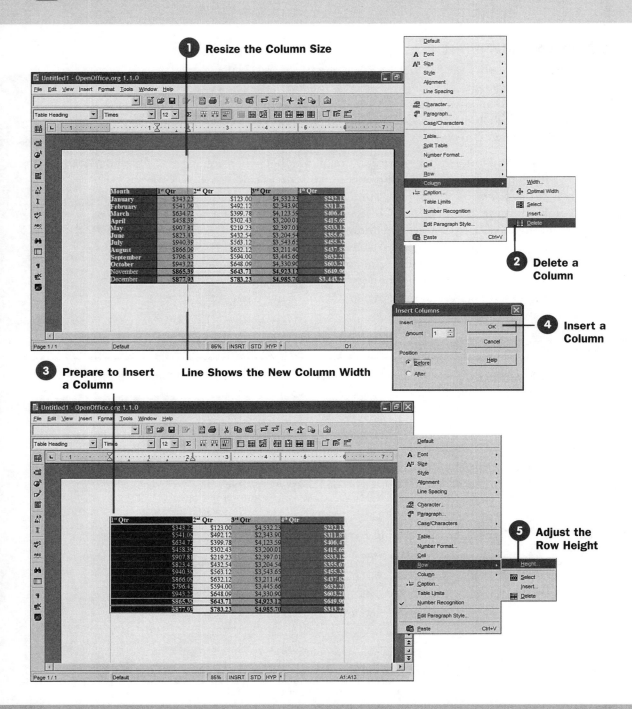

1 Resize the Column Size

2 Delete a Column

4 Insert a Column

3 Prepare to Insert a Column

Line Shows the New Column Width

5 Adjust the Row Height

① Resize the Column Size

Adjusting a column's size is extremely simple. Move your mouse pointer to an edge of the column you want to resize (to either increase or decrease the column width). The mouse pointer changes to a double arrow. Click the edge of the column and drag the column left or right. When you release the mouse, Writer resizes the column to its new size. If you shrink a column's width too narrow, the text may not all fit on one line, and Writer will be forced to double the height of the rows to hold the extra data.

② Delete a Column

Select a column you want to delete by right-clicking that column. A menu appears. Select **Column**, **Delete** to delete the column from the table. The column to the right of the deleted column increases in size to maintain the same table size. If you don't prefer the wide column that results, you can drag its left edge to the right to reduce its size and put the columns back to a uniform size.

③ Prepare to Insert a Column

Select an entire column if you want to insert a new column before or after the selected column. If you don't select the entire column, Writer attempts to insert a single cell at the position of the cursor, and you almost never want to do this because, generally, tables should retain a rectangular shape to take advantage of proportional spacing and other formats available to rectangular tables. (Calc is a better tool for creating nonrectangular tables of data.)

Right-click the selected column and choose **Column**, **Insert** from the menu. The **Insert Columns** dialog box appears.

④ Insert a Column

Click **Before** if you want to insert the column before the selected column and click **After** if you want the new column to appear after the selected column in your table. You can insert more than one column by adjusting the **Amount** value. When you click **OK**, the column appears in your table.

Once the new column arrives, you'll fill it with data and adjust any column or table widths as necessary.

NOTE

You can make a column width adjustment by dragging a column's edge on the horizontal ruler atop the document. Most users are more comfortable dragging the actual column edge to resize a column, though, because a vertical line moves as you drag your mouse to show the new column size.

 TIP

If you want to insert a new row instead of a new column, select **Row**, **Insert** from the right-click menu.

5 Adjust the Row Height

Adjusting a row's height isn't as simple as dragging the row divider up or down. To adjust one or more rows, select the row or rows you want to adjust and then right-click the selection. Select **Row, Height** from the menu to display the **Row Height** dialog box. Adjust the **Height** value to adjust your row height up or down. If you click the **Fit to size** option, the row adjusts to match the height of the row's data. If, therefore, the row contains a large font, the **Fit to size** option adjusts the row to handle that large font size well.

27 Insert Graphics in a Document

Before You Begin

✔ **14** Set Up Page Formatting

✔ **15** Create a Multicolumn Newsletter

See Also

→ **28** Draw with Writer

KEY TERM

Gallery—A collection of graphics supplied by OpenOffice.org programs that you can insert into your documents.

KEY TERM

Anchor—A Writer place-holder that shows itself as an icon of a boat anchor. Anchors show the location of objects such as graphic images, footnotes, and end-notes. The anchor shows where you inserted an object. If you move the object, the anchor stays in place.

Writer enables you to put pictures in your documents. Those graphic images can have captions and borders, and you can specify how the text around such images wraps.

Writer supports the inclusion of all the following kinds of graphic images:

- Graphic images from a file, such as bitmapped images
- Graphic images from OpenOffice.org's *gallery*
- Graphic images you scan into your document
- Graphic images produced in OpenOffice.org's other products such as Draw and Impress
- A Calc chart

When you insert a graphic image, Writer places an *anchor* at that location. You will see the anchor when editing but not when you print your document. The anchor shows where you inserted the actual image. You can format a graphic image to appear on the left or right of text, or above or below the text in which you insert the graphic. Therefore, the anchor and the actual image may not appear together. When you want to move an image, move its anchor and not the image itself.

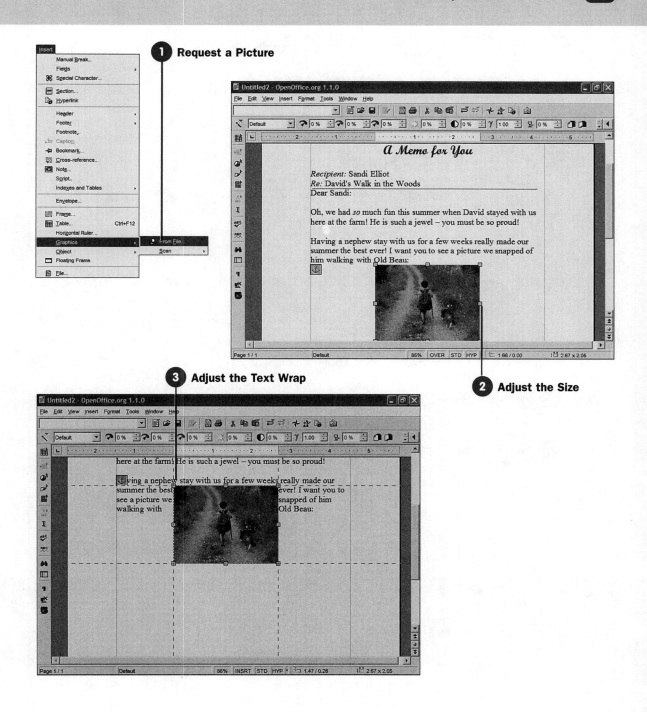

1 Request a Picture

3 Adjust the Text Wrap

2 Adjust the Size

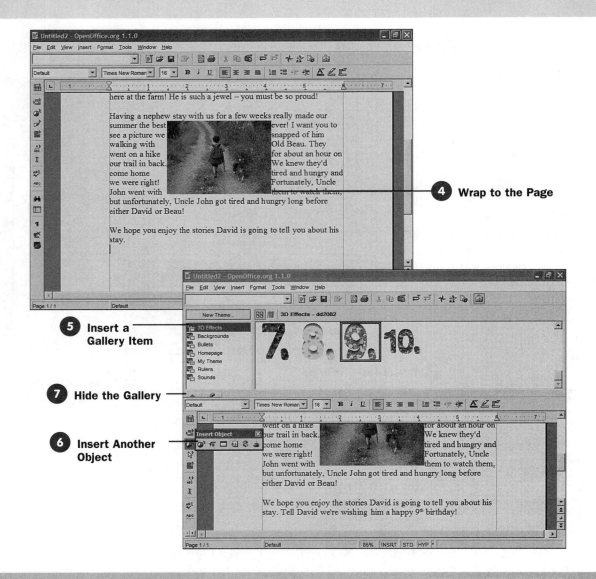

④ Wrap to the Page

⑤ Insert a Gallery Item

⑦ Hide the Gallery

⑥ Insert Another Object

① Request a Picture

To insert a graphic image from a file, first place your text cursor where you want the image to go. Then, select **Insert**, **Graphics**, **From File** from the menu. Writer displays the **Insert Graphics** dialog box, which is nothing more than a file-selection dialog box where you navigate to the file you want to insert. Once you select the graphic image you want to place in your document, click the **Open** button to insert the image.

If you want to scan an image directly into Writer, select **Insert**, **Graphics**, **Scan** instead and select the scanning method you want to use to scan the picture. (Some scanners support multiple scanning methods.) As long as you have a *TWAIN*-compliant scanner attached to your computer (which most scanners are), Writer will scan the image and bring that image into your document.

2 Adjust the Size

Once Writer brings the graphic image into your document, you can make adjustments to suit your needs. Typically, Writer imports graphic images and centers them at the location you inserted them. No text wraps to either side of the image, and the image often is not sized properly for your document.

To resize the image, drag any of the eight resizing handles inward to reduce the image size or outward to increase the image size.

3 Adjust the Text Wrap

If you want to embed the image inside text, having the text wrap around the image instead of the image consuming space without any text wrapped around it, click to select the image. Then, right-click the image and select **Wrap**, **Page Wrap** from the menu.

4 Wrap to the Page

Once you've elected to wrap to the page, you now can drag the image up or down to the middle of text, and the text will wrap around the image. As you drag the image, grid lines will show to reflect where the dragged image will appear when you release your mouse button. When you release your mouse button, the image is anchored into place and surrounding text will wrap around the sides.

You're not limited to keeping the image in the middle of the text. If you'd prefer to move the image over to the left or right margin, right-click the image and select the **Alignment** option for either **Left**, **Centered**, or **Right** alignment. Often, text is easier to read if

NOTE

OpenOffice.org supports all popular graphic file formats, including JPG, GIF, and BMP files.

KEY TERM

TWAIN—A scanner hardware interface format recognized by all of today's computers.

TIP

If you want to add a caption to your image, right-click the image and select **Caption** to display the **Caption** dialog box. You can add a sequential number before your caption so that you can reference all your images from the document by number.

it wraps only on the left or right side of an image instead of the image falling directly in the center of the text.

5 Insert a Gallery Item

You may insert one of OpenOffice.org's gallery images if you wish instead of importing your own graphic image. The gallery contains a collection of *clip art*, such as fancy numbers, buttons, and graphic borders that you may want to use to spruce up your page.

You must display the gallery before you can drag items from the gallery into your document. To display the gallery, select **Tools**, **Gallery**. The top half of your screen shows the gallery, organized in the following categories: **3D Effects**, **Backgrounds**, **Bullets**, **Homepage**, **My Theme**, **Rulers**, and **Sounds**. Some of the gallery images are useful for creating and designing Web pages. The **Sounds** category contains various sounds you can insert into a document, although this feature is often overused at first and then never used later after its novelty wears off.

To insert a gallery image, click to select that image and drag it to the place in your document where you want the image to go. As with graphic images you insert, once the gallery image appears in your document, you can resize it and align it with text in the way that fits your needs best.

6 Insert Another Object

By long-clicking the **Insert Object** button on your **Main** toolbar, you are given the chance to insert a chart (see **29** **Add a Chart or Spreadsheet to a Document**), mathematical expression (see **30** **Use Mathematical Formulas in Documents**), *floating frame*, and other kinds of objects into your document.

7 Hide the Gallery

Click the gallery's **Hide** button to hide the gallery and return your document's editing area to its normal size.

28 Draw with Writer

If you don't have any graphic images to insert into your documents, you can draw your own! Writer supports a drawing toolbar that supplies you with the following drawing tools:

- Line drawing
- Rectangle drawing
- *Ellipse* drawing
- *Polygon* drawing
- Curve drawing
- Freeform drawing
- *Arc* drawing
- Ellipse pie
- Circle segment
- Text drawing
- Animated text
- *Callout* drawing

Using one of the drawing tools usually requires only that you select the tool you want to use, click your mouse where you want the shape to begin, and then click your mouse where you want the shape to end.

1 Open the Draw Functions Toolbar

To add a drawing to your Writer document, you must display the **Draw Functions** toolbar. Long-click the **Draw Functions** button on the **Main** toolbar to display the **Draw Functions** toolbar. On the **Draw Functions** toolbar appear 12 items available to you, plus the pointer when you want to select from a drawing instead of drawing a new element.

Before You Begin

✔ **27** Insert Graphics in a Document

See Also

→ **29** Add a Chart or Spreadsheet to a Document

KEY TERMS

Ellipse—A round shape such as a circle or an oval.

Polygon—A multisided shape.

Arc—Half an ellipse, such as a half-moon.

Callout—A caption that points to an item to describe that item.

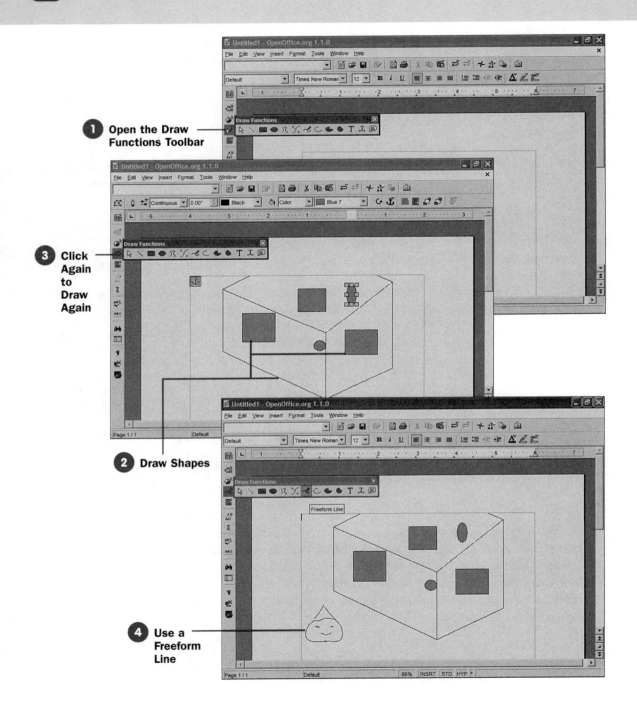

1 Open the Draw Functions Toolbar

3 Click Again to Draw Again

2 Draw Shapes

4 Use a Freeform Line

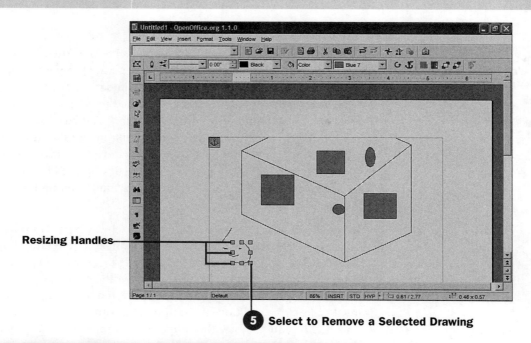

Resizing Handles

5 Select to Remove a Selected Drawing

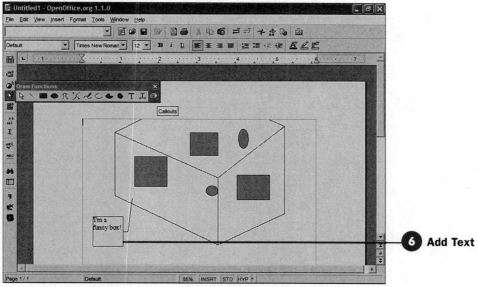

6 Add Text

② Draw Shapes

Click one of the **Draw Functions** toolbar's buttons, such as the **Line** button, to draw a shape (in this case, a line) in your document. The first thing that occurs is Writer hides the **Draw Functions** toolbar and changes the button that was the **Draw Functions** toolbar button to the **Line** button. The authors of Writer knew that you are more likely to draw multiple lines than to pick a different shape to draw next. Once you draw your first line, you therefore can easily add a second line by clicking the **Line** button on the **Main** toolbar instead of first displaying the entire **Draw Functions** toolbar again.

To draw any of the **Draw Toolbar** shapes, click where you want the shape to begin. For example, if you've selected the **Line** shape, click once on your document to anchor the line's starting point. Drag your mouse in the direction you want the shape to go, and when you release your mouse, the shape will appear in your document. The shape will have resizing handles around it. You may click any handle to resize the shape. For example, you can extend or shorten a line by dragging one of its resizing handles in or out. You can also move a shape to a different location by moving the mouse pointer over the shape until it changes to show four arrows pointing in the compass directions. Drag the shape to where you want it to go.

③ Click Again to Draw Again

If you want to draw the same shape, click the shape's button on the **Main** toolbar and continue drawing. If you ever draw a shape that you don't want, click to highlight that shape's resizing handles and press the **Delete** key to remove the shape.

④ Use a Freeform Line

Pick a different shape, such as the **Freeform** shape. To draw a different shape, long-click over the shape currently showing on the **Main** toolbar until the **Draw Functions** toolbar appears. Click to select a different shape, such as the **Freeform** drawing tool. Unlike the line, ellipses, and other shapes, you can drag the **Freeform** drawing shape to any position, and a line will follow your movement, drawing as you drag your mouse.

5 Select to Remove a Selected Drawing

Writer keeps track of each line and every other shape you add to a drawing. Therefore, you can click to select any piece of the drawing that you drew and resize or remove that part of your drawing. In complicated drawings, determining exactly what is selected can be tricky, so study the resizing handles closely to determine if you've selected the proper shape to remove before you press the **Delete** key. Fortunately, you can always undo any piece of the drawing that you delete to get it right back.

6 Add Text

Callouts are often useful to add to some drawings. You can use a callout as a text balloon showing that someone on your drawing is speaking. For more traditional technical and business drawings, callouts are useful for labeling items on a drawing. To add a callout, select the **Callout** drawing tool, add the callout, and resize and move the callout so it hovers exactly where you want it to land on your drawing. Click inside the callout and type whatever text you wish to use for the callout. All the usual formatting tools work on the callout's text, such as italics and boldface. If the callout is too large for the text you type, resize the callout box.

The **Callout** tool isn't the only way to add text to your drawing. Click the **Text** tool to draw a text box where you can type text inside the box. The primary difference between a text box and a callout is that a callout has a line pointing to another item the text refers to. If you want to get really fancy, you can add animated text to your drawing by selecting the **Text Animation** tool from the **Draw Functions** toolbar. When you add animated text to a text box, the text might scroll across the text box area as a marquee does. Right-click animated text that you place and select **Text**; then click the **Text Animation** tab to change the way the text animates.

29 **Add a Chart or Spreadsheet to a Document**

Before You Begin

✔ **27** Insert Graphics in a Document

See Also

→ **39** Create a New Spreadsheet

→ **67** Add a Chart to a Spreadsheet

 NOTE

This task explains how to copy a *static* chart or spreadsheet into Writer—that is, one that will not change if you change the original in Calc after copying to Writer. To keep a link to the original Calc spreadsheet, select **Edit**, **Paste Special**, **DDE Link** to paste the chart or spreadsheet.

 TIP

If you have dual monitors or can position both Writer's and Calc's windows on the same screen, you can drag a selected chart from Calc to Writer without using the Clipboard.

Calc produces excellent charts and graphs. In many documents, you'll need to include a chart and possibly a spreadsheet to make a point more clear. Business reports, for example, are full of charts, spreadsheets, and text, all working together to demonstrate the financial health of a company.

You'll find that copying charts and spreadsheets into a Writer document is extremely simple to do. Both require that you start in Calc, because Calc is the source of such charts and spreadsheets. All you need to do is select the chart or spreadsheet and drag or copy it into your document. Writer recognizes the copied chart or spreadsheet, and you can resize and format the chart or spreadsheet using Writer's tools.

1 Select Calc's Chart

Start Calc and load the spreadsheet that has the chart you want to copy to your Writer document. Select the entire chart by clicking it to display its resizing handles.

2 Copy to the Clipboard

Press **Ctrl+C** or click the **Copy** toolbar button to copy the chart to the Windows Clipboard.

3 Paste the Chart into Writer

Return to your Writer document and click where you want the chart to appear. Generally, plan to give the chart plenty of room. In other words, you'll usually give the chart the full margin width. Even so, the chart will probably come into your document too wide.

Press **Ctrl+V** (or click the **Paste** toolbar button) to paste the chart into your Writer document.

4 Adjust the Size

Drag the chart's resizing handles to adjust the chart's size.

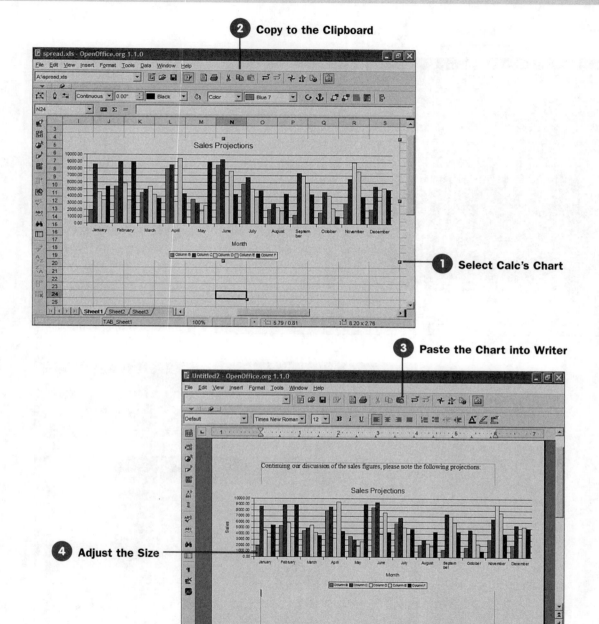

2 Copy to the Clipboard

1 Select Calc's Chart

3 Paste the Chart into Writer

4 Adjust the Size

---

6 Copy to the Clipboard

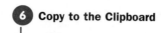

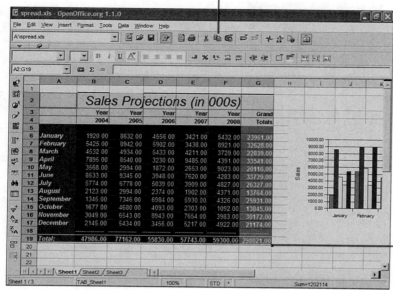

5 Select a Spreadsheet

7 Paste the Spreadsheet into Writer

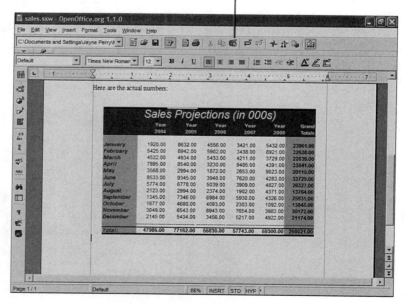

⑤ Select a Spreadsheet

To bring a spreadsheet into a Writer document, you must start in Calc. Open the spreadsheet you want to copy to the Writer document. Select the entire spreadsheet or just the portion of the spreadsheet you want to copy to Writer.

⑥ Copy to the Clipboard

Press **Ctrl+C** or click the **Copy** toolbar button to copy the spreadsheet to the Windows Clipboard.

⑦ Paste the Spreadsheet into Writer

Return to your Writer document and click where you want the spreadsheet to appear. Click **Paste** (you can also press **Ctrl+V**) to paste the spreadsheet into your Writer document.

 TIP

As with charts, if you have dual monitors or can position both Writer's and Calc's windows on the same screen, you can drag the spreadsheet from Calc to Writer without using the Clipboard.

5

Using Writer's Advanced Features

IN THIS CHAPTER:

If you've read some of the Writer tasks that appear earlier, you already know that Writer provides tremendous power and a lot of features. The ability to accept charts and spreadsheets with ease, for example, is enough to turn some Microsoft Word users into Writer users the next time Microsoft releases a "new" Office version for several hundred bucks (see **29** **Add a Chart or Spreadsheet to a Document**).

Writer provides even more advanced features than you've already experienced if you've read tasks that came before. Despite being considered advanced, these features are simple to use. In addition to providing you the ability, for example, to put complex mathematical expressions in your documents (see **30** **Use Mathematical Formulas in Documents**), Writer also can work behind the scenes, automatically making corrections as you type. This chapter provides you with the tools you'll need to take your words to their next level and to create powerful and correct documents.

30 Use Mathematical Formulas in Documents

Before You Begin

✔ **27** Insert Graphics in a Document

✔ **29** Add a Chart or Spreadsheet to a Document

🔍 KEY TERM

Formula editor—A tool included in the OpenOffice.org programs with which you can compose complex math equations.

By its very nature, the inclusion of advanced mathematical formulas isn't the simplest to explain. Math experts will understand, and those who cloud up at long division may want to skip the whole thing. Probably, if you have the need to include mathematical formulas, then you understand the math behind what you're including in your document.

This task shows you how to include such an advanced mathematical expression in your document. Writer provides many options for many types of formulas. An entire chapter, written for experts in math, is justified for this feature due to its power. Yet, such time simply cannot be given here to this math feature of Writer. Therefore, you'll see some fundamental ways to include such expressions in your document in this task but not an exhaustive demonstration. Far too many combinations of far too many expressions exist to cover it all in a task.

Having said that, you may be amazed at how simple Writer makes it for you to enter such formulas. With Writer's *formula editor*, you can build an extremely complex expression.

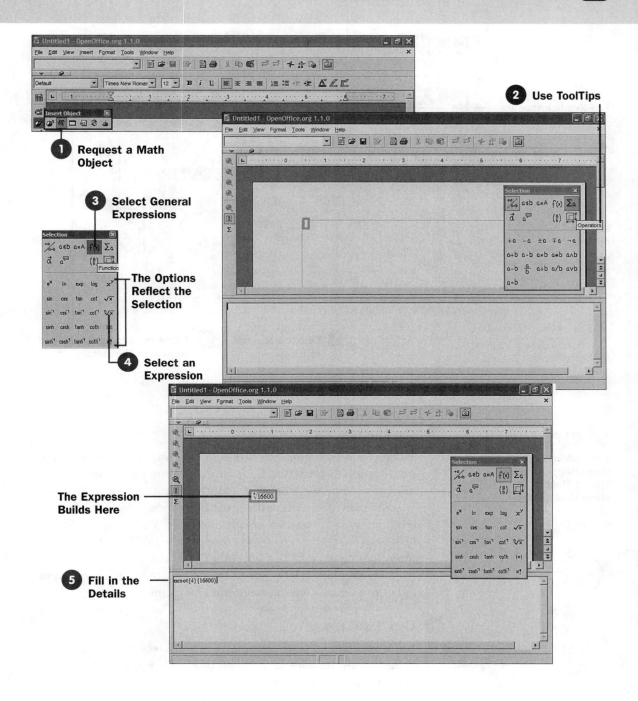

1 Request a Math Object

2 Use ToolTips

3 Select General Expressions

The Options Reflect the Selection

4 Select an Expression

The Expression Builds Here

5 Fill in the Details

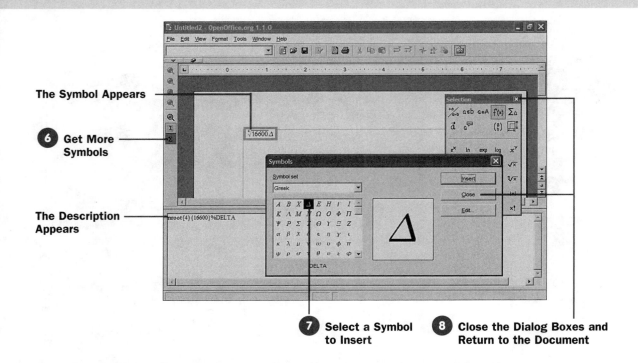

The Symbol Appears

6 Get More Symbols

The Description Appears

7 Select a Symbol to Insert

8 Close the Dialog Boxes and Return to the Document

 TIP

If the **Selection** dialog box doesn't appear, select **View, Selection** from the menu to display it.

1 Request a Math Object

When you need a mathematical formula, long-click the **Main** toolbar's **Insert Object** button to display a floating toolbar that contains the **Math** object. Select the **Math** object. When you do, a new window pane will open in the lower half of your screen to provide a place to build your mathematical formula. The formula editor is always at work in this lower window pane to build mathematical formulas you request. The **Selection** dialog box appears also. From the **Selection** dialog box, you select the kind of formulas you want to build, such as sums, relations, and functions.

2 Use ToolTips

Hover your mouse pointer over any of the **Selection** dialog box's items to view more information on that item. The ToolTip that appears provides an explanation of what the symbol stands for.

③ Select General Expressions

When you click a button in the top half of the **Selection** dialog box, the available expressions in the lower half change. Click the **Functions** button (the one that looks like **f(x)**), and the lower half of the dialog box changes to reflect all the functions you can build inside the formula editor.

④ Select an Expression

Click to select the **nth Root** button in the lower half of the **Selection** dialog box. As soon as you do, the formula editor displays an expression that represents an nth root.

⑤ Fill in the Details

You now must fill in the details, replacing the placeholder symbols with actual values. To write a formula that represents the 4th root of the number 16,600, for example, you would replace the first placeholder, <?>, with **4** and the second placeholder with **16600**. Have patience, because the formula editor takes its time parsing your expression before producing the formula with all the proper symbols in the document at the top of your screen.

The OpenOffice.org programs all support a symbolic mathematical language. When you type the language in the formula editor, the formula editor interprets what you type and builds the formula above in your document. As you work with the formula editor over time, you will get accustomed to the language used there. Once you learn some of the language, you can type the language directly instead of selecting from the **Selection** dialog box if you find that typing the language is easier. For example, instead of selecting the **nth Root** button, you could have typed `nroot{4}{16600}`, and the formula editor would have known what you wanted to build.

⑥ Get More Symbols

To add more symbols, such as a delta symbol, to your formula, click the **Symbols** button on your **Main** toolbar. The **Symbols** dialog box appears.

NOTE

You won't see math symbols in the formula editor, but as you build formulas, the symbols will appear above in your document.

7 **Select a Symbol to Insert**

When you click to select a symbol, a description of that symbol, in the formula editor's math language, appears in the lower window pane, and the symbol itself appears above next to the first part of your formula. You can continue adding symbols (in this case, adding more symbols would represent multiplication of them).

8 **Close the Dialog Boxes and Return to the Document**

Click the **Close** button to close the **Symbols** dialog box when you're done inserting symbols. You can jump back and forth between the **Symbols** dialog box and the **Selection** dialog box as you build more complicated expressions.

Click to close the **Selection** dialog box when you're through building your formula.

Click anywhere in your document to hide the formula editor's window pane and to return to your document.

31 About Writer's Automatic Correction Tools

Before You Begin

✔ **4** Type Text into a Document

✔ **25** Format a Table

See Also

→ **32** Use AutoCorrect to Improve Your Typing

Many of Writer's tools work in the background to make your writing as accurate and as well formatted as possible. If you've read previous chapters already, you've seen the following two automatic helpers:

- **AutoComplete**—Finishes common words before you type them. For example, when you begin typing **following**, Writer's word-completion feature finishes the word for you after you type **follo** (press **Enter** to accept the suggestion or keep typing if you meant something else, such as *follows*). You can keep typing or accept the suggestion. See **4** **Type Text into a Document** for more information.

- **AutoSpellcheck**—As you type words, Writer monitors your progress, and if you type a word incorrectly, such as **wondoes**, the spelling checker corrects the word so you can continue with the rest of the document. See **8** **Check a Document's Spelling** for more information.

Another form of automatic help provided by Writer is the AutoFormat feature you use to format tables. After specifying the number of rows and columns in your table, as **24** **Create a Table** explains, you can click the **AutoFormat** button to display a wide range of formats you can choose from to make your table look better than the standard black text on a white background.

Writer provides even more automatic correction tools to help ensure your writing is as accurate as possible. Often, Writer fixes problems without you ever being aware of them, thanks to its *AutoCorrect* feature. As you type, Writer analyzes potential errors and makes corrections or suggested improvements along the way.

If AutoCorrect recognizes a typing mistake, it immediately corrects the mistake.

Following are just a few of the mistakes AutoCorrect recognizes and corrects as you type:

- AutoCorrect corrects two initial capital letters at the beginning of sentences. For example, "LAtely, we have been gone" becomes "Lately, we have been gone."

- AutoCorrect enables you to enter shortcuts such as your initials, which, when typed into a document, convert to your full name.

- AutoCorrect replaces common symbols with predefined characters. When you type **(c)**, for example, Writer converts the characters to a single copyright symbol (©).

- AutoCorrect replaces common spelling transpositions, such as "teh" with "the."

If AutoCorrect corrects something that you don't want corrected, press **Ctrl+Z** and AutoCorrect reverses its action. If you type an entry in the AutoCorrect list that you do not want corrected in the future, such as *QBasic*, which Writer incorrectly changes to *Qbasic*, you can add QBasic to Writer's exception list so that Writer does not make that correction in the future.

KEY TERM

AutoCorrect—The capability of OpenOffice.org programs to analyze what you just typed and replace with a corrected version if needed.

TIP

The initial AutoCorrect word list and options are preset, but you can add your own frequently misspelled (or mistyped) words to the list. You will most certainly want to add your initials to the AutoCorrect table, for example, so that you need only type your initials when you want to enter your full name in a document.

32 Use AutoCorrect to Improve Your Typing

Before You Begin

✔ **31** About Writer's Automatic Correction Tools

KEY TERM

Smart quotes—The rounded quotes that curl in or out, depending on whether they begin or end a quoted phrase. Both single quote marks and regular quotations can be smart quotes. The term originally started with Word and applies to a word processor's capability to recognize whether a quote mark should be open or closed.

NOTE

The **AutoCorrect/ AutoFormat** menu option is badly worded. Nothing on the resulting dialog box enables you to control the AutoFormat feature of tables. The **AutoFormat** part of the name only applies to quote marks in this case.

Writer gives you complete control over the way it handles AutoCorrect entries. You can modify the correction list, add your own corrections that you want Writer to make, and add to a list of exceptions so that Writer stops correcting things you don't want corrected.

If you find Writer correcting certain words and phrases that you don't want corrected, you can add those words and phrases to Writer's exception list. In addition to autocorrecting words and phrases, the AutoCorrect feature performs some formatting changes for you, most notably changing straight quotes into custom, rounded quotes, sometimes called *smart quotes*.

➊ Request the AutoCorrect Dialog Box

Select **Tools, AutoCorrect/AutoFormat** from the menu to display the **AutoCorrect** dialog box. It is from this dialog box that you control the way AutoCorrect operates on your words. Click the **Replace** tab to display the **Replace** page if it's not already displayed.

➋ Scroll to See Replacements

Scroll down the list to see all the replacements that Writer will make on your behalf. Many of the replacements replace common misspellings, such as *believe* for when you accidentally type *beleiv*.

➌ Delete an Entry

If you want Writer to stop making one of the replacements, select that entry in the list and click the **Delete** button to the right of the dialog box. For example, you may be writing a book and want to designate your headings using a common format such as A-heads, B-heads, C-heads, and so on, indicating each succeeding level of subheadings throughout the text. If you prefix your third-level headings with (c), Writer immediately replaces the (c) with the copyright symbol, unless you delete that entry from the table.

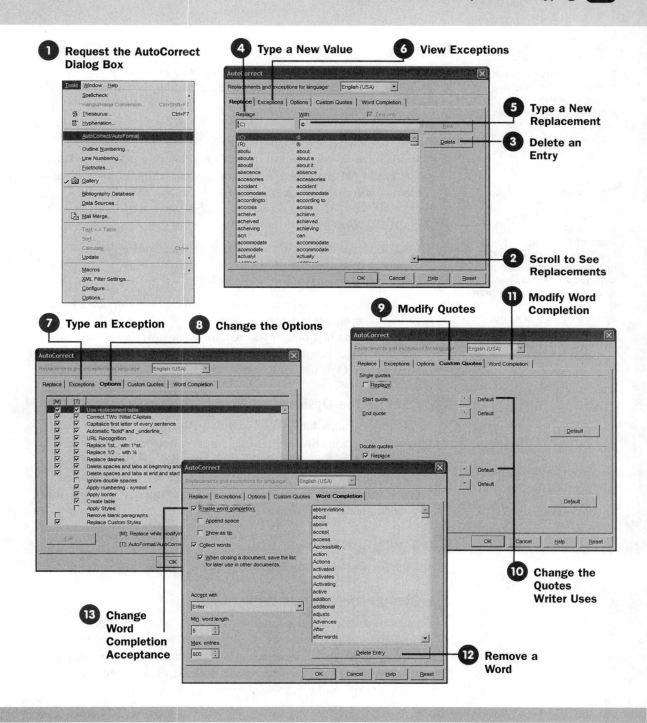

1 Request the AutoCorrect Dialog Box

4 Type a New Value

6 View Exceptions

5 Type a New Replacement

3 Delete an Entry

2 Scroll to See Replacements

9 Modify Quotes

11 Modify Word Completion

7 Type an Exception

8 Change the Options

10 Change the Quotes Writer Uses

13 Change Word Completion Acceptance

12 Remove a Word

TIP

You can change any entry in the table by selecting it, changing either the **Replace** or the **With** word, and then clicking the **Replace** button.

 TIP

Two columns appear, labeled **M** and **T**, next to most of the options. Keep the **T** column checked for options you want automatically made as you type. Keep the **M** option checked if you want the option to be applied when you select **Format, AutoFormat, Apply** from the menu to manually autocorrect a document.

④ Type a New Value

To add your own AutoCorrect entries, click the **Replace** text box and type your value there. This will be the value you want Writer to replace.

⑤ Type a New Replacement

Type the value you want to replace the other one with in the **With** text box. Click the **New** button that appears to the right of the dialog box when you finish the entry.

⑥ View Exceptions

Click the **Exceptions** tab to display the **Exceptions** page.

⑦ Type an Exception

If you regularly use a lowercase abbreviation that you don't want Writer to capitalize, type the exception abbreviation in the **Abbreviations** text box. If you regularly use a word with two initial capital letters, such as *QBasic*, type that exception in the **Words with TWo INitial CApitals** text box.

⑧ Change the Options

Click the **Options** tab to display the **Options** page. Scroll through the list of options that Writer uses for its AutoCorrect corrections. Instead of entering an exception, for example, for *QBasic* on the **Exceptions** page, you might elect to uncheck the option labeled **Correct TWo INitial CApitals** so that Writer stops trying to correct all such entries.

⑨ Modify Quotes

Click the **Custom Quotes** tab to display the **Custom Quotes** page.

⑩ Change the Quotes Writer Uses

You can change the quotes that Writer uses when you open or close either single quotes or double quotes (regular quotation marks). To use a different start quote, for example, when you type an opening straight quote mark, click the straight quote button labeled **Start quote** and select a new quote from the symbols that appear. More than likely, you'll be replacing a straight quote with a curly quote. You can replace all four kinds of quotation marks used by Writer on the **Custom Quotes** page.

⑪ Modify Word Completion

Click the **Word Completion** tab to display the dialog box's **Word Completion** page. Here, you work with word completion entries to modify the way Writer completes your typing for you (such as offering *abbreviation* when you type **abb**).

⑫ Remove a Word

If you want Writer to stop completing a certain word for you, click to select the word and click the **Delete Entry** button.

⑬ Change Word Completion Acceptance

If you want to change the character used to accept a completed word, click to select either **End**, **Enter**, **Space**, or **Right** from the **Accept with** list. For example, if you select **End**, when you type **abb** and Writer replaces the word with *abbreviation*, you'll have to press the **End** key to accept the suggestion; otherwise, Writer erases the suggestion and lets you complete the word.

The other options on the **Word Completion** page enable you to request an automatic space after a completed word and show the suggested word as a ToolTip instead of having Writer complete the word at your cursor's position.

When you finish making changes to the **Word Completion** page, click **OK** to close the dialog box and return to your document.

㉝ About Headers and Footers

Headers and *footers* can give your documents a consistent appearance. You can select certain pages to receive headers and footers. Writer also supports the use of odd- and even-numbered headers and footers. For example, you might want a page number to appear in the upper-right corner of the header on odd pages and in the upper-left corner of the header on even pages. You can put both a header and a footer on a page or use one or the other.

Before You Begin

✔ **⑭** Set Up Page Formatting

✔ **⑯** About Styles and Templates

See Also

➜ **㉞** Add a Header or Footer

Headers and footers can contain graphics, so you can place your company's logo at the top of every page. Writer also supports the use of *fields*, such as page numbers, the time, the date, and even chapter numbers. When you insert one of these fields, Writer inserts the actual value. If your document, for example, is 50 pages, the pages will automatically display 1 through 50. If you delete a page from your document, Writer instantly renumbers the pages.

Footer —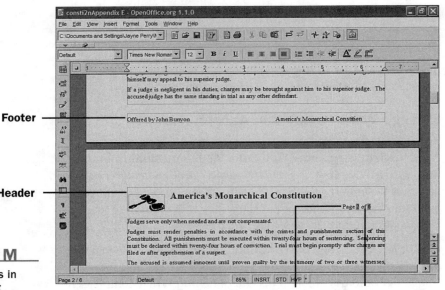

Header —

Page Number Changes   Total Page Count Changes

Headers and footers appear on each page of the section or document.

As with paragraphs, pages can have styles. **14** **Set Up Page Formatting** discusses page styles. If you define and name a new page style somewhere in your document, from the **Format**, **Stylist**, **Page Styles** list, all pages until you revert back to the previous page style or a new page style can use a header or footer that's different from the ones on surrounding pages.

If you attempt to insert a header or footer onto a page that already has a header or footer, Writer warns you that the other header or footer exists and lets you verify that you want to delete the contents of the existing header or footer before continuing. Writer won't overwrite a header or footer without you verifying that you really want to add a new one.

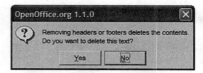

Writer won't overwrite a header or footer without you verifying that you really want to add a new one.

 Add a Header or Footer

The **Insert**, **Header** and **Insert**, **Footer** menu options provide you with the tools you need to add headers and footers to your document's pages. Each header and footer is saved in the page's current style. If your document has multiple page styles, your document can have multiple headers and footers, too. The **Insert**, **Fields** menu option inserts placeholder fields that Writer updates as necessary.

Here are the fields you'll find helpful for headers and footers:

- Date
- Time
- Page Number
- Total Document Page Count

The total document's page count is nice to use when you want to add a header or footer that reads, for example, **Page 4 of 17**.

1 **Request a Header**

Select **Insert**, **Header**, **Default**. Writer inserts a header block at the top of every page in your document of the current page style. If you want to insert a footer instead of a header, you would instead select **Insert**, **Footer**, **Default**. You can insert both a header and footer on the same page.

Before You Begin

✔ **33** About Headers and Footers

See Also

→ **35** Add a Footnote or Endnote

TIP

Sometimes you won't want a header or footer to appear on a page. Simply define a new page style for that page and don't add the header or footer.

1 Request a Header

2 Insert Graphics

3 Type the Text

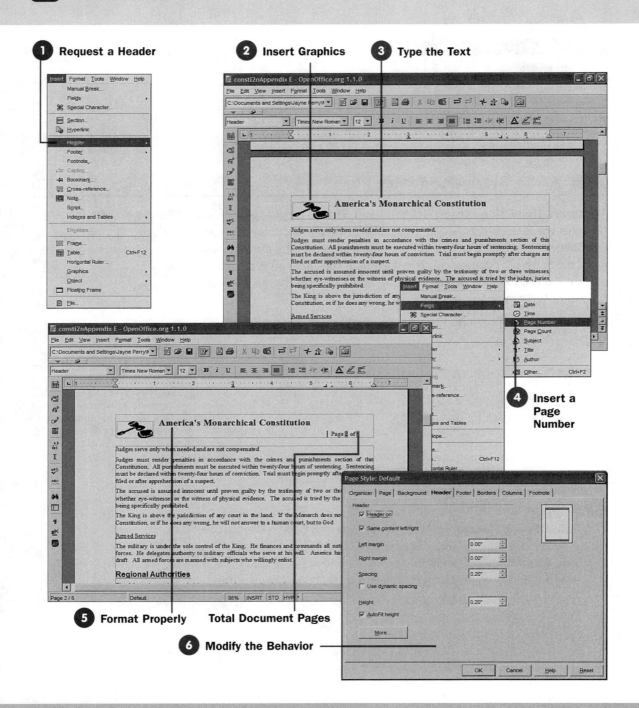

4 Insert a Page Number

5 Format Properly

Total Document Pages

6 Modify the Behavior

② Insert Graphics

Feel free to insert a graphic image in your header or footer. You can insert from the galley, from a graphics file, or you can scan an image into the header or footer (see ㉗ **Insert Graphics in a Document**).

If the header or footer is not wide enough to display the graphic image, you can change the text's point size or use multiple header or footer text lines to give the graphic image a large enough block in which to appear. Even then, you may want to adjust the size of the image some, so click the image and drag the sizing handles inward or outward as needed.

③ Type the Text

Type the text that goes in the header or footer. If you want to end the first line early and start a second line of text, press **Enter** while typing within the header or footer block.

④ Insert a Page Number

Select **Insert**, **Fields**, **Page Number** to insert a page number placeholder in your header or footer. You can set up a page number by typing **Page** followed by a space before you insert the page number field. You can also insert a total document pages field that updates as your document grows and shrinks.

⑤ Format Properly

All the regular character formatting options work on header and footer text, so you can format the text any way you prefer. You can also use the ruler to set tabs if needed.

⑥ Modify the Behavior

Select **Format**, **Page** and click the **Header** tab to display the **Header** page. (There's an identical **Footer** page in the same dialog box.) The **Header** page enables you to control left and right headers for facing pages, margin spacing, and height. By adjusting the **Height** value, you can set the height of a header or footer to be large enough for a graphic image without having to format surrounding text large enough to show the image. As you adjust the

TIP

If you don't want any text in the same header or footer that contains a graphic image, but the single line for the header or footer isn't large enough to display the graphic, insert a blank space before or after the image and set the font size for the space to 36 points or another setting that gives the graphic enough room to display.

TIP

Set a right tab if you want the page number to align with the right edge of the page.

header settings, the preview area updates to show you visually what your header or footer will look like.

35 Add a Footnote or Endnote

Before You Begin

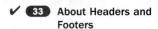 ✔ **33** About Headers and Footers

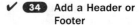 ✔ **34** Add a Header or Footer

KEY TERMS

Footnotes—A note at the bottom of a page referenced by number somewhere on the page.

Endnotes—A note at the end of a document referenced by number somewhere in the document.

TIP

You also can long-click the **Insert** icon on the **Main** toolbar at the left of your screen and then click the **Insert Footnote Directly** button on the toolbar that appears to insert a footnote.

In addition to headers and footers, Writer supports the inclusion of *footnotes* and *endnotes* in your documents. A footnote differs from a footer in that it appears only on the page in which it's referenced. An endnote appears at the end of your document, referenced somewhere in the text. You can place both footnotes and endnotes in your documents. Once you set up footnotes or endnotes, Writer takes over the administration of them. Therefore, if you add a footnote between two others, Writer renumbers all the footnotes accordingly. The same goes for endnotes, so if you delete an endnote, Writer renumbers all the other endnotes affected by the deletion.

When you're ready to insert a footnote or endnote, a footnote or endnote anchor appears at the location in the text where you inserted the footnote or endnote. Writer takes care of numbering footnotes and endnotes for you as you add them.

1 Determine a Location

Click inside your document where you want the footnote or endnote anchor to go. The anchor will become a sequential number (or some other text that you will specify) attached to the footnote or endnote. For your first footnote, the number will be **1**, and the footnote numbered **1** will always apply to that anchor. An endnote anchor numbered **21** will refer to an endnote with the same number. Again, these numbers update automatically if you insert or remove footnotes and endnotes from among others.

2 Request a Footnote

Select **Insert**, **Footnote** to insert either an endnote or a footnote at the selected location. The **Insert Footnote** dialog box appears, where you can provide the specifics of the footnote or endnote.

1 Determine a Location

2 Request a Footnote

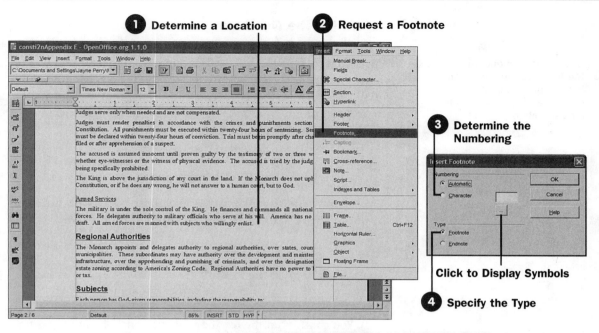

3 Determine the Numbering

Click to Display Symbols

4 Specify the Type

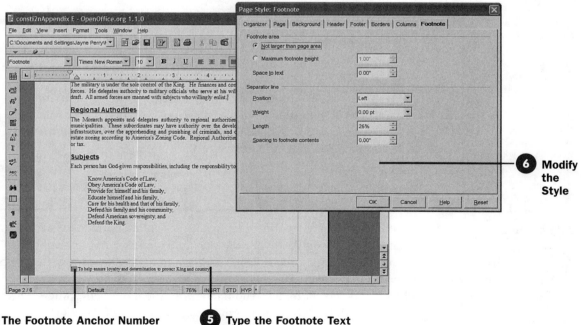

6 Modify the Style

The Footnote Anchor Number

5 Type the Footnote Text

NOTE

If you add a footnote to a multicolumned document, the footnote appears at the bottom of the column where you placed the footnote's anchor.

③ Determine the Numbering

Generally, you'll leave the **Automatic** numbering option selected. This enables Writer to handle the sequential numbering for you of your footnotes and endnotes. If you want to use a different character, such as an alphabetic letter, type the letter that will belong to the footnote or endnote. You can use a special symbol, such as a Greek letter if you wish, by clicking the ellipses (...) button.

④ Specify the Type

Click either **Footnote** or **Endnote** to tell Writer where you want the current note handled (either at the end of the page or at the end of the document). Click **OK** to close the **Insert Footnote** dialog box.

⑤ Type the Footnote Text

Writer drops down to the footnote (or back to the endnote) section after numbering your anchor point and adding the footnote (or endnote) reference number. Type the text for your footnote (or endnote). You can format the text however you wish, including using italics and different fonts.

⑥ Modify the Style

If you want to change the way Writer formats your footnotes or endnotes, select **Format**, **Page** and then click the **Footnote** tab to display the **Footnote** page. Here, you can specify the maximum height of your note as well as determine where the note will go on the page and how thick the dividing line will be between the text on the page and the footnote at the bottom.

---

36 Save a Document as a PDF File

Before You Begin

✔ Create a New Document

✔ Print a Document

Adobe Systems, Incorporated designed a special file format called *PDF* that is readable on the Windows, Mac, and Linux platforms. Many electronic books (often called *eBooks*) conform to the PDF format so that Web users can download such books and read them online, save them to their computers for a later reading, or print them on their printers. The problem with the typical file format, such as Microsoft Word's DOC file format, is that Web browsers cannot read these files and they are not supportable on some of the major computing platforms in use today (although usually a plug-in utility program is available for most computers that do allow non-Windows users to read PC-based DOC files).

Writer (and the other OpenOffice.org programs) supports the PDF format in the following way: When you compose your document, you then can save that document in the PDF format. Once your document is in the PDF format, you can distribute it onto the Web, where most users will be able to read your document.

Almost all computers sold in the past few years support the use of PDF files. For users of older PCs that cannot yet read Adobe's PDF format, the Adobe Reader is available free for download from http://www.adobe.com/products/acrobat/readstep2.html, where the download is quick. Again, almost every computer in use today can read PDF files. So Writer's native capability to save documents in the PDF format gives you the ability to compose documents that most others can read.

Adobe sells Adobe Acrobat, a program that converts documents to PDF format, for several hundred dollars (full retail; wholesale often finds the price still high, at a little more than $300). Writer saves you money!

1 **Request PDF Export**

Select **File**, **Export to PDF** to display the **Export** dialog box, where you save your document to the PDF format.

2 **Type a Filename**

Type the filename you want to use for your PDF document in the **File name** text box. Make sure the **File format** box reads **PDF— Portable Document Format (pdf)**. Leave the **Automatic file name extension** check box selected to ensure that your exported document retains the proper .pdf filename extension.

KEY TERM

PDF—The name (and file-name extension) given to documents that conform to Adobe Systems' *Portable Document Format*. This format is readable by Web browsers and most computers.

TIP

If you want to convert Microsoft Word documents to PDF, use Writer as your intermediary! Open the Word document in Writer and then save the document using Writer's PDF file-saving feature.

NOTE

Not only are PDF documents readable on virtually every computing platform, but your graphics, tables, headers, footers, multiple columns, and all other formatting remains intact also.

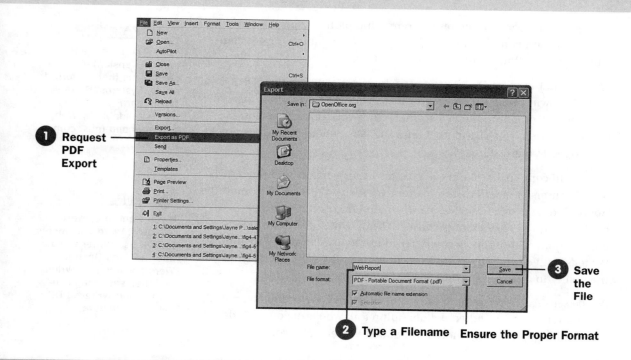

Request PDF Export

② Type a Filename   Ensure the Proper Format

③ Save the File

---

③ Save the File

Click the **OK** button to save the file.

Don't confuse the common Web page format (HTML) with PDF files. You'll often make PDF files available on a Web page for your users to download and read, but the Web page itself, the page that delivers your PDF document, must be in the standard HTML format. So when creating documents for others to download from the Web, always use PDF, not HTML.

PART II

Crunching Numbers with Calc

IN THIS PART:

6

Getting to Know Calc

IN THIS CHAPTER:

Spreadsheets—OpenOffice.org documents that hold one or more sheets (called *workbooks* in Microsoft Excel).

Sheets—Numerical information presented in a tabular row and column format with text that labels and discusses the data (also, loosely, called *spreadsheets*).

This chapter introduces topics related to Calc, OpenOffice.org's *spreadsheet* program. A spreadsheet is a collection of one or more *sheets*. OpenOffice.org's Calc is to numbers what Writer is to text; Calc has been called a "word processor for numbers." With Calc, you can create numerically based proposals, business plans, business forms, accounting spreadsheets, and virtually any other document that contains calculated numbers. If you've heard of, or have seen, Microsoft Excel, OpenOffice.org's Calc is OpenOffice.org's answer to Excel... only without the price tag.

If you are new to electronic spreadsheets, you may have to take a little more time learning Calc's environment than you have to take to learn other programs such as Writer. Calc starts with a grid of cells in which you place information, not unlike Writer's tables (see **23** **About Writer Tables**). This chapter orients you to Calc by offering tasks that explain how to enter and edit data in Calc spreadsheets as well as how to navigate them.

37 About Sheets and Spreadsheets

See Also

→ **38** Set Calc Options

→ **39** Create a New Spreadsheet

→ **45** Edit Cell Data

NOTE

Many people loosely use the term *spreadsheet* for single sheets inside a Calc *spreadsheet*. This lax term is used because Excel's sheets are called *spreadsheets*, but a Calc *spreadsheet* is technically the name for multiple sheets. It gets confusing! You'll often know by the context if *spreadsheet* is to refer to a single sheet or a collection of sheets.

Calc enables you to create and edit one or more sheets that you store in spreadsheets. Typically, people work with a single sheet for simple applications, such as a worksheet that an investor might use to analyze a single stock investment.

Typically, Calc helps users prepare financial information, but you can manage other kinds of data in Calc, such as a project timeline. Calc even supports simple database routines (see Chapter 10, "Using Calc as a Simple Database"). If your project requires multiple closely linked financial sheets, you'll keep those sheets in one large spreadsheet file.

A simple example may help solidify the difference between a *spreadsheet* and a *sheet* in your mind. A company with several divisions might create a spreadsheet with annual sales for each division, and each division might be represented with its own tabbed sheet inside the spreadsheet. Any time you create, open, or save a Calc file, you are working with a spreadsheet. Often, that spreadsheet contains only one sheet. When that's the case, the terms *spreadsheet* and *sheet* really are basically synonymous.

Sheet Area
Name of Active Cell   Active Cell
Column Headings
Function Bar   Object Bar   Formula Bar

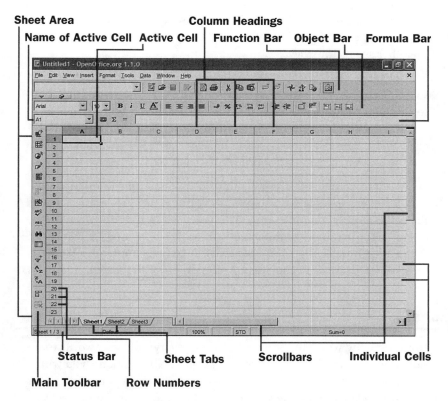

Status Bar   **Sheet Tabs**   **Scrollbars**   **Individual Cells**

Main Toolbar   Row Numbers

A sheet is a collection of rows and columns that holds text and numbers.

All Calc files end in the .sxc filename extension. Your spreadsheet name is the Calc name you assign when you save the file. You can save Calc sheets and spreadsheets in HTML and other spreadsheet formats, such as Microsoft Excel and Star Calc. When you save your sheet as an HTML file, you can embed your sheet data inside a Web page. To save your work, select **File**, **Save**; then name your Calc spreadsheet, specify the location, and select the format if you want to save the spreadsheet in a non-Calc format. To load an existing Calc file, use **File**, **Open**.

A sheet is set up in a similar manner to a Writer table (see **23** **About Writer Tables**), except that Calc sheets can do much more high-end, numeric calculating than Writer tables can.

Initially, blank Calc spreadsheets contain three sheets, named **Sheet1**, **Sheet2**, and **Sheet3**. When you click a sheet's tab, Calc brings that sheet

 TIP

Give your sheet a name other than **Sheet1**. Doing so helps you keep track of what data is on each sheet. Right-click the sheet tab labeled **Sheet1**, select **Rename Sheet** from the menu, and enter a different name, such as 2004 Payroll.

KEY TERM

Cell reference—The name of the cell, composed of its column and row intersection, such as **G14**. This is also called the *cell address*.

NOTE

No matter how large your monitor is, you see only a small amount of the **Sheet Area**. Use the scrollbars to see or edit information in the off-screen cells, such as cell **M200**.

into view. Initially, you'll probably stay with one sheet per spreadsheet, so you'll typically never have to click the secondary sheet tabs to bring the other sheets into view.

Each sheet column has a heading; heading names start with **A**, **B**, and so on. Each row has a heading, starting with **1**, **2**, and so on. The intersection of a row and column, called a *cell*, also has a name, which comes from combining the column number and row name, such as **C4** or **A1**. **A1** is always the top-left cell on any sheet. The gridlines throughout the sheet help you to distinguish between cells.

Every cell in your spreadsheet contains a unique name or address to which you can refer when you are tabulating data. This name is called the *cell reference*, and it is unique for each cell in the sheet. The active cell or cells are always highlighted with a dark border (**45** **Edit Cell Data** shows how to select multiple cells). A cell's location, also known as its *reference*, appears in the **Sheet Area** portion of the screen.

38 Set Calc Options

Before You Begin

✔ **37** About Sheets and Spreadsheets

See Also

→ **40** Open an Existing Spreadsheet

→ **45** Edit Cell Data

NOTE

All options are available for all OpenOffice.org programs at all times. For example, you can control the display of a grid in Calc from Impress, and you can request that Draw print all drawings in black and white from within Calc.

Not everybody works the same way, so not every Calc user wants to use Calc the same way. By setting some of Calc's many options, you will make Calc conform to the way you like to do things. For example, you may want Calc to hide the grid lines that normally distinguish between rows and columns to reduce onscreen clutter. If so, Calc has an option to display or hide the grid lines.

As a matter of fact, Calc has an option for just about anything! Table 6.1 describes Calc's options. You'll learn a lot about what Calc can do just by looking through the options available to you.

TABLE 6.1   Calc Spreadsheet Options

Calc Option Category	Explanation
General	Describes general Calc settings, such as the default unit of measurements and data-entry settings (see **41** **Enter Simple Data into a Spreadsheet**).
View	Describes how Calc appears on the screen and which Calc special elements (such as grid lines) appear by default.

Calc Option Category	Explanation
Calculate	Describes how Calc displays dates and interprets search criteria when you search for data inside your spreadsheet (see **47 Find and Replace Data**).
Sort Lists	Describes the sorting order for Calc's various lists of data, such as days of the week.
Changes	Describes how Calc interprets revisions that you or someone else makes to spreadsheets.
Grid	Describes the grid Calc uses so you can accurately place objects in your document exactly where you want them.
Print	Describes how Calc handles the printing of empty sheet pages (you can either print blank sheets or omit their printing). You can also control whether Calc can print only selected sheets or the entire spreadsheet.

① Request Options

Select **Options** from Calc's **Tools** menu. The **Options** dialog box appears. From the **Options** dialog box, you can change any of Calc's options as well as the options for the other OpenOffice.org programs.

② Change Overall Options

Select any option in the **OpenOffice.org** category to modify OpenOffice.org-wide settings, such as pathnames. For example, if you don't like the pathname you see when you open or save a file, click the **Paths** option and change it to a different default file path.

If you're new to OpenOffice.org, consider leaving all the OpenOffice.org options "as is" until you familiarize yourself with how the OpenOffice.org programs work.

③ Open the Spreadsheet Category and Set General Options

Click the plus sign next to the **Spreadsheet** option to display the seven Calc-specific options listed in Table 6.1, at the beginning of this task.

NOTE

The placement grid described by the **Grid** option is not the row and column grid that you see in a sheet's background. The placement grid helps you accurately put objects such as graphics in a sheet exactly where you want them.

TIP

Often, you'll work in one OpenOffice.org program and realize that you need to change an overall option. For example, if you want to print several kinds of OpenOffice.org documents to a file (instead of to your printer) to send to others via email, you can change the **OpenOffice.org** option labeled **Print**, from within Calc, to apply that setting to all OpenOffice.org programs.

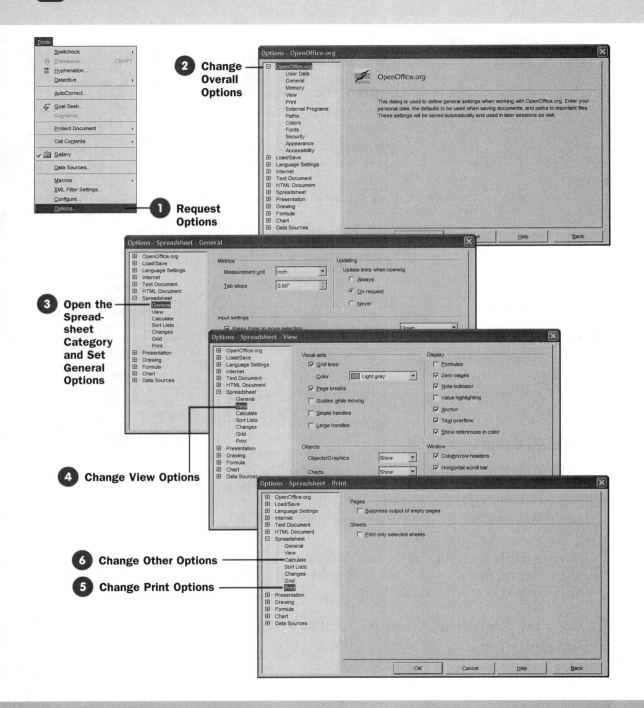

Click the **General** options category; the dialog box changes to show options you can select to make changes to the general Calc options. The **Metrics** section enables you to specify how you want to handle measurements and tab stops, such as in inches or metrically. The **Updating** section enables you to specify when Calc is to update links you put in a sheet, such as to a Web page. The **Input settings** section enables you to specify how you want to enter data into spreadsheets, such as whether to move to the next cell when you press **Enter** or stay in the current cell.

④ Change View Options

Click the **View** category under the **Spreadsheet** category; the dialog box changes to show options that handle Calc's onscreen display. For example, you can hide and change the color of Calc's grind lines in the background of sheets from within the **Visual aids** section. The **Display** section determines how special values such as zeroes, formulas, and anchors are to be shown. The **Objects** section determines how Calc shows objects such as charts and graphics. The **Window** section specifies the display of various Calc screen elements, such as the scrollbars and sheet tabs, that contain the name of the sheets in the current spreadsheet.

⑤ Change Print Options

Click to select the **Print** category under the **Spreadsheet** category. Only two options appear: **Suppress output of empty pages** and **Print only selected sheets**. With a judicious use of these options, you can save a lot of paper in some documents if you don't print every blank page or all sheets in the spreadsheet.

⑥ Change Other Options

Continue viewing and changing the remaining options in the **Spreadsheet** category by first selecting the category and then looking at the individual options.

When you're done specifying Calc options, click the **OK** button to close the **Options** dialog box.

39 Create a New Spreadsheet

Before You Begin

✔ **37** About Sheets and Spreadsheets

See Also

→ **40** Open an Existing Spreadsheet

→ **41** Enter Simple Data into a Spreadsheet

NOTE

Unlike Writer, AutoPilot offers no help for creating spreadsheets.

Calc offers two ways to create new spreadsheets: You can create a completely blank, new spreadsheet (if you choose this approach, you must decide what to put in the spreadsheet and where that information should go), or you can use a spreadsheet template to open a preformatted spreadsheet. **16** **About Styles and Templates** explains what templates are.

Although Calc does not come with templates when you first install OpenOffice.org, you can easily create a template to reuse later. This task shows you how to open a blank spreadsheet. **18** **Use a Template** explains how to create a new spreadsheet based on a template you may have created and saved previously.

1 **Request a New Spreadsheet**

Select **Spreadsheet** from the **File**, **New** menu option. Calc creates a blank spreadsheet. Alternatively, click the **New** toolbar button to open a new blank Calc spreadsheet quickly.

2 **Compose Your Spreadsheet**

Create your spreadsheet in the blank work area of cells that Calc gives you. You'll enter text, numbers, and formulas, depending on the needs of your spreadsheet. You can print your spreadsheet (see **46** **Print a Spreadsheet**) at any time.

3 **Save the Spreadsheet**

After creating your spreadsheet, select **File**, **Save** and type the name of your spreadsheet. Calc uses the filename extension .sxc for your spreadsheet. You can select another file format, such as Microsoft Excel; doing so saves the spreadsheet with the .xls Excel extension. Other file formats include StarCalc (.sdc), text (.txt), and HTML (.html).

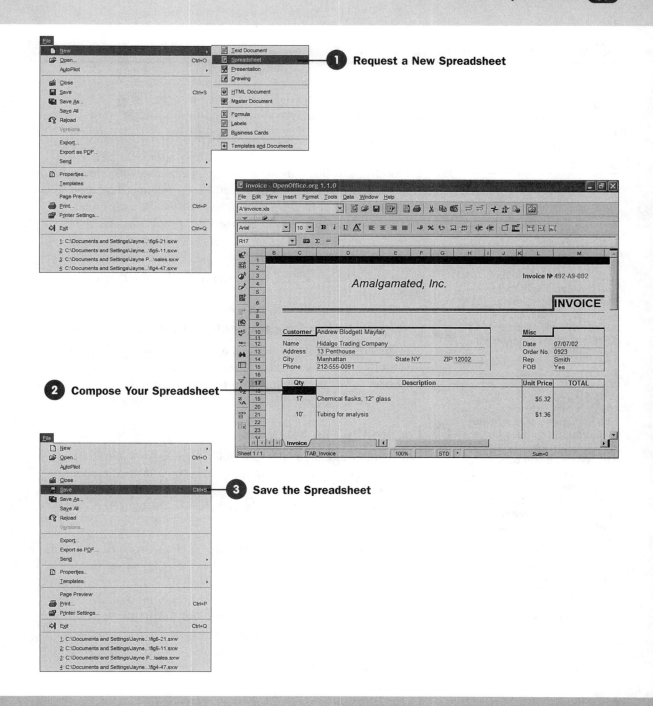

1 Request a New Spreadsheet

2 Compose Your Spreadsheet

3 Save the Spreadsheet

40 Open an Existing Spreadsheet

Before You Begin

✔ **37** About Sheets and Spreadsheets

✔ **39** Create a New Spreadsheet

See Also

→ **45** Edit Cell Data

NOTE

Microsoft Excel uses the .xls file extension. You'll see any Excel spreadsheets that reside in the folder you open from within Calc along with any Calc spreadsheets that also appear in that folder.

TIP

You can open spreadsheets from your computer's disk or from elsewhere in the file system. If you want to open a spreadsheet located on the Web, preface the filename with http:// or ftp:// to open spreadsheet files from those sources. For example, you could preface a filename with http://www. SimpleRentHouses.com to open a file from that site (assuming you have access to that site's files).

Opening an existing spreadsheet to edit in Calc is simple. You tell Calc that you want to open a spreadsheet file and then locate the file. Calc then loads the spreadsheet into the row-and-column-based editing area.

One important Calc feature is its capability to open documents you create in other spreadsheet programs. Most notably, Calc opens Microsoft Excel spreadsheets (called *workbooks* in Excel) with ease. Although Calc might not fully support 100% of Microsoft Excel's advanced features, Calc does a super job of loading Excel spreadsheets into Calc's workspace so that you can edit the spreadsheets using Calc's interface.

● Request a Spreadsheet

Select **Open** from the Calc **File** menu to display the **Open** dialog box.

● Navigate to the Spreadsheet's Location

The spreadsheet that you want to open might not appear at the default location shown in the **Open** dialog box, so navigate to the folder in which the spreadsheet you're looking for resides using the **Look in** drop-down list.

● Locate the File You Want

When you locate the folder that holds the spreadsheet file, select the file you want to open. Then click the **Open** button to open the selected file in Calc's editing workspace. The **Files of type** option enables you to select files of a specific type only, such as the Microsoft Excel spreadsheets.

If the default **Editing view** option on the **OpenOffice.org Options** page is set, Calc opens the document at the point where it last saved the spreadsheet. For example, if the spreadsheet is large enough to span six screens and you previously made edits to the third screen of the sheet before saving and closing the spreadsheet last week, Calc displays that place on screen 3 where you last quit editing. The **Editing view** option enables you to get right back to work where you left off.

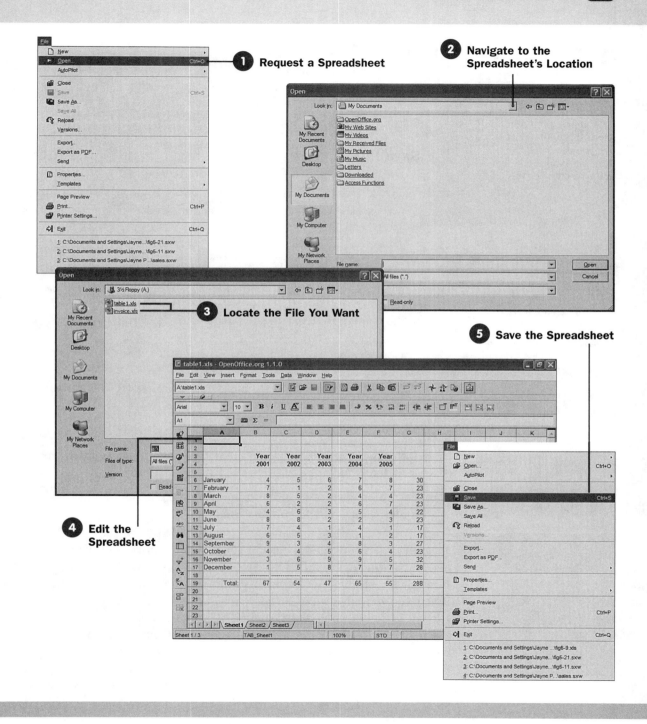

① **Request a Spreadsheet**

② **Navigate to the Spreadsheet's Location**

③ **Locate the File You Want**

④ **Edit the Spreadsheet**

⑤ **Save the Spreadsheet**

TIP

Feel free to open more than one spreadsheet by holding the **Ctrl** key while clicking multiple filenames. Calc opens each spreadsheet that you select in its own window. Use the **Window** menu to select an open spreadsheet to edit.

4 Edit the Spreadsheet

After the file opens in the Calc workspace, you can edit the file. Navigate to where you wish to make edits (see **45 Edit Cell Data**) or move to the end of the document and add to it (see **41 Enter Simple Data into a Spreadsheet**).

5 Save the Spreadsheet

Once you've made all the changes you wish to make, select **File**, **Save** to save your spreadsheet. Your recent changes will be saved in the spreadsheet file for your next editing session.

41 Enter Simple Data into a Spreadsheet

Before You Begin

✔ **39** Create a New Spreadsheet

✔ **40** Open an Existing Spreadsheet

See Also

→ **45** Edit Cell Data

→ **46** Print a Spreadsheet

Often, entering worksheet data requires nothing more than clicking the correct cell to select it and then typing the data. The various kinds of data behave differently when entered, however, so you should understand how Calc accepts assorted data.

Calc works with the following kinds of data:

- **Labels**—Text values such as names and addresses, as well as date and time values.

- **Numbers**—Numeric values such as 34, –291, 545.67874, and 0.

- **Dates and times**—Calc accepts date and time values that you type in virtually any format.

- **Formulas**—Expressions that compute numeric results. (Some formulas work with text values as well.)

This task walks you through a short editing session just to give you a feel for entering data into a Calc sheet. Keep in mind that Calc's interface is different from most other programs you may have worked with, unless you've worked with electronic spreadsheet programs before. Having said that, some of the editing skills you acquire in one OpenOffice.org program apply to the other OpenOffice.org programs as well. For example, both Calc and Writer offer the capability to display or hide the **Main** toolbar. The **Main** toolbar changes slightly depending on which program you use, but most of its functions are similar across the OpenOffice.org programs.

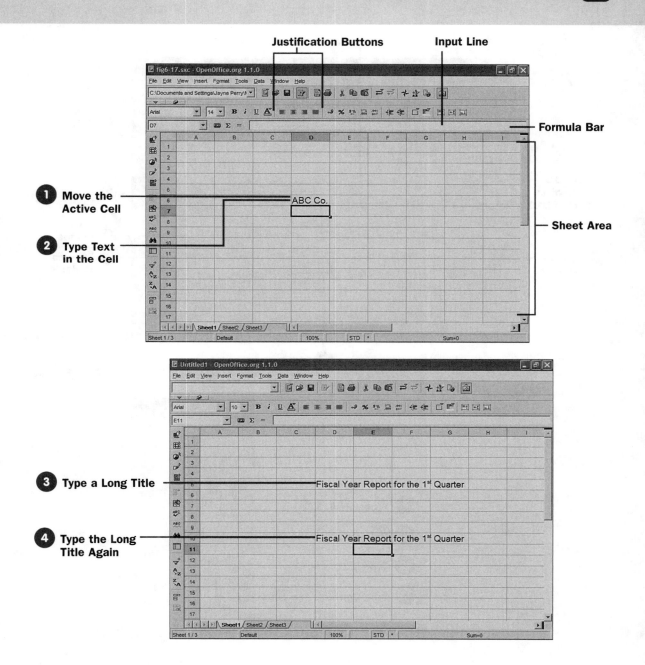

Justification Buttons

Input Line

Formula Bar

1 Move the Active Cell

2 Type Text in the Cell

Sheet Area

ABC Co.

3 Type a Long Title

Fiscal Year Report for the 1st Quarter

4 Type the Long Title Again

Fiscal Year Report for the 1st Quarter

No Data in E5 to Overwrite D5

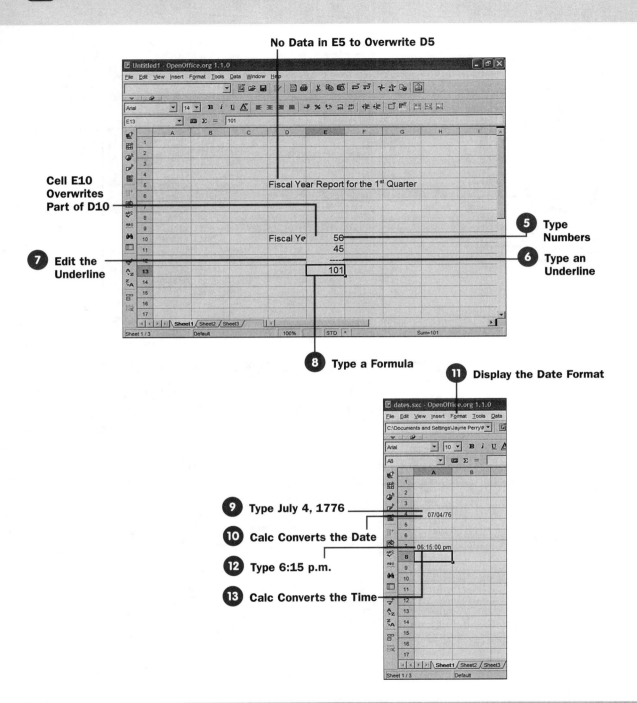

Cell E10 Overwrites Part of D10

7 Edit the Underline

8 Type a Formula

5 Type Numbers

6 Type an Underline

11 Display the Date Format

9 Type July 4, 1776

10 Calc Converts the Date

12 Type 6:15 p.m.

13 Calc Converts the Time

① Move the Active Cell

Click cell **D5** to make **D5** the active cell. The cell's dark outline indicates that the cell is selected. Also, the cell name appears in the **Sheet Area**.

② Type Text in the Cell

Type **ABC Co.** into cell **D5**. To enter the text, simply type the text, and it appears both in the cell as well as in the **Input** line toward the top of the screen. When you press **Enter**, the activedifferently when entered, however, so you should understand cell moves down one row. Instead of **Enter**, you can press the **right arrow** button or **Tab**, and the cell to the right of the cell becomes active next.

Text always appears left-justified in a cell, although you can click one of the justification buttons to center or right-justify text in a cell. To correct a mistake, press **Backspace** and type the corrected text.

If you press the **Esc** button at any point during text entry but before you move to another cell, Calc erases the text you typed in the cell and restores the original cell. In addition, you can press **Ctrl+Z** (for undo) or click the **Undo** button to back up to a cell's previous state.

③ Type a Long Title

Replace the text in cell **D5** by typing **Fiscal Year Report for the 1st Quarter**. As you type, the text spills into cells **E5**, **F5**, and finally ends in **G5**. The important thing to note is that only cell **D5** holds the text value **Fiscal Year Report for the 1st Quarter**. Although it *looks* as though pieces of the title spill into the cells to the right, Calc is showing the full text in cell **D5** because no values appear to the right of **D5**. If any data resided in cells **E5**, **F5**, or **G5**, Calc would *not* have shown the full value in **D5**.

④ Type the Long Title Again

Move to cell **D10** and type the same title, **Fiscal Year Report for the 1st Quarter**. As with cell **D5**, the full text shows because nothing appearsdifferently when entered, however, so you should understand in the cells to the right of **D10**.

NOTE

You can change the action of the **Enter** key from the **Options, Spreadsheet, General** dialog box page.

TIP

You'll see that when you type 1st, Calc's AutoCorrect feature converts it to 1st.

TIP

Instead of typing the title twice, select the title and click **Copy** (or press **Ctrl+C**). You then can paste the title where you want it by clicking the cell and then clicking **Paste** (or pressing **Ctrl+V**).

⑤ Type Numbers

Type the following numeric values into cells **E10** and **E11**, respectively: **56** and **45**. You'll see that as soon as you type cell **E10**'s value, the long text in cell **D10** no longer displays. The long text is still in cell **D10**, but Calc doesn't display the text because then you would be unable to see the number in cell **E10**.

Calc usually recognizes any entry that begins with an alphabetical character as text. Some textual data, such as price codes, telephone numbers, and ZIP Codes can fool Calc into thinking you are entering numeric data because of the initial numeric value. Calc treats numeric data differently from text data when you type the data into cells. If you want Calc to treat a number (such as a ZIP Code) as a text entry so that it does not perform calculations on the cell, precede the contents with a single apostrophe ('). For example, to type the ZIP Code 74137, type **'74137**; the apostrophe lets Calc know to format the value as text. Knowing this enables you to enter text-based numbers such as ZIP Codes and product codes that require a leading zero. Without the quote, Calc interprets a value with a leading zero as a number and removes the zero and right-justifies the number.

Also notice that, unlike text values, Calc right-justifies numeric values. You'll also see when you enter formulas that Calc right-justifies the results of those formulas.

⑥ Type an Underline

You can put a line, composed of dashes, below the two numbers you just entered. Type **- - - - -** in cell **D7** and press **Enter**. The dashed line doesn't look correct because Calc left-justified the line since the line is not numeric but text.

⑦ Edit the Underline

Click the underline to make it active. Then click the **Align Right** button that resides in the group of justification buttons and Calc right-justifies the underline.

8 Type a Formula

Type **=E10+E11** in cell **E13**. You've just typed your first formula in Calc. The moment you press **Enter**, Calc displays the formula's answer instead of the formula itself.

Click cell **E13** to make it active again. You'll see the formula in the **Input** line. So when you click a formula's cell, Calc shows you both the formula and the value. If you want to change the formula, either press **F2** to display the formula once again inside the cell itself or click to edit the formula in the **Input** line.

9 Type July 4, 1776

Type **July 4, 1776** in cell **A4**.

10 Calc Converts the Date

Press **Enter** and Calc converts your date to a different format. Calc converts the date to **07/04/76**. Calc does retain the date's full value inside the cell, and only the date's display appears in the *mm/dd/yy* format.

11 Display the Date Format

Calc supports almost every national and international date and time format. To determine which format Calc is to display dates (and times) in, select **Format**, **Cells**, click the **Numbers** tab, and then click the **Date** entry under **Category**. You can change the way Calc displays any cell's date by modifying its format. **59** **Format Cells** goes into detail about how to format cells.

12 Type 6:15 p.m.

Type **6:15 p.m.** in cell **A7**.

13 Calc Converts the Time

Press **Enter** and Calc converts your time to a different format. Calc converts the time to **06:15:00 pm**. Calc does retain the time's full value inside the cell, and only the time's display appearsdifferently when entered, however, so you should understand in the *hh:mm:ss am/pm* format.

NOTE

For now, do not make changes to the formula but rather click cell **E13** and press **F2**. Calc colorizes the formula and highlights each formula value's cell so you can easily see the cells that comprise the formula. Press **Enter** to keep the current value.

NOTE

Type the **am** or **pm** designation when entering time values or enter the time using a 24-hour clock. Either **6:15 pm** or **18:15** work to enter the same time in the cell.

42 **About Moving Around Calc**

Before You Begin

✔ **41** Enter Simple Data
into a Spreadsheet

See Also

→ **43** About Calc
Formulas

NOTE

If you select multiple cells, the selection is considered to be a single set of active cells.

Your mouse and arrow keys are the primary navigation keys for moving from cell to cell in sheets. Unlike Writer, which uses an insertion point, Calc uses its active cell, the highlighted cell, to indicate your current position in the sheet.

The active cell has a darkened border around it and accepts whatever data you enter next. As you press an arrow key, Calc moves the cell pointer in the direction of the arrow to a new cell, making the new cell the active one. Once you begin typing inside a cell, the insertion point appears. Unlike in Writer, though, the insertion point is not your primary means of traversing spreadsheets; rather, the active cell is.

If you're working with a rather large sheet, you might find the **Navigator** dialog box useful. Press **F5** to display the **Navigator** dialog box, where you can select a range of cells that you might have previously named or enter a cell address, such as **C141**, to jump to that cell. You may also click any object in the **Navigator** dialog box, such as a sheet name, or select a range name to jump to.

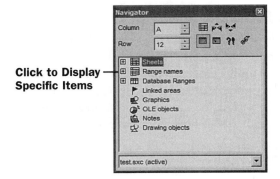

Click to Display Specific Items

Use the Navigator dialog box to move around a spreadsheet efficiently.

Table 6.2 lists the most commonly used navigational keystrokes within Calc. Use your mouse to scroll with the scrollbars.

TABLE 6.2   Using the Keyboard to Navigate Calc

Press This Key...	To Move
Arrow keys	The direction of the arrow, one cell at a time
Ctrl+up arrow, Ctrl+down arrow	The topmost or bottommost cell that contains data or, if at the end of the range already, the next cell that contains data
Ctrl+left arrow, Ctrl+right arrow	The leftmost or rightmost cell that contains data or, if at the end of the range already, the next cell that contains data
PageUp, PageDown	The previous or next screen of the worksheet
Ctrl+Home	The upper-left corner of the worksheet (cell A1)
Ctrl+PageUp, Ctrl+PageDown	The next or previous sheet within the current spreadsheet

43   About Calc Formulas

Without *formulas*, Calc would be little more than a simple row-and-column-based word processor. When you use formulas, however, Calc becomes an extremely powerful timesaving, planning, budgeting, and general-purpose financial tool.

On a calculator, you typically type a formula and then press the equal sign to see the result. In contrast, all Calc formulas begin with an equal sign. For example, the following is a formula:

=4*2-3

The asterisk is an operator that denotes the times sign (multiplication). This formula requests that Calc compute the value of 4 multiplied by 2 minus 3 to get the result. When you type a formula and press **Enter** or move to another cell, Calc displays the result and not the formula on the worksheet.

When you enter **=4*2-3** in a cell, the answer 5 appears in the cell when you move away from the cell. You can see the formula in the **Input** line atop the sheet if you click the cell again to make it active. When entering a formula, as soon as you press the equal sign, Calc shows your

Before You Begin

✔ **37** About Sheets and Spreadsheets

See Also

→ **44** Copy and Move Formulas

🔍**KEY TERM**

Formulas—Equations composed of numeric values and often cell addresses and range names that produce a mathematical result.

formula in the **Input** line area as well as in the active cell. If you click the **Input** line first and then finish your formula there, the formula appears in the **Input** line as well as in the active cell. By typing the formula in the **Input** line, you can press the **left-** and **right-arrow** keys to move the cell pointer left and right within the formula to edit it. When you enter long formulas, this **Input** line's editing capability helps you correct mistakes that you might type.

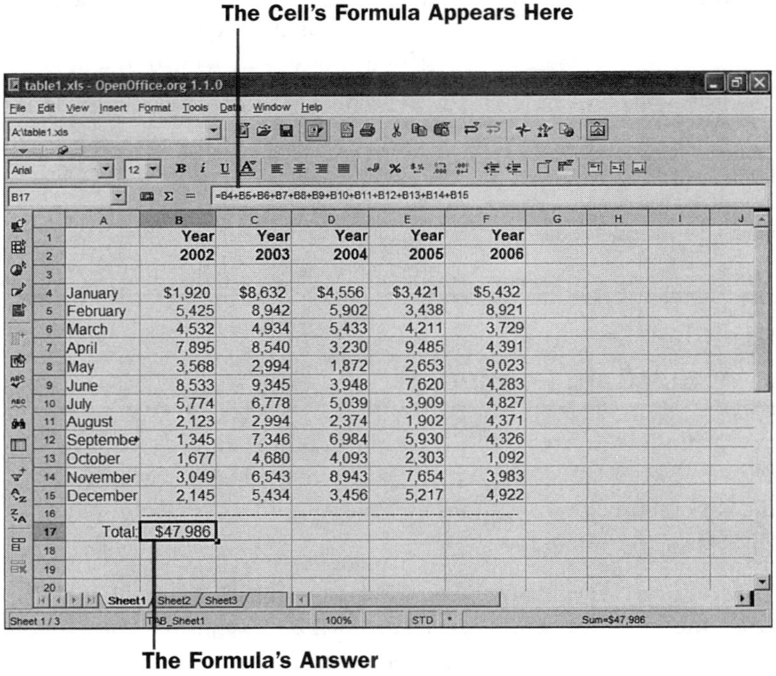

The Cell's Formula Appears Here

The Formula's Answer

Calc displays a formula's result in the cell.

Table 6.3 lists the primary math operators you can use in your worksheet formulas. Notice that all the sample formulas begin with the equal sign.

TABLE 6.3   The Primary Math Operators Specify Math
Calculations

Operator	Example	Description
^	=7 ^ 3	Raises 7 to the power of 3 (called *exponentiation*)
/	=4 / 2	Divides 4 by 2
*	=3 * 4 * 5	Multiplies 3 by 4 by 5
+	=5 + 5	Adds 5 and 5
−	=5 - 5	Subtracts 5 from 5

KEY TERM

Operator hierarchy model—A predefined order of operators when equations are being calculated.

NOTE

Formulas can contain cell addresses, cell names, and other values besides numbers. See **48** About Calc Ranges for more information about range names.

You can combine any and all the operators in a formula. When combining operators, Calc follows the traditional computer (and algebraic) *operator hierarchy model*. Therefore, Calc first computes exponentiation if you raise any value to another power. Calc then calculates all multiplication and division in a left-to-right order (the first one to appear computes first) before addition and subtraction (also in left-to-right order).

The following formula returns a result of 14 because Calc first calculates the exponentiation of 2 raised to the third power and then divides the answer (8) by 4, multiplies the result (2) by 2, and finally subtracts the result (4) from 18. Even though the subtraction appears first, the operator hierarchy forces the subtraction to wait until last to compute.

=18 - 2 ^ 3 / 4 * 2

If you want to override the operator hierarchy, put parentheses around the parts you want Calc to compute first. The following formula returns a different result from the previous one, for example, despite the same values and operators used:

=(18 - 2) ^ 3 / 4 * 2

Instead of 14, this formula returns 2,048! The subtraction produces 16, which is then raised to the third power (producing 4,096) before dividing by 4 and multiplying the result by 2 to get 2,048.

To add three cells together, you could type the following in another cell:

=D3+K10+M7

Calc adds the values in **D3**, **K10**, and **M7** and shows the result in place of the formula. The cells **D3**, **K10**, and **M7** can also contain formulas that reference other cells.

44 Copy and Move Formulas

Before You Begin

✔ **43** About Calc
       Formulas

See Also

→ **49** Create a Range

Relative reference—A cell that is referenced in relation to the current cell.

Absolute reference—A cell reference that does not change if you copy the formula elsewhere.

You can copy, move, and paste one cell into another using standard copy-and-paste tools such as the Windows Clipboard. When you copy formulas that contain cell addresses, Calc updates the cell references so they become *relative references*. For example, suppose that you enter this formula in cell **A1**:

`=A2 + A3`

This formula contains two cell references. The references are relative because the references **A2** and **A3** change if you copy the formula elsewhere. If you copy the formula to cell **B5**, for example, **B5** holds this:

`=B6 + B7`

The original relative references update to reflect the formula's copied location. Of course, **A1** still holds its original contents, but the copied cell at **B5** holds the same formula referencing **B5** rather than **A1**.

A dollar sign ($) always precedes an *absolute reference*. The reference **B5** is an absolute reference. If you want to sum two columns of data (**A1** with **B1**, **A2** with **B2**, and so on) and then multiply each sum by some constant number, for example, the constant number can be a cell referred to as an *absolute reference*. That formula might resemble this:

`=(A1 + B1) * $J$1`

In this case, **J1** is an absolute reference, but **A1** and **B1** are relative. If you copy the formula down one row, the formula changes to this:

`=(A2 + B2) * $J$1`

Notice that the first two cells changed because when you originally entered them, they were relative cell references. You told Calc, by placing dollar signs in front of the absolute cell reference's row and column references, not to change that reference when you copy the formula elsewhere.

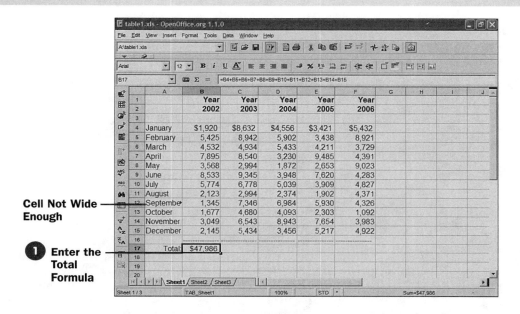

Cell Not Wide Enough

1 Enter the Total Formula

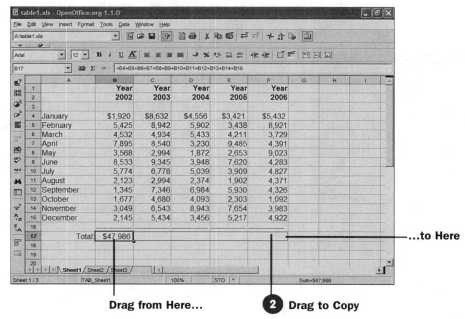

Drag from Here...

2 Drag to Copy

...to Here

Align Right Button

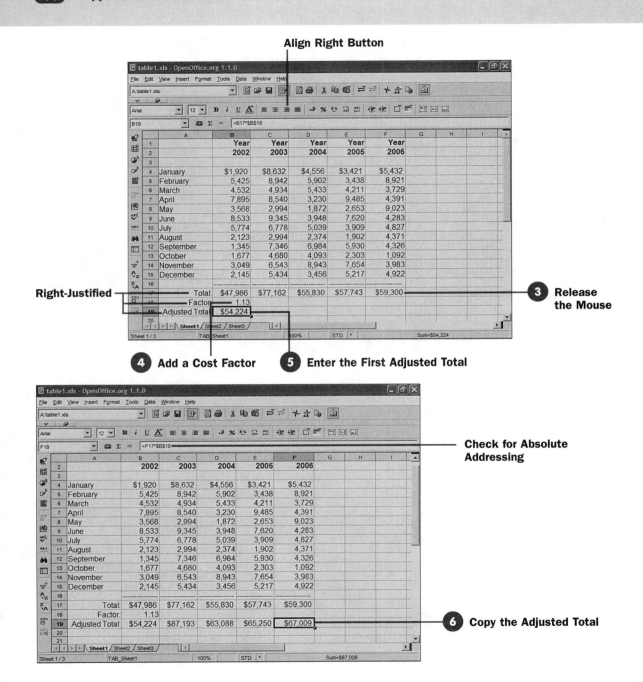

Right-Justified

Release the Mouse 3

4 **Add a Cost Factor**   5 **Enter the First Adjusted Total**

Check for Absolute Addressing

6 **Copy the Adjusted Total**

$B5 is a partial absolute cell reference. If you copy a formula with $B5 inside the computation, the $B keeps the B column intact, but the fifth row updates to the row location of the target cell. For example, if you type the formula

=2 * $B5

in cell **A1** and then copy the formula to cell **F6**, cell **F6** holds this formula:

=2 * $B10

You copied the formula to a cell five rows and five columns over in the worksheet. Calc did not update the column name, **B**, because you told Calc to keep that column name absolute. (It is always **B** no matter where you copy the formula.) Calc added five to the row number, however, because the row number is relative and open to change whenever you copy the formula.

1 **Enter the Total Formula**

For this sheet, assume you want a formula for each past year and projected year into the future. You would type the formula to total the first year in cell **B17**. One formula that would total this year would be

```
=B4 + B5 + B6 + B7 + B8 + B9 + B10 + B11 + B12 + B13 +
B14 + B15
```

Notice that cell **A12** does not display all of the month of September's name. The column is not wide enough to display the full month. Calc warns you that this cell's contents aren't fully displayed with a small triangle along the right side of the cell. You can widen cells like this that you find are too narrow by dragging the dividing line between the name of column **A** and column **B** to the right to give every month name enough room to display properly.

A quick way to resize a column to ensure that it is wide enough for all its data is to double-click the column divider between the column you want to widen and the one on its right. Calc automatically resizes the column width to hold the widest value in the column.

TIP

Most of the time, you'll use relative referencing. If you insert or delete rows, columns, or cells, your formulas remain accurate because the cells that they reference change as your worksheet changes.

TIP

There are several better ways to total a column. The most tedious but easiest to understand is this step's way. One better way would be to type this formula: **=Sum(B4:B15)**. **51** **About Calc Functions** explores Sum( ) and other Calc functions.

NOTE

When you drag your mouse across multiple cells, you are indicating a range that you want to work with.

NOTE

Look at the Input line for cell **F17**. You'll see that Calc copied the formula from **B17** using relative addressing. It wouldn't make sense to put the total for column **B** in cell **F17**. When Calc saw that you wanted to copy the formula, and because the formula contains relative cell references, Calc copied the formula as though it referred to cells relative to **B17**.

NOTE

The figure's cells are formatted to display dollar signs in some places and not in others. **59** Format Cells explains how to format cells the way you want them to look. The labels for **Factor** and **Adjusted Total** are right-justified (with the **Align Right** button); however, they first enter their respective cells left-justified because they contain text.

TIP

You don't need to leave spaces between operators such as multiplication (*) in formulas. Doing so makes them easier to read and to check for errors, however.

2 Drag to Copy

Once you type a formula in cell **B17**, you can copy that cell to the Windows **Clipboard** with **Ctrl+C** and then paste the cell into **C17**, then **D17**, then **E17**, and finally **F17**. Calc offers an easier way though. Drag the lower-right corner of cell **B17**, where you'll see a small square, to the right, and Calc highlights each empty cell along the way as you copy.

3 Release the Mouse

Once you release your mouse button over cell **F17**, you will see that Calc totals all five columns for you where you copied the total formula.

4 Add a Cost Factor

To demonstrate absolute cell addressing, add a cost factor of 1.13 below **Year 2002**'s total. You then can multiply the total to create an adjusted total in cell **B19**. If you also want to multiply the remaining totals by the adjustment factor, you *cannot* use relative addressing for the cost factor. In other words, if you multiply cell **B17** by cell **B18** and store the result in **B19** with the formula =B17*B18, and then copy that formula to cell **C19**, cell **C19** would hold this formula: =C17*C18. However, **C18** is blank! So Calc would multiply **C17** by zero, which is not the correct adjustment factor.

5 Enter the First Adjusted Total

To enter the correct adjusted total in cell **B19**, you would type =B17 * B18.

By using absolute addressing in cell **B18** (that is, B18), when you copy it to the remaining years, all the cells you copy to will also use **B18** instead of a different cell for the factor.

6 Copy the Adjusted Total

To copy the adjusted total to the other years, you can use **Ctrl+C** and then paste with **Ctrl+V** into each year's adjusted total cell, but it's simpler just to drag the small square in the first cell's lower-right corner (the mouse pointer changes to a plus sign when you point to this square) across through the cells that are to receive the copied formula.

When you release your mouse after making such a copy with one or more absolute cell addresses in the range, the absolute address remains the same and the relative addresses inside the cells change. This sounds less obvious than it is. In other words, when you copy the formula =B17 * B18 to cell **C19**, cell **C19** gets this formula: =C17 * B18. Cell **D19** gets =D17 * B18, and so on.

NOTE

You can make only the row or only the column of a cell address absolute. In the cell reference **M$15**, the column named **M** is relative and will change if you copy a cell that contains this reference elsewhere, but the absolute row number, **$15**, will not change.

45 Edit Cell Data

Entering numeric data is error-prone at its best; the faster you edit cell values accurately, the faster you compose accurate sheets. If you have already moved to another cell when you recognize that you have entered an error, you can quickly correct the mistake as follows:

1. Move the cell pointer to the cell you need to correct. (Click the cell to move the pointer there.)

2. Press **F2**, which is the standard Windows editing shortcut key. You know Calc is ready for your edit when you see the insertion point appear in the cell. You can also click and edit the **Input** line to change the cell's contents.

3. Use the **arrow keys** to move the insertion point to the mistake.

4. Press the **Insert** key to change from Overtype mode to Insert mode, or vice versa. As with Writer, Overtype mode enables you to write over existing characters, whereas Insert mode shifts all existing characters to the right as you type the correction.

5. Press **Enter** to anchor the correction in place.

Inserting cells, as opposed to inserting data inside a cell, requires that the existing sheet cells move to the right and down to make room for the new cell. Perhaps you created a sheet of employee salaries and failed to include the employees who work at another division. You can easily make room for those missing entries by inserting new cells. You can insert both new rows and new columns in your sheets.

Use the **Delete Contents** dialog box not only to delete cells but also to delete entire rows and columns.

Before You Begin

✔ **41** Enter Simple Data into a Spreadsheet

See Also

→ **48** About Calc Ranges

TIP

If you want to reverse an edit, click the **Undo** button. To reverse an undo, select **Edit, Restore**.

TIP

If you want to delete multiple rows or multiple columns, select cells from each column or row you want to delete before displaying the **Delete Contents** dialog box.

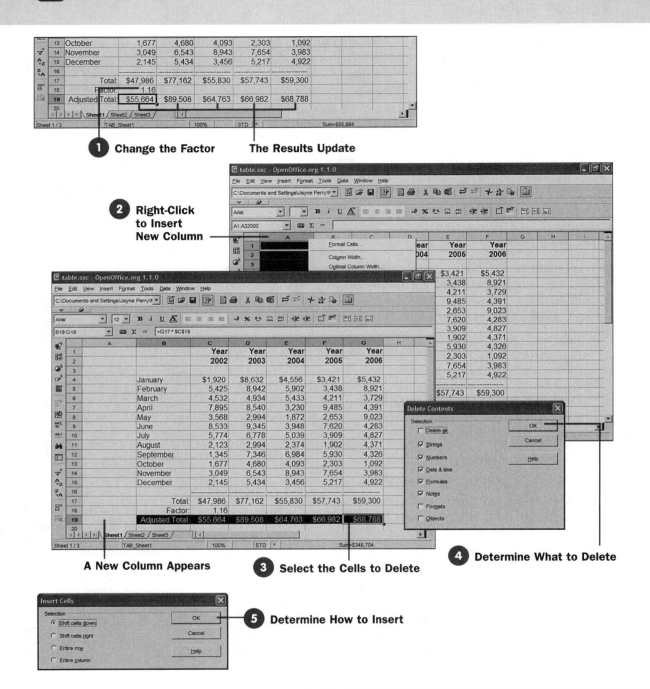

1 Change the Factor   **The Results Update**

2 Right-Click to Insert New Column

A New Column Appears   **3** Select the Cells to Delete   **4** Determine What to Delete

5 Determine How to Insert

Deleting rows and columns differs from deleting specific contents inside cells. When you want to erase a cell's specific contents, the other cells to the right and below that cell don't shift to fill in the empty space. To erase a cell's contents, click the cell to move the cell pointer there and press **F2** to edit the cell's contents. Press **Backspace** to erase the cell. Even quicker, you can press **Ctrl+X** or select **Edit, Cut** to remove the contents and send them to the Clipboard, where you can paste them elsewhere or ignore them.

TIP

You can just as easily insert more than one column. For example, if you want to insert three new columns, select three column names that are to *follow* the new columns before selecting the **Insert Columns** option. Calc inserts three columns.

1 Change the Factor

To change the factor, you click cell **B18** and press **F2** to enter editing mode. You'll see the insertion point at the end of the cell's contents. Press **Backspace** once to erase the **3** and then type **6**. Press **Enter**. You have just changed the factor from **1.13** to **1.16**.

2 Right-Click to Insert New Column

To insert a column before another, click a column name that is to *follow* the new column. Then right-click your mouse and a menu appears. Select **Insert Columns** (even if you want to insert only one column). Calc moves the sheet's contents to the right by one column.

3 Select the Cells to Delete

To delete the contents of one or more cells, click to select the cell or drag your mouse to select multiple cells. Press the **Delete** key to delete the contents.

4 Determine What to Delete

Calc opens the **Delete Contents** dialog box. You can select what from the cell you want to delete. Usually, you'll immediately press **Enter** or click **OK** to delete the data from the cells you selected. Doing this maintains any formatting in the cells you deleted.

You can remove the formatting as well by clicking **Formats** in the **Delete Contents** dialog box before clicking **OK**. Or, you can remove only the formatting but keep all the data. The options you select before performing the deletion determine exactly what you want to delete.

TIP

If you were to insert four quarter values after each year in this sample sheet, you would want to shift the entire columns to the right as you insert the quarterly data to retain all the year information appropriately.

5 Determine How to Insert

To insert a cell before another, you must first consider the implications of what you're doing. Other cells reside in the sheet. If, for example, you wanted to insert a cell before the final **Adjusted Total** value, how is Calc supposed to handle the value that's in the cell? Should Calc delete it, move it to the right, or move it down?

If other data were to appear to the right of a cell you try to insert, you must tell Calc how to handle the insertion. When you click to select a cell (or drag to select a range of cells) and select **Insert**, **Cells**, the **Insert Cells** dialog box appears. From the dialog box, you tell Calc whether you want the cells to the right of the newly inserted cell to shift down or to the right, or if you want the entire row or the entire column moved so that all the data in the affected row or column moves.

46 Print a Spreadsheet

Before You Begin

✔ **39** Create a New Spreadsheet

✔ **40** Open an Existing Spreadsheet

See Also

→ **61** Set Up Calc Page Formatting

TIP

If you select **File**, **Export as PDF**, Calc saves your document in the common PDF format, which you can send to any computer with Adobe Acrobat Reader. See **36** Save a Document as a PDF File for more information about PDF files.

Once you're done creating your spreadsheet, you'll want to print it to paper. Calc supports the standard printing options that most Windows programs support. If your document has color charts and you have a color printer, the charts will print just fine. Otherwise, the charts will print in shades of black and gray (and still look fine!).

Be sure to save your spreadsheet before you print it. Actually, it's a good idea to select **File**, **Save** to save your work throughout the editing of your sheets. If your printer jams or the Windows print queue messes up during the printing process (rare, but it can happen), you could lose the changes you made to the spreadsheet before you printed it.

Before you print, consider looking at the **Page Style** dialog box by selecting **Format**, **Page** and then clicking the **Sheet** tab. From the **Sheet** page, you can specify whether you want to print using any of the following options:

- **Top to bottom, then right**—Prints the sheet down one column at a time.

- **Left to right, then down**—Prints the sheet across one row at a time.

- **Spreadsheet elements**—Requests the printing of any or all of the following: column and row headers, the sheet's grid, notes, graphics, charts, formulas (instead of their results), and zero values (instead of blanks).

- **Scaling**—Use this option to reduce the size of the printout to fit on one page (if the sheet is small enough) and to specify exactly how many pages you want Calc to attempt to print the sheet to. The scaling options often enable you to squeeze a sheet that's larger than a single page onto one printed page.

TIP

If your sheet produces errors, you might want to print it with the formulas showing so you can more easily locate the problem in the sheet.

TIP

If you have a fax modem, you can select your fax from the **Name** list to send your document to a fax recipient.

① Request a Page Preview

Select the **Page Preview** option from the **File** menu. Calc shows you the current sheet. If you want to print a different sheet, you need to click that sheet name before selecting **File**, **Page Preview**. It's easy to forget that a spreadsheet can have multiple sheets. When one does, you'll preview (and print) each sheet individually.

② Review a Sample of the Printed Document

Look over the preview of the sheet to see if it appears to be properly formatted. Click the **Zoom In** or **Zoom Out** button to increase or decrease the preview.

③ Close the Preview

Once you've previewed what your sheet will look like printed, click the **Close Preview** button. If you need to make further edits to your sheet, do so now.

④ Prepare to Print

Once you're satisfied that the sheet is ready to print, select the **Print** option from the **File** menu. The **Print** dialog box appears.

⑤ Select a Printer

Select the printer you want to print to using the **Name** drop-down list.

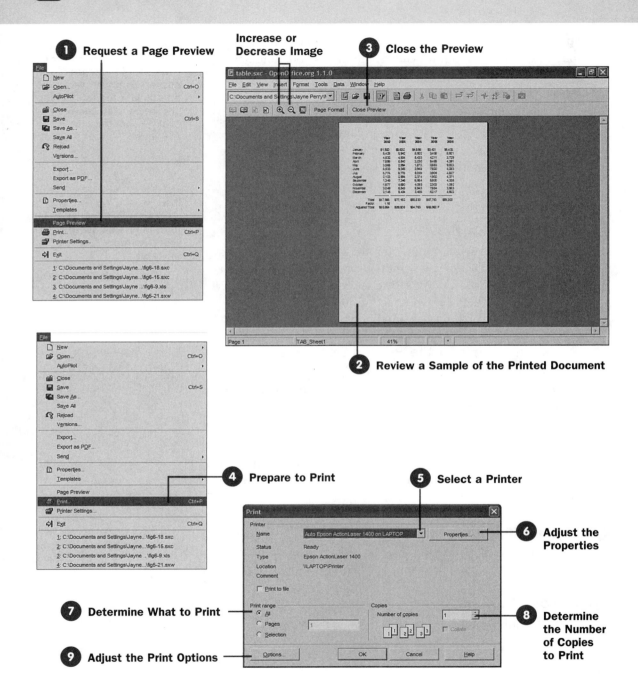

1 Request a Page Preview

Increase or Decrease Image

3 Close the Preview

2 Review a Sample of the Printed Document

4 Prepare to Print

5 Select a Printer

6 Adjust the Properties

7 Determine What to Print

8 Determine the Number of Copies to Print

9 Adjust the Print Options

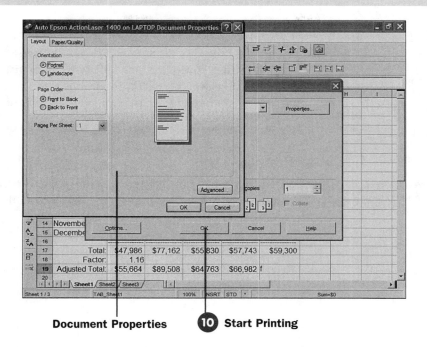

Document Properties   **10** **Start Printing**

6 Adjust the Properties

If you want to adjust any printer settings, click the **Properties** button. The dialog box that appears when you click **Properties** varies from printer to printer. Close the printer's **Properties** dialog box once you've made any needed changes.

7 Determine What to Print

Click to select either **All** or **Pages** to designate that you want to print the entire sheet or only a portion of it. If you clicked **Pages**, type the page number or a range of page numbers (such as **2-5** or **1-10, 15-25**) that you want to print.

8 Determine the Number of Copies to Print

Click the arrow button next to the **Number of Copies** option to determine how many copies you want to print.

⑨ Adjust the Print Options

Click the **Options** button to display the **Printer Options** dialog box. From the **Printer Options** dialog box, you can adjust several print settings, such as whether you want graphics, tables, and drawings printed or omitted from the printed sheet.

Click the **OK** button to close the **Printer Options** dialog box.

⑩ Start Printing

Once you've determined how many pages and copies to print, click the **OK** button to print your sheet and close the **Print** dialog box.

7

Working with Calc Data

IN THIS CHAPTER:

This chapter teaches you how to manage and organize your Calc spreadsheets to make them really work for you. You'll be surprised how Calc follows and updates formulas as you modify worksheet data. If you really want to master Calc, you must understand how to set up and work with cell ranges. Therefore, this chapter's material will greatly enhance your Calc expertise. You will learn to use range names and references to produce more powerful Calc formulas and functions.

In addition to learning about Calc's range features, you'll also see how Calc's built-in *functions* save you many steps when you need to perform calculations. By using functions, you'll leverage the use of common calculations such as averages and advanced calculations such as trigonometric calculations.

47 Find and Replace Data

Before You Begin

✔ **40** Open an Existing Spreadsheet

✔ **42** About Moving Around Calc

See Also

➜ **52** Enter Calc Functions

You'll find yourself working with small, single worksheets quite a bit in Calc because each sheet usually represents one aspect of a financial analysis, such as weekly sales figures for a division. Nevertheless, you'll also work with large spreadsheets quite often too. Many times, a company needs to consolidate numbers from several different regions, companies, or departments into a single spreadsheet. Therefore, you'll combine numerous smaller sheets into a spreadsheet and consolidate them, report totals from them, and analyze them against one another.

Whether you have one large sheet or multiple smaller ones, being able to locate numbers and text easily is important. Calc provides powerful find and replace tools you can use to locate and change the data you want.

1 Find Data

Select the **Find & Replace** option from the **Edit** menu to display the **Find & Replace** dialog box. You can also click the **Find** button on the **Main** toolbar or press **Ctrl+F** to display the **Find & Replace** dialog box.

2 Enter Search Data

Type the data you want to find in the **Search for** text box.

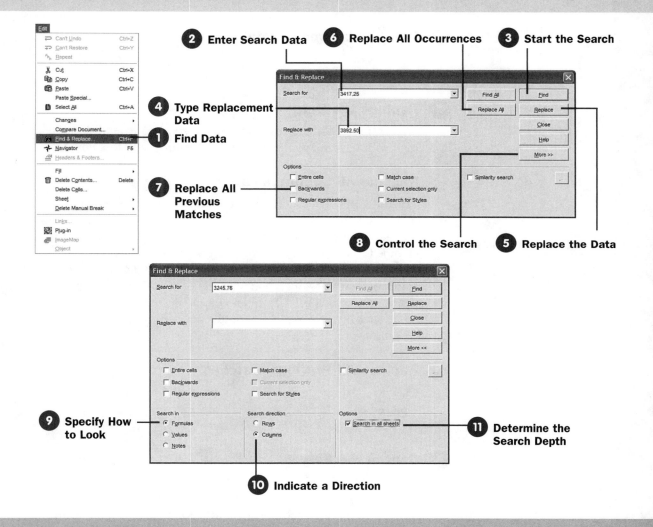

Enter Search Data ②

Replace All Occurrences ⑥

Start the Search ③

④ **Type Replacement Data**

① **Find Data**

⑦ **Replace All Previous Matches**

⑧ **Control the Search**

⑤ **Replace the Data**

⑨ **Specify How to Look**

⑪ **Determine the Search Depth**

⑩ **Indicate a Direction**

③ **Start the Search**

Click the **Find** button. Calc searches from the current cell cursor's position in the sheet to the end of the sheet. If Calc finds the data anywhere within a cell, Calc highlights that cell. (If you click the **Find All** button instead of **Find**, Calc will highlight every cell that contains the matched data.)

TIP

If you've searched for the same data before, you can click the down arrow to open the **Search for** drop-down list box and select the data to search for it once again.

4 Type Replacement Data

If you want Calc to replace found data with new data, type the new data into the **Replace with** text box.

5 Replace the Data

Click **Replace**. If the **Search for** data is found, Calc replaces that data with the data you entered in the **Replace with** text box.

6 Replace All Occurrences

Instead of **Replace** (or after you perform one or more replacements), if you click the **Replace All** button, Calc replaces all the matches with your replacement data throughout the sheet. Such a change is more global and possibly riskier because you may replace data you didn't really want replaced. By clicking **Find** before each replace operation, you can be sure that the proper data in the correct cell is being replaced, but such a single-occurrence find and replacement takes a lot of time in a long spreadsheet.

7 Replace All Previous Matches

Click to select the **Backwards** option before doing a find or replacement if you want to find or replace from the current cursor's position back to the start of the sheet.

8 Control the Search

To control the way Calc searches the current sheet, or to enable Calc to search all sheets within the current spreadsheet, click the **More** button. Calc expands the **Find & Replace** dialog box with additional options.

NOTE

Selecting **Formulas** enables Calc to locate your search term in either formulas or results. Selecting **Values** only returns a match if your search term is found in an actual number or text and not if it's the result of a formula.

9 Specify How to Look

Perhaps you only want Calc to search formulas for calculated results that match your search term. If so, click to select **Formulas** in the **Search in** section. If you want Calc to search only in values and text you've typed, but not formulas, click to select **Values**. (The **Notes** option is available if you want to search for text inside notes you've attached to cells within the sheet.)

⑩ Indicate a Direction

Although Calc normally searches from left to right and from the top row down, you can specify that Calc search completely down the first column of data before searching the second column, moving from column to column only after searching down the entire previous column. Click to select the **Columns** option if you want to search down entire columns before moving to the next one.

⑪ Determine the Search Depth

If you want Calc to search throughout all sheets inside the current spreadsheet, click to select the **Search in all sheets** option. Unless you check this option, Calc only searches the currently active and displayed sheet within the current spreadsheet.

When you finish finding and replacing all the data for this search session, click the **Find & Replace** dialog box's **Close** button to close the dialog box and return to the sheet's work area.

48 About Calc Ranges

A selected group of cells comprises a *range*. A range is always rectangular, and it might be a single cell, a row, a column, or several adjacent rows and columns. The cells within a range are always contiguous, but you can select multiple ranges at the same time. You can perform various operations on ranges, such as moving and copying. If, for example, you want to format a row of totals in some way, you first select the range that includes the totals and then apply the format to that range.

The next figure shows three selected ranges on a sheet. You can describe a range by the cell reference of the upper-left cell of the range (the *anchor point*) and the cell reference of the lower-right cell of the range. As you can see from the figure, multiple-celled ranges are designated by listing the anchor point, followed by a colon (:), followed by the range's lower-right cell reference. Therefore, the range that begins at C8 and ends at E12 has the range of C8:E12. To select more than one range, in case you want to apply formatting or calculations to different areas of your worksheet at once, hold **Ctrl** while selecting the ranges.

Before You Begin

✔ **44** Copy and Move Formulas

See Also

→ **49** Create a Range

🔍 KEY TERM

Range—One or more cells, selected adjacent to each other in a rectangular manner, that you can name and treat as a single entity or group of cells in formulas.

Range A6:A17

Range C8:E12

Range G6:G17

A sheet can have multiple ranges selected at one time.

Ⓚ**EY TERM**

Anchor point—One corner of a range of cells; typically, the upper-left cell in a range is considered the anchor point, although any of the four corner cells can be considered an anchor point also.

Keep in mind that a single cell, if selected, can be considered a range. So, D5:D5 is a range composed solely of the cell D5. In this case, the anchor point is the entire range, which is only one cell.

The true power of Calc shows when you use ranges of cells, as opposed to specifying every individual cell, in formulas. (**49** **Create a Range** explains how to name ranges.) Instead of referring to the range F2:G14, you can name that range MonthlySales and then refer to MonthlySales in your formulas by name.

All the following are valid formulas. Cell references or range names appear throughout the formulas:

```
=(SalesTotals)/NumOfSales
=C4 * 2 - (Rate * .08)
=7 + LE51 - (Gross - Net)
```

When you enter formulas that contain range references, you can either type the full reference or point to the cell reference. If you want to include a complete named range in a formula (formulas can work on complete ranges), select the entire range, and Calc inserts the range name in your formula. Often, finding and pointing to a value is easier than locating the reference and entering it exactly.

If, for example, you are entering a formula, when you get to the place in the formula that requires a cell reference, don't type the cell reference (such as G23); instead, point to and click on the cell you want to use in the formula, and Calc adds that cell reference to your formula. If you enter a formula such as =7 +, instead of typing a cell reference of LE51, you can point to that cell and press **Enter** to end the formula or type another operator to continue the formula. Immediately after typing the cell reference for you, Calc returns your cell pointer to the formula (or to the Formula bar if you are entering the formula there) so that you can complete the formula.

After you assign a name to a range, you don't have to remember that range's address, such as R31, when you use it in formulas. Suppose that you are creating a large worksheet that spans many screens. If you assign names to cells when you create them—especially to cells that you know you will refer to later during the worksheet's development— entering formulas that use those names is easier. Instead of locating a cell to find its address, you need only to type its name when entering a formula that uses that cell.

TIP

Range names are absolute. If a formula in one cell refers to a range named Commission, Calc considers the reference to be absolute (see **44** Copy and Move Formulas). Also, you don't use the dollar sign as you would when making cell addresses absolute (such as B10).

49 Create a Range

To name a range, you only need to select a range and assign a name to it. Calc supports the naming, renaming, and deleting of range names. Once you've named a range of cells, you no longer have to refer to that group of cells by their cell addresses.

Calc keeps track of your ranges and changes them as needed. If you insert a cell in the middle of a range, or even entire rows and columns somewhere inside a range, Calc reassigns the range name to the new cell range. This holds true if you delete cells from a range as well. (If you delete only cell contents, the range is unaffected.)

1 Select a Range

Click the anchor cell in a range you want to define. While holding down your mouse button, drag your mouse to the last cell in the range. Calc highlights the cells within the range as you drag the mouse.

Before You Begin

✔ **48** About Calc Ranges

See Also

→ **50** Fill Cells with Data

TIP

Give your ranges meaning-ful names. The name Payroll05 is obviously a better name than XYZ for payroll data in the year 2005. The better you name ranges, the fewer errors you'll type in your sheets because you'll more accu-rately refer to cells.

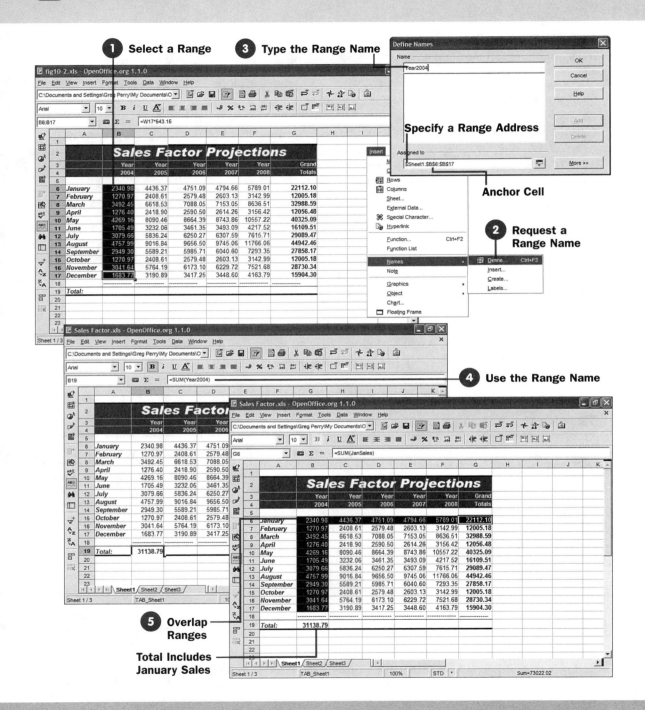

1 Select a Range

3 Type the Range Name

Specify a Range Address

Anchor Cell

2 Request a Range Name

4 Use the Range Name

5 Overlap Ranges

Total Includes January Sales

② Request a Range Name

Select **Insert**, **Names**, **Define** from the menu. (You can also press the shortcut **Ctrl+F3**.) The **Define Names** dialog box appears. This is where you name ranges and manage them.

③ Type the Range Name

Type a name for your selected range in the **Name** text box. Click **Add** to add the name to your sheet. A spreadsheet can contain as many names as you need. Click **OK** to close the **Define Names** dialog box. You can now use your range name in formulas.

④ Use the Range Name

Where you would otherwise use the cell addresses, such as in a Sum() function, use the range name instead. The Formula bar always displays the range name inside formulas.

⑤ Overlap Ranges

Two or more cells can appear in different ranges. Depending on the kind of sheet you're creating, overlapping range names can be common. Multiple rows might comprise one range, whereas columns within some of those rows might define a different range. You can name any range you wish, regardless of whether part or all of that range appears in other range names.

Name as many ranges as you can because the more range names you create, the less error-prone your sheets will be. By referring to ranges by name, you are less likely to make a mistake than if you reference the cells within that range by their addresses.

TIP

51 About Calc Functions explains how to use functions such as the Sum() function.

---

50 Fill Cells with Data

Calc often predicts what data you want to enter into a sheet. By spotting trends in your data, Calc uses educated guesses to fill in cell data for you. Calc uses data *fills* to copy and extend data from one cell to several additional cells.

Before You Begin

✔ **39** Create a New Spreadsheet

✔ **45** Edit Cell Data

See Also

→ **52** Enter Calc Functions

---

1 Type the Initial Label   Fill Handle

2 Drag to Other Cells

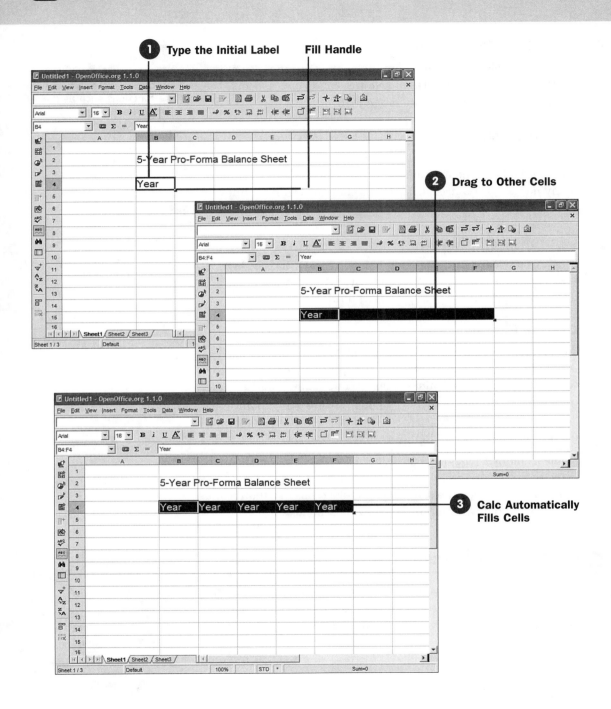

3 Calc Automatically Fills Cells

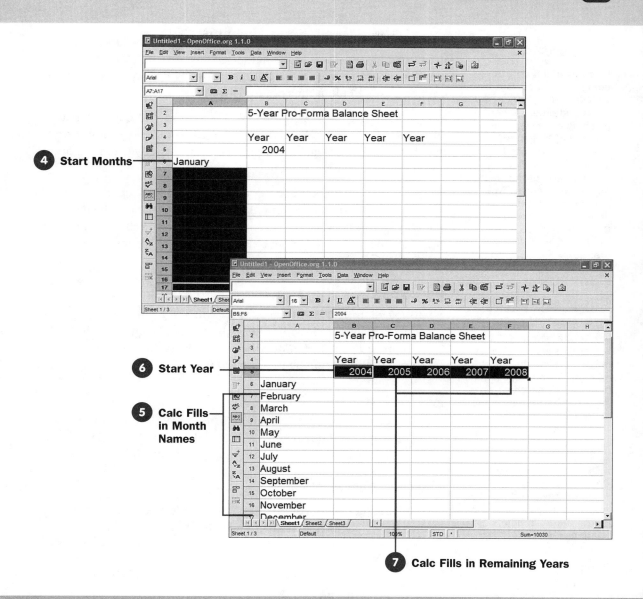

4 Start Months

6 Start Year

5 Calc Fills in Month Names

7 Calc Fills in Remaining Years

One of the most common data fills you perform is to use Calc's capability to copy one cell's data to several other cells. You might want to create a pro forma balance sheet for the previous five-year period, for example. You can insert a two-line label across the top of each year's

KEY TERM

Fills—The automatic placement of values in sheet cells based on a pattern in other cells.

data. The first line would contain five occurrences of the label **Year**, and the second line would hold the numbers **2004** through **2008**. After entering all the data in year 2004's column, you only need to select that column and drag to fill in the remaining columns.

Even if the only fill Calc performed was this copying of data across rows and columns, the data fill would still be beneficial. Calc goes an extra step, however: It performs smart fills, too. Calc actually examines and completes data you have entered.

Using Calc's fill capability to enter the years 2004 through 2008 across the top of the sheet requires only that you type **2004** under the first Year title and type **2005** under the second title. Select both cells and then drag the fill handle right three more cells. When you release the mouse button, Calc fills in the remaining years.

① Type the Initial Label

Type your first label, such as **Year**. This will be the value you will fill succeeding cells with. Although you could copy the value to the Clipboard with **Ctrl+C** and then paste the value to other cells with **Ctrl+V**, the fill handle is quicker to use.

② Drag to Other Cells

Click and drag the cell's fill handle to the rest of the cells in which you want the label to appear. As you drag the fill handle to the right, Calc highlights each cell that will receive the filled data.

③ Calc Automatically Fills Cells

When you release your mouse button, Calc fills the remaining cells in the range with your label. Calc fills with numeric data, too, not just text inside cells. When you drag *integers*, Calc extends the range by increasing the integer by one.

④ Start Months

To see Calc's smarter fill capability, you can type a month name and drag that month's fill handle across or down the sheet to fill in the rest of the months.

⑤ Calc Fills in Month Names

When you release your mouse, Calc fills in the remaining month names for you.

⑥ Start Year

Type the initial year. Any single number, such as a year or any other number that does not have a decimal point, whose fill handle you drag will increment by one in each cell you drag the fill handle to.

⑦ Calc Fills in Remaining Years

When you release your mouse, Calc fills in the remaining years by incrementing the years for you throughout the range.

◢ NOTE

If you drag the fill handle fewer than **11** additional months, Calc only fills in those months. Therefore, you would drag the **January** cell's fill handle down only five more cells if you wanted to show the months January through June only.

51 About Calc Functions

Entering individual formulas can get tedious. Suppose you want to add all the values in a column of 100 cells. You would type a formula such as =F2+F3+F4+... and would likely run out of room in the cell before you complete the formula. In addition, such long formulas are likely to produce errors when you have to type so much.

Fortunately, Calc includes several built-in functions that perform many common mathematical calculations. Instead of writing a formula to sum a row or column of values, for example, you would use the Sum() function.

Function names always end with parentheses, such as Average(). A function accepts zero or more *arguments*. A function might use zero, one, or more arguments, depending on how much information the function needs to do its job. When using multiple arguments in a function, separate the arguments with semicolons. If a function contains only a single argument, do not use a semicolon inside the parentheses. Functions generally manipulate data (numbers or text), and the arguments inside the parentheses supply the data to the functions. The Average() function, for example, computes an average of whatever list of values you pass in the argument. Therefore, all the following compute an average from the argument list:

Before You Begin

✔ **43** About Calc Formulas

See Also

➜ **52** Enter Calc Functions

◢ KEY TERM

Arguments—Values appearing inside a function's parentheses that the function uses in some way to produce its result.

TIP

When you begin to enter a formula, ToolTips pop up after you start to type the formula's name to help guide you through the formula's required contents. When you type =A into a cell, a ToolTip pops up that reads =AVERAGE. You can take advantage of Calc's AutoComplete feature by pressing **Enter** when you see the ToolTip if that's the function you're entering and not another, such as =**Abs()**.

TIP

When you insert rows within the Sum() range, Calc updates the range inside the Sum() function to include the new values.

```
=Average(18; 65; 299; $R$5; 10; -2; 102)
=Average(SalesTotals)
=Average(D4:D14)
```

When you type a function name, whether you type it in uppercase or lowercase letters, Calc converts the name in your formula to all uppercase letters.

As with some functions, Average() accepts as many arguments as needed to do its job. The first Average() function computes the average of seven values, one of which is an absolute cell reference. The second Average() function computes the average of a range named SalesTotals. No matter how many cells comprise the range SalesTotals, Average() computes and displays the average. The final Average() function shows the average of the values in the range D4 through D14 (a columnar list).

Functions improve your accuracy. If you want to average three cell values, for example, you might type something such as this:

```
=C2 + C4 + C6 / 3
```

However, this formula does not compute an average! Remember that the operator hierarchy forces the division calculation first. If you use the Average() function, as shown next, you don't have to worry as much about the calculation's hierarchy:

```
=Average(C2; C4; C6)
```

The Sum() function is perhaps the most common function because you so often total columns and rows. Instead of adding each cell individually, you could more easily enter the following function:

```
=Sum(F2:F101)
```

You can use functions inside other formulas. The following formula might be included in a cell that works on sales totals:

```
=CostOfSales * Sum(Qtr1; Qtr2; Qtr3; Qtr4) / SalesFactor * 1.07
```

Table 7.1 describes common built-in functions for which you'll find a lot of uses as you create spreadsheets. Remember to start every formula with an equal sign and to add your arguments to the parentheses, and you are set.

TABLE 7.1 Common Calc Functions

Function Name	Description
Abs()	Computes the absolute value of its cell argument. (Good for distance- and age-difference calculations.)
Average()	Computes the average of its arguments.
Count()	Returns the number of numerical arguments in the argument list. (Useful if you use a range name for the argument list.)
Max()	Returns the highest (maximum) value in the argument list. (Useful if you use a range name for the argument list and you need to pick out the highest value.)
Min()	Returns the lowest (minimum) value in the argument list. (Useful if you use a range name for the argument list and you need to pick out the lowest value.)
Pi()	Computes the value of mathematical pi (requires no arguments) for use in math calculations.
Product()	Computes the product (multiplicative result) of the argument range.
Roman()	Converts its cell value to a roman numeral.
Sqrt()	Computes the square root of the cell argument.
Stdev()	Computes the argument list's standard deviation.
Sum()	Computes the sum of its arguments.
Today()	Returns today's date (requires no arguments).
Var()	Computes a list's sample variance.

 NOTE

Calc supports many functions, including complex mathematical, date, time, financial, and engineering functions. Select **Help** to get more details on all the functions you can use.

52 Enter Calc Functions

Computing totals is so common, Calc makes the Sum() function even easier to use by placing the **Sum** button on the **Function** toolbar. Just click a blank cell below or to the right of a range of values, click **Sum**, and Calc computes the sum and writes the proper Sum() function for you.

You'll have to type the remaining functions yourself when you want to use them, but doing so is far from a chore. **About Calc Functions** lists some of the most common functions you'll use. For the rest, use Calc's **Help** feature to find the function you want to use and then type that function and its arguments to get the result you want.

Before You Begin

✔ **51** About Calc Functions

See Also

→ **53** Use the Function AutoPilot

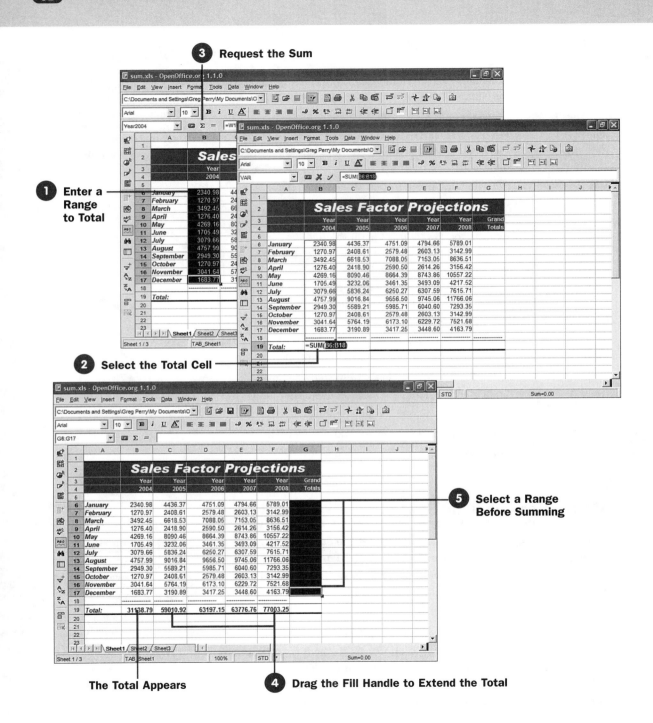

3 Request the Sum

1 Enter a Range to Total

2 Select the Total Cell

5 Select a Range Before Summing

The Total Appears

4 Drag the Fill Handle to Extend the Total

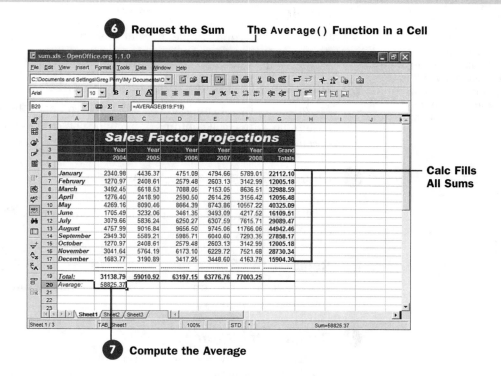

6 Request the Sum   The Average() Function in a Cell

**Calc Fills
All Sums**

7 Compute the Average

---

1 **Enter a Range to Total**

Type the range of values you want to get a total of. The range can
be a row or a column of numbers.

2 **Select the Total Cell**

Click to select the cell that you want to hold the total.

3 **Request the Sum**

Click the **Function** toolbar's **Sum** button. Calc analyzes the current
cell and guesses at the row or column that is to comprise the sum.
For example, Calc might highlight the column of cells above the
current cell and indicate its range in the Sum() function.

If the range is correct, press **Enter** to accept the sum; otherwise, type a different range inside the Sum() function's argument list and then press **Enter**. The sum then appears in the cell.

4 Drag the Fill Handle to Extend the Total

As with any other formula or cell label, you can drag the formula's fill handle, whose cell contains a function such as Sum(), to another cell to extend that formula.

5 Select a Range Before Summing

Calc doesn't make you request one sum at a time. Just select all the cells at the end of a set of rows or columns before clicking **Sum**.

6 Request the Sum

When you click the **Sum** button, Calc automatically sums the entire column or row you selected.

7 Compute the Average

Although other functions aren't represented on the **Function** toolbar, you can easily type functions that you need. To get a yearly sales average, for example, you can type =Average(B19:F19) in cell B20 to learn your average projected sales over the next 5 years.

53 Use the Function AutoPilot

Before You Begin

✔ 51 About Calc Functions

✔ 52 Enter Calc Functions

See Also

➡ 55 Work with Dates and Times

Some functions require more arguments than a simple cell or range. Calc contains many financial functions, for example, that compute loan values and investment rates of return. If you want to use one of the more advanced functions, or if you're unsure exactly which arguments are required for a function you're about to use, be sure to take advantage of Calc's **Functions** AutoPilot.

With AutoPilot, you can

- Select from a list of functions organized by category

- Build your functions one argument at a time

3 Select a Function to Build

1 Request the Functions AutoPilot

2 Select a Category

Result Builds Here

Scroll to Additional Arguments

5 Search for a Function

Hide AutoPilot   **Create a Floating Toolbar**

4 Request the Function List

6 Follow the Function Pattern

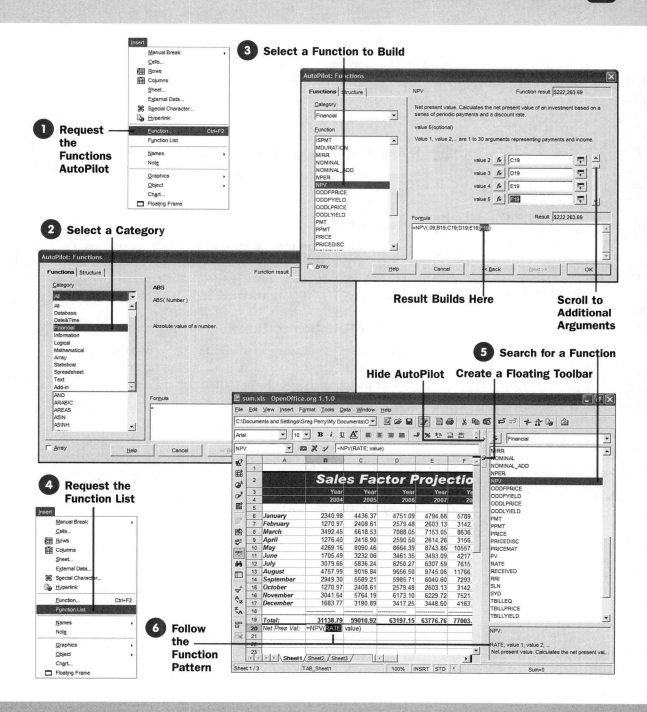

TIP

In the **Functions** AutoPilot, you can type either specific values, cell addresses, or ranges (by name or by their address), or you can click to select cells from the current sheet. Click to scroll the scrollbar if more arguments are needed than will show on the current **Functions** AutoPilot dialog box.

TIP

You can hide the Function List at any time by clicking its **Hide** button. Also, you can turn the **Function List** pane into a floating toolbar that you can move to any location on your screen by clicking the **Floating** button.

From the **AutoPilot** dialog box, you don't need to memorize long function argument list requirements. The AutoPilot works like a wizard, helping you create your functions.

If you need only a reminder of what a function is named or what it's for, just request the *Function List*.

❶ Request the Functions AutoPilot

When ready for the **Functions** AutoPilot, select **Insert**, **Function** from the menu.

❷ Select a Category

Select the category from which you wish to write a function. For example, if you are wanting to compute the net present value of a series of cash flows, you would first select the **Financial** category and scroll down until you reach the **NPV** function entry.

❸ Select a Function to Build

When you see the function you wish to use in the **Functions** list, double-click to select that function name. Calc displays a list of fields to match every argument that function needs.

For example, if you selected the **NPV** function, Calc would display the fields that match the NPV( ) argument list: rate of return, and one or more values representing the cash flow. As you add arguments, Calc displays the current result in the **Functions** AutoPilot dialog box's **Result** area. Click **OK** when you finish the function.

❹ Request the Function List

If you don't need the **Function** AutoPilot's help, select **Insert**, **Function List** from the menu to display the **Function List** pane at the right of your screen.

❺ Search for a Function

Open the function category list to select the function category you want to choose from. Scroll the list of functions in that category to find the one you want to use.

6 Follow the Function Pattern

Select the function that you want to use in your sheet. The function's argument list pattern appears at the bottom of the **Function List**. If you double-click the function in the **Function List**, Calc inserts the function's format in your cell and highlights each argument (such as RATE) while you fill in each argument with a value, cell, or range.

After entering the arguments, press **Enter**. Calc then completes the function and displays the results.

54 Reference Data Outside This Sheet

If all your data resided in the current sheet, referencing other cells would be simple. You'd only need to know the other cell's address, such as D4. What if the cell is in another sheet inside the current spreadsheet? If Sheet1 needs to reference cell G6 in a sheet named Sheet3, you cannot use the simple G6 reference.

Perhaps the data you need isn't even in another sheet but resides across your network somewhere. Or, perhaps, the data resides across the world, accessible from the Internet. That's no problem for Calc. You can insert network addresses and Web address links anywhere in a spreadsheet to display data from that location.

1 Prepare for Entries

Set up your sheet so it's ready for entries from other sheets and even from other locations. Of course, you can always add the labels after you reference data from other locations too.

2 Enter a Sheet Reference

To reference a cell from another sheet, preface your cell address with the sheet's name followed by a period, followed by that sheet's cell you want to reference. For example, to display in the current sheet the value from cell G19 of a sheet named Division2, you'd type the following value in the current sheet's cell:

```
=Division2.G19
```

Before You Begin

✔ **41** Enter Simple Data into a Spreadsheet

✔ **45** Edit Cell Data

See Also

→ **63** Conditionally Format Data

💡 TIP

If you use a spreadsheet with multiple names, consider renaming the default sheet names of Sheet1, Sheet2, and Sheet3 to names that are more meaningful, such as Division1Sales, Division2Sales, and Division3Sales. Right-click the sheet name's tab and select **Rename** to rename, insert, or delete any sheet.

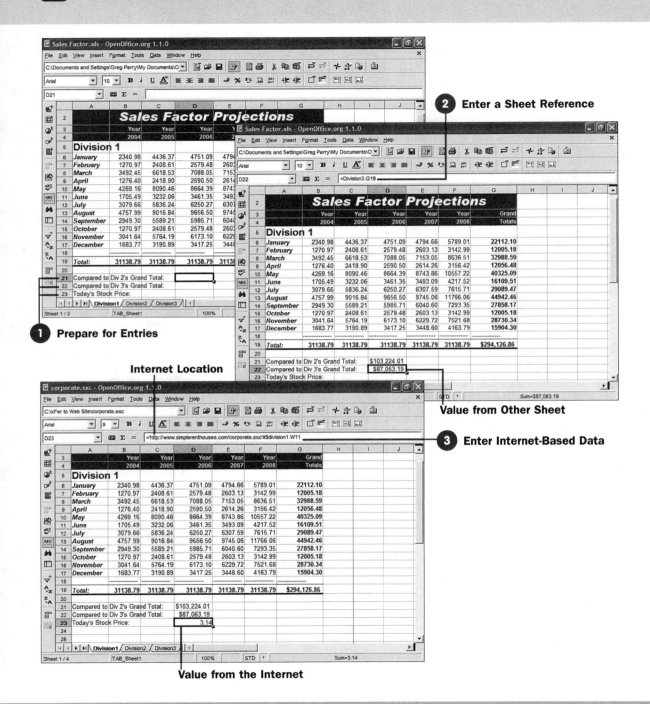

② Enter a Sheet Reference

① Prepare for Entries

Internet Location

Value from Other Sheet

③ Enter Internet-Based Data

Value from the Internet

Calc locates the value in cell G19 of the sheet named Division2 and places it in the current cell.

3 Enter Internet-Based Data

If you want to reference a value from a spreadsheet stored on the Internet, feel free to do so. Obviously, an always-on Internet connection is best for such a reference. Otherwise, Calc will dial your modem connection to get the value every time you recalculate the spreadsheet.

Use the following pattern:

```
='http://www.YourDomain.com/Spreadsheet.sxc'#Sheet1.Cell
```

That's quite a mouthful! Here is one such example:

```
='http://www.simplerenthouses.com/
➥corporate.sxc'#Division1.W11
```

To read such a long reference, it helps to begin at the right. This references cell W11 in the sheet named Division1 in a spreadsheet named Corporate.sxc on a Web site named www.SimpleRentHouses.com; keep in mind that you must enclose the Web page reference inside single quote marks.

TIP

You aren't limited to displaying values from other sheets. You may also want to use those values in calculations and functions. For example, the following duration function uses arguments from three other sheets:

```
=Duration(Region1.G45,
Accounting.PValue,
Finance.FutValue*.9)
```

Two of the values are range names given to individual cells: PValue and FutValue.

NOTE

Calc adds a dollar sign ($) to your external sheet name to keep it an absolute reference. Also, Calc will rename your Web page reference to all lowercase letters if you type any in uppercase.

---

55 Work with Dates and Times

Calc supports almost every national and international date and time format. Calc converts date and time values that you type to a special internal number that represents the number of days since midnight January 1, 1900. Although this strange internal date representation of days since 1-1-1900 might not make sense at first, you'll use these values to compute time between two or more dates. You can easily determine how many days an account is past due, for example, by subtracting the current date from the cell in the worksheet that contains the due date.

Before You Begin

✔ **41** Enter Simple Data into a Spreadsheet

✔ **52** Enter Calc Functions

See Also

→ **59** Format Cells

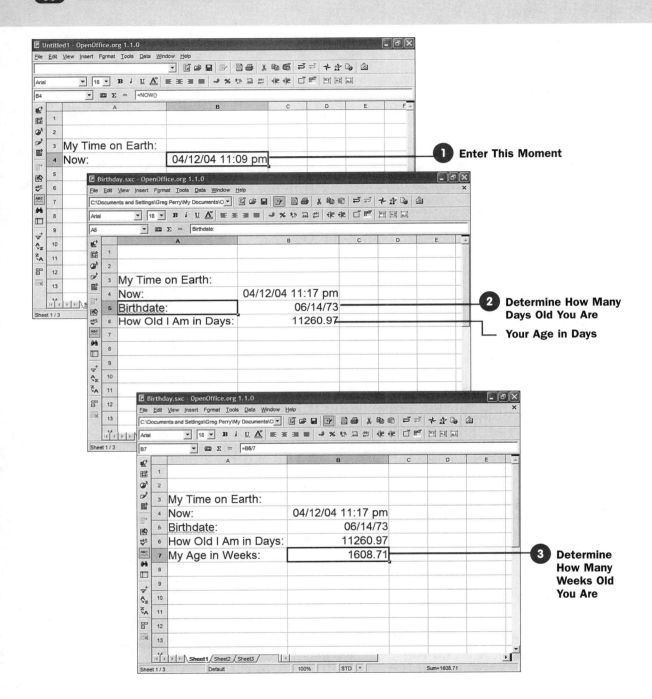

1 Enter This Moment

2 Determine How Many Days Old You Are

Your Age in Days

3 Determine How Many Weeks Old You Are

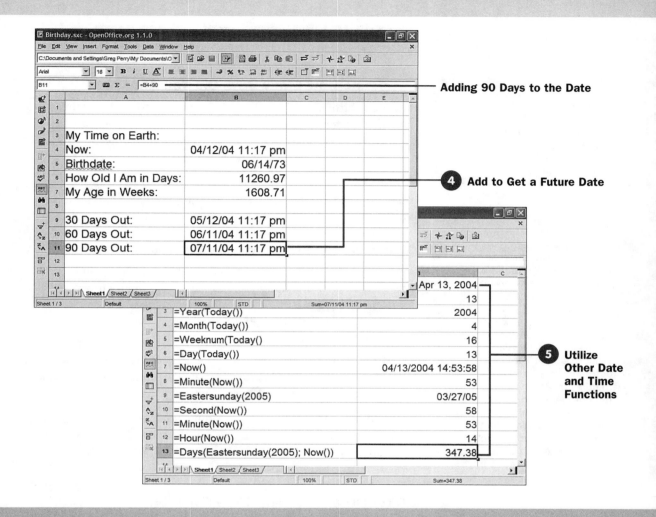

Adding 90 Days to the Date

4 Add to Get a Future Date

5 Utilize Other Date and Time Functions

If you enter a date in a longer format, such as July 4, 1776, Calc usually converts the date to another format (such as 7/4/76 18:15). You can enter a date, a time value, or both. You can format the date and time values you enter (see **59** Format Cells) to take on any format you wish.

 TIP

The date and time functions are useful for calculating durations for past due and other calculations related to date and time values.

1 **Enter This Moment**

Type =Now() in a cell. When you press **Enter**, Calc converts the function to the computer's currently set date and time. You can use

TIP

Remember that Now() and the other date functions operate as number of days since January 1, 1900. Therefore, when you add or subtract dates, with or without using Calc's date functions, the result is always a number of days.

NOTE

Generally, you'll use date formats to hide the time when you work with date arithmetic. When working with time values, a day has 24 hours in it, so you'll need to multiply by 24 to obtain the number of hours represented by the value. When you subtract two date and time values, if you multiply by 24 you'll get the number of hours represented. For example, if you subtract a cell containing your birth date from a cell containing today's date, then multiply the result by 24, you'll learn how old you are in hours.

this to calculate values based on this moment, such as the number of days old you are.

② Determine How Many Days Old You Are

Enter your birth date. Type the date in any format. Although you can format the date using the **Format** menu, don't worry about the format now; concentrate on what occurs when you use date arithmetic.

Subtract your birth date from the current date to determine how many days old you are. Digits to the right of the decimal indicate partial days since midnight of your birth date.

③ Determine How Many Weeks Old You Are

Because the dates work in days, you can divide your age in days by seven to determine approximately how old you are in weeks.

④ Add to Get a Future Date

What will be the date one month from today? Sure, it's simple to look at a calendar, but when you write general-purpose spreadsheets, you've got to be able to apply such formulas to dates to age accounts receivables and other calculations.

By adding **30**, **60**, and **90** to today's date, you can display the date when future payments will come due. Calc understands how many days different months have in them, so adding **60** to April 12th properly returns June 11th and not June 12th.

⑤ Utilize Other Date and Time Functions

Several date and time functions are available to make working with dates and times simpler. Today() returns the date only (without the time, unlike Now()). Day() returns today's day of the month of whatever date you use as its argument. Weeknum() returns the week number (within the year, from 1 to 52) of the date inside its argument list. Weeknum() requires two arguments: a date and either 1 or 2 to indicate that the start of the week is Sunday or Monday, respectively. Month() returns the month number of its date argument. Year() returns the year of the date given as its argument. You'll use these functions to pick off what you want to work with in another formula or label: either the day, month, or year by itself instead of working with the complete date.

Eastersunday() returns the date of Easter given the year of its argument. You can add to or subtract from Eastersunday() to get the days around the holiday, such as Good Friday, which displays for any year with the following calculation:

=Eastersunday(yearCell) - 2.

Second() returns the second number of its time argument. Minute() returns the minute number of its time argument, and Hour() returns the hour number of its time argument.

Days() requires two date arguments and returns the number of days (and partial days) between two dates. Therefore, to determine the number of days between today and Easter, you could enter the following:

=Days(Eastersunday(Year(Today())+1); Now())

Although at first glance this appears convoluted, it's a simple set of arguments.

TIP

You can enter a time value, a date value, or both. If you don't enter a date with a time value, Calc displays only the time in the cell.

56 About Names as Addresses

The makers of OpenOffice.org designed Calc to be watching over your shoulder, ready to help you when possible. One way that Calc does this is to look at the labels you place in your spreadsheets and use them as range names when appropriate.

Consider the sheet in the following figure. The totals do not align well with any specific row or column. In other words, cell B4 is going to hold the total of the four Miami estimates, not G7, where the total could easily be placed by selecting G7 and clicking the **Sum** button. To compute the total projections of Miami, for example, requires more than clicking the **Sum** button, because the total entry for Miami does not fall right below the column of Miami-related data. As you see in **52** **Enter Calc Functions**, the **Sum** button is useful when you are totaling a column or a row and the total is to appear directly at the end of that column or row.

Of course, you could type the Sum() function in the appropriate cells of column B, but doing so (especially if the table were much larger) is time-consuming and error-prone. To total the Miami sales projections, for example, you would enter this into cell B4:

=Sum(H4; H10)

Before You Begin

✔ **48** About Calc Ranges
✔ **49** Create a Range

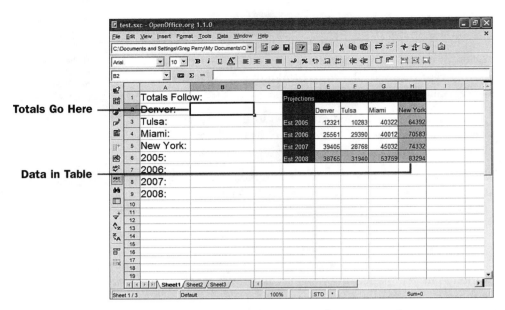

Totals Go Here ———

Data in Table ———

Totals do not always fall at the end of a row or column.

TIP

You rarely can name too many ranges. If you create a spreadsheet that you plan to add to quite a bit, create range names as you go so that subsequent formulas you enter will be able to rely on those names. For very small sheets, though, sometimes naming ranges is more trouble than its worth.

Likewise, you would have to enter every other range for the rest of the totals.

One improvement would be to create and name the following ranges from the sheet: Est2005, Est2006, Est2007, Est2008, Denver, Tulsa, Miami, and New York. At least entering the Sum() functions would be simpler. For Miami's total, you would type =Sum(Miami) into cell B4. If you added data to the table, your range names would expand appropriately, keeping the totals accurate.

In spite of some advantages to the range names, naming six ranges for this small table is a lot of work. It's simpler and quicker—although, as just stated, more error-prone and more difficult to maintain—if you create the ranges individually for totals.

Fortunately, Calc is smart. Notice the headings over the columns of data: Denver, Tulsa, Miami, and New York. These are not range names; rather, they are just labels typed over the columns to label the data. The same is true for the rows with these labels: Est 2005, Est 2006, Est 2007, and Est 2008.

Although the column labels are not range names, you can often treat such column and row headings as though they are range names!

Therefore, you can enter the following formula into Denver's total cell B2:

`=Sum(Denver)`

Summed Values Under Label   **Label Used**

Denver's total computed correctly without range names.

Calc did *not* generate a new range named Denver. All Calc did was make an educated guess that you wanted to calculate the column under the heading Denver. Calc did not confuse the labels Denver in the table with Denver: in column A because column A's Denver: has a colon following it.

You won't want to rely on Calc's capability to calculate from labels in large and complex sheets because you'll be rearranging such sheets occasionally, and range names are better suited for sheets that you edit often. For smaller sheets, though, using the labels as column and row headings for summing and performing other routine functions makes a lot of sense.

One thing you must keep in mind when using cell labels inside functions and calculations is to enclose the labels in quote marks if they

NOTE

If you copy or move a cell that uses a heading or row name to another place in the sheet, Calc moves the cell using absolute addressing (see **44** Copy and Move Formulas).

have a blank in them. For example, the following two cell entries would produce errors in this sheet:

```
=Sum(New York)
```

```
=Sum(Est 2007)
```

To correct these entries, you must use quotes like this:

```
=Sum('New York')
```

```
=Sum('Est 2007')
```

If a label is nothing more than a number, as the year 2004 would be if used as a label in the table, you would not be able to use that label in such calculations, even if you enclosed it inside quotes.

The next figure shows the completed sheet with all the totals. As you can see, all the totals work fine, even though no range names exist.

Note Required Quotes

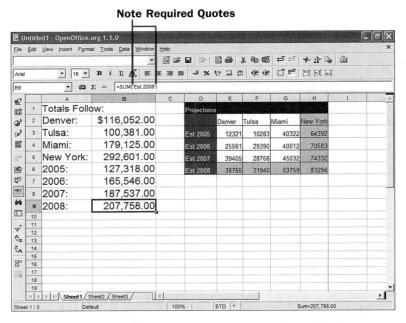

All totals entered using the table's column and row labels.

8

Formatting Spreadsheets with Calc

IN THIS CHAPTER:

KEY TERM

AutoFormat—The process that Calc uses to format spreadsheets from a collection of predetermined styles.

Calc makes it easy to make even simple spreadsheets look professional. *AutoFormat* quickly formats your sheets within the boundaries you select. If you want to format your spreadsheet by hand, the formatting commands you learn in this chapter will enable you to pinpoint important data and highlight that data. Others can then look at your spreadsheets and easily find your highlighted information.

During this chapter, you'll learn how to change the appearance of your spreadsheets so they look as good as possible. Specifically, you will learn how to select from a list of AutoFormats styles, you'll learn how to format selected cells and ranges, and you'll learn how to leverage your spreadsheet designs so you can reuse them again with little trouble.

57 Freeze Row and Column Headers

Before You Begin

✔ **41** Enter Simple Data into a Spreadsheet

See Also

→ **60** Center a Heading over Multiple Columns

Often, you'll enter lots of data into a spreadsheet—perhaps daily sales figures, for example. As you add more and more data, your sheets will grow to be quite large. Perhaps at the end of each month, quarter, or fiscal year, you close your books so that you can consolidate the data and begin anew the next time period.

Until you restart the data entry for the next time period, the data can consume many rows and columns as time goes by. Eventually your data will take more than one screen, which can lead to a problem: If you initially put labels across the top of the sheet to label the columns and put labels down the left column to label the rows of data, when you page down or move too far to the right, the column and row headings will scroll off the screen. In order to keep track of what the purpose of your sheet's values are, you can freeze the scrolling of row and column headers so that those headers remain on the screen while the rest of the data scrolls under or to the right of them.

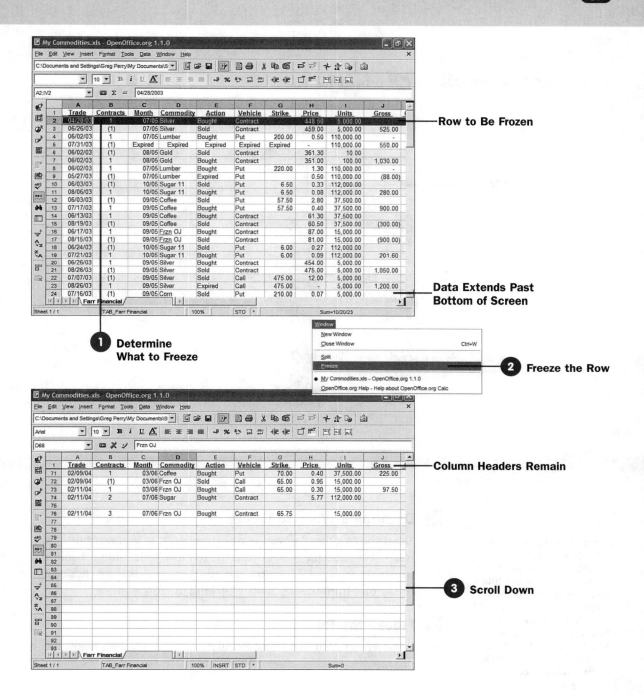

Row to Be Frozen

Data Extends Past Bottom of Screen

① **Determine What to Freeze**

② **Freeze the Row**

Column Headers Remain

③ **Scroll Down**

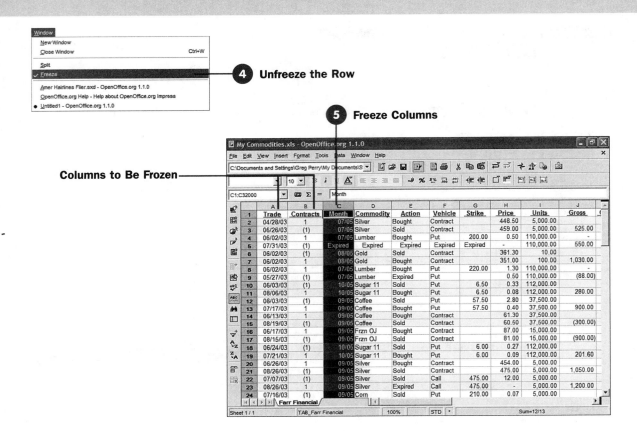

Unfreeze the Row

Freeze Columns

Columns to Be Frozen

TIP

You can freeze as many contiguous rows or columns as you need. For example, your sheet title and column headings might span three rows. All rows below those three frozen rows will scroll up and down, but the three remain in place so you'll know what the columns represent.

1 Determine What to Freeze

Select the row that *follows* the row (or rows) that you want to freeze. For example, if you want the top row with column headings to remain in place no matter how much data falls below it, select the second-from-the-top row by clicking the row number.

2 Freeze the Row

Select **Freeze** from the **Window** menu to freeze all rows below the top row.

③ Scroll Down

Scroll down the sheet. The top row remains in place while the data below scrolls upward. No matter where you are in the worksheet, you know the labels that go with the data because the headings are never scrolled off the screen.

④ Unfreeze the Row

To unfreeze rows or columns you've frozen, select **Freeze** from the **Windows** menu once again to deselect the option. You don't need to select any rows or columns first to unfreeze them.

⑤ Freeze Columns

To freeze one or more columns, click the column name of the column that falls to the right of the last column you want to freeze. When you once again select **Freeze** from the **Windows** menu, Calc will freeze the column (or columns) so when you scroll to the right, the column titles remain on your screen.

 TIPS

Calc inserts a thick line between the frozen rows (or columns) and the data so you'll know where the break occurs.

If you want to freeze both row and column headings, click to select the cell that intersects the row and column following the headings you want to freeze before selecting **Windows, Freeze.**

---

58 AutoFormat a Spreadsheet

Although you can format individual cells to make them look the way you want, many Calc users take advantage of Calc's AutoFormat feature to apply formatting to an entire spreadsheet. If you enter straight text, numbers, or formulas while building your sheets, without regard to the formatting as you go, when you finish with the data, you can apply one of several AutoFormats that Calc offers. Many times, you will have to do nothing more because AutoFormat works so well to make your spreadsheets look good.

Calc offers several AutoFormat styles from which you can choose. The AutoFormat feature analyzes your spreadsheets looking for data that is probably heading information. With only a few mouse clicks, your entire spreadsheet changes its appearance.

Before You Begin

✔ **41** Enter Simple Data into a Spreadsheet

See Also

→ **59** Format Cells

→ **61** Set Up Calc Page Formatting

 TIP

Calc also offers AutoFormat for charts so your charts can take on one of several predesigned looks (see **67** Add a Chart to a Spreadsheet).

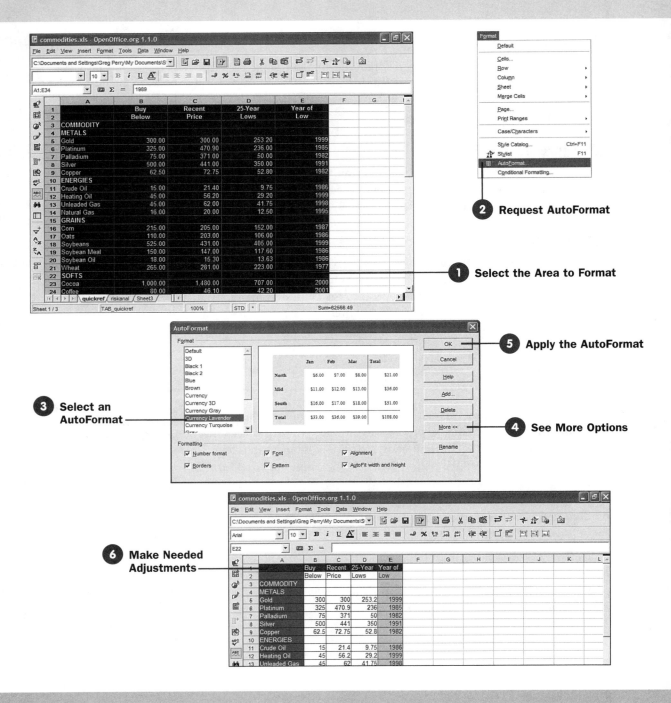

2 Request AutoFormat

1 Select the Area to Format

5 Apply the AutoFormat

3 Select an AutoFormat

4 See More Options

6 Make Needed Adjustments

1 Select the Area to Format

AutoFormat works best after you have created an entire spreadsheet to format. Create your spreadsheet, but for now don't worry about formatting it to look any certain way. Once you create your spreadsheet, select the area you want to format.

2 Request AutoFormat

Once you've selected the area you want to format, select **AutoFormat** from the **Format** menu. The **Main** toolbar also has an **AutoFormat** button that you can click to request AutoFormat.

3 Select an AutoFormat

The **AutoFormat** dialog box scrolls to show numerous formats from which you can choose. As you click each sample AutoFormat, Calc displays a preview of it to give you an idea of what your spreadsheet will look like if you were to go with that AutoFormat option.

4 See More Options

Click the **AutoFormat** dialog box's **More** button to see additional formatting options. You can limit whether AutoFormat applies a number format, font format, alignment format, borders, grid pattern, or *AutoFit* by selecting from those six options, which appear at the bottom of the **AutoFormat** dialog box.

5 Apply the AutoFormat

Click **OK** to apply the AutoFormat to your spreadsheet.

6 Make Needed Adjustments

Keep in mind that AutoFormat does a lot of formatting, and often you'll be completely satisfied with the format you choose. Other times, you'll want to make some minor adjustments. For example, if your heading takes more than one row, AutoFormat may not have realized that when formatting your sheet. Therefore, you'll have to manually apply cell formatting to that extra row (see **59** Format Cells).

NOTES

You'll often select your entire sheet, with **Ctrl+A**, to format with AutoFormat.

The **AutoFormat** dialog box's preview image does not contain a preview of your data. To really see what your spreadsheet looks like with the current AutoFormat applied, you'll have to click **OK** to see the actual results of your selected AutoFormat. You can always select another AutoFormat or click **Undo** to get rid of an AutoFormat you dislike.

KEY TERM

AutoFit—The capability of AutoFormat to keep the original widths and heights of the cells it formats.

Before You Begin

✔ **58** AutoFormat a
Spreadsheet

See Also

→ **60** Center a Heading
over Multiple
Columns

→ **61** Set Up Calc Page
Formatting

NOTE

If you increase the size of characters in a row, Calc does not increase the row's height to match the new character height. Therefore, after increasing or decreasing the font used for data or text in a row, you'll often have to adjust the height.

TIP

You can change the height or width of multiple rows and columns by selecting several rows or columns before making an adjustment.

Now you see how to pretty things up, one cell at a time, if that's what you want. Calc offers many ways to change the look of your spreadsheets, such as enabling you to do the following:

- Align data inside cells (such as left- and right-justification)

- Modify row and column heights and widths

- Change the font

- Format data values such currency, date, and time values

If you've used other OpenOffice.org programs such as Writer, you'll feel at home with many of Calc's formatting tools because the menus and options are similar to those of the other OpenOffice.org programs.

① **Drag to Adjust the Row Height and Column Width**

If you want to increase or decrease the height of a row, just drag the row divider up or down for that row. To increase or decrease any column width, click to drag a column divider left or right. You must click to drag within the column names or row numbers area to adjust the height and width; you cannot drag the sheet's grid lines themselves to make height and width adjustments.

If you shrink a column too small, Calc displays ### to let you know that there's not enough room for the data to show completely. Your data will still be stored inside the column completely, but the value cannot show until you increase the width of the column.

The **Format** menu contains **Row** and **Column** options that you can choose to specify an exact height or width of selected rows or columns. By selecting the **Optimal** option on either menu, Calc will adjust to include the tallest or the widest data value within the selected rows or columns.

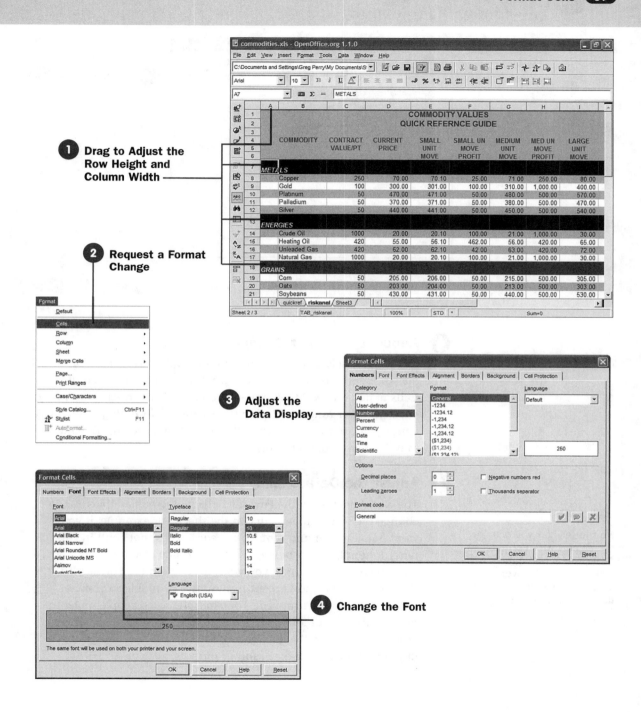

1 Drag to Adjust the Row Height and Column Width

2 Request a Format Change

3 Adjust the Data Display

4 Change the Font

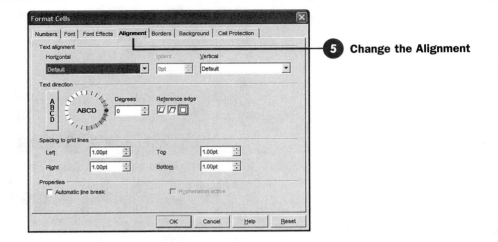

5 Change the Alignment

② Request a Format Change

To change a selected cell's font, alignment, display format, or background, select **Format**, **Cells** from the menu. The **Format Cells** dialog box will then appear. You can also right-click over any selected cell or range to display the **Format Cells** dialog box, where you can modify all the cells' formatting, such as alignment, font, background, and colors.

③ Adjust the Data Display

The **Numbers** tab on the **Format Cells** dialog box enables you to change the way data appears on the sheet. For example, if you want a dollar sign and cents to appear in cells that contain currency amounts, you would click the **Currency** category and then select the currency format you want to see from the **Format** list. Various **Number** and **Percent** formats are available so you can control how numbers appear. For example, some people prefer to display negative amounts with parentheses around them, whereas others prefer to see the minus sign. You control how your sheets display numbers with the **Number** formats.

NOTE

No matter how you change the display with **Format Cells**, the actual data inside each cell never changes—only the way the data displays changes.

If you use dates or times inside your spreadsheets, you'll almost always want to change the format of those values by using the **Date** and **Time** categories. Often, companies have standards they enforce for published reports that indicate how date and time values are to display, and you'll want to format yours accordingly. You'll also see scientific and other formats available to you for many different data displays.

The **Format Cells** dialog box shows a preview of how your selected data will look as you select from the various formatting options.

You can control the number of decimal places displayed as well as whether you want leading zeroes to appear (such as **012.31**). The **Thousands separator** option determines whether a comma (or decimal, depending on your country) separates digits to show the places of the thousands, such as **34,321,567.43**, and the **Negative numbers red** option ensures that negative values stand out when you need them to.

④ Change the Font

Click the **Font** tab to select the **Font** page in the **Format Cells** dialog box. You can choose from various fonts and typefaces (such as bold and italics), and you can specify a font size, in points, to use. See **12 Apply Character Formatting** for information on fonts, typefaces, and point sizes.

Many of these font-related options, such as bold and italics, as well as various number formats, are available from your **Object** toolbar's buttons.

⑤ Change the Alignment

Not only can you left-justify, center-justify, and right-justify data within cells from the **Alignment** page of the **Format Cells** dialog box, you can also orient text vertically or to whatever angle you prefer.

When you click the **Alignment** page's first **Text Direction** button (the button with the letters **ABCD** dropping down the screen), Calc changes all selected cells to vertical orientation.

TIP

Additional font-related options are available if you click the **Font Effects** tab. You can change the color of text and data that you display as well as control a shadow effect, which may be beneficial to make your titles stand out.

If you want to angle text, such as titles at the top of columns, select a different **Degrees** value or click the rotating text pointer to the slant you desire. When you click **OK**, Calc rotates the selected text to your chosen angle. Although you don't want to overdo this text-slanting capability of Calc's, a 45-degree angle for certain column headings really makes them stand out, as opposed to falling as they normally do horizontally across the column. All the text within the selected cells that you choose to slant prints at the angle you choose.

Although not as common in spreadsheets as they are in Writer documents, you can add special borders to certain cells from the **Borders** tab of the **Format Cells** dialog box. The **Background** tab controls the background color of selected cells, and the **Cell Protection** tab controls the protection of data to ensure that it cannot be changed (see **69** **Protect Spreadsheet Data**).

60 Center a Heading over Multiple Columns

Before You Begin

✔ **59** Format Cells

See Also

→ **61** Set Up Calc Page Formatting

 **NOTE**

The **Align Center** button does not accomplish what you want by itself when you attempt to center a title over multiple columns. The alignment (or justification) buttons only align text within single cells, not across multiple cells.

If you want to center a title over multiple columns, you might find that you have trouble adjusting the title just right. You must first type the title into the most central column over the sheet below. Even then, the title usually doesn't align properly, so you must go back and edit the column, inserting spaces, until the title is just right.

Then, you adjust the data below the title. Typically, adjusting the data below forces you to adjust the title once again. In other words, centering a title (or any column heading) over multiple columns can get tricky if you rely solely on adding spaces yourself to accomplish the centering.

1 Make Room for the Centered Title

When you create your spreadsheet, leave room atop the columns for the title. It's best to create the columns, enter some or all the data, and adjust the column widths before worrying with the title. You can also type a title atop these columns as a placeholder and then perform the actual centering once you finish the spreadsheet's columns. Many users prefer to add the title after completing the rest of the sheet, which makes a lot of sense. Often, I'll add a placeholder title first and find that I must adjust it some later once I've completed the rest of the sheet.

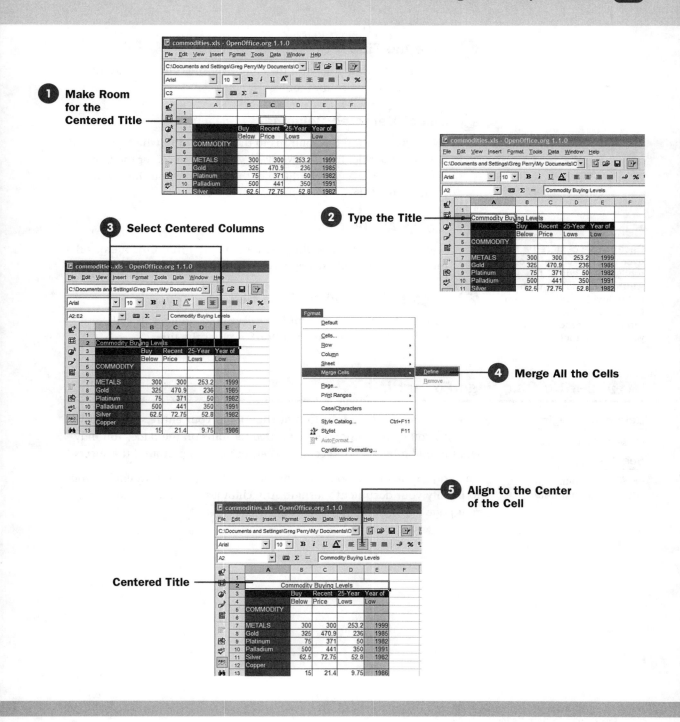

1 Make Room for the Centered Title

3 Select Centered Columns

2 Type the Title

4 Merge All the Cells

5 Align to the Center of the Cell

Centered Title

2 **Type the Title**

Type the title that you want to center over the columns. Put the title atop the first column only.

3 **Select Centered Columns**

Select the title and the columns to the right within which you want to center the title. In other words, if you want to center the title over five columns, select all five of those columns on the row that contains the title.

NOTE

Once you've centered a title over multiple columns correctly, if you adjust the width of the columns that fall below the title, the centered title will adjust to remain centered without your intervention.

4 **Merge All the Cells**

Select **Format**, **Merge Cells**, **Define** to request that Calc merge all the selected cells into a single cell.

5 **Align to the Center of the Cell**

Now that you've merged all five cells into a single wide cell, you can click the **Align Center** button to center the title.

---

61 **Set Up Calc Page Formatting**

Before You Begin

✔ **59** Format Cells

See Also

→ **63** Conditionally Format Data

You will often need to make format changes to your entire spreadsheet. Perhaps you want to change the printed margins on the page. You may want to add a background color or even put a border around the sheets.

The **Page Style** dialog box contains all of Calc's options that enable you to modify your document's format. Any changes you make to the current page apply to all pages in your sheets.

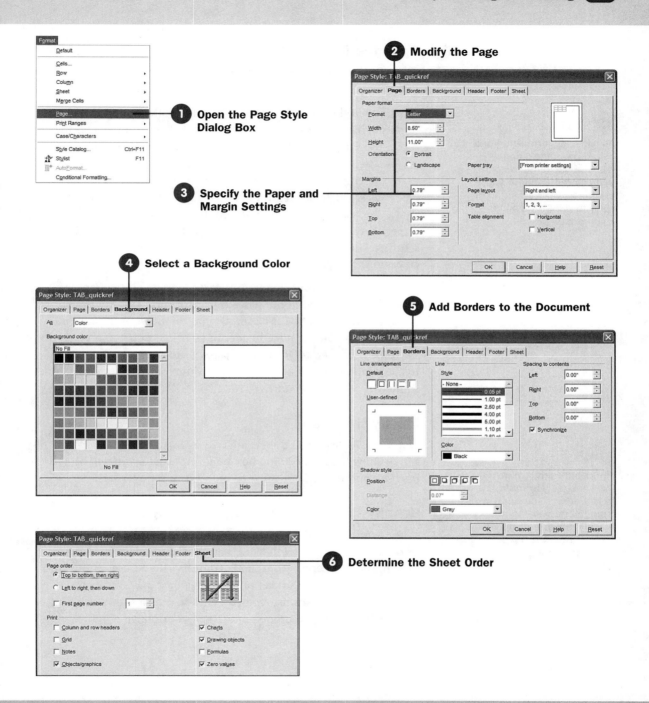

1 Open the Page Style Dialog Box

2 Modify the Page

3 Specify the Paper and Margin Settings

4 Select a Background Color

5 Add Borders to the Document

6 Determine the Sheet Order

❶ Open the Page Style Dialog Box

Select **Page** from the **Format** menu to open the **Page Style** dialog box.

The **Page Style** dialog box contains several categories you can use to modify the pages in your document. Click each tab across the top of the **Page Style** dialog box to select from the dialog box pages. The **Organizer** page determines the default style currently used and enables you to select a different style. See **64** **About Calc Styles and Templates** for help with understanding and using styles. The **Page** dialog box page enables you to format your paper's settings, such as selecting a page length as well as margin settings. The **Background** page enables you to place a background color on the page.

The **Header** and **Footer** pages in the **Page Style** dialog box provide you with the ability to place a header and footer on the pages of your printed sheets. For example, you might want to place a company logo on the page header of your first page, and you'd do so inside a header. **33** **About Headers and Footers** explains how to use headers and footers in Writer documents, and they work the same way in Calc spreadsheets.

❷ Modify the Page

Once you've displayed the **Page Style** dialog box, click the **Page** tab to show the **Page** dialog box page. From here you will modify page-layout information such as margins and paper size.

❸ Specify the Paper and Margin Settings

When you change the type of paper you use in your printer, such as going from letter size to legal, you'll need to select the proper option, such as **Legal**, from the **Format** list. If you use a nonstandard paper size, one that is not letter, legal, or one of the other options in the **Format** list, you can click to adjust the **Width** and **Height** settings to the unique settings of your paper.

TIP

As with any formatting and color commands, don't overuse background colors. Use colored paper in your printer for best effect if you want to print on a single-colored background.

NOTE

You cannot undo many of the changes you make from **Page**. If you apply a change and want to undo it, you'll have to display the **Page** dialog box page again and change the incorrect setting back.

You also may want to change the orientation of your printed page from portrait to landscape. Many spreadsheets are wide, and the landscape mode is perhaps used more for spreadsheets than for any other documents. In addition, you can give your margins more or less room by adjusting the **Left**, **Right**, **Top**, and **Bottom** measurements. If you have multiple paper trays in your printer, such as one with your letterhead and one with blank paper in it, you may want to select a different tray from the **Paper tray** option. Finally, the **Layout settings** options enable you to control how the pages print in relation to one another; for example, if you plan to bind your output into a booklet, you may want the left and right margins to be mirrored to leave more room in the middle for the binding or hole punching.

④ Select a Background Color

Click the **Background** tab to add a background color to your sheet. Although you may want to use colored paper for extensive coloring, you might want to lightly highlight a report page that appears inside your document with a highlighted background color.

⑤ Add Borders to the Document

Click the **Borders** tab to display the **Borders** page. Here, you can specify which edges you want to use as a border (one or two sides, the top and bottom, or all four sides) and the line thickness of the border (from the **Line** list). If you want to add an additional effect to your border, you can adjust the position and color of shading. Shading a border softens the border's look.

⑥ Determine the Sheet Order

Click the **Sheet** tab to display the **Sheet** page. Here, you specify the elements from your spreadsheet that you want to print as well as the order of those printed elements. For example, you specify whether you want Calc to print your spreadsheet from top to bottom (an entire column) before printing the next column, or print from left to right (an entire row) before moving down to print the next row.

NOTE

All large spreadsheets will consume multiple printed pages. By specifying "by column" or "by row" order printing, you determine where the page breaks are likely to fall.

The **Print** section of the **Sheet** page specifies exactly what you want to print. You may elect to print the spreadsheet's grid lines, headers, graphics, or any combination of the three. Also, you can request that zero values print as blanks or as zeroes.

Finally, the **Scale** section enables you to change the scale of your spreadsheet when you print it so that you might be able to fit a large spreadsheet on fewer pages. Calc will squeeze your sheets as much as possible in an attempt to honor your request. For example, if your spreadsheet takes a page and a half to print, you can almost always click the **Fit printout on number of pages** option and change the setting to **1** so that Calc reduces the size of the spreadsheet's output to one page.

62 Attach a Note to a Cell

Before You Begin

✔ **46** Print a Spreadsheet

✔ **47** Find and Replace Data

See Also

→ **64** About Calc Styles and Templates

TIP

Suppose you notice an anomaly in a report, such as a division's forecast is lower than expected. You can attach a note to that cell to follow up and find out where the problem lies.

NOTE

You can attach a note to a single cell only, not a range of cells.

You've seen the yellow sticky notes that some people plaster all over their desks. The reason for their popularity is that these notes work well for reminders. You can put them on just about anything, and although they stick for a while, they come right off without removing what's underneath and without leaving sticky gunk behind.

Calc offers the electronic equivalent of these notes. You can attach notes to cells inside your spreadsheets. The notes can remain yours alone, meaning you don't print them when you print the sheets, or you can print the notes for others to see when you print the spreadsheet's contents.

❶ Locate a Cell for the Note

When you want to attach a note to a cell, click to select the cell.

❷ Request the Note

Select **Note** from the **Insert** menu to request a note. Calc then displays the yellow note box beside the cell with a callout pointing to the cell the note goes with.

❸ Enter the Note Text

The text cursor appears inside the note so that you can type the note's text. As you type, the note expands to make more room if needed. You can also drag the note's edges to expand or contract the size of the note.

1 Locate a Cell for the Note

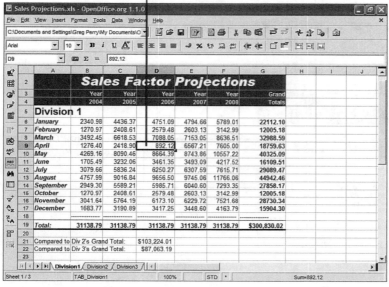

3 Enter the Note Text

2 Request the Note

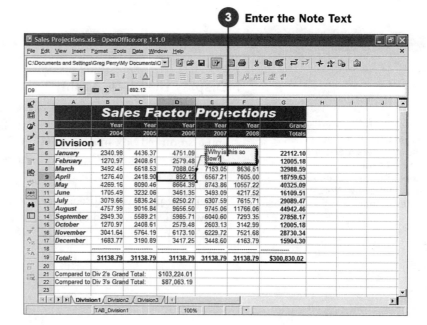

4 Display the Note Again

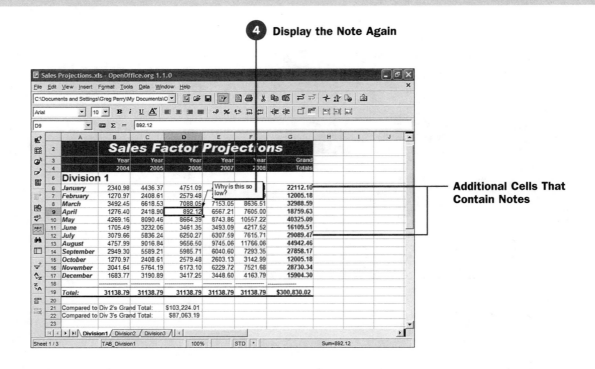

Additional Cells That Contain Notes

4 Display the Note Again

Once you enter the note, you go about working in your spreadsheet as usual. Calc indicates which cells contain notes by displaying a small red box in each cell's upper-right corner that contains a note. To see the note in any cell, hover your mouse pointer over that cell, and Calc displays the note.

When you print your spreadsheet, you must right-click and select **Show Note** on any and all cells with notes that you want printed with the spreadsheet.

63 Conditionally Format Data

Conditional formatting enables you to make your spreadsheets respond to the data they contain. When certain conditions arise, you can draw attention to particular cell entries by automatically making those cells display differently from the cells around those exceptions.

Most often, users place conditional formats on cells that they want to watch (for example, for extraordinarily high or low conditions that might require special attention).

The way you indicate if a condition is met is to specify a value and a condition that must become true before the format takes place. Here's a list of the available conditions:

- Less than
- Greater than
- Equal to
- Not equal to
- Less than or equal to
- Greater than or equal to
- Between (requires two values for the condition)
- Not between (requires two values for the condition)

Before You Begin

✔ **59** Format Cells

✔ **61** Set Up Calc Page Formatting

See Also

→ **69** Protect Spreadsheet Data

✎ **KEY TERM**

Conditional formatting— The process of formatting cells automatically, based on the data they contain. When the data changes and triggers a predetermined condition, Calc automatically changes the cell's format.

➊ Request Conditional Formatting

Click to select the cell or range on which you want to apply a conditional format. Select **Conditional Formatting** from the **Format** menu. The **Conditional Formatting** dialog box appears.

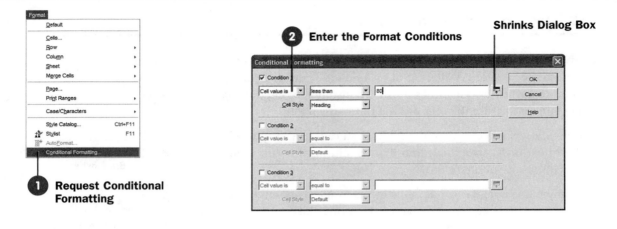

Shrinks Dialog Box

2 Enter the Format Conditions

1 Request Conditional Formatting

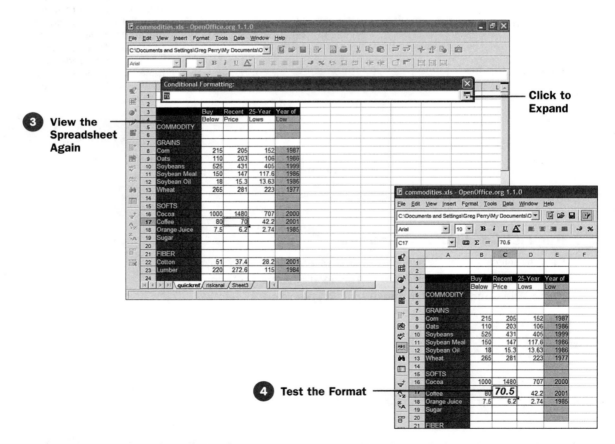

Click to Expand

3 View the Spreadsheet Again

4 Test the Format

2 Enter the Format Conditions

You can apply up to three conditions for the cell you've selected to format conditionally. Most often, you'll probably only need to use a single conditional format.

Click to select either **Cell value is** or **Formula is** to indicate how the conditional format is to apply. If the format depends on a value, as it usually will, select **Cell value is**. If the format depends on a formula, select **Formula is** and enter a cell reference for that formula to the right of the option.

Select the **Cell Style** setting that you want Calc to use for the data's display if the condition is met by data within the cell. Any time the data changes to make the condition true, Calc applies the format style to the cell.

Select the condition, such as **Less than**. If the cell's value ever goes below the value you enter next to the condition, Calc changes the cell's format to match the style you select. Two of the conditions, **Between** and **Not between**, require two values for the condition to be matched. If you select either of these conditions, Calc provides two text boxes so you can enter both values that define the condition.

3 View the Spreadsheet Again

The **Conditional Formatting** dialog box consumes quite a bit of space, and while you're filling it in, you may need to see your data on the sheet beneath the dialog box. If so, click the **Shrink** button. Calc temporarily shrinks the **Conditional Formatting** dialog box to a thin line so you can view the spreadsheet once again.

Click the **Shrink** button once again to return the **Conditional Formatting** dialog box to its original size so that you can complete the formatting. After setting up the conditional format, click **OK** to apply it.

4 Test the Format

If the cell never matches the condition, the cell's format will remain unchanged. If, however, the cell does pass the condition, Calc applies the format so it becomes noticeable to anyone looking at the spreadsheet.

NOTE

The available formats are **Default**, **Heading**, **Heading1**, **Result**, and **Result2**. If you want to display a different format, you'll have to select one of these styles and change its format so it appears the way you prefer (see **64** **About Calc Styles and Templates**).

NOTE

Calc constantly monitors cell contents. Every time you enter a new value or the spreadsheet recalculates, Calc tests all the conditional formats and applies any of those formats if needed.

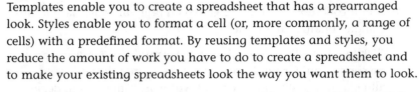

64 About Calc Styles and Templates

NOTES

16 **About Styles and Templates** describes how to use templates and styles in Writer documents. If you need to review terminology, you can review that task because the background is the same whether you're applying templates and styles to Calc spreadsheets or to Writer documents.

 TIP

Templates are more global than styles. A template is a model for a spreadsheet, and a style is a model for a cell or range of cells. Often, a template contains several cell styles that you can choose from.

NOTE

In reality, you always use a template when you create new Calc spreadsheets. Calc uses a default template named **Default** unless you specify another template. The font, margin, and cell-formatting settings offered when you create a new spreadsheet come from this default template.

Templates enable you to create a spreadsheet that has a prearranged look. Styles enable you to format a cell (or, more commonly, a range of cells) with a predefined format. By reusing templates and styles, you reduce the amount of work you have to do to create a spreadsheet and to make your existing spreadsheets look the way you want them to look.

Suppose you find yourself producing a spreadsheet of weekly payroll figures. Management requests that you format out-of-town payroll figures in a sheet different from the corporate office's payroll numbers. Each goes on its own sheet inside the same spreadsheet, although management requests that you lightly shade the background on the noncorporate payroll figures and use a different table format for them.

If your spreadsheet takes on the same general look each week, even though it contains two very different sheets, you can create a template that acts like a preformatted, fill-in-the-blank spreadsheet. In the future, you start with that template so you no longer have to worry with formatting the same spreadsheet each week. You also can create styles for individual sections within each sheet so you can quickly apply those styles to ranges of cells that are to take on that appearance.

A template is to an entire spreadsheet what a style is to selected cells. When creating a spreadsheet that's to look like another you often create, such as a weekly payroll report or invoices, you can start with a template that you've already set up, and you only need to fill in the details.

A template may contain several styles. When you want to use a style that's available to your current template, you can easily select that style and apply it to existing cells or cells you're about to fill in.

The **Stylelist**, available from the **Format** menu or by pressing **F11**, is a dialog box that lists every style available in the current spreadsheet. Each style has a name. If you create a new spreadsheet using **File**, **New**, **Spreadsheet**, the styles in the Stylelist will display the default template's styles. If you create a new spreadsheet using a predefined template, the styles in the **Stylelist** dialog box come from the styles defined in that template.

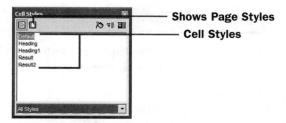

Shows Page Styles

Cell Styles

The Stylelist dialog box displays the current styles available to you.

You can also see the styles available to you in a different way. You can display a catalog of styles that shows the styles in a format you may prefer over the **Stylelist** dialog box. Select **Format**, **Style Catalog** (or press **Ctrl+F11**) to see the **Style Catalog** dialog box. You can select cell styles and page styles as well as modify and easily organize the collection of styles.

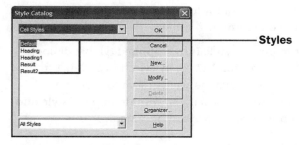

Styles

The Style Catalog lists styles by style types.

When you want to use a template, you'll select **File**, **New**, **Templates and Documents** to choose the template you want to work from.

✎ NOTE

When you first install Calc, you won't find any preexisting Calc templates. OpenOffice.org comes with several templates for Writer and Impress but none for Calc. You can build your own templates and save them in the template area (see **66** Create a Calc Template).

65 Create a Calc Style

Before You Begin

✔ **64** About Calc Styles
       and Templates

See Also

→ **66** Create a Calc
       Template

Using a style is simple. You can apply a style to selected cells to format those cells with the style's formatting. Calc comes with several styles, and you can add your own.

Suppose you routinely create income statements for various departments. You might develop three separate sets of character formats that work well, respectively, for the title of the income statements, the data that comprises the body of the income statements, and the profit or loss line at the bottom of the income statement.

Instead of defining each of these cell formats every time you create the income statement, you can create three styles and store the styles under their own names (such as **IS Heading**, **IS Data**, and **IS ProfitLoss**). The next time you create the income statement, you need only to select a style such as **IS Title** before typing the title. When you then type the title, the title looks the way you want it to look without your having to take the time to designate any format.

 TIP

The Stylelist provides existing styles, and you can define your own from text you select before displaying the Stylelist.

One of the easiest ways to apply a style is to keep the **Stylelist** dialog box showing at all times by pressing **F11** (or by selecting **Stylelist** from the **Format** menu). If you don't have the screen room to keep the Stylelist showing, you can display it when you want to apply a style and then click its **Close** button to hide the Stylelist once again.

1 Select the Cell Text for the Style

When you want to apply a predefined style to text, first select the cell or range. The format of the cell will completely change depending on which style you apply, but the data inside the cell will not change.

2 Display the Stylelist

Press **F11** to display the **Stylelist** dialog box. If you see the page styles and not the cell styles, click the **Cell Styles** button. The style names will then appear that you can apply to your selected cells.

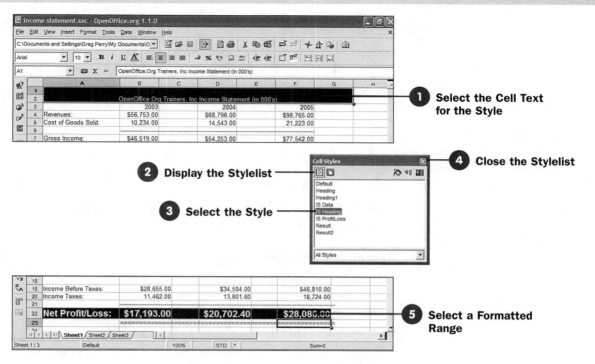

1 Select the Cell Text for the Style

2 Display the Stylelist

3 Select the Style

4 Close the Stylelist

5 Select a Formatted Range

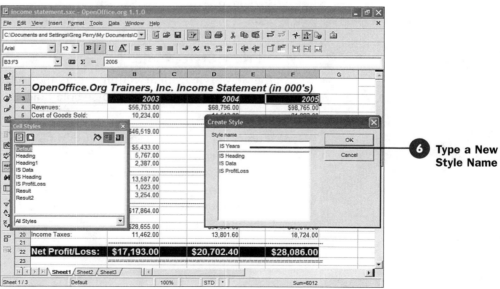

6 Type a New Style Name

③ Select the Style

Double-click the style in the Stylelist that you want to apply to the selected range. Depending on the arrangement of your screen and windows, you can usually see the style immediately applied to your selected text. If you want to try a different style, double-click another in the list. Feel free to keep the **Stylelist** dialog box showing or click **Close** to hide it, depending on how much you plan to use the Stylelist during the rest of your editing session.

④ Close the Stylelist

Once you've applied the styles, close the **Stylelist** dialog box to return to your formatted spreadsheet.

⑤ Select a Formatted Range

You can easily add your own styles. You add styles to Calc's Stylelist by example. In other words, format a cell or range to match a style you want to create and then tell Calc to create a new style based on that format.

To add the new style to the **Stylelist** dialog box, press **F11** to display the **Stylelist** dialog box after selecting the formatted range in the sheet.

⑥ Type a New Style Name

Click the **New Style from Selection** button, the second button from the right atop the **Stylelist** dialog box. Calc displays the **Create Style** dialog box.

Type a name for your style (one that does not already exist in the Stylelist, unless you want to replace one). When you click **OK**, Calc creates the new style based on your selected text. The next time you select that kind of cell and select the new style, Calc applies the new style's formatting to the cell without you having to worry about the formatting details for that cell ever again.

---

66   **Create a Calc Template**

Templates contain formatting for complete spreadsheets. Think of a template as a model for a spreadsheet. All the OpenOffice.org programs support templates. If you create a new spreadsheet without specifying a template, Calc uses the **Default** template style to create the empty spreadsheet and to set up initial font, margin, and other formatting-related details.

The **Template Management** dialog box, available from the **File**, **Templates**, **Organize** menu option, lists all templates currently available to you. You work with templates, selecting and adding them, from the **Template Management** dialog box.

1 **Request a Template**

Select **File**, **New**, **Templates and Documents** to open the **Templates and Documents** dialog box. Click the **Templates** icon to see folders of templates such as **Default** and **Presentations** (used for Impress, see **85** **Use an Impress Template**). To open a template folder, double-click it to see all the available templates in that folder. Double-click the **Default** folder to see its contents.

2 **Choose a Template**

Decide which template you want to work with.

After clicking to select a template, you can click the **Preview** button to see a preview of the template at the right of the **Templates and Documents** dialog box. If you then click the **Document Properties** button, the preview goes away and the template's properties will display, showing you who created the template, how long ago the template was created, the template's size, and the last time the template was modified.

Click the **Open** button to create a spreadsheet based on the template.

Before You Begin

✔ **64** About Calc Styles and Templates

✔ **65** Create a Calc Style

See Also

→ **72** Import and Export Sheet Data

NOTES

Calc templates use the filename extension .stc.

If you've recently installed Calc or have not added new templates, you may only see a Writer template named **letter**.

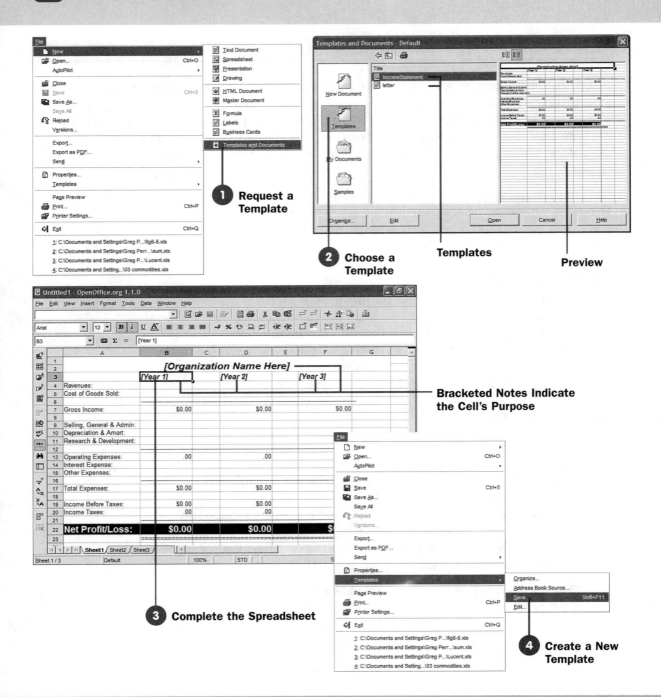

1 Request a Template

2 Choose a Template

Templates

Preview

Bracketed Notes Indicate the Cell's Purpose

3 Complete the Spreadsheet

4 Create a New Template

③ Complete the Spreadsheet

Once Calc creates a new spreadsheet based on the template, you then fill in the specific details to complete the spreadsheet. When designing templates, use placeholder text for names, titles, years, and other common data to be requested from inside brackets. The placeholder text indicates that you should fill in those cells with more specific data. These bracketed notes are not a requirement in any way; they serve to tell you what is expected in those cells. When you develop your own templates, remember to add as many of these bracketed notes as you can so whoever uses the template in the future will know what is expected. Not all cells in a spreadsheet template will need these bracketed placeholders, though. Many cell contents require data that is obvious from the labels around those cells.

You might wonder what the difference is between creating a template and creating a spreadsheet and saving the sheet to be reused as a starting point later. If you start a new spreadsheet based on a template, when you save the spreadsheet, Calc knows to save the spreadsheet in a new spreadsheet file and will not overwrite the template. The template is always ready to be used. If you were to start with an actual spreadsheet that you use as your model, you can easily overwrite that model by performing a **File**, **Save** operation.

④ Create a New Template

Feel free to create your own templates! Remember to include placeholder instructions to the user of your template, such as **[Type Discount Rate Here]**.

After you create and format a spreadsheet that you may need to re-create in the future, save the spreadsheet and then remove all the data specific to that particular spreadsheet, keeping all the formulas and formatting intact.

When you select **File**, **Templates**, **Save**, Calc opens the **Templates** dialog box, where you can assign a name and category folder for your template (such as **Default**). The next time you create a new document from a template, your new template will appear in the list.

> **TIPS**

Templates are easier to maintain as models of spreadsheets than storing actual spreadsheets that you reuse over and over.

If your template spreadsheet contains formulas, you should protect those cells so that anybody who creates a spreadsheet from the template doesn't inadvertently overwrite those formulas with data (see **69** Protect Spreadsheet Data).

9

Creating Advanced Spreadsheets

IN THIS CHAPTER:

A picture is worth a thousand words—and worth even more numbers! Your spreadsheet data might contain a ton of numbers, but many times you can present data better with a chart or graphic. The actual raw data supplied by a worksheet is accurate and vital information for analysis, but for trends and overall patterns, charts demonstrate the data's nature quickly and effectively. After you create and format your worksheets, use Calc to quickly create a chart that depicts your data graphically. After Calc generates the chart, you then can customize the chart to look exactly the way you want.

You can easily import graphics into your spreadsheets, as you might do, for example, with a graphic logo for your company or pictures of inventory items. The distinction between numbers, text, and graphics is blurred these days thanks to modern technology, and Calc handles virtually any data you want to store in a spreadsheet.

Once you create spreadsheets with data, charts, and graphics, you'll want to protect the contents so you (or another user of your spreadsheet) don't accidentally overwrite something you shouldn't. You can protect cells to maintain their integrity. Calc's other capabilities, such as being able to check certain cells for accuracy, are explored in this chapter.

67 Add a Chart to a Spreadsheet

Before You Begin

✔ 50 Fill Cells with Data

See Also

→ 68 Insert Graphics into a Spreadsheet

Although Calc can produce professional-looking graphs from your spreadsheet data, you don't need to know a lot about graphing and charting unless you want to create extremely sophisticated graphs. Instead, you'll simply tell Calc what data you want to see in the chart and select the type of chart you want Calc to produce, and Calc does the rest.

Table 9.1 describes each of Calc's chart types. Different charts reflect different kinds of data. If you create one chart and realize it's not the best type of chart to use, you can request that Calc switch to a different type.

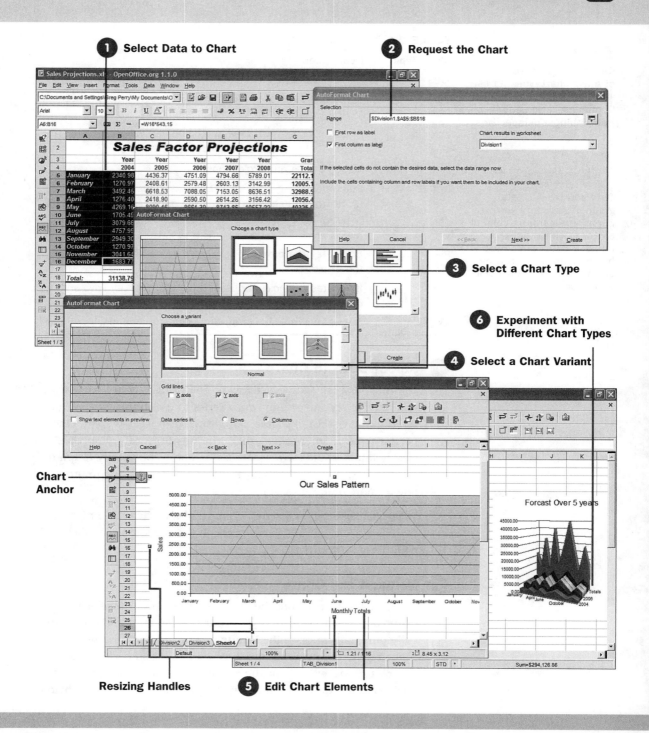

1 Select Data to Chart

2 Request the Chart

3 Select a Chart Type

6 Experiment with Different Chart Types

4 Select a Chart Variant

Chart Anchor

Resizing Handles

5 Edit Chart Elements

NOTE

Calc supplies 3D versions of these chart types for use when you must chart data in multiple time periods or from multiple perspectives.

KEY TERM

Data series—A single group of data that you might select from a column or row to chart. Unlike a range, a data series must be contiguous in a row or column with no empty cells in between.

TABLE 9.1 Calc Chart Options

Chart Type	Description
Area	Emphasizes the magnitude of changes over time.
Bar	Compares data items. A bar chart is a column chart with horizontal lines.
Column	Shows changes over time and compares values. A column chart is a bar chart with vertical bars.
Line	Shows trends and projections.
Net	Puts in each category an *axis* that radiates from the center of the graph (useful for finding the data series with the most penetration, as needed in market research statistical studies).
Pie	Compares the proportional size of items against the parts of the whole.
Stock	Illustrates a stock's (or other investment's) high, low, and closing prices.
XY (Scatter)	Shows relationships of several values in a series.

1 Select Data to Chart

You must first tell Calc exactly what you want to chart. To do this, you must select one or more *data series* to use in the chart. A data series might consist of a time period such as a week or year. One person's weekly sales totals (from a group of several salespeople's weekly totals) could form a data series. Some charts only graph a single series, such as a pie chart, whereas other charts can graph one or more data series, such as a line chart.

When you select a data series, include labels if available next to the series. Calc can use those labels on the chart itself to label what is being charted.

2 Request the Chart

Select **Insert**, **Chart** from the menu to display the **AutoFormat Chart** dialog box. Calc analyzes your selected data and automatically puts that range in the **Range** text box (using an absolute range reference, including the sheet name). If you decide to use a different range, either type the range in the **Range** box or click the **Shrink** button to select a different range before clicking the **Shrink** button once again to restore the **AutoFormat Chart** dialog box and continuing with the chart.

Calc will probably have already checked either the **First row as label** option or the **First column as label** option. In doing so, Calc wants to use either the first row or column in your selection for the labels on the data points that will be graphed. If you don't want labels, or if your selected data series doesn't include labels, click to uncheck either of these options. If you selected multiple data series, you still could select the row or column that precedes the series to be used for the labels.

Click **Next** to continue with the chart building so you can select the type of chart you want to build.

❸ Select a Chart Type

Scroll through the various charts offered and select the chart you wish to build. The preview area updates as you select different chart types to give you a good idea of what your chart will look like. Use the preview area to determine as early as possible the best chart type for the data series you selected. For example, if you selected only a single data series, such as 12 monthly gross sales figures, you would want to select a simple chart type and most likely a line chart. The line will show the direction and trend of the sales over the year. A chart type that compares multiple data series against others, such as an area chart, would make little sense when charting a single series.

Click the **Next** button once you've selected a chart type.

❹ Select a Chart Variant

Each chart type includes several variables. You'll now want to choose one of those variants that displays your selected data the best. You may also want to hide or display grid lines on both axes of the chart, or only on one or the other. As you select from the options and variants, Calc updates the preview to show you what your chart will look like.

Click **Next** to continue building the chart. Calc displays one more dialog box where you enter a title for your chart, indicate if you

TIP

Calc will display the chart you build next to the data in the current sheet. If you would prefer the chart to appear in a sheet by itself, click the **Chart results in worksheet** option and select a different sheet. Doing so keeps your data and chart separated into different sheets.

TIP

During the chart-building process, you can generate the chart immediately without having to click **Next** to run through each of the possible steps. Click **Create** at any point to generate the chart with the options you've selected so far.

KEY TERM

Legend—Tells a chart's audience what series each colored line or bar represents.

want a *legend* to display, and type labels for the two (or three, depending on whether the chart is a regular 2D or a 3D chart) chart axes.

5 Edit Chart Elements

Once Calc displays your chart (next to the data or in its own sheet, depending on your selection when you built the chart), you are free to edit any and all the elements in the chart. By double-clicking the title, for example, you can change the title. The resizing handles that appear when you click the chart enable you to resize the chart to any proportion you prefer. The chart's anchor appears anytime you select the chart, in case you want to move the chart or delete it (by moving or deleting the anchor).

6 Experiment with Different Chart Types

When first mastering the nuances of Calc's charting capabilities, start with a single data series to get a feel for the charting dialog boxes and to learn the terminology. Then, you can experiment with charting additional data series within the same chart to make data comparisons that sometimes are easier to study in chart form as opposed to lists of numbers inside a large worksheet.

---

68 Insert Graphics into a Spreadsheet

Before You Begin

✔ **61** Set Up Calc Page Formatting

✔ **67** Add a Chart to a Spreadsheet

See Also

→ **73** About Advanced Spreadsheet Printing

NOTE

Calc supports all popular graphic file formats including JPG, GIF, and BMP files.

Calc enables you to put pictures in your spreadsheets. Perhaps you'll want to accent a motivational message next to sales figures or perhaps insert your logo at the top of the sheet.

When you insert a graphic image, Calc places the image's anchor at that location. You will see the anchor when editing but not when you print your spreadsheet. The anchor shows where you inserted the actual image, but you can adjust the placement of the image. For example, you might adjust the image so that it appears right-justified; the anchor will remain where you last placed it, even when you change the position of the picture. When you want to move an image, move its anchor and not the image itself.

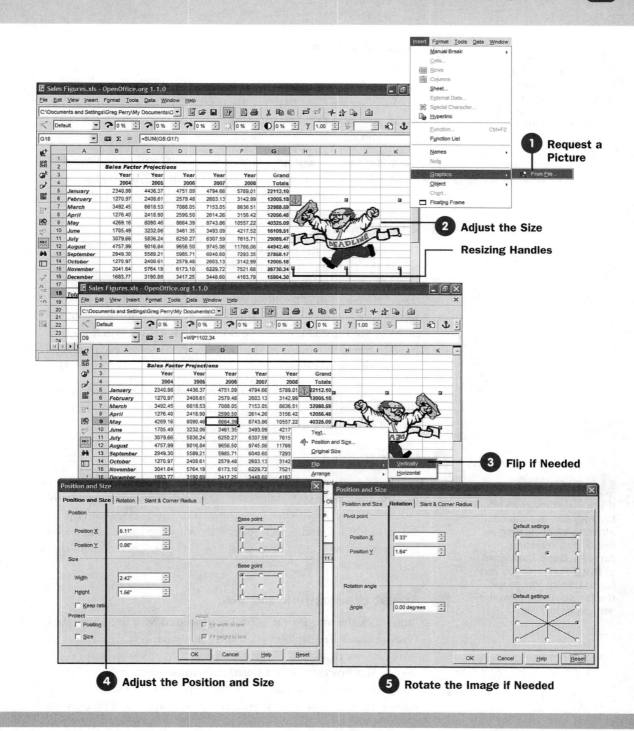

CHAPTER 9: Creating Advanced Spreadsheets

TIP

Click the **Insert Graphics** dialog box's **View** button and select **Thumbnails** to see previews of your graphics before you import them.

1 Request a Picture

To insert a graphic image from a file, first select the cell where you want the image to go. Then, select **Insert**, **Graphics**, **From File** from the menu. Calc displays the **Insert Graphics** dialog box, which is nothing more than a Windows file-selection dialog box where you navigate to the file you want to insert.

Once you select the graphic image you want to place in your document, click the **Open** button to insert the image. The image appears in your spreadsheet at the location you first selected.

2 Adjust the Size

Once Calc brings the graphic image into your spreadsheet, you can make adjustments to suit your needs. Typically, Calc imports graphic images and centers them at the location you inserted them. No text wraps to either side of the image because, unlike a word processed document, a spreadsheet relies on the exact placement of data inside the rectangular grid. Therefore, you'll usually have to move the image so that it doesn't overwrite any important data in your spreadsheet.

Often, your imported image is not sized properly for your spreadsheet. To resize the image, drag any of the eight resizing handles inward or outward to reduce the image size.

3 Flip if Needed

TIP

If you insert multiple graphics, they can overlap each other. By right-clicking an image and selecting **Arrange**, **Send Backward** or **Bring Forward**, you can control which image gets the top spot when layered with other images.

Depending on your image and your data, you may want to flip, or reverse, the image so it points the other direction, either vertically or horizontally. Right-click over the graphic and select the **Flip** menu to flip the image so it faces differently. Be sure to check your image after reversing it because if any text appears in the image, it will also be reversed.

4 Adjust the Position and Size

Right-click the image and select **Position and Size** to display the **Position and Size** dialog box. From this dialog box, you can resize, move, or slant the graphic image using exact measurements. The **Position X** and **Position Y** values determine where the image appears on the page from the upper-left corner. The **Size** values determine how large your image will appear. If you do resize an image, be sure that you click to select the **Keep ratio** option so that Calc resizes the width in proportion to any height changes you make (or so Calc resizes the height in proportion to any width changes you make) to keep your image clear and in the correct ratio as the original. If you fail to maintain the ratio, your image can look skewed and stretched. Checking the **Protect** area ensures that you don't inadvertently move the image with your mouse later.

5 Rotate the Image if Needed

Click the **Position and Size** dialog box's **Rotation** tab to display the **Rotation** page. Here, you can rotate the image any angle by specifying a value in the **Angle** field. The image rotates around the center of your image.

69 Protect Spreadsheet Data

When developing spreadsheet templates (see **66** **Create a Calc Template**) or creating spreadsheets that others less savvy in Calc will work with, you may want to protect certain cells from being changed. This protection helps ensure that formulas do not get changed and that fixed data remains fixed.

In addition to protecting individual cells and ranges, you can password-protect entire spreadsheets to keep them secure and to limit access to them.

1 Select Cells to Protect

Select the cell or the range of cells you want to protect. (Hold **Ctrl** and click to select multiple cells in a range.) These cells can contain data, be empty, or contain formulas. Also, if you've stored a graphic image in a cell, you can protect that image from being moved or overwritten.

2 Request Cell Protection

Select **Format**, **Cells** from the menu. The **Format Cells** dialog box appears.

TIP

If you rotate or resize the image too much and want to begin again with the original position and size, click the **Position and Size** dialog box's **Reset** button to restore the values to the original image state.

Before You Begin

✔ **59** Format Cells
✔ **66** Create a Calc Template

See Also

→ **71** Ensure Valid Data Entry

NOTE

Cells you designate as protected are only protected if you also protect the spreadsheet.

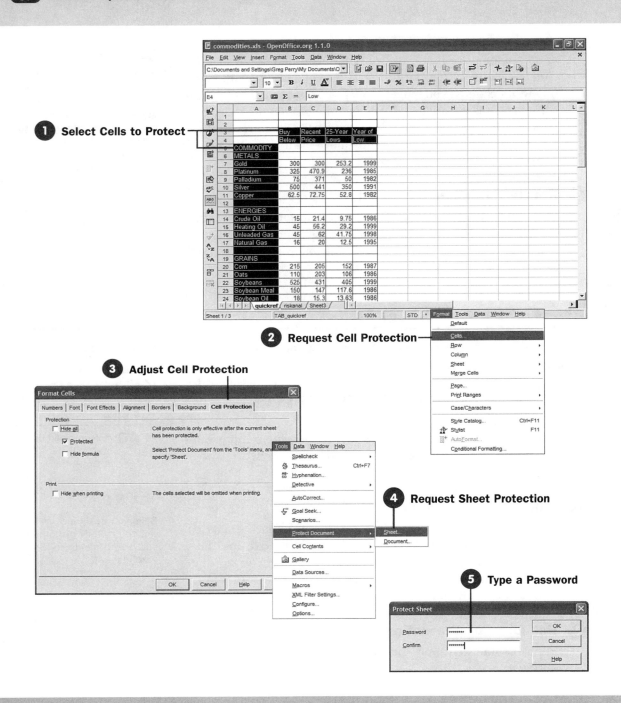

1 Select Cells to Protect

2 Request Cell Protection

3 Adjust Cell Protection

4 Request Sheet Protection

5 Type a Password

3 **Adjust Cell Protection**

Click the **Cell Protection** tab to display the **Cell Protection** page within the **Format Cells** dialog box. If you click to select the **Hide all** option, the contents of the selected cells will not appear when the spreadsheet is viewed. The **Protected** option keeps the selected cells from being changed. The **Hide formula** option hides any formulas in the protected cells, if any formulas reside there.

Click the **Hide when printing** option if you don't want the cells to appear when the user prints the spreadsheet. Once you've indicated the protection, click **OK** to close the **Format Cells** dialog box and apply the protection to your spreadsheet.

4 **Request Sheet Protection**

Select **Tools, Protect Document, Sheet** to open the **Protect Sheet** dialog box.

5 **Type a Password**

In the **Protect Sheet** dialog box, type a password, press **Tab**, and type the password once more. The password does not show on the screen in case someone is looking over your shoulder. The second typing of the password ensures that you typed it correctly the first time.

Once you type the password and click **OK**, you've protected the spreadsheet. Any cells that you now designate as protected (or have before) will now be protected. No user can change the contents of those protected cells without first removing the protection from the entire sheet by selecting **Tools, Protect Document, Sheet** once again and entering the correct password.

NOTE

When you hide formulas, the user cannot see them but can still see the cell values that result from the formulas.

70 Combine Multiple Cells into One

Sometimes you'll need to merge multiple cells into a single cell. Perhaps you want to pad a label with several surrounding blank cells to add spaces that can't be easily removed from the label.

Before You Begin

✔ **57** Freeze Row and Column Headers

✔ **60** Center a Heading over Multiple Columns

1 Select Multiple Cells

2 Request Merged Cells

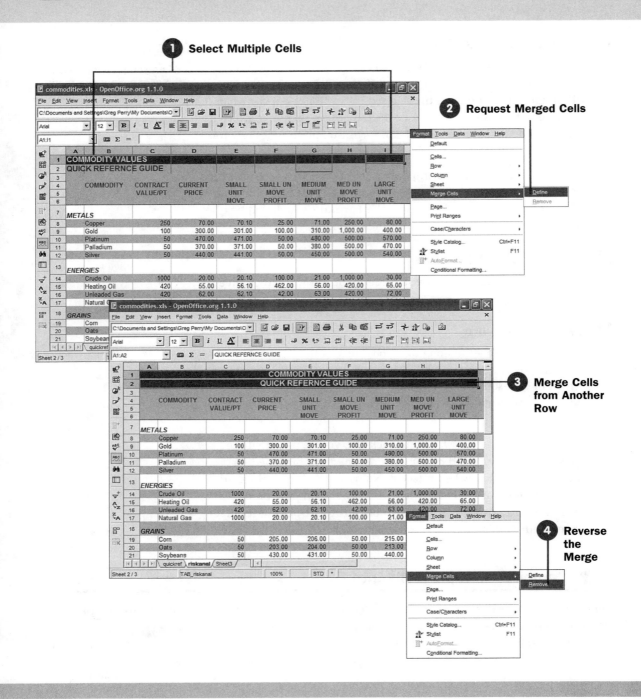

3 Merge Cells from Another Row

4 Reverse the Merge

Not only can Calc merge multiple cells into a single cell, but it can also turn a single cell with multiple values back into multiple cells once again.

❶ Select Multiple Cells

Select the cells that you want to merge into a single cell. Generally, this requires that you select empty cells to the right or to the left of one or more labels.

❷ Request Merged Cells

Select **Format**, **Merge Cells**, **Define** from the menu. Calc merges the cells into a single cell for you.

❸ Merge Cells from Another Row

If you have other cells from a subsequent row that you want to merge into one, continue selecting adjacent cells in each row and merging them from the **Format**, **Merge Cells**, **Define** menu. You might do this, for example, if your spreadsheet uses a multiline title atop the data; by merging the title's cells into a single cell, you can more easily center the title over the data.

❹ Reverse the Merge

To reverse the merge, select **Format**, **Merge Cells**, **Remove**.

TIP

One of the most common reasons to merge two or more cells into a single cell is to center titles over multiple columns (see **60** **Center a Heading over Multiple Columns**).

NOTE

If you select cells from two or more rows to merge, Calc merges those cells' contents into a single cell on a single row. Usually, you'll want to merge only adjacent cells from the same row.

71 Ensure Valid Data Entry

Not only can you conditionally format data so that the format changes based on the data (see **63** **Conditionally Format Data**), you can also set up *data validity* rules to help maintain accurate spreadsheets. Once you set up data validity rules, you or those who use your spreadsheets are limited on what they can enter into certain cells.

Without data validity checks, anybody can enter any value into any cell (assuming the cell is not protected). Once you set up data validity checks, if someone violates any criterion you set up, such as entering a negative payroll amount, that you deem impossible, Calc flags the entry as an error. If a user types a value that violates any data validity check you've set up, Calc displays an error message you define for that situation.

Before You Begin

✔ **63** Conditionally Format Data

✔ **69** Protect Spreadsheet Data

KEY TERM

Data validity—A check to determine whether data entered into a cell is valid, defined by a set of criteria that you set up.

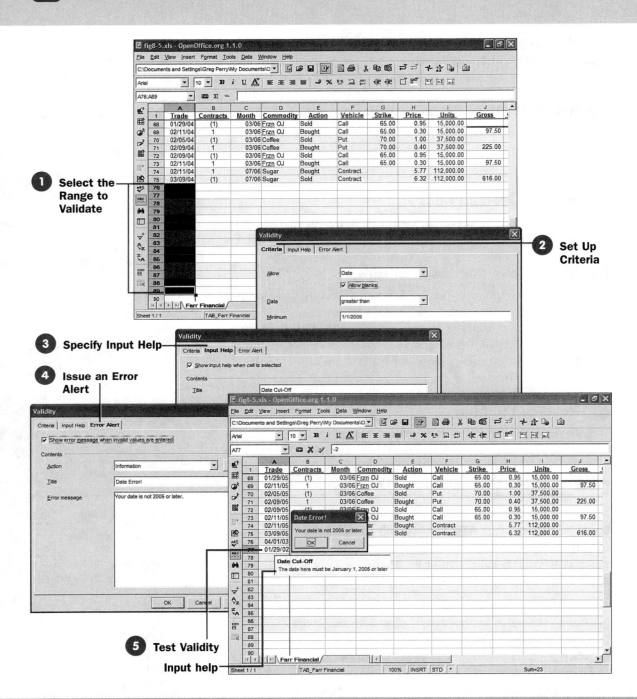

1 Select the Range to Validate

2 Set Up Criteria

3 Specify Input Help

4 Issue an Error Alert

5 Test Validity

Input help

① Select the Range to Validate

Select the cell or range that you want to create a data validity check for. For example, you may want to create a range of dates and disallow any entry into the range that is not a valid date.

To add the data validity check, select **Data**, **Validity** to display the **Validity** dialog box.

② Set Up Criteria

On the **Criteria** page, you set up the criteria to which the range must conform before the user can enter a value. For example, if you require a date that falls after January 1, 2005, you would select **Date** from the **Allow** field. Keep the **Allow blanks** option checked if you want to allow blanks in the range without the blanks violating the criteria.

Select a condition from the **Data** field that the range must meet. For example, to allow the entry of dates January 1, 2005 and after, you would select **greater than**. Then, you'd type **1/1/2005** in the **Minimum** field. The **Maximum** field appears if you select either **between** or **not between** so that you can define the two fields that limit the input range.

③ Specify Input Help

Click the **Input Help** tab to display the **Input Help** page in the **Validity** dialog box. Here, you set up a floating ToolTip that appears whenever the user selects the cell. The title and message that you type in the **Title** and **Input help** fields appear when the cell becomes active. The purpose of the **Input help** field is to let your users know the kind of data you allow in the cell.

④ Issue an Error Alert

The **Error Alert** page describes what happens if and when the user violates the criteria you set up on the **Criteria** page. The **Action** field can be set to **Stop**, **Warning**, **Information**, or **Macro**, depending on what you want to happen when the violation occurs. When you select **Stop**, Calc disallows any entry into the cell until the user enters data that conforms to the criteria. **Warning** or **Information** allows the data but shows a pop-up

NOTE

The **Allow** field enables you to set up criteria for dates, times, whole numbers, or decimals. You can also limit the number of characters that can be typed into a text cell.

TIP

Usually, cells don't require both a title and input help if the criteria is simple. A title such as **Must be more than 0** is usually sufficient.

NOTE

The **Macro** option starts a macro program that you or someone else may have written. See **127** About OpenOffice.org Macros for more information about macros.

dialog box with the title and error message you enter in the **Title** and **Error message** fields of the **Error Alert** page.

5 **Test Validity**

Test your data validity check by typing data in the cell. When you select the cell, the **Input Help** message should appear, telling you what data the cell expects. If you enter a value that violates the criteria, Calc responds with a warning or a pop-up dialog box, depending on how you set up the error alert.

72 Import and Export Sheet Data

Before You Begin

✔ **46** Print a Spreadsheet

See Also

→ **73** About Advanced Spreadsheet Printing

KEY TERMS

Import—To load data from a non-Calc program into Calc.

Export—To save data from Calc so another program can use the data.

As with all the OpenOffice.org programs, Calc works well with data from similar programs such as Microsoft Office and StarOffice. Most of the time, you can load an Excel spreadsheet directly into Calc and work with the spreadsheet as though you had originally created it in Calc. When you load a spreadsheet from another program into Calc, you are using Calc's automatic *import* feature to bring that data into Calc's workspace. If you want to use Calc data in another program, you must *export* the spreadsheet data.

Although Calc imports virtually all Excel spreadsheets, Calc may have problems importing the following Excel items. If your imported spreadsheets contain any of these items, you may need to adjust the imported spreadsheet manually to eliminate the sections with these items or make a note that the items will not be appearing:

- AutoShapes
- OLE objects
- Advanced Office form fields
- Pivot tables
- Non-Calc-supported chart types
- Excel's conditional formatting
- Esoteric Excel functions and formulas

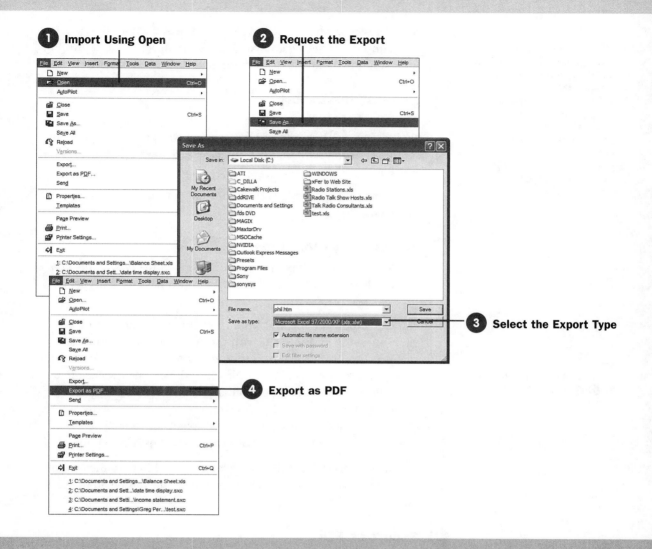

1 **Import Using Open**

2 **Request the Export**

3 **Select the Export Type**

4 **Export as PDF**

1 Import Using Open

To import an Excel or StarOffice spreadsheet into Calc, simply use **File**, **Open** to request the file. Browse the files from the **Open** dialog box until you find the spreadsheet you want to import and then click **OK** to import the file into Calc. Almost always, assuming the spreadsheet doesn't contain some advanced or esoteric

TIP

After importing the spreadsheet, save the spreadsheet with **File**, **Save** and select the Calc extension .SXC from the **Save as type** list box to convert the spreadsheet to Calc's native format. This also preserves the file's original Excel or StarOffice format.

feature, such as those listed in this task's introduction, the spreadsheet imports perfectly, and you can continue editing and printing it as though you had created the sheet originally in Calc.

② Request the Export

Although Calc's **File** menu contains an **Export** command, you should only use this command when you want to export your current spreadsheet data to a PDF file (see 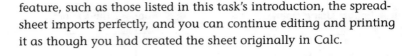 **Save a Document as a PDF File**).

To export your spreadsheet in a non-Calc format, select **File**, **Save As**.

③ Select the Export Type

The **Save As** dialog box opens, and you select the type of file you want Calc to convert your spreadsheet to in the **Save as type** list box.

 TIP

The dBASE file format is useful when you use Calc as a database, as you learn in **74** **About Calc Databases**.

You can export the file to a Data Interchange Format with the .dif extension, a dBASE file with the .dbf extension, one of several versions of Excel (most commonly, the .xls extension is used for Excel spreadsheets), a StarCalc file with the .sdc extension, a SYLK file with the .slk extension, a text-based comma-separated values file (known as a *CSV* file) with the .csv or .txt extension, or an HTML document with the .html extension, which you would use if you wanted to display your spreadsheet as a Web page.

When you click **Save**, Calc converts the spreadsheet to the format you selected and saves the file under the name you typed in the **File name** field.

④ Export as PDF

Calc's **File**, **Export** and **File**, **Export as PDF** commands do the very same thing. They both convert your spreadsheet to Adobe's PDF format (see **36** **Save a Document as a PDF File**) and save the file with the .PDF filename extension. PDF files are useful for eBooks and for offering to Web page visitors as downloads because PDF files are readable on many kinds of computer systems. A primary advantage of PDF files is that they look the same no matter what kind of system you view them on.

73 About Advanced Spreadsheet Printing

Printing Calc spreadsheets offers some challenges that other kinds of documents, such as Writer documents, do not require. For example, once you develop a comprehensive spreadsheet, you may want to print the spreadsheet with all its notes showing, perhaps even with formulas showing instead of values. Such reports serve as documentation to the spreadsheet and can help you pinpoint errors in the spreadsheet that might be more difficult to locate searching and scrolling around the screen.

The **Format, Page** menu option displays the **Page Style** dialog box. The **Sheet** tab displays the **Sheet** page, where you can specify the kinds of items you wish to print or to suppress during printing. For example, if you want to print formulas instead of the values they equate to, you would click to select the **Formulas** option in the **Print** area of the **Sheet** page.

Before You Begin

✔ Print a Spreadsheet

✔ **61** Set Up Calc Page Formatting

TIP

Before printing, be sure to view a preview with **File, Page Preview.** The preview ensures that your printed spreadsheet will look exactly the way you want it to look before you send the spreadsheet to paper.

TIP

If your spreadsheet contains one or more charts along with data, you can print just the charts by unchecking every option in the **Print** section except the **Charts** option.

Requests Grid Printing ——

Requests That Notes Print

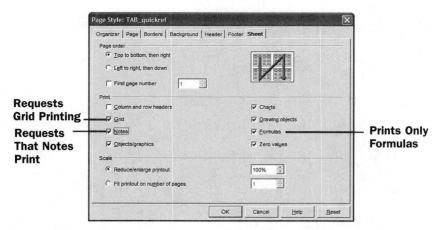

Prints Only Formulas

The Sheet page specifies how you want your spreadsheet to print.

Normally, the gridlines that separate cells are suppressed during printing, but to help with your row and column alignment when studying large spreadsheets, you may opt to select the **Grid** option so that Calc prints the gridlines to paper. In addition, Calc normally suppresses notes that you've attached to cells but will print those notes along with the rest of the spreadsheet if you click to select the **Notes** option.

The **Print** dialog box itself enables you to print only a selected range. If, for example, you wanted to print only certain rows in your spreadsheet, select those rows and then select **File, Print** from the menu. Click the **Print** dialog box's **Selection** option before clicking **OK** to start printing.

Prints Selected —
Range Only

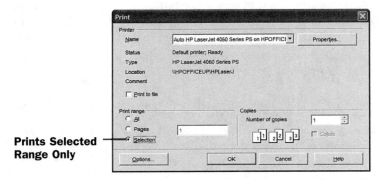

Calc can print only selected ranges if you wish.

10

Using Calc As a Simple Database

IN THIS CHAPTER:

🔍**KEY TERM**

Database—A collection of data that is often organized in rows and columns to make searching and sorting easy to do.

Although OpenOffice.org doesn't include a *database* program as complete (or as complex) as Microsoft Access, OpenOffice.org does support the use of Calc-based database tables from which you can store, edit, sort, and report from the data as though you were using a standalone database program.

Everyone trudges through a lot of data at work and at home. With the proliferation of computers, information overload seems to be the norm. A database program such as Calc enables you to organize your data and turn raw facts and figures into meaningful information. Calc processes data details so you can spend your valuable time analyzing results. Suppose that your company keeps thousands of parts in a Calc database, and you need to know exactly which part sold the most in Division 7 last April. Calc can supply the answer for you.

This chapter introduces you to the world of databases with Calc. The nature and use of databases are not difficult to master, but you must understand something about database design (see **74** About Calc Databases) before you can fully master Calc's capability to process database data.

74 About Calc Databases

Before You Begin

✔ **39** Create a New Spreadsheet

See Also

→ **75** Create a Calc Database

→ **76** Import Data into a Calc Database

NOTE

Calc's row-and-column format makes it a useful tool as a database program and as a spreadsheet program. The difference between the two is how you access, change, and sort the data in the spreadsheet.

Before using a database, you need to learn how a database management system organizes data. With Calc, you can create, organize, manage, and report from data stored in your Calc spreadsheet.

A database typically contains related data. In other words, you might create a home-office database with your household budget but keep another database to record your rare-book collection titles and their worth. In your household budget, you might track expenses, income, bills paid, and so forth, but that information does not overlap the book-collection database. Of course, if you buy a book, both databases might show the transaction, but the two databases would not overlap.

Technically, a database does not have to reside on a computer. Any place you store data in some organized format, such as a name and address directory, could be considered a database. In most cases, however, the term *database* is reserved for organized, computerized data.

When you design a database, consider its scope before you begin. Does your home business need an inventory system? Does your home business often need to locate a single sales contact from a large list of contacts? If so, a Calc database works well. Only you can decide whether the inventory and the sales contacts should be part of the same system or separate, unlinked systems. The database integration of inventory with the sales contacts requires much more work to design, but your business requirements might necessitate the integration. For example, you might need to track which customers bought certain products in the past.

To keep track of data, you can break down each database sheet into *records* and *fields*. A database's structure acts just like a Calc worksheet because the rows and columns in a worksheet match the records and fields in a database. This similarity between databases and spreadsheets is why Calc works well for simple database management.

In the following figure, the database's records are the sheet's rows, and the fields are the columns. This database is a simple checkbook-register database; you usually organize your checkbook register just as you would organize a computerized version of a checkbook, so you will have little problem mastering Calc's concepts of records and fields.

Five Records   **Six Fields**

Checkbook Register Database					
Date	Number	Description	Amount	Deposit	Balance
04/01/05		Starting Balance		904.11	$904.11
04/03/05	3432	Pearson Education	97.80		806.31
04/07/05	3433	Allied Cable TV	21.64		784.67
05/03/05	3434	West Highland Gas	52.02		732.65
05/15/05		North-End Job Payment		1,803.09	2,535.74

A database contains records and fields that associate to Calc's rows and columns.

NOTE

Not all database values relate to each other. Your company's loan records do not relate to your company's payroll, but both might reside in your company's accounting database. You probably would keep these in separate Calc spreadsheets, although for a small company, one spreadsheet with multiple sheets representing separate databases might be manageable.

KEY TERMS

Records—The rows in a database representing all the data for a single item. A single employee record would consist of one employee's data, such as employee number, first name, last name, address, birth date, hire date, and so on.

Fields—The columns in a database representing individual descriptions of the records. A field in an employee database might be the last name field or the hire date.

75 Create a Calc Database

Before You Begin

✔ **74** About Calc
Databases

See Also

→ **76** Import Data into a
Calc Database

NOTE

A field can consist of a calculated value that contains a formula based on other data in the record.

TIP

60 Center a Heading over Multiple Columns shows you how to center your database title in a wide column across the top of the fields.

NOTE

You can sort database records into many different orders. For example, you can sort a checkbook record into alphabetical order based on whom you wrote checks to. This, however, makes the calculated **Balance** field nonfunctional for that view of your data. Only when sorted by date would a calculated balance field be useful.

You already know how to create a Calc database if you know how to create a Calc spreadsheet. A database consists of records and fields (see **74** About Calc Databases), and a sheet inside a spreadsheet consists of rows and columns that perform the same purpose as records and fields when you type data into them.

Each field in your database must have a name. The simplest way to designate a field name is to type a label atop each column in your database. That label, such as **Address** or **DateHired**, becomes the name of that field. A field contains as many values as you have records in the database. For example, if your database has 100 rows, your database has 100 records, and each field in the record contains 100 values (some may be blank).

1 Type the Field Names

To create field names for your database, you only need to type a one-line label atop each column in your spreadsheet's database. First, label your spreadsheet with an appropriate title that describes the database you're creating.

2 Enter the Data

Type the data that falls beneath the field names. Reserve one row for each record in your database. Use the standard data-entry techniques you'd use for any spreadsheet (such as pressing **Tab** or **Enter** at the end of a value, and so on).

You may enter formulas if you wish. In a database that represents a checkbook register, for example, the **Balance** field (column) should be calculated and consist of a running total from your very first deposit that you used to set up the account in the first record.

3 Request a Data Range

Once you've entered some or all of your database records (you can always add more later), you must define a *data range* for the data so that Calc will know which rows and columns hold database data. Select your database rows and columns that will make up your database. If you include the column titles above each column, Calc makes those titles the field names that you can refer to later when accessing the database.

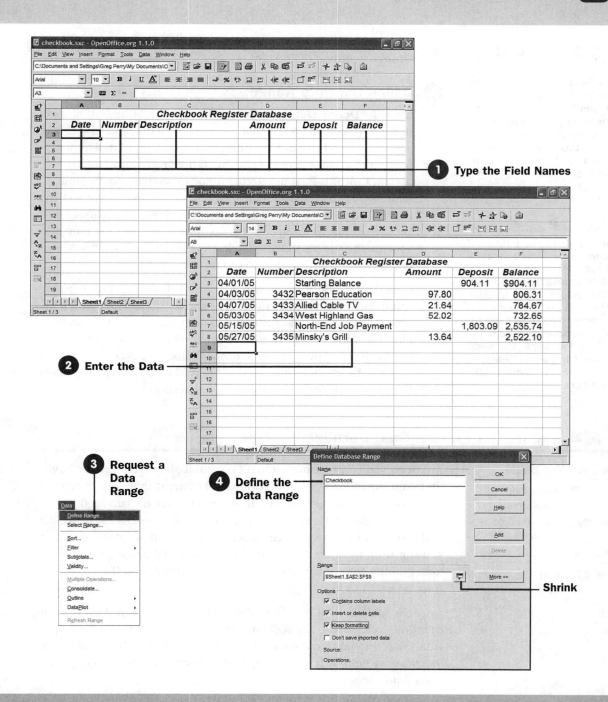

1 Type the Field Names

2 Enter the Data

3 Request a Data Range

4 Define the Data Range

Shrink

KEY TERM

Data range—A range you define that specifies exactly which rows and columns comprise the records and fields of your database. If you include column title cells, Calc makes those titles the field headings in your database.

TIP

If you plan to add data later to the database, click to check the **Insert or delete cells** option so that Calc automatically updates the data range when you append data to the end of it or remove rows from within the range. The **Keep formatting** option maintains the cell formats with the data.

Select **Data**, **Define Range** from the menu to display the **Define Database Range** dialog box.

④ Define the Data Range

Click the **Define Database Range** dialog box's **More** button to display extra options you'll often need to define the data range. If you've included column titles and you want Calc to make them field names, make sure to select the **Contains column labels** option. Calc fills in your selected range for you (using absolute addressing with the sheet name preceding the range), but you can change the range if you wish to. The **Shrink** button collapses the **Define Database Range** dialog box in case you want to look at your sheet once again without closing the dialog box (click **Shrink** again to restore the dialog box to its original size).

Click **Add** to add the data range to Calc's stored databases. You can define multiple data ranges per sheet, but generally you'll be able to track your data better if you keep each sheet a separate database range. If you ever want to remove a defined data range, display the **Define Database Range** dialog box once again but click the **Delete** button instead of the **Add** or **OK** button to remove the data range from Calc's database collection.

76 Import Data into a Calc Database

Before You Begin

✔ **74** About Calc Databases

✔ **75** Create a Calc Database

See Also

➔ **77** Sort Calc Database Data

Although you can type data into a Calc database, if you already have that data stored elsewhere, you can usually import that data directly into Calc by first saving the data in a format that Calc can read. For example, suppose your company uses an Access database for its records and you want to import the customer table into Calc's database so that you can work with the data more easily. You would first export that customer table's data in Excel's XLS spreadsheet format and then open that spreadsheet in Calc.

Once the table is open, you must define the data range and save the file as a Calc spreadsheet. See **72** **Import and Export Sheet Data** for help with importing non-Calc spreadsheets into Calc and **75** **Create a Calc Database** for help with converting your imported data to a Calc spreadsheet data range.

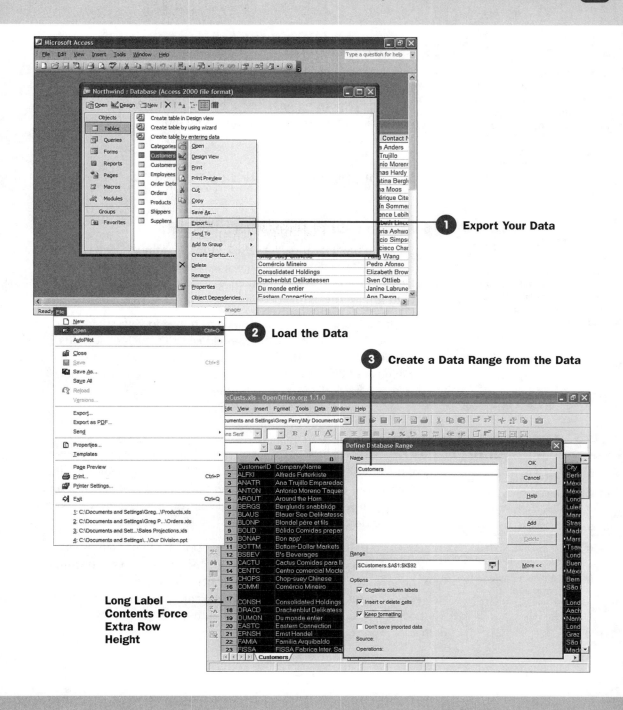

1 Export Your Data

2 Load the Data

3 Create a Data Range from the Data

Long Label
Contents Force
Extra Row
Height

1 Export Your Data

In Access, or wherever your data resides, export that data to an Excel spreadsheet. In Access, you can right-click over a table name, select the **Export** option, select the Excel XLS spreadsheet format, and click **Export All** to export the entire table.

2 Load the Data

Select **File**, **Open** and then select the exported data to load the data into Calc.

3 Create a Data Range from the Data

Select all the data including the column headings. Once you've selected all the data that is to reside in the database, select **Data**, **Define Range** to define the data as a data range and to name the data range. This name becomes your database name for this data.

Click **Add** to save the data range and return to your spreadsheet. If you don't perform any database-related tasks, such as sorting or filtering, you can work with the data just as you would any spreadsheet data. The data, when defined in a data range, however, is also available to you for analysis as a database.

Sort Calc Database Data

Before You Begin

✔ **76** Import Data into a Calc Database

See Also

→ **78** Filter Data That You Want to See

→ **79** Compute Table Totals and Subtotals

One of the reasons some people create a database data range from their spreadsheet data is to sort the data using Calc's database-related sorting tools. Once you set up the database, you can sort on amounts or text *ascending* or *descending*.

By sorting your data, you can often gain insights into it, such as where the top and bottom values lie, without having to resort to extra work to find those values (such as writing **Max()** or **Min()** functions in cells outside your database's data range). Also, you can print parts of the list in ZIP Code order as you might do when printing a list of names and addresses for a mailing.

1 Request the Sort

2 Specify Sort Criteria

3 Adjust Sorting Options

4 Check the Sort

KEY TERMS

Ascending—The sort method where lower values are sorted early in the list and higher values fall at the end of the list, as is the case with an alphabetical list of names.

Descending—The sort method where higher values are sorted early in the list and lower values fall at the end of the list, as would be the case where payroll amounts are sorted from highest to lowest.

NOTE

When you sort a data range, you sort on one or more fields (columns), but all the data in all the rows of the data range sort along with your key sorting fields.

TIP

You'll almost always want to keep the **Range contains column labels** option checked so that Calc does not consider your field names at the top of the columns to be part of the data that it sorts. Also, keeping **Include formats** selected ensures your sorted data remains formatted properly.

1 Request the Sort

Once you've defined the data range for the data you want to sort, select **Data**, **Sort** from the menu to display the **Sort** dialog box.

2 Specify Sort Criteria

Set up your sorting criteria by selecting a field name from the **Sort by** list box. The field names will be those fields you designated as field names (the labels atop the columns) when you created the data range.

You can select optional second and even third sort criteria by selecting a field name from the next two **Then by** list boxes. For example, if you sort initially by **City**, then by **CompanyName**, if two or more companies in your data range reside in the same city, the company names will be listed together and sorted alphabetically within that city's name, as long as you keep the **Ascending** options selected. If you change **Ascending** to **Descending** on any of the sort criteria field names, that criteria will sort from high to low instead of from low to high values.

3 Adjust Sorting Options

Click the **Options** tab to display the **Options** page in the **Sort** dialog box. The **Options** page enables you to adjust the way Calc sorts your data. You can make the sorts case sensitive so that lowercase letters are distinguished from (and considered to follow) uppercase letters. Therefore, eBay would follow Zsoft if you sort on company names. (Without the **Case sensitive** option checked, eBay would sort before Zsoft because eBay precedes Zsoft in the alphabet.)

If you specify a range after **Copy sort results to**, Calc will sort the data but place it at that range, keeping your original data range intact. Otherwise, Calc sorts your original data. The **Custom sort order** option enables you, if you've created a *custom sort list*, to change the way Calc sorts your data from the normal alphabetical or numerical order to an order based on a different ranking system you define.

Because Calc databases are almost always stored with the rows representing records and the columns representing fields, keep the option labeled **Top to bottom (sort rows)** selected so that Calc sorts all rows properly. If you select the **Left to right (sort columns)** option, Calc sorts an entire column's data before looking at the next column, which can really mess up your data unless your original data imported was transposed for some reason.

When you click the **OK** button, Calc sorts your data in the order you requested.

4 Check the Sort

Once Calc finishes the sort, check the data to ensure that Calc sorted properly. For example, if you sorted by **City** field, you would make sure that the **City** column appears in alphabetical order.

78 Filter Data That You Want to See

Databases can grow to be enormous. Without some way to filter the data, finding what you want is tedious. Calc's **Find and Replace** command works well enough to locate values that you want to find, but by being able to apply a filter to your database, you can actually hide data that does not currently interest you without removing that data from your database. When you're done with the filtered data, you can easily return to the full database view.

Calc supports two kinds of filters, both of which are related:

- *AutoFilter* filters, where you specify values to filter by

- Standard dialog box filters, where you can specify a range of values to filter by

1 Request a Standard Filter

Once you define your data range, you can request a filter by selecting **Data**, **Filter**, **Standard Filter**. Calc displays the **Standard Filter** dialog box.

1 Request a Standard Filter

2 Specify the Filter Criteria

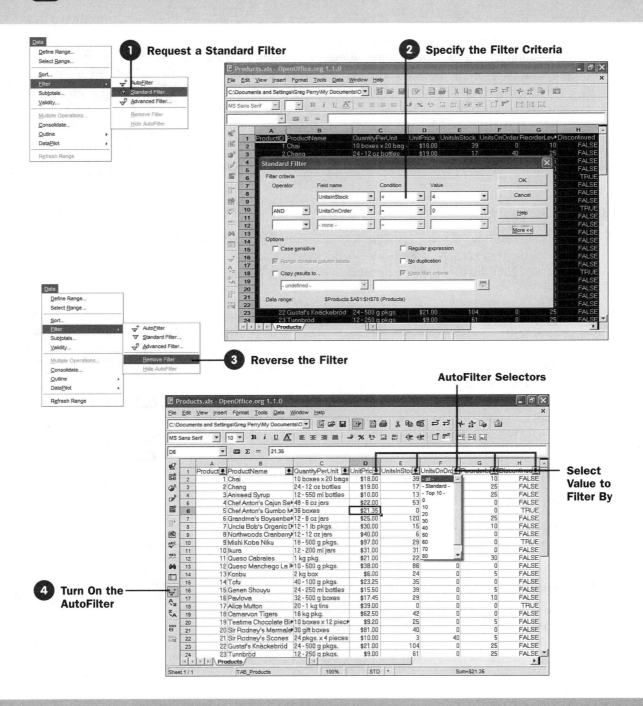

3 Reverse the Filter

AutoFilter Selectors

Select Value to Filter By

4 Turn On the AutoFilter

2 Specify the Filter Criteria

Select from the **Field Name** dialog box. All the fields defined by the data range's column names will appear when you open the **Field Name** list box. Select a condition in the **Condition** list box, such as an equal sign or less-than sign, and then enter a quantity (you can also click the **Value** list box's down arrow to see a list of possible values) stating what you want to filter by. For example, if you enter **UnitsInStock**, **<**, and **4**, you are requesting that you only want to see the database records whose **UnitsInStock** field contains four or fewer items.

You may add additional criteria to filter down your data even further by selecting **AND** or **OR** from the **Operator** column and entering second and even third criteria.

Click **OK** to apply the filter and view the results.

3 Reverse the Filter

To restore your data to its original state once you've viewed, printed, stored, or saved the filtered data, select **Data**, **Filter**, **Remove Filter** to remove the filter and return your complete data range to your spreadsheet.

4 Turn On the AutoFilter

To use the AutoFilter feature, select **Data**, **Filter**, **AutoFilter** (or click the **AutoFilter** button from the **Main** toolbar). Arrows appear to the right of each field name.

When you click one of the field name arrows, a list of values opens to display all possible unique values in that field, with scrollbars if needed to display the entire list. When you select any value in that list, Calc immediately filters on that value, displaying only those records that match that criteria. For example, if you click an inventory's **Discontinued** field and select **True**, only those discontinued items would appear in the filtered data that appears.

Once you create the filter, you can print, sort, save, or copy the filtered data and return to the full database by selecting **Data**, **Filter**, **AutoFilter** once again.

 TIP

Click the **More** button to see additional filter options, such as the ability to make your criteria case sensitive so a match is made against text fields only if the uppercase and lowercase letters match your criteria's uppercase and lowercase letters. Also, you can request that the filtered data be copied to a range you specify instead of the filtering taking place right in your data range itself.

TIP

For quick filters when you want to filter based on exact matches, use the AutoFilter feature, which is faster than displaying the **Standard Filter** dialog box every time you want to filter the database.

79 **Compute Table Totals and Subtotals**

Before You Begin

✔ **76** Import Data into a
 Calc Database

✔ **77** Sort Calc Database
 Data

✔ **78** Filter Data That
 You Want to See

NOTE

The 2nd Group and 3rd Group tabs are for performing statistical analysis, which you may want to do when you have multiple divisions in multiple areas, or countries, and want to group first by area, then by division, and then by an individual field, such as sales per customer. The resulting summarized groups would show a subtotal of each customer, then each division, and finally each area, with a grand total at the bottom.

When working with any kind of financial database information, the ability to calculate subtotals and totals, based on sorted data, becomes necessary. For example, you might want to see all the total sales from a given region or ZIP Code. If any sales are down in one area, you can get your Marketing Department to step up their efforts in that area.

Calc can summarize database data for you based on any of the following criteria:

- **Sum**—The added total of data

- **Count**—The number of items in the data range

- **Average**—The calculated intermediate value in a range of data

- **Min or max amounts**—The lowest or highest value in the data

- **Product**—The multiplied result of the data values

- **Standard deviation (of a sample or population)**—A statistic that measures how well dispersed values in a data range are

- **Variance (of a sample or population)**—The square of the standard deviation used for statistical measurements

1 Request the Summary Information

Click anywhere within the data range that you want to summarize. Select **Data**, **Subtotals** to open the **Subtotals** dialog box.

2 Specify Summary Criteria

The **Subtotals** dialog box opens with the **1st Group** tab displayed. This is where you specify the first grouping you want to see. Often, you'll select only one group, even though Calc supports up to four subtotal groups. Specify the **Group by** value (such as a date), followed by a selection of the field you want a subtotal for (such as **CustomerID**). You then must tell **Calc** how the subtotals are to be grouped, such as by **Count**. In this case, you are requesting a count of each customer's order, grouped by date. If a customer orders three times on one day, that customer's daily orders should appear together when you click **OK** to display the summary.

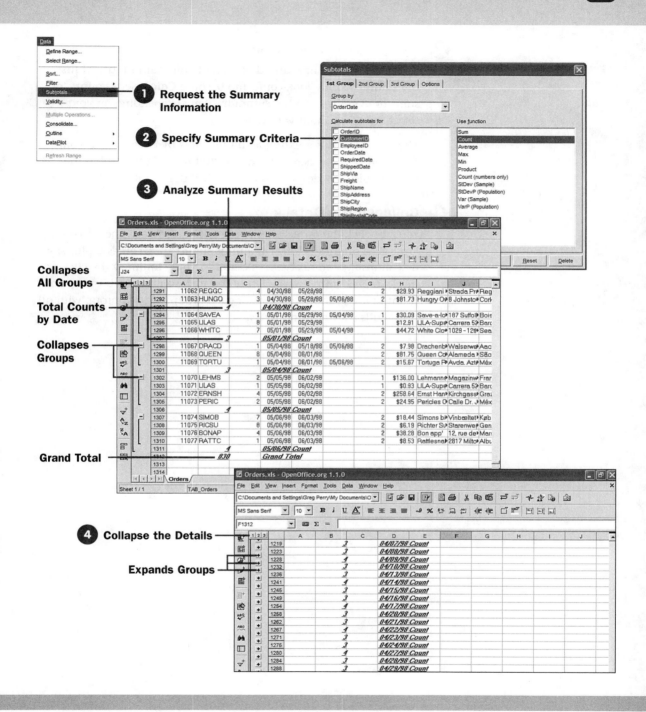

1 Request the Summary Information

2 Specify Summary Criteria

3 Analyze Summary Results

Collapses All Groups

Total Counts by Date

Collapses Groups

Grand Total

4 Collapse the Details

Expands Groups

3 Analyze Summary Results

Calc produces a summarized version of your data range. At first, the summary may look confusing because Calc inserts counts (or sums or averages or other summary items, depending on your selection) throughout your data.

The count totals, for example, might show by each date in your data how many orders you had on that date. At the end of the report, Calc provides a grand total of all the counts.

4 Collapse the Details

You can click the minus sign to the left of a row number to collapse that group's detail. The minus sign then becomes a plus sign. By collapsing various types of detail in your summary (by clicking the **1**, **2**, or **3** button to the left of the row number), you can get a count of the grand total only, of each group, of each group with all the details shown, respectively.

PART III

Impressing Audiences with Impress

IN THIS PART:

11

Learning About Impress

IN THIS CHAPTER:

KEY TERM

Presentation—A set of screens, called *pages* or *slides*, that you present to people in a room or over the Internet.

NOTE

Remember, the term *presentation* refers to an entire Impress collection of slides (or pages), whereas the term *slide* or *page* refers to an individual screen within that presentation. *Slide* is more common than *page* due to Microsoft Office PowerPoint's use of the slide terminology.

Have you wanted to wow your audiences with professional *presentations*? You can with Impress. This chapter introduces you to Impress. You'll soon be designing and creating effective presentations. By using the predefined presentation tools of Impress, you generate good-looking presentations without needing to worry about design, format, and color specifics. After Impress generates a sample presentation, you need only follow a few simple procedures if you want to modify and tweak the presentation into your own unique version.

The primary purpose of Impress is to help you design, create, and edit presentations and printed handouts. Because Impress provides a wide variety of predefined templates, you don't have to be a graphics design specialist to create good-looking presentations.

Impress slides can hold many kinds of information. Here are a few of the things you can add to an Impress presentation:

- Data you insert into Impress, including text, charts, graphs, and graphics

- Writer documents

- Live data from the Internet, including complete Web pages

- Calc worksheets

- Multimedia content such as video and sound files

- Graphics from graphics programs such as Draw

80 Set Impress Options

See Also

✔ **81** Create a New Presentation

✔ **83** Run a Presentation

 TIP

Even if you're familiar with Calc or another OpenOffice.org set of options, initially learning about Impress's options helps you see a preview of what Impress is able to do.

Not everybody works the same way, so not every Impress user wants to use Impress the same way. By setting some of Impress's many options, you will make Impress conform to the way you like to do things. For example, you may want Impress to create all new presentations using the AutoPilot guide (see **81** **Create a New Presentation**) or you might always want to begin with a completely empty presentation and add all the initial elements. The Impress options you set control these and many other Impress aspects.

As a matter of fact, Impress has an option for just about anything! Table 11.1 describes Impress's options. You'll learn a lot about what Impress can do just by looking through the option categories available to you.

1 Request Options

2 Change the Overall Options

3 Open the Presentation Category and Set General Options

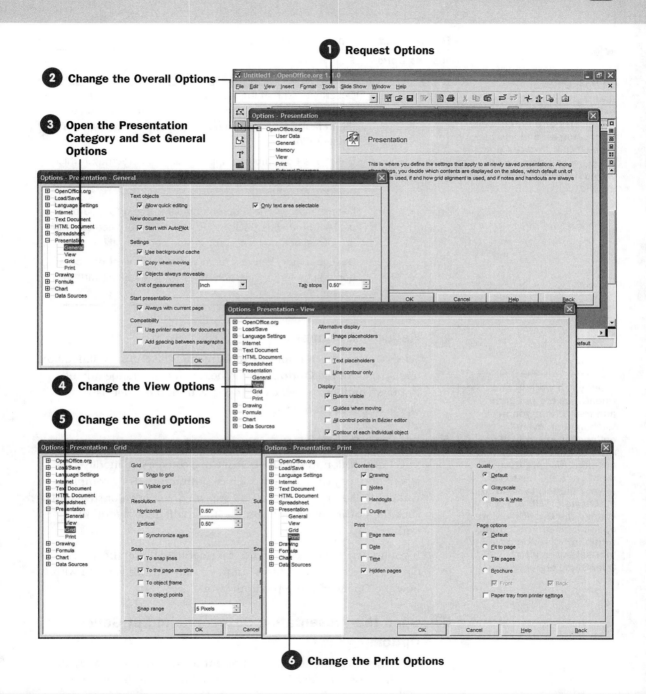

4 Change the View Options

5 Change the Grid Options

6 Change the Print Options

NOTE

All options are available for all OpenOffice.org programs at all times. For example, you can control the display of a grid in Calc from Impress, and you can request that Impress print the date and time on all pages of output from within Calc.

TABLE 11.1   Impress Presentation Options

Impress Option Category	Explanation
General	Describes general Impress settings, such as the initial use of AutoPilot when you create new presentations and sets the default unit of measurements for elements within a presentation.
View	Describes how Impress appears on the screen and which Impress special elements, such as rulers and text placeholders, are shown.
Grid	Determines whether Impress displays a grid for you on your presentation slide backgrounds to help you place elements on your slides more accurately and consistently.
Print	Describes how Impress handles the printing of presentations, such as printing presentation notes along with the presentation.

❶ Request Options

Select **Options** from Impress's **Tools** menu. The **Options** dialog box appears. From the **Options** dialog box, you can change any of Impress's options as well as the options from the other OpenOffice.org programs.

TIP

Often you'll work in one OpenOffice.org program and realize that you need to change an overall option. For example, if you want to print several kinds of OpenOffice.org documents to a file (instead of to your printer) to send to others via email, you can change the **OpenOffice.org** option labeled **Print**, from within Impress, to apply that setting to all OpenOffice.org programs.

❷ Change the Overall Options

Select any option in the **OpenOffice.org** category to modify OpenOffice.org-wide settings such as pathnames. For example, if you don't like the pathname you see when you open or save a file, click the **Paths** option and change it to a different default file path.

If you're new to OpenOffice.org, consider leaving all the OpenOffice.org options "as is" until you familiarize yourself with how the OpenOffice.org programs work.

❸ Open the Presentation Category and Set General Options

Click the plus sign next to the **Presentation** option to display the four Impress-specific options listed in Table 11.1 at the beginning of this task.

Click the **General** options category; the dialog box changes to show options you can select to make changes to the general Impress options. The **Text Objects** section enables you to specify how you wish to edit text objects inside your presentations—either quickly when they're available by clicking them or only after you click the **Option** bar's **Allow Quick Editing** button. The **New Document** section determines whether you want AutoPilot to start when you first create a new presentation. The **Settings** section describes how you want Impress to use its *background cache* when displaying objects in a presentation (without the cache, Impress runs more slowly, although on recent computers you'll hardly notice the difference). In addition, you can specify how you wish to handle copying and moving presentation objects, and you may also specify how you want to handle measurements and tab stops, such as in inches or metrically. The **Start Presentation** section determines whether you want Impress to jump to the most-recently edited slide or the first slide when you open a new presentation. The **Compatibility** section determines how you want Impress to handle the printing and paragraph-spacing capabilities of Impress.

KEY TERM

Background cache—A memory area that Impress can use to speed some operations. Instead of waiting for Impress to load all objects needed in a presentation from the disk drive, you can have Impress preload certain presentation objects into the background cache memory area so those objects more rapidly appear when it becomes time for them to display.

4 Change the View Options

Click the **View** options category under the **Presentation** category; the dialog box changes to show options that handle Impress's onscreen display. The **Alternative display** section determines how and when Impress shows slide elements such as text and images. If you choose to show *placeholders* only, Impress will not display actual text and graphics but rather will show placeholders for them to speed your screen's display. During the editing of a large presentation, you can often speed up the editing process by electing to show placeholders instead of actual text and graphics. When running your presentation for others, of course, Impress will show the actual text and graphics during the presentation. The **Display** section determines how special elements such as the rulers are to show while you work within Impress.

KEY TERM

Placeholders—Fast-loading logos that take the place of slower-loading graphic images and long spans of text.

5 Change the Grid Options

Click to select the **Grid** category under the **Presentation** option category. The **Grid** section allows you to determine whether you wish to use the snap-to grid and whether to make the grid visible.

KEY TERMS

X-axis—The horizontal axis on a slide (or drawing) with the lower-left corner of your slide having an X-axis value of 0 and increasing as you move up the slide.

Y-axis—The vertical axis on a slide (or drawing) with the lower-left corner of your slide having a Y-axis value of 0 and increasing as you move to the right on the slide.

TIP

If you are new to spreadsheets, perhaps it's best to accept Impress's default option settings. Read through them now to familiarize yourself with Impress terminology, however. Once you've created some presentations, you'll better understand how these options impact your work.

The **Resolution** section specifies the width between each grid point measurement (decrease the width for detailed slides). If you click to check the **Synchronize axes** option, when you change the *X-axis*, the *Y-axis* adjusts symmetrically at the same time, instead of changes to one axis not affecting the other. The **Snap** section allows you to determine how you want to use the snap-to grid to align objects. If you plan to produce many freeform presentation slides, you'll want to turn off all snap-to items. If you create commercial presentations, such as for business meetings, advertisements, and education classes, that show relationships and textual backgrounds and layouts, you may wish to require that some objects move toward the closest snap-to grid for consistency and alignment of objects.

6 Change the Print Options

Click to select the **Print** category under the **Presentation** option category. The **Quality** section allows you to determine whether you want your slides printed in the default screen colors, in a more efficient grayscale, or in black and white (both printed without colors, thus saving color printer ink and toner). The **Print** section specifies what you want printed, such as the page name (if you've assigned one), date, time, and pages you've hidden within the presentation but may want to print. The **Page options** section allows you to determine how you want your presentations to fit the final page—whether they take up the actual size specified by the ruler on your drawing or whether you want Impress to shrink the slides enough to fit on the current page. You can also specify whether you want to print on the front and back of the page as well as use the printer's own paper tray settings instead of the default settings.

---

81 Create a New Presentation

Before You Begin

✔ **80** Set Impress Options

See Also

→ **82** Open an Existing Presentation

→ **83** Run a Presentation

You'll almost always begin a new presentation the same way—you'll start Impress, follow the AutoPilot guide, and build an initial but empty presentation. Perhaps you'll build an empty presentation based on a template supplied with Impress or from a template you built before and saved for reuse.

The creation of a presentation does take two steps:

1. Build your initial presentation with AutoPilot.

2. Fill in details by designing each slide inside the presentation.

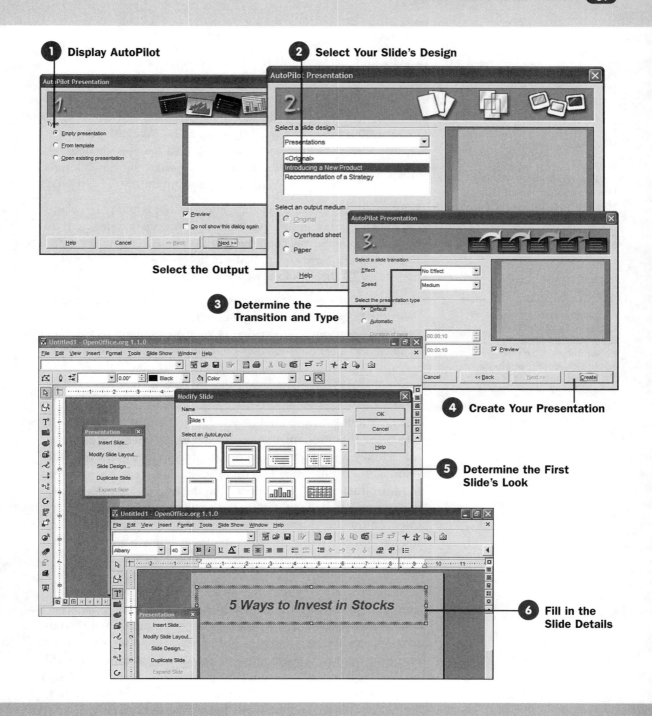

1 Display AutoPilot

2 Select Your Slide's Design

Select the Output

3 Determine the Transition and Type

4 Create Your Presentation

5 Determine the First Slide's Look

6 Fill in the Slide Details

5 Ways to Invest in Stocks

TIP

Plan your presentations! Think about your target audience. Presenting identical information to two audiences might require completely different approaches. A company's annual meeting for shareholders requires a different format, perhaps, from the board of director's meeting. After determining your target audience, create a slide outline before you begin.

TIP

Although most Impress users prefer AutoPilot's help, you can click the option labeled **Do not show this dialog again** on the initial **AutoPilot Presentation** dialog box to keep AutoPilot from running automatically the next time you start Impress.

In other words, you'll create an overall presentation that forms a collection of slides and then you'll work on the individual slides.

① Display AutoPilot

Select **Impress** from your Windows menu by selecting **Presentation** from the **OpenOffice.org** menu. Assuming the default AutoPilot setting is in effect (see **80** **Set Impress Options**), the **AutoPilot Presentation** dialog box appears. You can follow the dialog box's steps to create your presentation.

You can elect to create a new presentation that is empty by selecting the **Empty presentation** option, you can create a presentation from a template by selecting the **From template** option (see **85** **Use an Impress Template**), or you can open an existing presentation (see **82** **Open an Existing Presentation**).

If starting a new presentation from scratch, you would click to select the **Empty presentation** option. Keep the **Preview** option checked so you can see a preview of your presentation as you build it. To continue creating the new presentation, click the **Next** button.

② Select Your Slide's Design

The next AutoPilot step enables you to select your slide's design. By selecting either **Presentations** or **Presentation Backgrounds**, you are actually selecting from a short list of templates that come with Impress. For example, by selecting **Presentations** and then selecting **Introducing a New Product** from the list that appears below, you inform AutoPilot that you want to create a new presentation based on the stored template for introducing a new product. Even though you may have elected to create an empty presentation in step 1, Impress still offers these templates from which you can choose. The templates provide background colors and some default slide effects, but in reality, the templates are not that impressive... even though they belong to Impress! Impress does not come presupplied with scores of sample template presentations, only a couple. If you're just beginning to use Impress, you might want to use one of these AutoPilot template guides to create your first presentation so you won't have to supply as many color, screen, and design elements as you would if you began with a completely blank presentation. Having said that, if you select <**Original**>, Impress creates a blank presentation without any background color or assumptions of any kind because Impress won't use a template to begin your presentation. **85** **Use an Impress Template** explains more about the templates that you can use and create with Impress.

Generally, you'll be creating a presentation for the screen. For example, if you plan to give your presentation as a speech, you might display your presentation from a laptop's projection system to a large screen that the audience can follow. Rarely will you want to create a presentation for printed paper only. So unless you plan to present your presentation on a medium other than a screen, leave the **Screen** option checked. Click **Next** to move to the next AutoPilot screen.

3 Determine the Transition and Type

You now can select the kind of *transition* you want Impress to make as your presentation moves from slide to slide. If you leave **Effect** at its default setting of **No Effect**, Impress simply replaces each slide with the next as you move forward in your presentation. The **Speed** option determines the transitional speed. You can always change the speed later, so generally, unless you're familiar with the transition speeds, you should leave the default speed (**Medium**) as is until you see whether you need a faster or slower setting.

Your presentation type might be an automatic slide show, as might be the case if you want to set up your presentation in a kiosk-style setting where your presentation plays by itself. You might prefer an automatic presentation for a sales screen that advertises products as customers walk by. If you want an automatic presentation such as this, adjust the duration settings that determine how long each slide page remains on the screen and how long you want Impress to pause between presentations before repeating the presentation once again. See **100** **Make an Automatic Presentation** for help with creating and presenting automatic presentations.

For presentations you give and control yourself, leave the presentation type set to **Default** so that you control when each slide changes to the next as you give your presentation.

NOTE

If you plan to print your presentation for audience handouts, even though you will be giving the presentation on the screen during your talk, keep the **Screen** option selected. You can always print a screen-based presentation to paper without rerunning AutoPilot.

KEY TERM

Transition—The way one slide leaves the presentation screen and the next slide appears. You can select from a variety of Impress transitional effects, such as fading from one slide to another or having the new slide fly in from the side or from the top, overwriting the previous slide.

AutoLayout—A pre-designed slide layout for Impress presentation slides. Some AutoLayouts contain both text and graphics, whereas others are more suitable for title screens with large titles or for charts with very little to no text.

NOTE

Be sure to save your presentation when you finish building it. Even better, save your presentation after you complete each slide to ensure that the presentation is safely stored on your disk drive in case your computer has a problem of some kind and you must reboot. Impress presentation files use the .sxi filename extension.

4 Create Your Presentation

When you're ready to create the presentation, click the **Create** button.

5 Determine the First Slide's Look

Once AutoPilot ends, your presentation is far from over! What you accomplished with AutoPilot is creating the backgrounds, default transitions, and time durations of your overall presentation. Not one slide is finished yet because you have yet to add text or graphics to any slide. Actually, only one slide even exists—the very first one. Your job is to determine the kind of slide you want to modify the first default slide into by selecting an *AutoLayout* from the **Modify Slide** dialog box.

Click to select an AutoLayout slide and then click **OK**. Impress changes the first slide in your presentation to the AutoLayout format so that you can continue filling in the details and continue inserting new slides until you finish the presentation.

6 Fill in the Slide Details

AutoLayout slides provide you with placeholders for text and sometimes for graphics and charts. To add text, click a placeholder and replace the placeholder text with your own text. You'll continue inserting new slides, modifying the new slides by selecting an AutoLayout for them, and filling in their details as you build your presentation.

82 Open an Existing Presentation

Before You Begin

✔ **80** Set Impress Options

✔ **81** Create a New Presentation

See Also

→ **83** Run a Presentation

When you open a document in most programs, such as Writer or Calc, you usually start the program and then select **File**, **Open** from the menu. Opening a presentation from within Impress usually differs somewhat due to the importance of AutoPilot and its appearance every time you start Impress.

The opening **AutoPilot** dialog box gives you the option to open an existing presentation instead of creating a new presentation. If you want to open an existing presentation, Impress's **AutoPilot** dialog box helps by displaying a list of presentation files from which you can choose.

Remember that Impress presentations use the `.sxi` filename extension, and all filenames with that extension in the **detail** folder displays for you to choose from when you want to open an existing presentation.

❶ Request a Presentation

Select **Presentation** from the **OpenOffice.org** Windows menu. Impress opens the **AutoPilot** dialog box from which you can start a new presentation or, in this case, select an existing presentation. Click the option labeled **Open existing presentation** to see a list of presentations in your default folder.

Impress lists any Impress presentations you have in your folder by name, and it lists any PowerPoint presentations that might exist in your folder with the cryptic **PowerPoint Presentation** title. It's obvious (as long as you gave your presentations meaningful names) what the Impress presentations are because you see their filenames. Fortunately, Impress also gives you a way to see a graphic preview of any presentation, whether it's an Impress or a PowerPoint presentation. Just click to select any presentation in the list, and Impress shows a preview of the presentation's first slide in the dialog box's preview area.

Although you would think Impress would give you an **Open** button, instead you must click the **Create** button to open your selected presentation.

❷ Edit or Run the Newly Opened Presentation

Once Impress loads the presentation, you are free to run or edit it.

❸ Open Another Presentation

Once inside Impress, if you want to open a second presentation, select **File**, **Open** from the menu. Impress displays the **Open** dialog box from which you can select a presentation to open.

❹ Select a Presentation

From the **Open** dialog box, select the presentation you wish to open and click the **Open** button. Impress opens the presentation, and you can edit or run the presentation.

🔖 NOTE

Obviously, if you've turned off the option to begin with AutoPilot (see **80** **Set Impress Options**), Impress starts without AutoPilot. Whenever you're inside Impress and want to open an existing presentation, you do use the **File, Open** menu command to open an existing presentation.

🔖 NOTE

Microsoft PowerPoint uses the `.ppt` file extension, and PowerPoint presentations appear when you open presentations from within Impress.

💡 TIP

You can browse to a different folder to find a presentation by double-clicking **<Other position>** and selecting a file from the **Open** dialog box that appears.

💡 TIP

If you want to close your existing presentation before opening another one, select **File, Close** to do so. If you've made changes since you last saved the presentation, Impress gives you the opportunity to save the presentation before closing it.

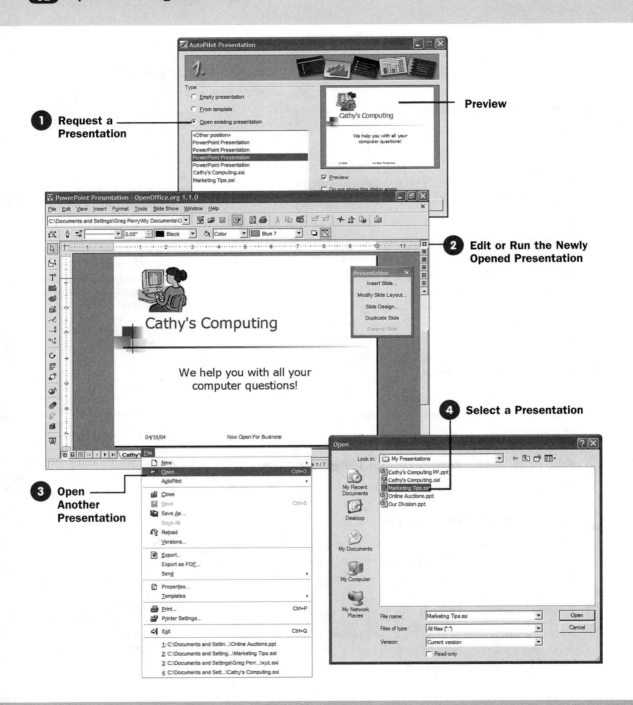

1 Request a Presentation

Preview

2 Edit or Run the Newly Opened Presentation

4 Select a Presentation

3 Open Another Presentation

83 Run a Presentation

Unlike a Writer document or a Calc spreadsheet or a Draw drawing, your Impress presentation is active from the beginning. That is, your presentation is meant to move, from slide to slide, from beginning to end, and possibly back and forth, depending on the exact order you desire.

Therefore, your audience doesn't just read a static document or spreadsheet when they view your presentation. When you want to show your audience an Impress presentation, you *run* the presentation. In Impress terminology, when you run a presentation, you show your audience a *slide show*.

You'll want to master some common presentation-controlling keystrokes before you give a presentation. When you master these keystrokes, you'll be able to step through your presentation, jump around the presentation, and control the entire presentation live. Table 11.2 lists the keystrokes you should know before running your presentation.

TABLE 11.2 Using the Keyboard to Navigate Through Presentations

Press This Key...	To Move...
+ (plus sign)	Into your presentation (useful for showing a close-up of small text and pictures)
- (minus sign)	Out of your presentation (useful for showing an overview of your information before you zoom in)
PageDown	Forward through your presentation one slide each time you press PageDown
PageUp	Backward through your presentation one slide each time you press PageUp
Home	To the first slide in your presentation
End	To the last slide in your presentation

1 Open Your Presentation

Select **File**, **Open** from the menu and select the presentation you want to run.

Before You Begin

✔ **81** Create a New Presentation

✔ **82** Open an Existing Presentation

See Also

→ **84** Print a Presentation

KEY TERMS

Run—The act of showing your Impress presentation to an audience so the presentation moves from slide to slide.

Slide show—Your running presentation, given this name due to its slide-by-slide format.

TIP

If you use your mouse pointer in your presentation, it's simple to move forward one slide at a time by clicking anywhere on your slide with your left mouse button.

1 Open Your Presentation

2 Start Your Presentation as a Slide Show

3 Specify Slide Show Settings

4 Start Your Show

Navigator

Cathy's Computing

We help you with all your computer questions!

04/19/04   Now Open For Business   1

② Start Your Presentation as a Slide Show

You now can select **Slide Show**, **Slide Show Settings** from the menu to prepare for your presentation. Impress displays the dialog box.

③ Specify Slide Show Settings

Many of your **Slide Show** dialog box settings are determined when you create your presentation, although you can always change them here at the **Slide Show** dialog box. You'll be able to select all or just a range of slides (from the **From** list box) as well as determine how your slide show will display (either in the default full-screen mode or in a smaller window). You can display the OpenOffice.org logo (assuming you'd want to do that) by clicking the **Show logo** option. Also, you can set the pause time between presentations that show from the **Auto** option.

For example, if the **Change slides manually** option is unchecked, you originally created this presentation to display automatically, without intervention. If you're speaking and using the presentation to support your speech, you'll probably not want the automatic changing of slides that occurs. Instead, you will want to move from slide to slide when you're ready to do so. If your audience has questions along the way or if you decide to cover a topic longer than you originally planned, you need full control over your presentation. So in such a case, ensure that **Change slides manually** is checked.

Once you've set the options that suit your current presentation, click the **OK** button to close the **Slide Show** dialog box.

④ Start Your Show

To start your slide show, select **Slide Show** from the **Slide Show** menu (or press **F9**) when you're ready to begin your presentation.

 TIP

Most presentations are given in front of an audience, often from a laptop plugged into an overhead projector. Walk through this task of running your presentation before your audience arrives to ensure that you have the overhead connected properly to your laptop.

TIP

Most presenters prefer to keep their mouse pointer showing during a presentation, although the **Mouse pointer visible** option can hide your mouse pointer if you wish. During your presentation, you can use your mouse pointer to point out items of interest to your audience.

TIP

Using the **Navigator visible** option, you can display the **Navigator** dialog box during your presentation so you can more easily navigate between pages and graphic elements instead of moving sequentially through your slide show.

84 Print a Presentation

Before You Begin

✔ **81** Create a New Presentation

✔ **82** Open an Existing Presentation

See Also

→ **93** Change a Presentation's Background

 TIP

If you want a preview of a simple printed copy of your presentation, one slide per printed page, just press **F9** and page through your presentation. You are, in effect, seeing a preview of what will appear on the printed page.

 TIP

By selecting multiple **Contents** options, Impress prints everything sequentially. For example, you might want to print notes, handouts, and the outline at once.

Unlike the other OpenOffice.org programs, such as Writer, Calc, and Draw, Impress offers no print preview. You cannot see a print preview of a presentation due to the slide-by-slide nature of presentations.

Although you learn some about Impress printing options in **80** Set **Impress Options**, it's critical to delve into the things you may want to print through Impress. In other words, Impress was not designed to be printed but presented. Having said that, you'll still make use of the printer on occasion with Impress as you see here.

1 **Request the Print Dialog Box**

Select **File**, **Print** from the menu.

2 **Request Print Options**

Click the **Options** button to display the **Printer Options** dialog box.

3 **Specify Printer Options**

Until now, setting up print options is routine and the same as the other OpenOffice.org programs. You now are at the place, at the **Printer Options** dialog box, where you determine the Impress settings you need.

The **Contents** area determines what you want to print. In today's modern world of fast, low-cost color printers, printing both graphics and text isn't as big of a deal, and your audience will appreciate it very much if you print a copy of your presentation to hand out. They will be able to concentrate on your speech and not worry about taking copious notes. Click to select the **Handouts** option to print multiple slides on one page. Your audience will be able to read the slides, but you won't waste as much paper as you would if you printed one slide per page. **102** **Create Presentation Handouts** explains how to produce effective audience handouts.

You may want to print only your speaker's notes by clicking to select the **Notes** option (see **101** **Add Notes to a Presentation**). The notes will print beneath the slides you've attached them to. You might choose to print your presentation's outline. To do that, click to select the **Outline** option.

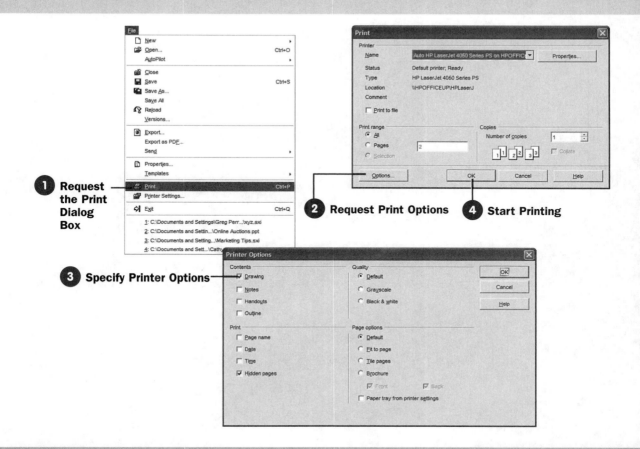

1 Request the Print Dialog Box

2 Request Print Options

3 Specify Printer Options

4 Start Printing

If you're printing a large presentation, you might want to save some color ink by printing a grayscale or black-and-white version of your presentation for your audience. Use the **Grayscale** and **Black & white** options in the **Print** dialog box to print using only black ink.

The **Print** section determines whether the date and time appear as well as whether you want to print slides you've set up as hidden. Click **OK** to close the **Print Options** dialog box.

4 **Start Printing**

Click the **Print** dialog box's **OK** button when you're ready to begin printing.

TIP

Hidden pages are great for notes to yourself as you develop your presentation, but you usually don't keep them around once you've handled them. You can also use hidden pages for different audiences, unhiding certain pages for audiences those pages were designed for and hiding them for other audiences.

12

Adding Flair to Your Presentations

IN THIS CHAPTER:

NOTE

Not only will too much text be difficult to read, presentation slides aren't designed to convey lots of textual information. That's your job as the presenter! Design your presentation to support and enhance the message you convey as you give your presentation.

When you first learn Impress, you should get a general overview of what presentations are all about and how to create them. Chapter 11, "Learning About Impress," covers all those topics, and if you have not ever worked with Impress, you may want to review the tasks in that chapter.

This chapter covers details, such as how to add text to your presentation slides. No matter how graphical you want your presentation to be, the presentation's words are what usually convey your information to your audience. You must enter and format text on the slides in a way that informs your audience without overwhelming them.

85 Use an Impress Template

Before You Begin

✔ **81** Create a New Presentation

✔ **83** Run a Presentation

See Also

→ **89** Format Presentation Text

NOTE

If you want to create your own Impress template, create the presentation skeleton to use as your template and save the presentation using **File**, **Save As** and select **OpenOffice.org Presentation Template** (**.sti**) as the file type. All Impress templates use the filename extension .sti.

When you use a template as a model for a presentation, you have to do less work because the template already has the backgrounds and slide information arranged for the initial presentation. Impress does not come fully loaded with lots of presentation templates. Actually, Impress only comes loaded with two templates—one named **Introducing a New Product** and another named **Recommendation of a Strategy**. Surprisingly, these are extremely limited, but they do get you started with templates you can use for your own presentations.

Creating a presentation using templates requires little more than selecting a few options using AutoPilot when you first start Impress.

 Select a Template

Select **Presentation** from the **OpenOffice.org** option of your Windows Start menu to start AutoPilot. Click to select the **From template** option. When you do, Impress lists the Impress templates available to you. As long as you've checked the **Preview** option, a preview image of the template appears in AutoPilot's preview area.

Select the template you want to use as the basis for your presentation and click **Next** to move to the next AutoPilot page.

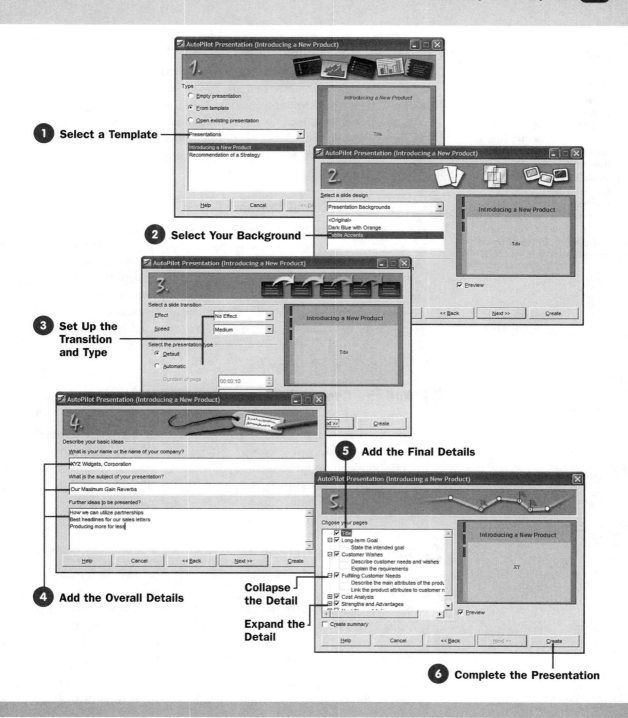

1 Select a Template

2 Select Your Background

3 Set Up the Transition and Type

4 Add the Overall Details

5 Add the Final Details

Collapse the Detail

Expand the Detail

6 Complete the Presentation

NOTE

If you're preparing a presentation for overhead slides, paper only, a computer screen (as opposed to an overhead projector), or to be placed on 35mm slides, select the appropriate option from the section titled **Select an output medium**. Often, these media produce the same presentation anyway, so you might want to start with the default **Original** option and change it if needed.

② Select Your Background

Select from the available backgrounds. Choose a background that will not overwhelm your audience. (With only two backgrounds available for your initial Impress installation, you don't have a lot to choose from.) Click to select the background you desire, and you can see that background's effect in the preview area. Click **Next** to move to the next AutoPilot page to continue selecting items from the template's available collection.

③ Set Up the Transition and Type

Select the kind of transition effect you want to apply to your slides as they change throughout your presentation and the speed at which you want the change to occur when one slide changes to another. If you want to create an automatic presentation, select the **Automatic** option and set the page duration and length of pause between presentations. **⑩⓪ Make an Automatic Presentation** explains how to create and present an automated presentation. If you're giving the presentation, leave the **Default** option selected. Click **Next** to move to the next **AutoPilot** page.

④ Add the Overall Details

In the fourth AutoPilot screen, Impress requests that you enter information that Impress will place throughout your presentation. You'll enter your company name, the subject of your presentation, and some additional ideas that you want to cover in the presentation. Impress scatters these details at appropriate places in the presentation it generates, based on the template's design. Click **Next** to move to the final **AutoPilot** page.

⑤ Add the Final Details

In the final **AutoPilot** page, Impress offers a list of details that you may or may not want in your presentation. The list changes depending on which of the two templates you chose when you first started the presentation. The new product details relate to the introduction of a new product, and the strategy template details relate to introducing a new strategy into your company plans.

Click the plus sign next to each group to see the details in that group. For example, you would click the plus next to **Fulfilling**

Customer Needs to see the two lines that will appear at that point in the presentation. Although the details are general, you'll be able to change them to your company's specific details once Impress generates your initial presentation.

Initially, all groups are selected (indicated by a check mark), but you can click to uncheck any group that you don't want to appear in your presentation. For instance, you may not want to discuss cost analysis in this presentation; if not, uncheck the group labeled **Cost Analysis** so that Impress won't include that group in this presentation.

6 Complete the Presentation

Click the **Create** button to generate the presentation based on the information you supplied as you went through the AutoPilot screens. Once Impress generates the presentation, you can change the general details to those that match your specific company needs. For example, you would replace the template-produced text that reads **Compare quality and price with those of the competition** with your own specifics in that area. You can also add and remove slides throughout the presentation, depending on your specific needs. The template did its job by designing a general presentation that you now can make specific.

NOTE

The first slide that Impress generates from the template will show your company name, presentation subject, and further ideas to be presented based on your answers in the fourth AutoPilot step.

---

86 About Impress Views

Views become important in Impress due to the nature of presentations. Impress supports the following views:

- **Drawing view**—Shows one slide at a time, allowing you to edit the slide and page back and forth among other slides. The Drawing view is the one you'll work in most often while building and editing your presentation.

- **Outline view**—Shows the title and secondary text of slides. You can easily and quickly scroll through your presentation, looking through the text. As you click any text, that text's slide shows in a preview window.

Before You Begin

✔ **82** Open an Existing Presentation

See Also

➔ **87** Enter Text into a Presentation

➔ **95** Insert Graphics into a Presentation

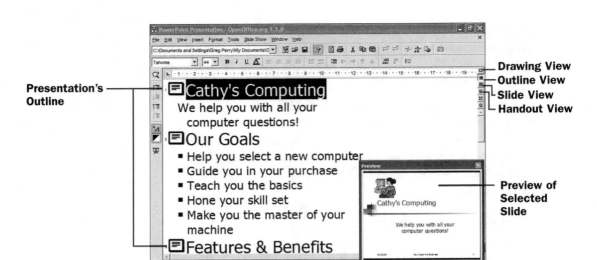

Presentation's Outline

Drawing View
Outline View
Slide View
Handout View

Preview of Selected Slide

The Outline view shows text from several slides at once, previewing the selected text's slide.

- **Slides view**—Shows multiple slides in a thumbnail form so that you can get a general overview of your slides, as many as 12 or more at a time. Depending on your monitor, you can probably make out most of the text and graphics on each slide. When you click to select a slide, that slide appears in a preview window so you can see more of that slide's detail. You can drag any slide from one location in your presentation to another while viewing the slides, making it simple to rearrange your presentation.

- **Notes view**—When you add speaker notes to your slides, you can view those notes, along with the slides the notes go with, in the Notes view. The notes appear at the bottom of the slide, with one slide and its notes showing at a time as you move through your presentation with **PageUp** and **PageDown**. See **101** **Add Notes to a Presentation** for help with adding notes.

- **Handout view**—If you want to print your presentation as a handout for your audience (see **84** **Print a Presentation** and **102** **Create Presentation Handouts**), you can get a preview of the presentation handout by displaying the **Handout** view. The **Handout** view shows four slides per page.

TIP

You can click the preview window's **Close** button to close the preview window and make more room for the slides. Select **View**, **Preview** to display the slide preview once again.

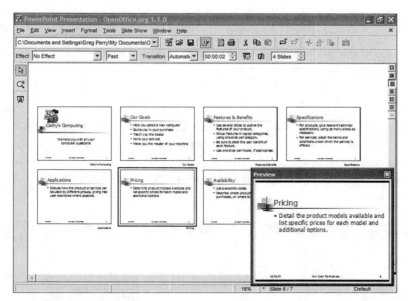

The Slides view shows several slides at once, allowing you to rearrange your presentation by dragging slides from one place to another.

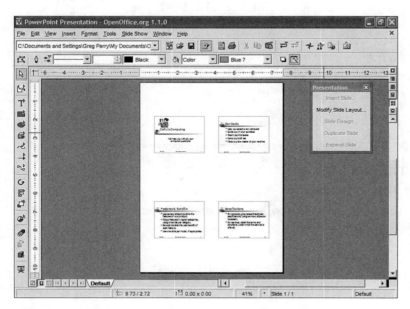

The Handout view shows how your audience's printed presentation will appear on each printed page.

NOTE

With four slides per page, your audience will be able to read your slides on their handouts, yet you use far less paper than if Impress printed one slide per page.

KEY TERM

Master slide—Also called a *master page* and refers to a page that determines the background and formatting styles in the current presentation. If you change the master slide, you change the entire presentation's format.

To change from view to view, select **View**, **Workspace** and then select the view you want to work with. You can also display the appropriate view by clicking the view's matching buttons on your vertical scrollbar. For example, if you're viewing notes inside the **Notes** view, you can return to the **Drawing** view to make edits more easily to your slide by clicking the vertical scrollbar's **Drawing view** button.

The buttons **Slide view**, **Master view**, and **Layer view** appear in your slide's lower-left corner. Generally, you'll work in the Slide view, but if you want to see a different view of the current slide, you can click another button. If you click the **Master view** button, Impress shows you the *master slide*.

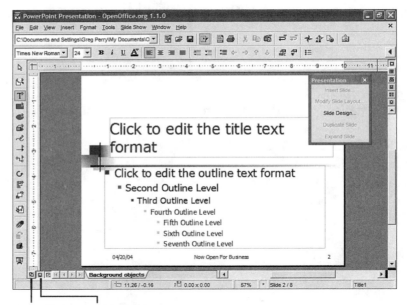

Slide View   Master View

The Master view shows you the contents of the master slide.

87 Enter Text into a Presentation

Generally, you'll add text and edit your slides in Drawing view and with the **Slide view** button selected at the bottom of your Impress screen. (**86** **About Impress Views** discusses both the Drawing view and the **Slide view** button.) You can make edits directly on the slide and see the results of those edits as you make them.

First, you must insert a new slide in your presentation. The new slide will hold the text you want to type. The format of the new slide determines how your text appears and whether graphics might appear with the text. When you want to edit some text, you'll actually be editing text within a text box that lies on a slide. To edit text in a text box, click that text box to activate the text box and to place the text cursor inside it.

Impress displays the text box surrounded by sizing handles. Impress treats a slide's title as a single object and the slide's bulleted set of items as another object. Both of these objects are text objects, and they will appear inside an editable text box when you click them.

1 **Request a New Slide**

To insert a brand new slide, click the **Insert Slide** button from the **Presentation** window. If you don't see the **Presentation** window, you can display it by selecting **View**, **Toolbars**, **Presentation**. The **Insert Slide** dialog box appears.

2 **Select the Type of Slide**

You must select the kind of slide you want to insert into your presentation at the current location. If you want to insert a slide with text and no graphics, you would select either the blank slide or one of the title slides in the window.

A new slide appears when you select a slide layout and click the **OK** button. Placeholders will let you know where text is expected.

3 **Add Text to the Slide**

Click any placeholder. If the placeholder rests in a title area, you'll be able to add a title to the slide. If the placeholder resides in an outline area, you will be able to add multiple lines of bulleted text to that area.

Before You Begin

✔ **81** Create a New Presentation

See Also

→ **89** Format Presentation Text

NOTE

If you've inserted an element other than text onto the slide, such as graphic image, sound, or video clip, you can click that object and move, edit, or delete it as well.

NOTE

The **Insert Slide** dialog box presents a series of available slides defined by an AutoLayout format Impress supplies for you.

TIP

You can request that the current date or time appear anywhere on a slide by selecting **Insert**, **Field** and selecting the **Date** or **Time** option. When you run your presentation, the current date or time appears at that location.

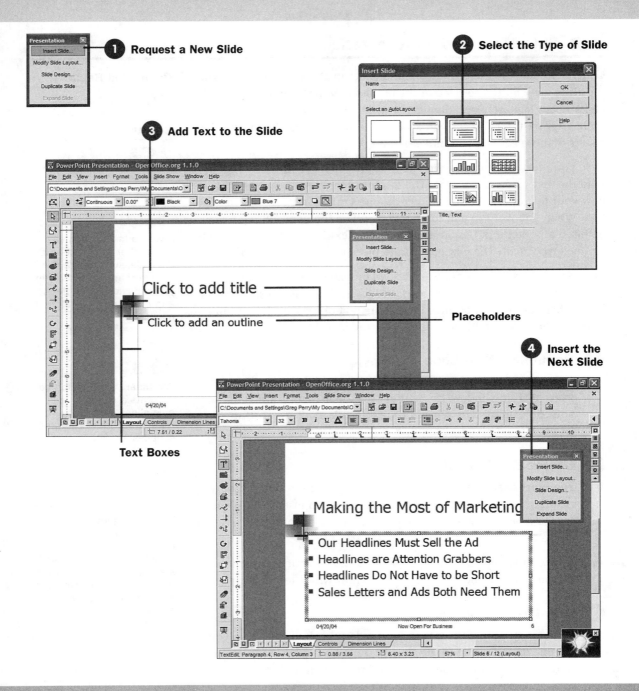

1 Request a New Slide

2 Select the Type of Slide

3 Add Text to the Slide

Click to add title

Click to add an outline

Placeholders

4 Insert the Next Slide

Text Boxes

Making the Most of Marketing

- Our Headlines Must Sell the Ad
- Headlines are Attention Grabbers
- Headlines Do Not Have to be Short
- Sales Letters and Ads Both Need Them

④ Insert the Next Slide

Once you finish with one slide, you can insert the next slide by clicking the **Insert Slide** button inside the **Presentation** window. The **Insert Slide** dialog box once again appears, letting you add more slides.

TIP

The **Presentation** window's **Duplicate Slide** option makes an exact copy of your current slide in case you want a duplicate. Sometimes, it's faster to duplicate and then edit a copy of the current slide than to start with a brand-new slide.

88 Find and Replace Text

When you work with large presentations, being able to locate text quickly, either to edit the text or to verify its accuracy, is vital. You don't want to step through a presentation slide by slide until you find text you want to see.

As with all of the OpenOffice.org programs, Impress offers a powerful find-and-replace command that enables you to locate text you want to find. Once Impress locates the text, you can request that Impress automatically replace it. If, for example, you realize that your company's Vice President's name is spelled *McGuire* instead of *MacGuire*, you can quickly make Impress change all the misspelled instances of the name, even if you're about to start your presentation in the next minute. (Just make sure you don't pass out those preprinted handouts of your slides!)

Before You Begin

✔ **82** Open an Existing Presentation

See Also

→ **89** Format Presentation Text

→ **90** Animate Text

① Find Text

Select the **Find & Replace** option from the **Edit** menu to display the **Find & Replace** dialog box. You can also press **Ctrl+F** to display the **Find & Replace** dialog box.

② Enter the Search Text

Type the data you want to find in the **Search for** text box. If you've searched for the same data before, you can click the down arrow to open the **Search for** drop-down list box and select the data to search for it once again.

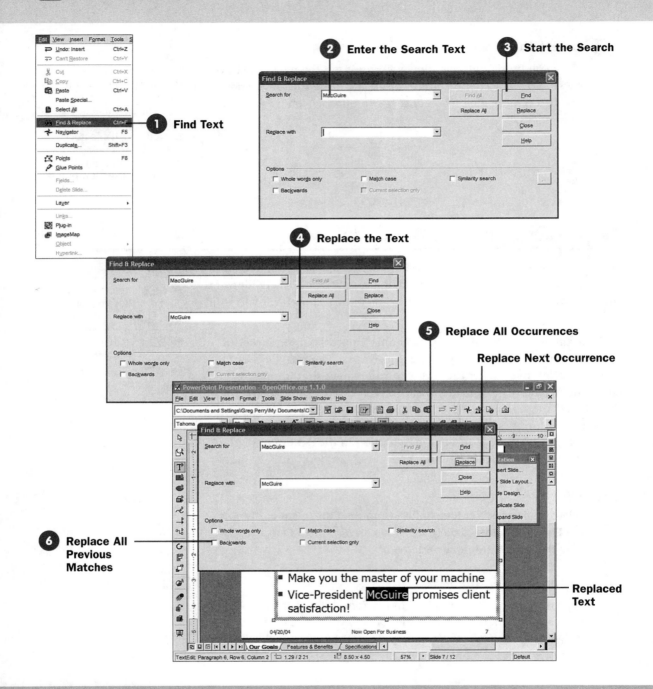

2 Enter the Search Text

3 Start the Search

1 Find Text

4 Replace the Text

5 Replace All Occurrences

Replace Next Occurrence

6 Replace All Previous Matches

Replaced Text

3 **Start the Search**

Click the **Find** button. Impress searches from the current position in the presentation to the end of the presentation. If Impress finds the text anywhere in the presentation, it displays the first slide that holds that text. (Unlike Writer and Calc, Impress doesn't offer a **Find All** button in its **Find & Replace** dialog box.)

4 **Replace the Text**

If you want Impress to replace found text with new text, type the new text into the **Replace with** text box.

If the **Search for** text is found, Impress replaces that text with the text you entered in the **Replace with** text box.

5 **Replace All Occurrences**

Instead of **Replace** (or after you perform one or more replace-ments), if you click the **Replace All** button, Impress replaces all the matches with your replacement text throughout the slide. Such a change is more global and possibly riskier because you may replace text you didn't really want replaced. By clicking **Find** before each **Replace**, you can be sure that the proper text is being replaced, but such a single-occurrence find-and-replacement opera-tion takes a lot of time in a long presentation.

6 **Replace All Previous Matches**

Click to select the **Backwards** option before doing a find or replacement if you want to find or replace from the current cursor's position back to the start of the presentation.

When you finish finding and replacing all the text for this search session, click the **Find & Replace** dialog box's **Close** button to close the dialog box and return to the presentation's slide-editing area.

89 Format Presentation Text

Before You Begin

✔ **87** Enter Text into a
Presentation

See Also

→ **90** Animate Text
→ **92** Use a Style

Although Impress's AutoLayout slides define preformatted text, there will be many times when you want to change the text format to something else. You can control many factors related to your presentation's text, including the following:

- Choose the alignment (such as left and right justification)

- Change the text size

- Change the font

- Animate the text (as described in **90** **Animate Text**)

- Change the text to a 3D format

If you've used other OpenOffice.org programs, such as Writer, you'll feel at home with some of Impress's formatting tools because the font-related options are similar to those of the other OpenOffice.org programs.

1 Select Text to Format

Locate the slide that contains the text you want to format. Select the text.

2 Change the Font

To change the selected text's font, alignment, display format, or background, select **Format**, **Character** from the menu. The **Character** dialog box appears. You can also right-click over the selected text to display the **Character** dialog box. Other right-click options are more specific, such as **Font**, **Size**, **Style**, and **Alignment**, in case you want to change one of those specific aspects of the text.

From the **Character** dialog box's **Font** page, you can change the font, the typeface (such as bold or italic), and the size of the text. A preview updates at the bottom of the **Font** page, showing you how your changes will affect your text. Click to select the **Font Effects** tab to change other aspects of the text, such as underlining and the text color. The **Position** tab determines how the text appears on the line (as normal, *superscript*, or *subscript* text). Click the **OK** button to close the dialog box and view your formatted text.

🔍EY TERMS

Superscript—Small text that begins above the text baseline, as is often used to indicate the square of a number.

Subscript—Small text that begins below the text baseline, as is often used to indicate numbers that drop below the line in chemical formulas.

1 Select Text to Format

2 Change the Font

3 Prepare for 3D

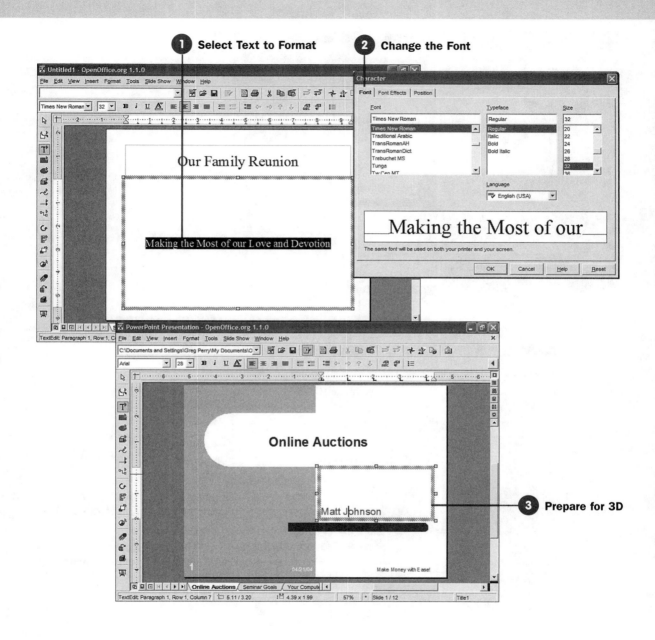

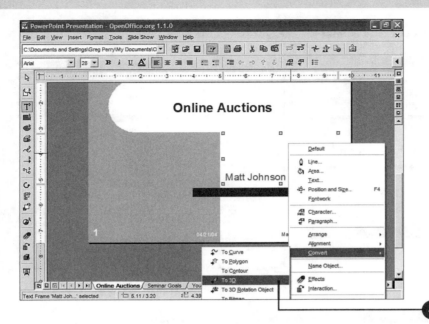

4 Request 3D Conversion

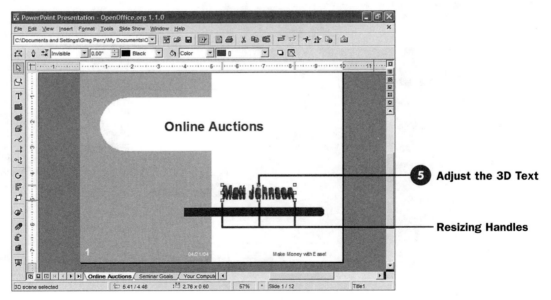

5 Adjust the 3D Text

Resizing Handles

③ Prepare for 3D

If you want to convert your text to 3D, you often can, depending on whether Impress can convert the font used to 3D. As appealing as 3D text sounds, I've found that Impress does not perform an adequate conversion. The text is often too dark and thick to work well. You can experiment and decide whether you like the 3D effect.

Click to select the text box that holds the text you want to convert to 3D. Impress selects the text and places the resizing handles around it.

④ Request 3D Conversion

You now must press the **Esc** key once. The resizing handles will stay around the text, but the selection outline goes away. Right-click the text to display the menu and then select **Convert, To 3D**. Impress converts the text to 3D.

⑤ Adjust the 3D Text

Once the text converts to 3D, drag the resizing handles up and down to make the text appear as clear as possible. Right-click the 3D text and select **3D Effects** to adjust the way Impress applies the three-dimensional style to your text.

NOTE

It seems as though Impress makes you jump through hoops to convert text to 3D!

NOTE

When converting text to 3D, Impress changes the text to a graphic image. If a text placeholder, such as **Type name here**, originally appeared where the text was, it may return once the 3D effect occurs. You may need to type a space over the placeholder to hide the placeholder text behind the 3D image.

90 Animate Text

One of the more interesting features of Impress is its capability to animate the various text elements of your slides, producing an animated effect as the slide appears during the presentation. Consider how captivating your presentation could be when any of the following occurs:

- The title and then the rest of the text flies onto the slide from the side.

- The title falls down from the top while the bottom half of the slide rises up from the bottom edge.

- The slide's graphics appear and the text slowly fades into view. (**98 Impress with Special Effects** describes how to animate graphics.)

Before You Begin

✔ **89** Format Presentation Text

See Also

→ **92** Use a Style

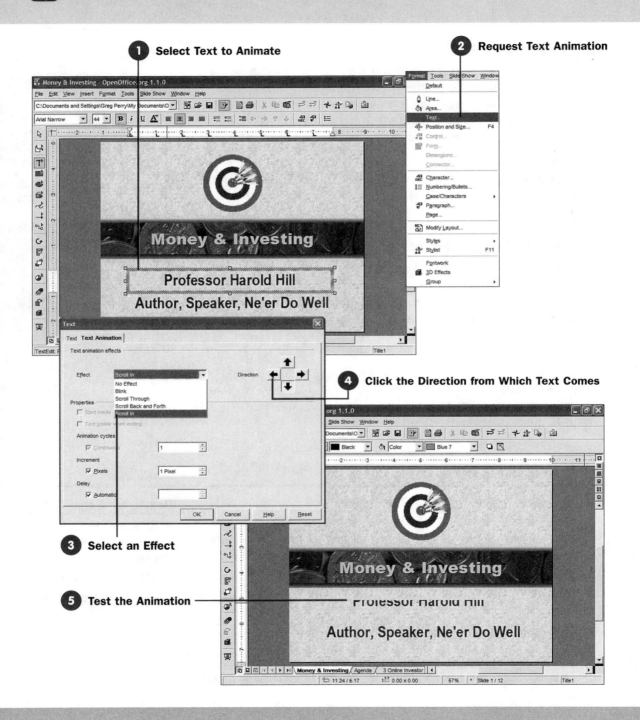

1 Select Text to Animate

2 Request Text Animation

4 Click the Direction from Which Text Comes

3 Select an Effect

5 Test the Animation

- Each bulleted item in the list comes onto the slide by each letter cartwheeling into view.

- Paragraphs of text fade in at different moments.

- The title of your slide bounces into view, and when it finally comes to rest at its anchored location, the rest of the slide appears.

1 Select Text to Animate

Click to select the text you wish to animate. Opening titles make good candidates for animated text, perhaps with some music in the background as your presentation's title flies in from the side of the screen. Self-running presentations should have slightly more animation than presentations that you give simply to keep the presentation from becoming stagnant. But even self-running presentations shouldn't overdo the effects at the expense of the content.

2 Request Text Animation

With the text still selected, click to open the **Format** menu and select **Text**. This displays the **Text** dialog box. Click the **Text Animation** tab to display the **Text Animation page** in the **Text** dialog box.

3 Select an Effect

Click the **Effect** list box to display the possible effects from which you can choose. Select an effect that you want Impress to use when bringing the text onto the screen during the presentation.

4 Click the Direction from Which Text Comes

Once you've selected an effect from the **Effect** list, the **Direction** arrows will activate. Click one of the arrows to indicate the direction from which the text is to arrive. For example, if you click the down arrow, the text will arrive on the screen from the top of the slide and drop downward until it rests in its proper position in the text box.

Depending on which effect you chose, you may or may not be able to change the **Properties** section. If the **Start inside** option is active, clicking it will make the animation begin inside the text

NOTE

The biggest problem with animation is not getting it to work but getting it to work far too well. Don't overdo animation. The animated effects are so fun to work with that it's tempting to add all sorts of fades, cartwheels, wipes, and bounces to the slides. After so many, your presentation will become so top-heavy with animation that the importance of the content will be lost on your audience and the presentation will take on an overdone appearance.

NOTE

You're sure to lose your audience's attention if you keep the animation continuous as you talk! Leave the **Continuous** option unchecked for presentations you'll be controlling while speaking. You can keep the **Continuous** option checked for any animations that take place on automatic presentations that run on their own.

KEY TERM

Pixels—An abbreviation for *picture elements*, which refers to the smallest addressable dot, or graphic element, on a screen or printer.

box instead of entering the text box first from the direction you indicate. In other words, if you selected the **Scroll Back and Forth** effect, the text will first enter its area from the direction you chose and then shake back and forth. If you've clicked to select the **Start inside** option, however, the text instantly appears inside its text box area and begins moving back and forth without any entrance. Click to select **Text visible when exiting** option to keep the text on the screen after the animation completes (for when you don't request a continuous animation). Click the **Continuous** option to keep the animation going after it has performed its first cycle. The **Continuous** option keeps the animation going until the next slide appears on the screen.

The **Increment** value determines how many *pixels* the animation moves at each step. The smaller the number, the slower the animation moves; the larger the number, the faster the animation moves. The **Delay** option determines how long Impress waits before repeating the animation if you've elected to use continuous animation.

5 Test the Animation

You don't have to run your entire presentation to test each text animation effect. Once you set up text for animation, click anywhere outside the text area (to remove the resizing handles) to see the effect immediately. To edit the effect, click the text once again and select the **Format**, **Text** menu option to adjust the animation.

---

91 About Impress Styles

Before You Begin

✔ **89** Format Presentation Text

See Also

➔ **92** Use a Style

Styles enable you to format text or graphics on your presentation's slides using a predefined format. By reusing styles, you reduce the amount of work you have to do to create and format a slide and to make your existing slides look the way you want them to look.

The terminology of styles is similar across all the OpenOffice.org products. Impress, however, uses styles in a more limited manner. With Writer, for example, you can select a word, sentence, or paragraph and select a new style from the **Style** dialog box to apply to that text. As soon as you do, the text takes on all the formatting that the style defines.

Impress limits your use of styles in the following ways:

- You must use styles applicable to slides you create with an AutoLayout. In other words, if you insert a blank, empty slide into your presentation, you will not be able to apply any styles to that slide. Instead, you must format the slide using the **format** menu without the use of styles. If you insert a new slide using one of the AutoLayout formats, such as the **Title and Text** AutoFormat slide, the presentation styles defined by that AutoFormat are available to you.

- You can only modify a style by changing one of the AutoFormat element's format and then changing the style. All existing slides that use that style, and all slides you add in the future to that presentation, use that modified style. In other words, if you add an AutoLayout slide with a title, as shown in the following figure, and you change the title's style, if you add a similar slide later, the new slide's title will take on the modified style, too.

NOTE

16 About Styles and Templates describes how to use styles in Writer documents. If you need to review terminology, you can review that task because the terminology is the same whether you're applying styles to Impress slides or to Writer documents.

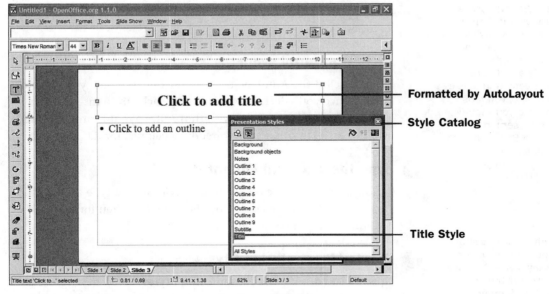

You can easily control your presentation's overall set of styles.

When you insert a new slide, you'll select an AutoLayout form that most closely matches the slide you want to insert. All styles for that AutoLayout are then available to you when you press **F11** or select **Format**, **Styles**, **Catalog** from the menu.

92 Use a Style

Before You Begin

✔ **91** About Impress Styles

See Also

→ **93** Change a Presentation's Background

> **NOTE**
>
> Impress's graphics styles are more lenient than the presentation text styles, although you'll probably use them less often. You can modify a style and apply it directly to a single graphic image, whereas any text style you modify (listed as *presentation styles* in the Style Catalog) causes all text that uses that style to change format.

> **TIP**
>
> If you only want this single occurrence changed, don't change any styles! You only want to modify the style used by this element of the slide if you want all other like elements to change too.

Using styles inside Impress differs from the other OpenOffice.org programs, as **91** **About Impress Styles** explains. The styles are linked to the AutoLayout forms that you use when you insert new slides into your presentation. You can only modify existing styles, and once you modify a style, all slides that use that style also change.

❶ Insert a New Slide

Select **Insert**, **Slide** to insert the next slide into your presentation. The **Insert Slide** dialog box lists the AutoLayout slides available to you. If you are creating a new presentation, the **Insert Slide** dialog box appears when you begin working on the first slide in the presentation.

❷ Select an AutoLayout

Click to select the AutoLayout that best suits the slide you wish to insert. Once you select the AutoLayout, click **OK** to insert a new slide into your presentation with that AutoLayout format. The slide will have presentation styles already developed for it.

❸ Type the Text and Format It

If you want to change a style in the Stylelist, first type the text that uses that style, such as a title on the slide, and then format the text any way you want the style to look.

❹ Display Presentation Styles

Press **F11** to display the **Presentation Styles** dialog box. Impress automatically highlights the style used by your selected text. For example, if you modified a title, the **Title** style will be selected in the **Presentation Styles** dialog box.

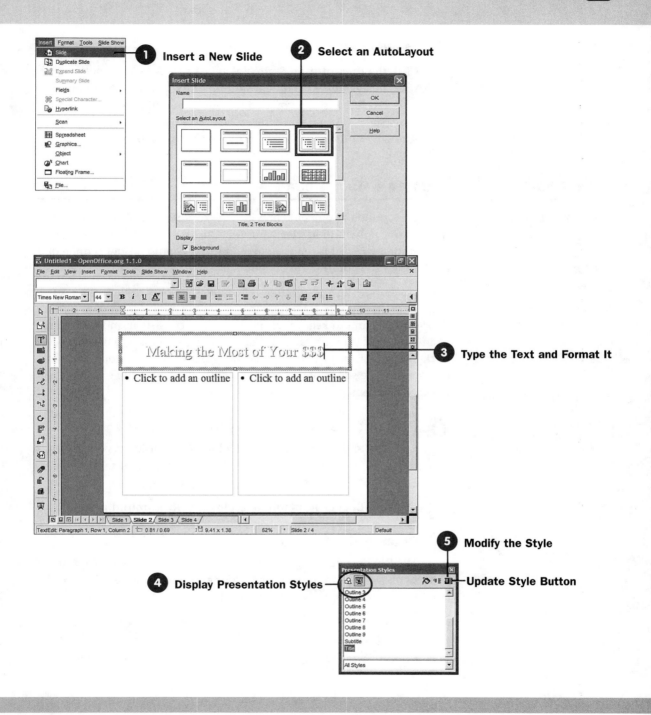

1 Insert a New Slide

2 Select an AutoLayout

3 Type the Text and Format It

5 Modify the Style

4 Display Presentation Styles

Update Style Button

5 Modify the Style

Click the **Presentation Style** dialog box's **Update Style** button. The selected style takes on the formatting of the text inside the current style. All future slides you add to your presentation with that same style (such as when you insert a new slide with a similar AutoLayout form) will take on the attributes of that style.

93 Change a Presentation's Background

Before You Begin

✔ 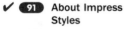 About Impress Styles

✔ **92** Use a Style

See Also

➔ **99** Add a Slide Transition

NOTE

Click the **Master view** button to change your entire presentation's background. Click the **Slide view** button to change only a single background.

The background of your slide provides the overall tone of your presentation. If your presentation's background appears in cool blue tones, your presentation will feel far more relaxed than if you use bright orange and red tones in the background of your slides.

You can change the background of a single slide or of your entire presentation. Often, presenters prefer to use the same background on all their slides. Doing so keeps their presentations consistent and maintains a similar mood throughout. All slides in a presentation use the same background specified by the master slide's background. If you want to change a single slide's background, you'll have to hide the master slide's background elements.

1 Request the Background Change

Click the **Slide view** button in the lower-left corner of your screen to change only the current slide's background. Then, select **Format**, **Page** to display the **Page Setup** dialog box.

Click the **Background** tab to display the **Background** page.

2 Change the Background

The **Background** page determines the background you want to apply to the current slide or to your entire presentation. You must select how you want to fill the background in the **Fill** section.

You can elect to show no background (a white background) by clicking the **None** option. The **Color** option enables you to select from a list of colors that appears. The **Gradient** option enables you to select from a list of *gradients* that you want to apply to the background. The **Hatching** option enables you to select from a list of various crosshatching patterns. The **Bitmap** option enables you to select from a list of background graphics, such as a brick wall or a sky pattern with clouds.

Click to select the type of fill you want and then, if the fill type produces a list of fills below, select the specific fill. Click **OK** to apply the fill and close the **Page Setup** dialog box.

③ Apply the Background to One or Multiple Pages

Impress asks whether you want to apply the background to a single page (the page you were on when you changed the background) or all pages.

④ Change the Master Slide

If you want to remove the master slide's background from view (assuming the master slide has a specified background you can see), you must click the **Master view** button to display the master slide.

⑤ Modify the Master Slide

Once the master slide appears, showing the background, title, and outline levels currently defined, click to select all the background images you want to remove and press **Del** to remove them from your presentation. When you once again click the **Slide view** button, the background images will be gone.

KEY TERM

Gradient—A transition from one color or pattern to another on the same slide.

NOTE

The **Page Settings** dialog box can apply the background to all pages in your presentation, except for the first slide. If you had first clicked the **Master view** button before changing the background, all slides, including the first one, would change. No matter what you do, the original background, determined by the master slide, shows also.

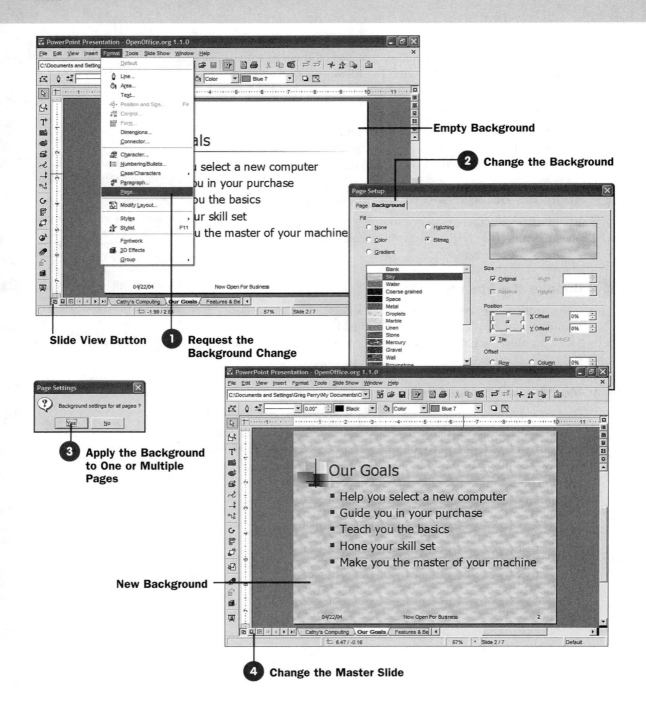

Empty Background

2 Change the Background

Slide View Button

1 Request the Background Change

3 Apply the Background to One or Multiple Pages

New Background

4 Change the Master Slide

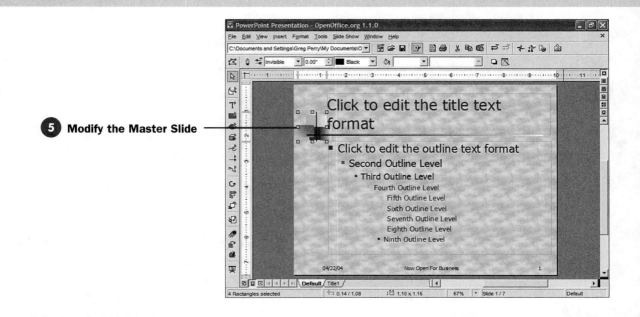

5 Modify the Master Slide

13

Making More Impressive Presentations

IN THIS CHAPTER:

The more pizzazz and flair you add to your presentations, the more responsive your audiences will be. Impress will help you drive home your point with several advanced features. Your presentations won't be boring. You can add charts and import graphics to spruce up your presentations. You can also animate graphics and determine special slide transitions so the movement from slide to slide follows the same tone as your presentation's.

The notes feature enables you to add your own private speaker's notes to your slides so you always remember important points you want to make. Your audience will also appreciate it when you print a copy of your presentation for them to take. Impress doesn't stop with live presentations; you can create automated presentations that repeat themselves, and you can easily put your Impress presentations on the Web for the world to view.

94 Insert a Chart into a Presentation

Before You Begin

✔ **93** Change a Presentation's Background

See Also

→ **95** Insert Graphics into a Presentation

 TIP

67 Add a Chart to a Spreadsheet, although a Calc-based lesson, describes charts and terminology related to them. If you are unfamiliar with OpenOffice.org charts, take a few minutes to review this task.

NOTE

Remember, Impress generates a sample chart for you, and you must change the chart's data and labels to suit your purpose.

A chart can summarize your presentation, and audiences often glean information from charts that they might not otherwise get from long lists of data or from you listing scores of numbers for them. So often you'll want to use charts in your presentations to make your data more available to your audience.

Impress (as does Writer) includes its own Calc-like charting capability. Impress accomplishes this by supporting the use of a mini-version of Calc right inside Impress. In other words, when you want to place a chart on an Impress slide, you can build the chart from within Impress, entering data into a spreadsheet as though Calc were inside Impress, ready to build your charts.

 Request a Chart

Select **Insert**, **Chart** from the menu. Impress places a sample chart directly in the center of your slide. You now must position the chart where you want it and change the data values used in the chart to match the data you want to portray in your presentation. In addition, you can change the chart type as well as all its labels.

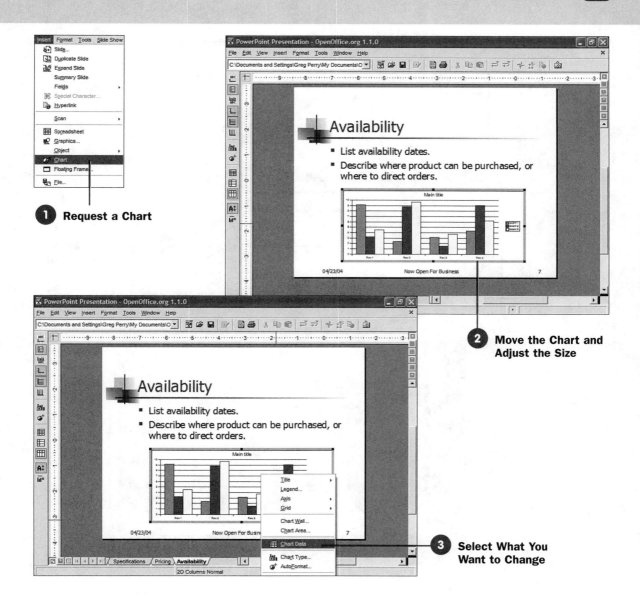

1 **Request a Chart**

2 **Move the Chart and Adjust the Size**

3 **Select What You Want to Change**

Add and Delete Rows and Columns

Transpose Rows and Columns

Sort Rows and Columns

Update the Chart

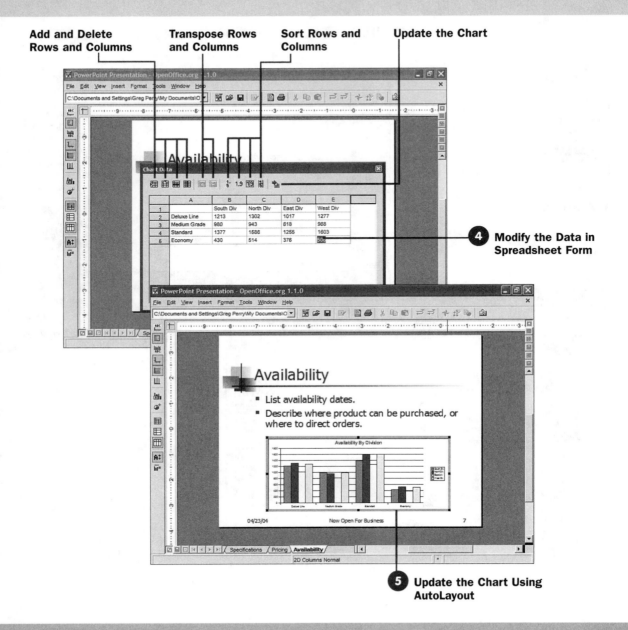

4 Modify the Data in Spreadsheet Form

5 Update the Chart Using AutoLayout

2 Move the Chart and Adjust the Size

The chart that Impress places on your slide appears in the center of the slide. Move the chart to where you want it to go. Even though this sample chart is not the chart you want to present, you can go ahead and position as well as resize the chart to make it easier to see later, along with the rest of your slide's contents. You now must enter data and edit the chart so it reflects the information you need in the slide.

3 Select What You Want to Change

Right-click the chart to display a menu showing you all the chart-related elements you can now change. You'll certainly want to modify the chart data because you don't want to use the chart's sample data for your presentation. In addition, you'll always want to modify the title so that your chart is labeled on your slide as well as on any printed handouts you might make from your presentation. Generally, the legend and the axis labels need to be changed. Finally, the chart type might very well need to be changed to reflect your data's intent.

TIP

67 Add a Chart to a Spreadsheet describes each chart type and the best use for each one.

4 Modify the Data in Spreadsheet Form

When you select **Chart Data** from the right-click menu, a small spreadsheet appears in the center of your slide. This is a Calc-like spreadsheet add-in program. Although all of Calc's features aren't represented in Impress's spreadsheet, you can easily enter the data needed to create your chart in the rows and columns there.

Replace the sample row and column labels with your own data's label information. Replace the data inside the spreadsheet's body with your own data. You can add or delete rows or columns, simply by selecting a row or column that precedes the one you want to add or by selecting a row or column to delete. You may sort by rows or columns, as you might do if you wanted data to appear alphabetically in the chart.

5 Update the Chart Using AutoLayout

After editing the spreadsheet, click the **Apply to Chart** button to update the chart on your slide. Once you update the chart, you cannot right-click the chart to display the editing options again

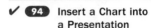

KEY TERM

OLE object—Abbreviation for *Object Linking and Embedding.* This term refers to an object that can be placed inside documents of different types, such as a Writer word processing document and an Impress presentation. You can place charts in Impress and Calc because OpenOffice.org converts the charts to OLE objects that both programs accept.

without first right-clicking the chart and selecting **OLE Object**, **Edit**. As soon as you update your chart with your data, Impress converts the chart to an *OLE object*. You must tell Impress that you want to edit that object when you want to make additional changes, such as changing the title or legend.

Once you've entered your specific data into the chart, the **AutoFormat** dialog box is the simplest place to update all the chart's details, such as titles and legends. After making the request to edit the chart as an OLE object, select **AutoFormat** from the right-click menu to modify the other chart features, including changing the chart's type, such as from a bar chart to a pie chart.

95 Insert Graphics into a Presentation

Before You Begin

✔ **94** Insert a Chart into a Presentation

See Also

→ **98** Impress with Special Effects

NOTE

Impress supports all popular graphic file formats, including JPG, GIF, and BMP files.

TIP

Click the **Insert Graphics** dialog box's **View** button and select **Thumbnails** to see a preview of your graphic before you insert it.

Impress enables you to put pictures throughout your presentation slides. Perhaps you'll want to stress your point when giving a motivational speech, for example, by showing a runner winning a race.

When you insert a graphic image, Impress places the image's anchor at that location. You will see the anchor when editing but not when you present your presentation. The anchor also does not show if you print your slides as handouts. The anchor shows where you inserted the actual image. The anchor and the actual image may not appear together, depending on how you format the image, but they will appear on the same slide. When you want to move an image, move its anchor and not the image itself.

1 Request a Picture

To insert a graphic image from a file, first select the slide where you want the image to go. Then, select **Insert**, **Graphics** from the menu. Impress displays the **Insert Graphics** dialog box, which is nothing more than a Windows file-selection dialog box where you navigate to the file you want to insert.

Once you select the graphic image you want to place in your presentation, click the **Open** button to insert the image. The image appears in your presentation at the location you first selected.

1 Request a Picture

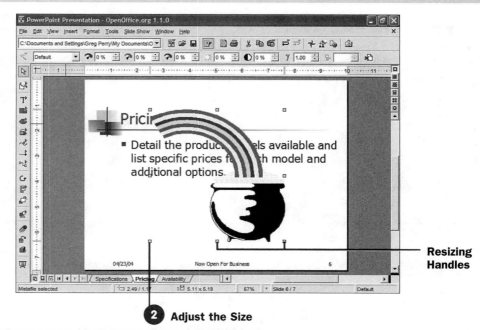

2 Adjust the Size

Resizing Handles

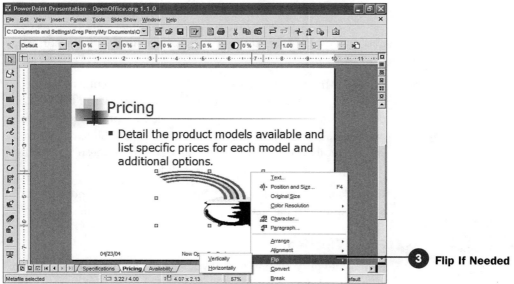

3 Flip If Needed

4 Adjust the Position and Size

5 Rotate the Image If Needed

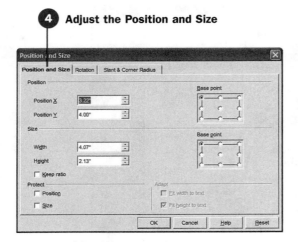

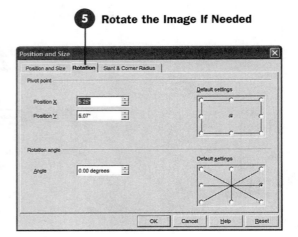

2 Adjust the Size

Once Impress brings the graphic image into your presentation, you usually need to make adjustments so the image suits your needs and rests on the slide in the proper position and with the correct size.

Typically, Impress imports a graphic image and centers it at the location you inserted it. No text wraps to either side of the image because, unlike a word processed document, a presentation relies on the exact placement of text and data on your slide. Therefore, you'll usually have to move the image so that it doesn't overwrite any important information on your slide.

To resize the image, drag any of the eight resizing handles inward to reduce the image size or outward to increase the image size.

 TIP

If you insert multiple graphics, they can overlap each other. By right-clicking an image and selecting **Arrange**, **Send Backward**, or **Bring Forward**, you can control which image gets the top spot when layered with other images.

3 Flip If Needed

Depending on your image and your data, you may want to flip, or *reverse*, the image so it points the other direction, either vertically or horizontally. Right-click over the graphic and select the **Flip** menu to flip the image so it faces differently.

4 **Adjust the Position and Size**

Right-click the image and select **Position and Size** to display the **Position and Size** dialog box. From this dialog box, you can resize, move, or slant the graphic image using exact measurements. The **Position X** and **Position Y** values determine where the image appears on the page from the upper-left corner. The **Size** values determine how large your image will appear. If you do resize an image, be sure you click to select the **Keep ratio** option so that Impress resizes the width in proportion to the height changes you make (or so Impress resizes the height in proportion to any width changes you make) to keep your image clear and in the correct ratio as the original. If you fail to maintain the ratio, your image can become stretched out of proportion. Checking the options in the **Protect** area ensures that you don't inadvertently move the image with your mouse later.

5 **Rotate the Image If Needed**

Click the **Position and Size** dialog box's **Rotation** tab to display the **Rotation** page. Here, you can rotate the image any angle by specifying a value in the **Angle** field. The *pivot point*, which remains at the center of your image unless you change the pivot point, determines where the imaginary spindle lies while the image rotates.

 TIP

If you rotate or resize the image too much and want to begin again with the original position and size, click the **Position and Size** dialog box's **Reset** button to restore the values to the original image state.

96 Add a Presentation Header and Footer

You must add headers and footers to your slides through the master slide (see **86** **About Impress Views**). Each header and footer is saved in the presentation's master slide so that the header and footer (you can have one or the other or both) reside on all slides throughout your presentation. You cannot add a different header or footer on different slides, although you can hide the header or footer from individual slides.

You may add the date, time, or slide number (referred to as the *page number*) in a header or footer area. When that slide appears during your presentation, the current date or time at that moment appears in the header or footer area.

Before You Begin

✔ **81** Create a New Presentation

See Also

→ **102** Create Presentation Handouts

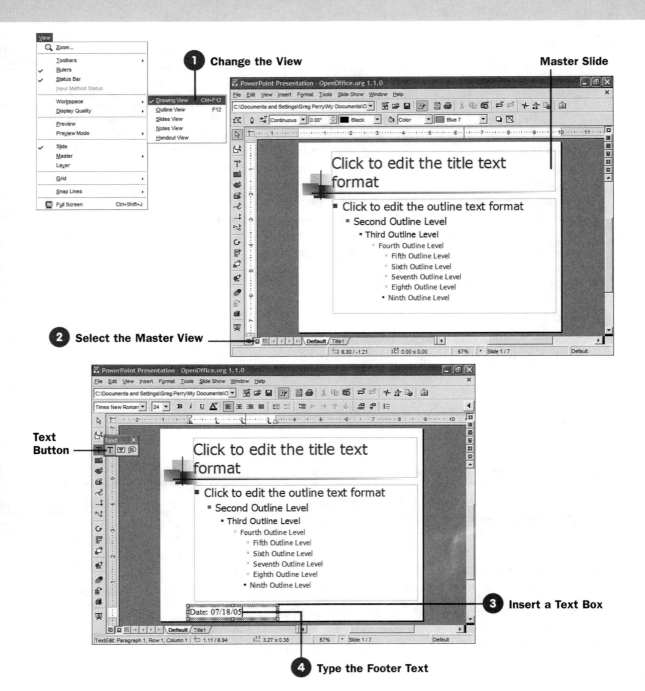

5 Request Layout Modification

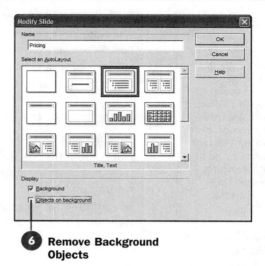

6 Remove Background Objects

1 Change the View

Select **View, Workspace, Drawing View** to enter the normal Drawing view. You can also press **Ctrl+F12** or click the **Drawing View** button above the vertical scrollbar to enter the Drawing view.

2 Select the Master View

Because you must add header or footer text to the master slide, your header or footer generally appears on all slides throughout your presentation. Click the **Master View** button to display the presentation's master slide.

3 Insert a Text Box

Your header and footer text must reside inside a text box. Long-click the **Text** tool on the **Main** toolbar. Click the **Text** button that appears. Your mouse cursor changes to a crosshair cursor, indicating that you can now place a text box anywhere on the slide.

NOTE

Technically, Impress does not support headers and footers. You can, however, add text to the top or bottom of your slides that acts just like Writer or Calc headers and footers. The rest of this task refers to such text as *header* and *footer* text, even though such text is just normal text that you place on your slides near their top or bottom.

TIP

If you don't want any text in the same header or footer that contains a graphic image, but the single line for the header or footer isn't large enough to display the graphic, insert a blank space before or after the image and set the font size for the space to 36 points or another setting that gives the graphic enough room to display.

 KEY TERMS

Variable date—The current presentation date as opposed to the fixed date.

Variable time—The current presentation time as opposed to the fixed time.

Fixed date—The date you created the slide as opposed to the variable date.

Fixed time—The time you created the slide as opposed to the variable time.

TIPS

If you want to remove the header or footer from multiple slides within your presentation, you must change each slide's layout one at a time.

Click the **Select** button atop the **Main** toolbar to stop adding text boxes to the slide and to return the mouse cursor to its normal pointing cursor shape.

Click the upper-left corner of your footer's (or header's) text box and drag your mouse down and to the right to draw the text box. When you release your mouse button, Impress places the text box in that position and inserts the text cursor inside it so you can type the header or footer text.

4 Type the Footer Text

Type the text that you want to appear in the footer (or header). If you want to display the time or date, you may want to label the time or date or leave the value to itself to appear. Generally, you'll want to insert the date or time that's current when you give your presentation, so select **Insert**, **Fields**, **Date (variable)** or **Time (variable)** to insert either the *variable date* or *variable time*. (In a similar manner, you can insert a *fixed date* or *fixed time* also.)

5 Request Layout Modification

To hide the header or footer on any single slide, locate the slide you wish to modify. Select **Format**, **Modify Layout** to display the **Modify Slide** dialog box.

6 Remove Background Objects

Click to uncheck the **Objects on background** option to hide the header or footer. This might remove other items as well. After confirming that you wish to remove the background objects by clicking **Yes**, Impress removes your header or footer from that one slide but not from the other slides.

97 Add Sound to a Presentation

You can add sound to your presentations to accent an effect or to get your audience's attention during slide transitions. Impress supports the following sound file extensions and formats:

- AU and SND files (SUN/NeXT)
- WAV (Microsoft Windows)
- VOC (Creative Labs SoundBlaster)
- AIFF (SGI/Apple)
- IFF (Amiga)

Surprisingly, there appears to be no way to provide timed narration throughout an entire presentation, as you might want for an automatic presentation. Nevertheless, Impress does support enough sound techniques to pique your audience's attention.

1 Select an Object to Apply Sound To

Click to select an object on a slide, such as a graphic image or text box. You can attach a sound to this item for a special effect.

2 Request Interaction

Select **Slide Show**, **Interaction** to add a sound to the selected image. The **Interaction** dialog box appears.

3 Play the Sound at Image Click

Click to open the **Action at mouse click** list box and select **Play sound**. You have just told Impress that you want to play a certain sound when you click the image.

Before You Begin

✔ **95** Insert Graphics into a Presentation

See Also

→ **99** Add a Slide Transition

→ **98** Impress with Special Effects

NOTE

As with all special effects, don't overdo the use of sound; otherwise, it will distract and not accent your presentation.

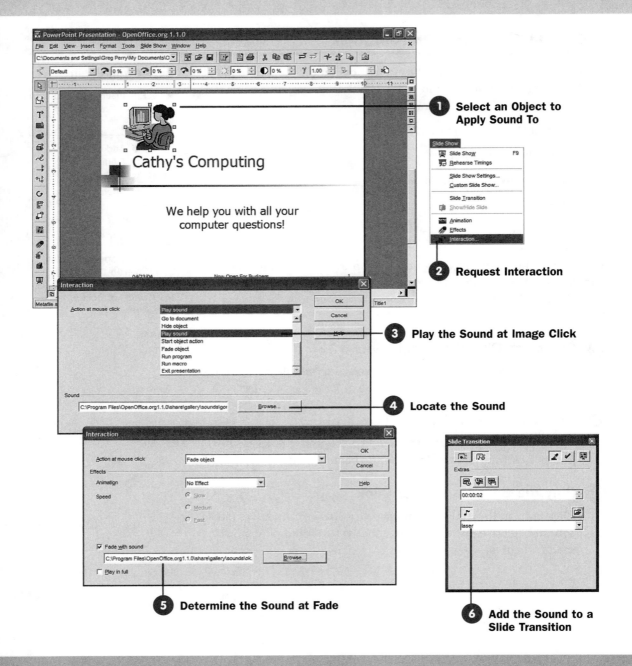

1 Select an Object to Apply Sound To

2 Request Interaction

3 Play the Sound at Image Click

4 Locate the Sound

5 Determine the Sound at Fade

6 Add the Sound to a Slide Transition

4 **Locate the Sound**

Browse your hard disk or network to locate the sound to play. Click OK to attach the sound to the image. When you give your presentation (assuming it's not an automatic presentation, where you cannot add sound linked to a mouse click because no human presenter will be there to click the mouse), you can click the image to produce the sound through the presentation computer's sound card. You can test the sound effect by clicking it from within the Drawing view without having to run your presentation. (To add sound during an automatic presentation, you can select an action such as **Action when slide appears**.)

5 **Determine the Sound at Fade**

Instead of adding the sound when you click an element, you can request that the element fade out and specify that a sound play during the fading process. When you change from that slide to the next one during your presentation, the image or text box will fade away and play the sound while doing so.

6 **Add the Sound to a Slide Transition**

When you transition from one slide to the next, you can specify a sound that will play during the transition. See **99** **Add a Slide Transition** for more information on setting up slide transitions.

NOTE

Obviously, you'll need sound amplification equipment so your entire audience can hear the sound when you trigger it with the mouse click.

98 Impress with Special Effects

Adding special effects to graphics and other presentation elements can really make your presentation come alive. You can make graphic images fly onto the screen, not unlike the animated text you can cause to roll into place (see **90** **Animate Text**). As with any special effects, don't overdo them. Reserve them for when you want to make an impression at a particularly critical part of your presentation.

Here are just a few of the effects you can apply to graphics and other presentation elements with Impress:

- The object flies in from outside the slide.

- A laser-like show produces the object.

Before You Begin

✔ **95** Insert Graphics into a Presentation

✔ **97** Add Sound to a Presentation

See Also

→ **99** Add a Slide Transition

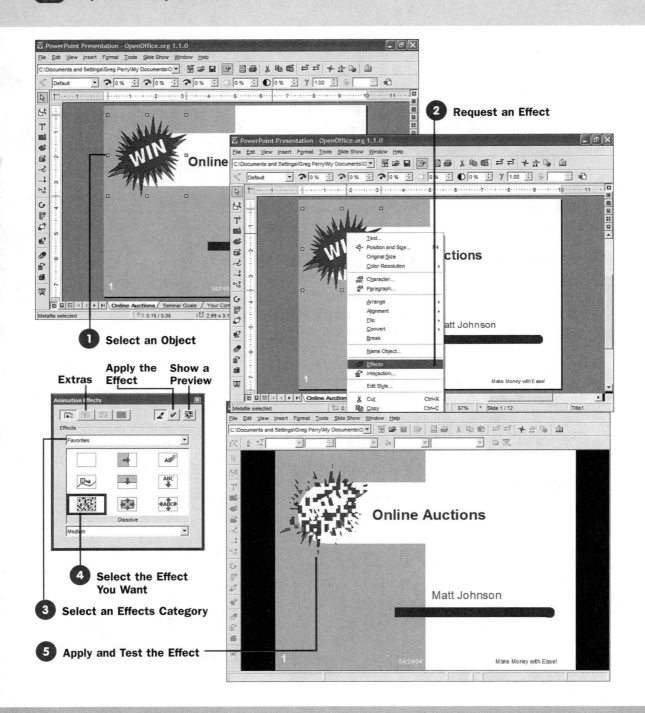

2 Request an Effect

1 Select an Object

Extras   **Apply the Effect**   **Show a Preview**

4 Select the Effect You Want

3 Select an Effects Category

5 Apply and Test the Effect

- The object fades into place.
- The slide sparkles, slowly producing the object from the moving glitter.
- The object (graphic text works well here) snakes into the slide from one of the edges.
- The object spirals into place.

❶ Select an Object

Click to select an object, such as a graphic image or a text box. You must first click to select the object before you can apply an effect to that object.

❷ Request an Effect

Right-click the selected object to produce a menu with the **Effects** option. Select **Effects**. The effects that you generate will apply to that selected object. The **Animation Effects** dialog box opens.

❸ Select an Effects Category

First click the down arrow to display the effects categories, such as **Favorites** and **Spiral**. As you select a different category, a different list of effects appears below. The **Favorites** category contains the most varied set of effects.

❹ Select the Effect You Want

Click to select the effect you wish to apply to your object. Click the list box at the bottom of the **Animation Effects** dialog box to adjust the speed of the effect that you wish to apply. To apply the effect, click the **Assign** button. If the **Extras** button is active, you can click it to turn that effect's sound on or off.

❺ Apply and Test the Effect

Once you've assigned the effect you desire, click the **Animation Effects** dialog box's **Close** button to return to your slide. Press **F9** to review your presentation and make sure that the overall special effect adds the flavor you want to your presentation. To change the effect, you only have to select the object once again and right-click the object to reach the **Effects** menu option.

NOTE

You can apply special effects to graphic objects as well as other presentation elements such as text boxes. The special effects are more pronounced than the simpler animated text you can also place in text boxes.

TIP

Some of these effects have sounds associated with them that you can keep or remove.

NOTES

If you right-click an object without first clicking to select that object, the **Effects** option doesn't appear on the menu.

Most of the special effects that appear in the **Animation Effects** dialog box are also available as slide transitions. See **Add a Slide Transition**.

TIP

Once you've assigned an effect, you can click the **Preview** button to see the effect in a small preview window. You can review various effects in the preview window without having to return to the slide to do it.

99 Add a Slide Transition

Before You Begin

✔ **97** Add Sound to a Presentation

✔ **98** Impress with Special Effects

See Also

→ **100** Make an Automatic Presentation

 TIP

Once you've assigned a transition, click the **Preview** button to display the **Preview** window. To see what the transition will look like, click **Assign** once again. You can keep selecting different transitions and clicking **Assign** to see their effect until you find the one you like best.

Adding a transition between slides is very much like adding special effects to graphics and other objects on your slides (see **98** **Impress with Special Effects**). Instead of applying a special effect to a graphic image, you apply the special effect to the next transition. For example, a rolling transition would bring the next slide into view, during an automatic slide show or when you request the slide during a presentation, by rolling it in from one of the edges as it slowly overrides the previous slide.

You can apply a different transition to each slide throughout your presentation. In addition, you can apply the same transition to multiple slides. As with any special effect, don't overdo it because it's your presentation's message that is more important than the look of the physical presentation itself.

① **Select the First Slide in the Transition**

Move to the slide that is to take on the transition. In other words, if you want the second slide in your presentation to appear on the screen through a special animated transition, display the second slide. Be sure the **Slide View** button is active so you can work with the slide and its transition.

② **Request a Transition**

Select **Slide Show**, **Slide Transition** from the menu. The **Slide Transition** dialog box appears.

③ **Select a Transition Effects Category**

First click the down arrow to display the transitional effects categories from the **Effects** area. Several categories, such as **Favorites**, **Spiral**, **Fly In** and **Roll** are available. As you select each category, a different list of transition effects appears below. The **Favorites** category contains the most varied set of transition effects.

④ **Select the Transition**

Click to select the transition you wish to apply to your slides. Then click the list box at the bottom of the **Slide Transition** dialog box to adjust the speed of the transitional effect you wish to apply. To apply the transition, click the **Assign** button.

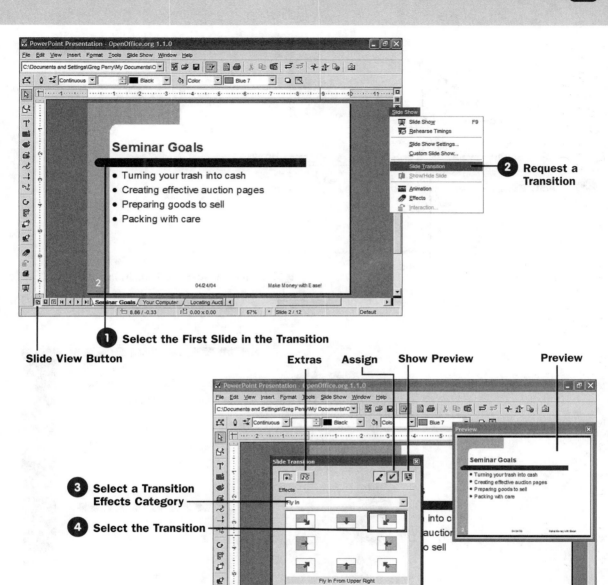

Slide View Button

1 Select the First Slide in the Transition

2 Request a Transition

Extras   Assign   Show Preview   Preview

3 Select a Transition Effects Category

4 Select the Transition

Manual

Automatic

Extras

Add Sound

Browse

5 Specify Extras

`explos`

Sound Name

6 Apply and Test the Transition

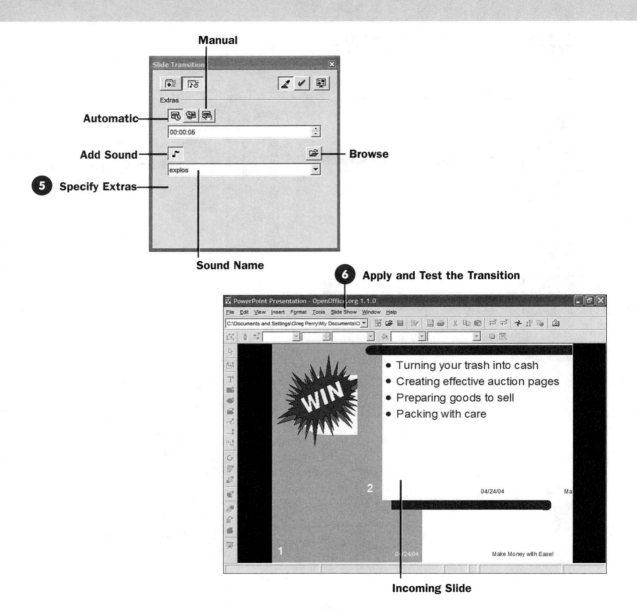

- Turning your trash into cash
- Creating effective auction pages
- Preparing goods to sell
- Packing with care

Incoming Slide

5 Specify Extras

Click the **Slide Transition** dialog box's **Extras** button to determine additional transition options. Select **Automatic Transition** when you want Impress to move to the next slide after the time you specify below the option passes. If you are controlling your own presentation, as opposed to creating an automatic presentation, you will want to click the **Manual Transition** button so the transition doesn't occur until you click your mouse button or press **Spacebar** during your presentation.

For an even more interesting effect, select a sound to play during the transition. Click the **Sound** button and then click **Browse** to locate a sound file that you wish to play during the transition. Click **Assign** to assign the extra options. If the **Preview** window is open when you click **Assign**, you will see the transition and hear the sound as it takes place.

6 Apply and Test the Transition

Once you've assigned the transition you desire, click the **Slide Transition** dialog box's **Close** button to return to your slide. Press **F9** to review your presentation and make sure that the transition works the way you desire. To change the transition to another, you only have to display the slide once again and select **Slide Show, Slide Transition** from the menu.

100 Make an Automatic Presentation

An automated slide show is useful for creating self-running demonstrations, product presentations, and conference information distribution. You can control each and every detail of a self-running slide show, add special and transition effects, and ensure that the show automatically runs within a given time frame.

1 Select Automation

Build your slide show. Once you've designed the slides and added the transitions, select **Slide Show, Slide Show Settings** to display the **Slide Show** dialog box.

Before You Begin

✔ 81 Create a New Presentation

✔ 82 Open an Existing Presentation

See Also

→ 103 Turn a Presentation into Online Web Pages

Determine which slides you want to use in the automatic presentation. Most often, you'll probably click the **All slides** option, but you can also start the automatic slide show after a specific slide that you choose from the list box next to the **From** option.

Click to select the **Auto** option and enter a time value that represents the amount of time you want Impress to pause between automatic showings. Checking the **Show logo** box displays the OpenOffice.org logo on the screen between presentations, and you cannot change the logo to something else. (The logo is a small price to pay for an absolutely free presentation program!)

The remaining **Options** section of the **Slide Show** dialog box enables you to select various options for your automated presentations, such as whether you want animations to show throughout the automatic presentation. Click **OK** to close the **Slide Show** dialog box.

2 **Rehearse and Time the Slides**

In many cases, your automatic slide show is ready to go without you doing anything further. Nevertheless, Impress offers one more service that improves upon your automatic presentation's timings. You can walk through a slide show in real time, selecting exactly when you want the next slide to appear. As you rehearse the presentation in this manner, Impress records the time frame that you use for each slide and prepares automatic transitions for you.

To rehearse the automatic presentation, click the **Slide View** button to display your presentation from a bird's-eye view perspective.

Click the **Rehearse Timings** button. Your presentation begins, and the first slide appears with a timer in the lower-left corner of your screen.

3 **Click the Timer to Advance**

When the first slide has been on the screen as long as you wish, click the timer. Impress advances to the next slide, using a transition and sound if you've set them up, and that slide's timer begins. Continue clicking each slide's timer after each slide has appeared until the presentation ends.

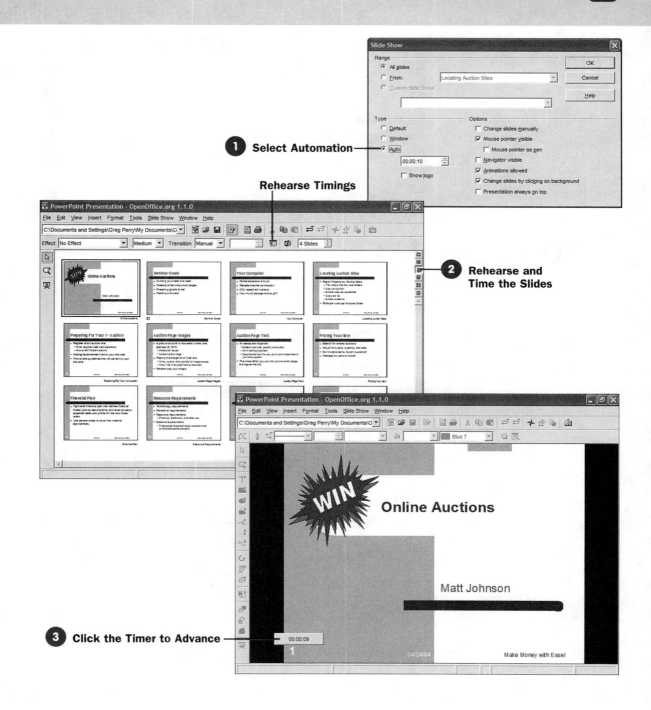

1 Select Automation

Rehearse Timings

2 Rehearse and Time the Slides

3 Click the Timer to Advance

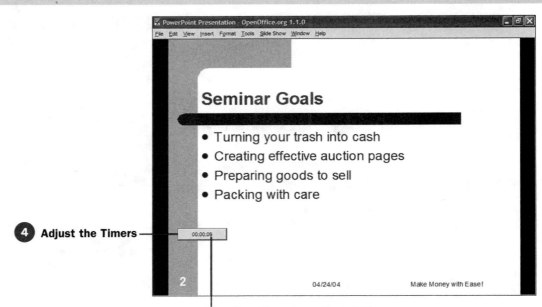

4 Adjust the Timers

The Timer Resets on Each Slide

Selected the Slide's Time

Slide Transition

Object Bar

Transition Speed

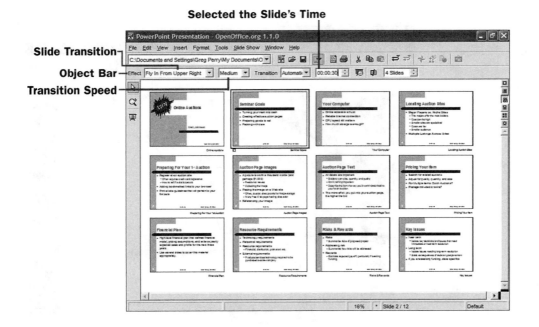

4 **Adjust the Timers**

When you return to the Slide view, the **Object** bar at the top of the screen displays the slide's transition, the transition time, and the amount of time you've given for the slide to appear during the automatic presentation. You can click to adjust any of these settings. If, for example, you want to decrease the time a slide appears, click the down arrow to reduce the amount of time the slide shows from the time applied during rehearsal.

101 Add Notes to a Presentation

Impress's Notes view enables you to create and edit notes for you or your presentation's speaker. When you display the notes, Impress shows the notes at the bottom of your slide while you work on your presentation. The Notes view shows the slide contents and, below it, a dialog box for your notes.

Therefore, the speaker's notes contain the slides that the audience sees as well as notes the speaker wrote to go along with each slide. Your audience does not see the speaker's notes during the presentation.

The Notes view is designed to allow printing of the notes for the speaker. However, the speaker can also display the Notes Page view during a presentation to eliminate paper shuffling. If the speaker's computer has two video cards and two monitors, as most laptop setups used for presentations will be able to provide (the laptop's monitor and the overhead projector plugged into the laptop's output port), Impress can send the slides to one monitor and the speaker's slides and notes are available on the speaker's computer to follow the presentation.

1 **Request the Notes View**

Select **View**, **Workspace**, **Notes View** to display your slides' Notes view. You can also click the **Notes View** button on the right side of your screen atop the vertical scrollbar.

2 **Click and Add Notes**

Click the text box with the placeholder text **Click to add notes**. Type your notes that go with the current slide. You can apply all the usual text-formatting commands to your notes (see **89** **Format Presentation Text**).

Before You Begin

✔ **84** Print a Presentation

See Also

→ **102** Create Presentation Handouts

TIPS

Generally, the **Notes** view is best used for short reminders that you want to remember for each slide. Don't plan to write your entire presentation's text in the note area because you'll get bogged down in the details (see **104** **About Giving Presentations**).

If your notes text is not large enough to read easily, expand the viewing area by using the **Zoom** command from the **View** menu.

1 Request the Notes View

2 Click and Add Notes

3 Continue Adding Notes

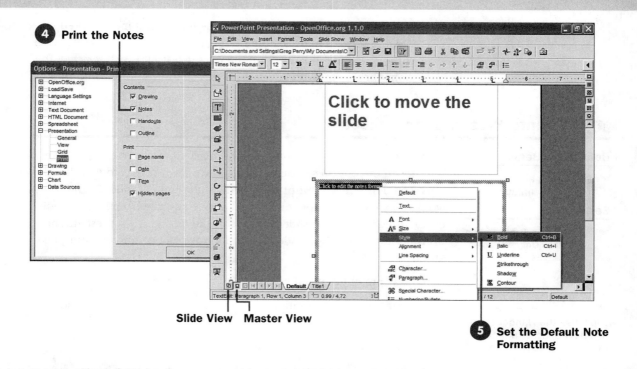

Print the Notes

Slide View **Master View**

Set the Default Note Formatting

3 Continue Adding Notes

Press **PageDown** to move to the next slide and add notes where needed throughout the rest of your presentation.

4 Print the Notes

If you prefer to print your notes instead of following along on your laptop as you give your presentation, you can print each slide and the notes that go with them. Select **Tools**, **Options**, **Presentation**, **Print** and click to select the **Notes** option.

5 Set the Default Note Formatting

If you want to set up a master format for your notes, you can click the **Master View** button to show the master slide. Select the place-holder text that reads **Click here to edit the notes format** and

NOTE

You don't have to add notes once you've completed all the slides. If you display the Notes view after creating each slide, you can add notes along the way.

then right-click the text to display the formatting menu. You don't have to select the text before right-clicking, but sometimes it's wise; if the note's text box and not the note text itself is still selected, the right-click menu won't display the needed formatting commands.

102 Create Presentation Handouts

Before You Begin

✔ **84** Print a Presentation

See Also

→ **103** Turn a Presentation into Online Web Pages

 TIP

You'll use the Handout view to select specific handouts from your presentation.

Handouts can benefit your audience because they can take home ideas and tips from your presentation. You control what goes into your handouts. You don't have to print every slide in the presentation. Doing so would only cost you paper and would not necessarily benefit your audience. Instead, select the slides that mean the most to your presentation. Consider the following handouts as important, depending on your presentation:

- Your presentation's title, goal, and your name
- Your contact information (Web site, phone number, email address, and so on)
- Critical ideas within your presentation
- Numerical examples the audience can study at their leisure
- Goals for the audience
- Take-home action items that the audience might want to do as a result of your presentation
- Products you or others sell that relate to your presentation and that will benefit your audience

KEY TERM

Handouts master slide—A slide that shows the formatting and number of slides per handout.

① Request the Handout View

Select **View**, **Workspace**, **Handout View** (or click the **Handout View** button atop your vertical scrollbar) to enter the Handout view. The *handouts master slide* appears.

② Modify the Handouts Master Slide

The handouts master slide appears, showing you the default settings for the handouts, such as four slides per page. Right-click the handouts master slide and select **Slide**, **Modify Slide** from the menu to display the **Modify Slide** dialog box.

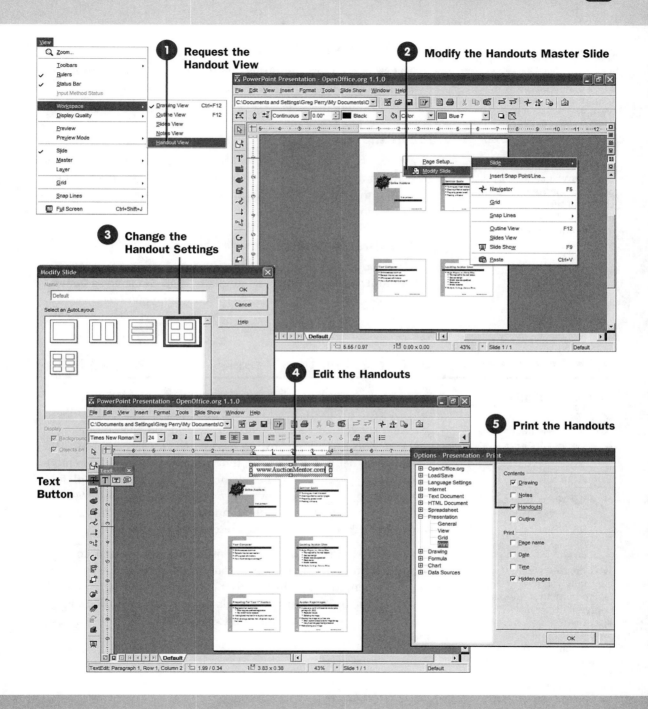

1 Request the Handout View

2 Modify the Handouts Master Slide

3 Change the Handout Settings

4 Edit the Handouts

Text Button

5 Print the Handouts

NOTE

After you click the **Modify Slide** dialog box's **OK** button, Impress warns you that changing the handouts master slide means you won't be able to undo any changes you made before changing this slide. In other words, if you changed your presentation right before changing the handouts master slide, you won't be able to undo those changes.

③ Change the Handout Settings

Click to select a different AutoLayout style for the handouts if you wish. For example, you may want to print six slides per handout instead of four. Click **OK** to apply your changes.

④ Edit the Handouts

With the handouts showing, you can edit, rearrange, and add elements to them. For example, you can add a text box (by first long-clicking the **Main** toolbar's **Text** button) at the top and throughout the handouts for your audience.

⑤ Print the Handouts

Select **Tools, Options, Presentation, Print** and select the **Handouts** option to print the handouts. **80 Set Impress Options** describes other options available to you when you're ready to print.

103 Turn a Presentation into Online Web Pages

Before You Begin

✔ **81** Create a New Presentation

✔ **82** Open an Existing Presentation

See Also

→ **104** About Giving Presentations

KEY TERM

Web hosting service—A company you hire or an inside computer support center that provides disk space where you can store Web pages and other online content. You might even host your own Web pages from your own computer if you have the knowledge and system software to do so.

Instead of a roomful of people, why not give your presentation to the world? You can by turning your Impress presentation into a set of Web pages. After converting your presentation to Web content, you must upload your pages to a *Web hosting service* (which will probably be the same service, either in-house or out, that hosts your Web site currently) and link to the presentation. When your site's visitors click the link for your presentation, they can enjoy your presentation from their Web browser. If the presentation is manual and not automatic, they can click forward and backward to watch the presentation.

Impress makes it surprisingly easy to convert your presentation to an online presentation. The most difficult part of the process is uploading the online presentation and linking to it (neither of which is Impress's role but rather tasks you must do outside Impress—or you can find someone who has the knowledge to upload and link to your presentation for you).

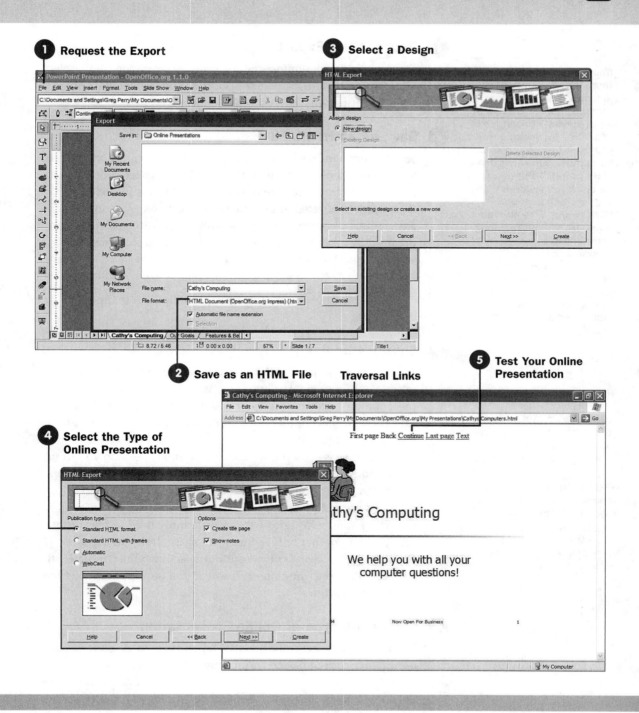

1 Request the Export

2 Save as an HTML File

3 Select a Design

4 Select the Type of Online Presentation

5 Test Your Online Presentation

Traversal Links

TIP

Impress actually supports three Web formats: HTML, Macromedia's *Flash* format (perhaps best if you use a lot of special effects), and PDF files (for documents you want to look the same on any computer that displays them). All three can be displayed inside a Web browser, although only HTML works with all Web browsers without requiring extra add-in products. Most browsers these days, though, are equipped to display PDF or Flash files without trouble. Plug-ins are available from Macromedia.com to play Flash and display PDF files.

KEY TERMS

HTML—Abbreviation for *Hypertext Markup Language* and refers to the code needed to make Web pages display properly inside a Web browser.

Flash—The name for an animated file format developed by Macromedia, Incorporated to give Web sites the capability to display animation using very little bandwidth.

① Request the Export

Once you finish designing and reviewing your presentation, select **File**, **Export** to display the **Export** dialog box, where you can export your presentation as a Web page.

② Save as an HTML File

Select a location in which to save the online presentation from the **Save in** drop-down list box at the top of the **Export** dialog box. Type a filename in the **File name** field and make sure **HTML Document** is selected in the **File format** list box. When you click **Save**, Impress converts your presentation to *HTML* code and stores the resulting Web pages, with a starting Web page named the same as your **File name** field and with each page in your presentation being saved as a separate Web page linked to that one.

Once you start the export, Impress opens the **HTML Export** dialog box.

③ Select a Design

The first page of the **HTML Export** dialog box requests that you select a design or create a new one. When you export your first presentation, you won't see any designs to choose from. As you save presentations in an online format, following through with the rest of the HTML export process, you will be able to save various Web site designs from the selections you make, keeping you from having to reselect them when you want to create similar Web presentations. For example, when you finish the process of exporting your first presentation to HTML, you then can save the HTML exporting options you chose so you later only need to select that name when another online presentation is to take on the same characteristics. Click **Next** to continue specifying the characteristics for this online presentation or **Create** if you decide to choose from an existing design.

④ Select the Type of Online Presentation

You now must select the type of Web page to create—either a standard HTML format or one with frames. If you select the framed Web site, Impress creates Web pages in a main frame with a table of contents to the left of the frame that contains a list of hyperlinks to the rest of your presentation. As you select from the **Publication type** options, the preview and related options change depending on your choice. For example, if you choose to create an automatic online presentation, Impress displays options that determine how long each slide is to be viewed before moving to the next slide (your own slide duration times will be in effect unless you specify a different duration setting here).

The **Automatic** option creates an automatic presentation where the slides advance online, just as they do in automatic presentations that you generate on your PC (see **100 Make an Automatic Presentation**). Reserve the **WebCast** option for when you have advanced server capabilities or can work with someone who does. You can use a WebCast presentation to control the presentation from your desk while teleconferencing with others who view your presentation, as you might do on a teleconferencing training call. For example, you could develop a presentation about reading stock charts and teach a phone class to a conferenced group of students around the world who would log in to your server's Web pages and view your presentation as you change slides and speak on the phone.

Finally, check the **Create title page** and **Show notes** options if you want a title page and your speaker notes generated for your online presentation. Click **Next** to continue exporting the online presentation.

You must now specify the type of graphics (such as **GIF** or **JPG**) that you want your presentation graphics saved as. If you choose the **JPG** option, you must specify a quality value. The closer your selected value is to **100%**, the more accurate your graphics will look, but the longer they will take to display in your users' Web browsers. Unless you know the kind of hardware most of your users will have, as you might if you were developing an in-house, online training presentation, select the **Low resolution (640 × 480 pixels)** option so your presentation loads as quickly as possible for everyone who views it online. Click **Create** to generate your online presentation. Impress asks you for a name to give to your Web page design. This name is little more than a collection of **HTML Export** dialog box settings you've given so far that you can choose from in the future instead of having to specify them again for this kind of presentation. If you did click to select **Save**, you can opt out of

> **NOTE**
>
> In spite of the advantages that a framed Web page seems to bring, such as the automatic table of contents, framed Web sites are generally frowned upon today due to the difficulties users often have bookmarking them. Table-based Web pages are simpler to maintain and maneuver.

TIP

You can review your online presentation from within a Web browser without uploading the files to a Web hosting service. Start your Web browser, select **File**, **Open**, and browse to the folder with your online presentation. Select the starting page, and your presentation begins inside your browser.

naming the design by clicking **Do Not Save** instead of entering a name and clicking **Save**.

Impress now generates your Web pages, creating JPG or GIF images and HTML files as needed. The name of the starting page, or the *home page* of your presentation, is the name you gave the HTML file when you first began exporting the presentation. This is the name you'll link to from other sites, once you transfer the generated online presentation files to your Web hosting service.

⑤ Test Your Online Presentation

Once you or someone you have help you transfers the generated files to the appropriate Web hosting service, and once you link to the files from within your Web browser (or type the address of the online presentation directly into your browser's **Address** box), your presentation is ready for you to review. Anyone viewing your presentation, even if it's an automatic presentation, can click the traversal links across the top of your presentation to move forward or backward throughout the presentation.

⟨104⟩ About Giving Presentations

Before You Begin

✔ ⟨81⟩ Create a New Presentation

✔ ⟨83⟩ Run a Presentation

✔ ⟨100⟩ Make an Automatic Presentation

 **NOTE**

Not every speech requires Impress's tools. A simple speech that you plan to give may be better presented without any overhead slides shown to your audience. However, you can still use Impress to develop your content and thoughts and to arrange the topics you wish to speak on.

Giving presentations seems to be as much of an art as a skill. Some extremely enjoyable, attention-getting speakers use absolutely no presentation handouts, notes, or overhead materials such as those Impress can produce. On the other hand, many professional speakers wouldn't enter a room without tools such as the ones Impress provides.

You must decide what is best for you, given your comfort level, your ability to capture an audience, your material, and the environment in which you plan to present your material. One thing is for sure—tools such as Impress are so powerful, it's easy to get caught up in special effects, color, and sound so much that your presentation's details take away from your message. You must keep in the forefront that your message should take priority over the presentation in every detail.

Don't add a special effect unless that effect accents the message you're trying to convey on that slide. Don't add sound to your presentation without ensuring that you won't be speaking when the sound starts. If you create automatic presentations, you might rely a little more on sound and special effects to keep the audience's attention because you won't be there to direct things, but the message you want to convey is still paramount to the technical aspects of your presentation.

Unlike tradition, seriously consider *not* passing out handouts of your presentation, or even letting your audience know you have them, until after your presentation ends. If you do, you may lose the interest of some audience members because they will assume all the information is in the handouts. Or they may think they can study the handouts later, and in doing so, they may miss connecting important points together that you make in your speech but that may not be explicit in the handouts. Do what you can to keep your audience attentive to your message—this may mean that you buck the trend and not pass out handouts before you speak.

Don't print, word for word, your speaker notes, either on slides or on a printed piece of paper you keep with you at the podium. You need to know your presentation well enough to give it cold, without any notes other than (perhaps) a card with key words that remind you of your presentation's order.

Unless you're teaching technical material, I'd suggest that you save questions for the end of your presentation. If you do not, you may be sidetracked from your presentation, you may go over time (upsetting both your audience and possibly the host conference personnel if you're speaking at a conference), and your entire presentation runs the risk of being derailed.

Finally, even though it should go without saying, how many times have you seen a speaker get up before the audience and not know how to work the equipment? You need to arrive before your audience and prepare your hardware, get your handouts ready to pass out after the talk, and test your entire presentation system before the presentation starts. If you cannot get the ball rolling when you're supposed to start the presentation, you lose control of the situation in your audience's eyes and you must fight to regain your audience.

TIP

Know your presentation but do not memorize it. Instead of coming across knowing your material inside and out, if you recite a memorized speech, you will come off sounding stiff and boring no matter how well you know your topic and no matter how interesting your topic is.

NOTE

As you can see, giving a presentation requires far more important tasks than using Impress to create slides. Make Impress an important part of your presentation but don't make Impress the center of your presentation. Impress should only serve your presentation and not the other way around.

PART IV

Drawing on Your Inner Artist with Draw

IN THIS PART:

14

Getting Ready to Draw

IN THIS CHAPTER:

KEY TERMS

Vector graphics—Graphics defined by geometric shapes such as lines, curves, rectangles, and polygons. Internally, vector graphics are stored as mathematical values, helping to decrease file size.

Snap lines—Also called *snap-to lines* and refers to logical lines that align the objects on your drawing to one another. When requested, an object shifts to the closest snap line as soon as you drag that object close to the snap line. Items aligned along the same snap lines will stay in alignment unless you move them relatively far from their snap lines.

With Draw, you can generate drawings and graphics. Draw supports all popular graphics formats, both for importing images as well as for the drawings you want to save. Here are just a few features Draw supports:

- *Vector graphics*—Use predefined geometric shapes to generate your drawings.

- **3D objects**—Create three-dimensional shapes to add depth to your images.

- **Light application**—Adjust the perceived light source on the objects you draw to add realism.

- **Object connections**—Logically connect objects so that when you move or resize one, other objects adjust accordingly.

Draw supports a gallery that contains numerous graphic images, animations, sounds, and Web graphics such as buttons, bullets, and backgrounds that you can use to spruce up your drawings. You can make your drawings more consistent by taking advantage of Draw's grids and *snap lines*.

If you're a graphic design artist, you'll be surprised at the tools you can get in Draw considering its free price. If you're not much of an artist, like this author, you'll be thankful that Draw's tools can help make your drawings more presentable when you need to create them.

105 Set Draw Options

See Also

→ **106** Create a New Drawing

→ **107** Open an Existing Drawing

TIP

Even if you're familiar with Calc or another OpenOffice.org set of options, initially learning about Draw's options now gives you a preview of what Draw is able to do.

Not everybody works the same way, so not every Draw user wants to use Draw the same way. By setting some of Draw's many options, you will make Draw conform to the way you like to do things. For example, you may want to hide Draw's image placeholding anchors because they distract you from your drawing. (**110** **Draw from Scratch** describes the use of anchors.) The options you set control this and many other aspects of Draw.

As a matter of fact, Draw has an option for just about anything! Table 14.1 describes Draw's option categories. You'll learn a lot about what Draw can do just by looking through the options available to you.

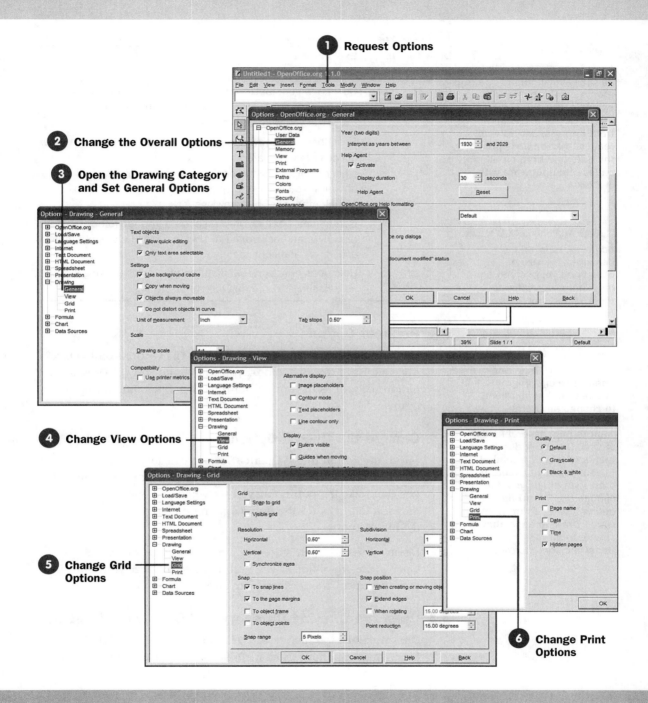

1 Request Options

2 Change the Overall Options

3 Open the Drawing Category and Set General Options

4 Change View Options

5 Change Grid Options

6 Change Print Options

NOTE

All options are available for all OpenOffice.org programs at all times. For example, you can control the display of a grid in Calc from Impress, and you can request that Impress print the date and time on all pages of output from within Draw.

KEY TERM

Scale—A ratio that describes the size of objects on your screen and how that size relates to their actual printed size.

TIP

Often you'll work in one OpenOffice.org program and realize that you need to change an overall option. For example, if you want to print several kinds of OpenOffice.org documents to a file (instead of to your printer) to send to others via email, you can change the **OpenOffice.org** option labeled **Print**, from within Draw, to apply that setting to all OpenOffice.org programs.

TABLE 14.1 Draw's Drawing Options

Draw Option Category	Explanation
General	Describes general Draw settings, such as the initial default unit of measurements for elements within a drawing and the *scale* you want your drawings to appear in.
View	Describes how Draw appears on the screen and which Draw special elements are shown, such as rulers and graphic placeholders. Only the contour, or *outline*, of graphics appear if you elect to display image placeholders in place of actual images in your drawings.
Grid	Determines whether Draw displays a grid for you on your drawing area background to help you place elements more accurately and consistently.
Print	Describes how Draw handles the printing of drawings, such as as adjusting the drawing size to fit the paper.

1 **Request Options**

Select **Options** from Draw's **Tools** menu. The **Options** dialog box appears. From this dialog box, you can change any of Draw's options as well as the options for the other OpenOffice.org programs.

2 **Change the Overall Options**

Select any option in the **OpenOffice.org** category to modify OpenOffice.org-wide settings such as pathnames. For example, if you don't like the pathname you see when you open or save a drawing to disk, click the **Paths** option and change it to a different default file path.

If you're new to OpenOffice.org, consider leaving all the OpenOffice.org options "as is" until you familiarize yourself with how the OpenOffice.org programs work.

3 **Open the Drawing Category and Set General Options**

Click the plus sign next to the **Drawing** option to display the four Draw-specific options listed in Table 14.1 at the beginning of this task.

Click the **General** options category; the dialog box changes to show options you can select to make changes to the general Draw options. The **Text objects** section enables you to specify how you wish to edit text objects inside your drawings—either quickly when they're available by clicking them or only after you click the **Option** bar's **Allow Quick Editing** button. The **Settings** section describes how you want Draw to use its background cache when displaying objects in a drawing (without the cache, Draw runs more slowly, although on recent computers you'll hardly notice the difference). In addition, you can specify how you wish to handle copying and moving your drawings' objects, and you may also specify how you want to handle measurements and tab stops, such as in inches or metrically. The **Scale** section shows the ratio of drawing size on your screen's rulers and how they relate to the actual printed drawing. The **Compatibility** section enables you to determine if you want Draw to use a different layout for the screen and printed drawings (typically you'll leave this option unchecked).

❹ Change View Options

Click the **View** options category under the **Drawing** category; the dialog box changes to show options that handle Draw's onscreen display. The **Alternative display** section determines how and when Draw shows elements such as text and images. If you choose to show placeholders only, Draw will not display actual text and graphics but rather will show placeholders for them to speed your screen's display. During the editing of a large drawing, you can often speed up the editing process by electing to show placeholders instead of actual text and graphics. When printing your drawings, of course, Draw will show the actual text and graphics on the drawings because the placeholders would be meaningless as artwork. The **Display** section enables you to determine how special elements such as the rulers are to show while you work within Draw.

TIP

If you are new to Draw, perhaps it's best to accept Draw's default option settings. Read through them now to familiarize yourself with the terminology, however. Once you've created some drawings, you'll better understand how these options impact your work.

❺ Change Grid Options

Click to select the **Grid** category under the **Drawing** option category. The **Grid** section enables you to determine whether to use the snap-to grid and whether to make the grid visible. The **Resolution** section specifies the width between each grid point measurement (decrease the width for detailed drawings). If you click to check the **Synchronize axes** option, when you change the X-axis, the Y-axis adjusts symmetrically at the same time, instead of changes to one axis not affecting the other. The **Snap** section determines how you want to use the snap-to grid to align objects. If you create many freeform drawings, such as an artist might do with a drawing tablet attached to the computer, you'll want to turn off all snap-to items. If you create commercial drawings and some educational drawings showing relationships and textual backgrounds and layouts, you may wish to require that some objects move toward the closest snap-to grid for consistency and alignment of objects.

6 Change Print Options

Click to select the **Print** category under the **Drawing** option category. The **Quality** section enables you to determine whether you want your drawing printed in the default screen colors or in a more efficient grayscale or black and white (both printed without colors, thus saving color printer ink and toner). The **Print** section specifies what you want printed, such as the page name (if you've assigned one), date, time, or pages you've hidden within the drawing but may want to print. The **Page options** section determines how you want your drawings to fit the final page—whether they should take up the actual size specified by the ruler or whether you want Draw to shrink the drawings enough to fit on the current page. You can also specify whether you want to print on the front and back of the page as well as use the printer's own paper tray settings instead of the default settings.

106 Create a New Drawing

Before You Begin

✔ **105** Set Draw Options

See Also

→ **107** Open an Existing Drawing

→ **110** Draw from Scratch

Unlike most other OpenOffice.org programs, Draw comes with no templates. Unlike common documents (such as memos) and presentations (such as those that might introduce a new product), drawings can differ from one another in such a major way that there isn't any way OpenOffice.org could provide templates that attempt to help you with what you might want to draw next.

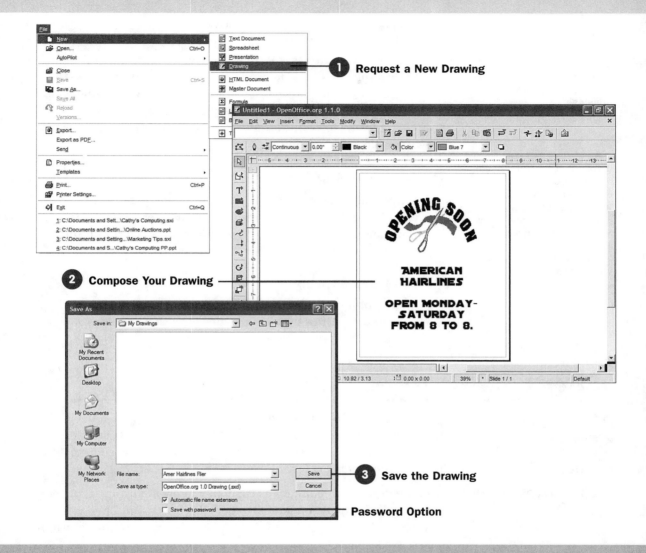

1 Request a New Drawing

2 Compose Your Drawing

3 Save the Drawing

Password Option

Most often, you'll create a brand-new drawing from scratch (or change one you've already created). Draw supplies drawing tools such as shapes and lines, and you can place graphic images and charts in your drawings also. Of course, you can put text throughout a drawing and add some effects to the text to make it look more artistic than plain text would look.

NOTE

Draw does support templates, and you can create your own by saving your drawing with the **File, Save As** menu option and selecting the **OpenOffice.org Drawing Template** option for the file type.

CHAPTER 14: Getting Ready to Draw

1 Request a New Drawing

Select **Drawing** from the **Windows** menu to create a new drawing. Draw displays a blank drawing area on which you can work. Of course, once inside Draw, you can select **File, New, Drawing** to display a fresh drawing area where you can create your drawing. Alternatively, you can click the **New** toolbar button to open a new, blank drawing area quickly.

2 Compose Your Drawing

Create your drawing in the blank drawing area that Draw provides. You'll draw lines, add shapes, type and format text, and edit your composition depending on your drawing's goals. You can print your drawing (see **109** **Print a Drawing**) at any time.

3 Save the Drawing

After creating your drawing, select **File, Save** and type the name of your drawing. Draw uses the filename extension .sxd for your drawing. Click **Save** to save your drawing.

107 Open an Existing Drawing

Before You Begin

✔ **106** Create a New Drawing

See Also

→ **108** About Drawing with Draw

Opening an existing drawing to edit within Draw is simple. You tell Draw that you want to open a drawing file and then locate the file. Draw then loads the drawing into memory, where you can edit the drawing on the drawing area.

One important Draw feature is its capability to open drawings that you create in other graphics programs. In addition to opening Draw files, Draw opens the following kinds of files as well as exports Draw drawings to these file formats:

- BMP (Windows Bitmap)
- DXF (AutoCAD Interchange Format)
- EMF (Enhanced Metafile)
- EPS (Encapsulated PostScript)
- GIF (Graphics Interchange Format)
- JPEG and JPG (Joint Photographic Experts Group)

- PCT (Mac Pict)

- PCZ (Zsoft Paintbrush)

- PNG (Portable Network Graphic)

- PSD (Adobe Photoshop)

- SDA and SDD (StarDraw 3.0 and 5.0)

- TGA (Truevision Targa)

- TIF and TIFF (Tagged Image File Format)

- WMF (Windows Metafile)

❶ Request an Existing Drawing

Select **Open** from Draw's **File** menu to display the **Open** dialog box.

❷ Navigate to the Drawing's Location

The drawing that you want to open might not appear at the default location shown in the **Open** dialog box, so navigate to the folder in which the drawing you're looking for resides using the **Look in** drop-down list.

❸ Locate the Drawing You Want

When you locate the folder that holds the presentation file, select the file you want to open. Then click the **Open** button to open the selected Impress file.

Draw opens the drawing and places it for you to view, edit, and print on Draw's drawing area. If the entire drawing is large, you may need to select the **View, Zoom** menu option and increase the zoom factor to see a close-up of your drawing's details before editing them.

❹ Edit the Drawing

After the file opens on the Draw workspace, you can edit the drawing (see ⓽ **Place Shapes on the Drawing Area** and ⓫ **Draw Lines**).

> **NOTE**
>
> Draw opens a few more graphic file types than those listed here, but the rest are far more obscure and less important these days.

> **TIPS**
>
> You can open drawings from your computer's disk or from elsewhere in the file system. If you want to open a drawing located on the Web, preface the filename with the http:// Web address or the ftp:// File Transfer Protocol address to open drawing files from those sources.
>
> Feel free to open more than one drawing by holding the **Ctrl** key while clicking multiple filenames. Draw opens each drawing that you select in its own window. Use the **Window** menu to select a currently opened drawing that you want to edit.

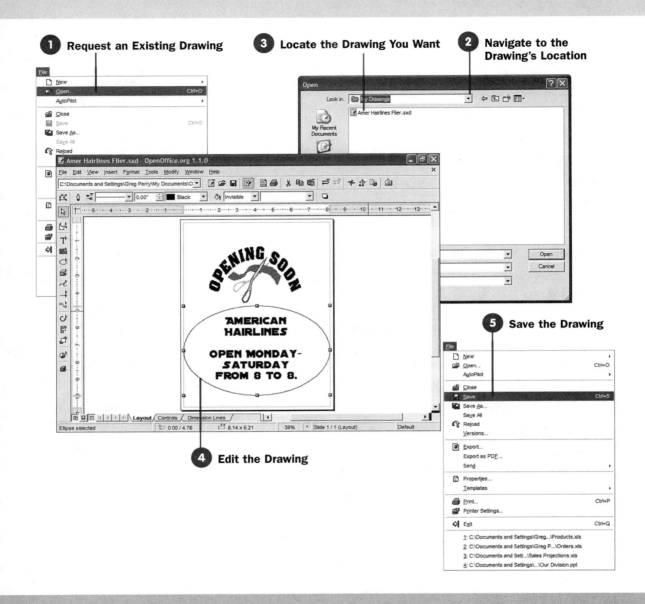

1 Request an Existing Drawing

3 Locate the Drawing You Want

2 Navigate to the Drawing's Location

5 Save the Drawing

4 Edit the Drawing

5 Save the Drawing

Once you've made all the changes you wish to make, select **File**, **Save** to save your drawing. Your recent changes will be saved in the drawing file for your next editing or printing session.

108 About Drawing with Draw

Without question, Draw is the most enjoyable of all the OpenOffice.org programs. Your imagination is the key to your creations. Well, that's a little too artsy…. Your artistic ability has most to do with how well you use Draw to produce drawings that people will enjoy. Still, Draw is fun to use, and it's the only one of the OpenOffice.org programs that both adults and children have fun using.

Draw supports all kinds of shapes. Here is only a sample of the shapes available to you as a Draw artist:

- Lines of all thicknesses, patterns, and lengths, including arrows and connectors

- Curves, circles, and ovals (ellipses of all kinds)

- Rectangles, squares, and polygons

- 3D blocks, 3D cones, 3D cylinders, 3D conclave holders, and 3D convex holders

- Artistic text

As you use draw, you place various shapes on the drawing area. You control all aspects of the shapes you place there, including their lighting effects, their rotation angles, their size, their interaction with other objects, their color, their line thickness, and more. You can always return to shapes you place on your drawing and delete, resize, and edit them.

One of the most powerful features of Draw is its capability to combine multiple shapes so that you can treat those shapes as a single object. You can temporarily combine multiple shapes to work with them currently or you can combine them into a single shape semi-permanently (you can, through menu commands, uncombine them).

As you place items on the screen, you are placing them on slides, not unlike Impress slides. (See the introduction in Chapter 11, "Learning About Impress," for a quick background about Impress slides.) You normally work from the Slide view (selected by clicking the **Slide View** button or by choosing **View**, **Slide** from the menu). A drawing might contain multiple slides, each having a tab at the bottom of your screen so you can quickly change slides. The slides never appear at the same time together.

Before You Begin

✔ **106** Create a New Drawing

✔ **107** Open an Existing Drawing

See Also

→ **110** Draw from Scratch

 TIP

Not only does Draw support multiple shapes, but you can control how those shapes overlap. You can combine or uncombine shapes to produce different effects when you place multiple images on the same plane.

Combined Shapes

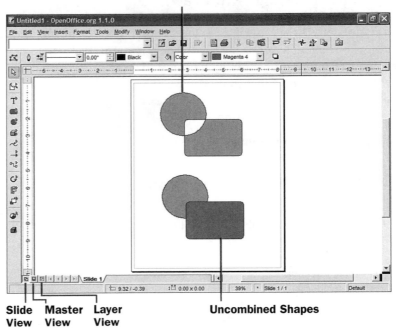

Slide   Master   Layer
View   View   View

Uncombined Shapes

You control the intersections of multiple shapes.

TIP

Whenever you want to place the same objects (such as a title and a background image) on all your drawing's slides, place those objects on the Master view so they appear on all slides you create in that drawing.

KEY TERM

Layers—Groups of items, such as your drawing's graphics and text, controls you place on a drawing, or dimension lines for three-dimensional space control.

In addition to the Slide view, two other views exist: the Master view and the Layer view. The Master view contains all the drawing elements that comprise your drawing's background. If you create a single drawing on a single slide, you won't need to work inside the Master view. If, however, you want to create multiple slides within the same drawing, the Master view determines the background of every slide.

In addition to the combining of multiple objects, Draw enables you to work with multiple *layers* within the same drawing. Layers are extremely advanced and are to be used when you add controls such as buttons to your drawing, as you might when creating graphical Web pages with Draw. Draw supports three layers: the **Layout** layer, which contains your drawing elements, the **Controls** layer, which holds buttons and other controls you may add to a drawing, and the **Dimension Lines** layer, which is to be used for rotating and placing objects in three-dimensional drawings. All three layers are available when you click the **Layer View** button. None of these layers is covered in this book due to their esoteric nature.

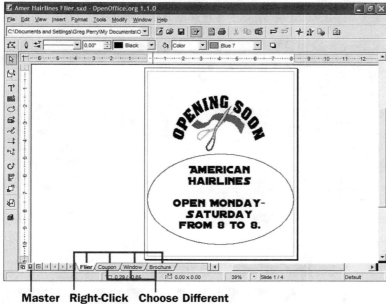

Master   Right-Click   Choose Different
View   to Rename   Slide

*One drawing can contain many slides, each its own drawing with a
background defined by the drawing on your Master view.*

At first, the terminology and concept of slides and layers within Draw
can be misleading. Neither slides nor layers act like transparency slides
that you can stack on top of one another to form a single drawing. You
don't need a "transparency" concept such as that in Draw because you
can always stack shapes and graphics on top of each other and
rearrange them so their stacked order changes. You reorder stacks of
individual objects, not the layers they reside on.

109 Print a Drawing

Once you're done creating your drawing, you'll want to print it to paper.
Draw supports the standard printing options that most Windows programs support. If your drawing uses color and you have a color printer,
the colors print just fine. Otherwise, the colored areas will print in
shades of black and gray (and still look fine!).

Before You Begin

✔ **106** Create a New
Drawing

✔ **107** Open an Existing
Drawing

See Also

→ **110** Draw from Scratch

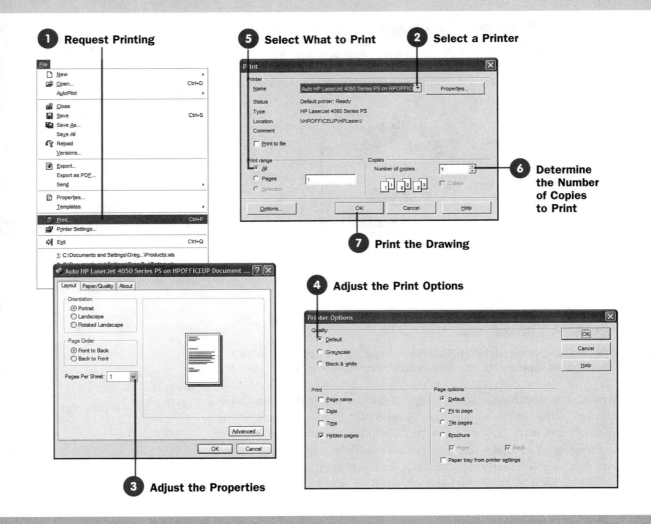

① **Request Printing**

⑤ **Select What to Print**

② **Select a Printer**

⑥ **Determine the Number of Copies to Print**

⑦ **Print the Drawing**

④ **Adjust the Print Options**

③ **Adjust the Properties**

Be sure to save your drawing before you print it. Actually, it's a good idea to select **File, Save** to save your drawing throughout the creation and editing of that drawing. If your printer jams or the Windows print queue messes up during the printing process (rare, but it can happen), you could lose changes you made to the drawing before you printed it.

① Request Printing

Select **Print** from the **File** menu. The **Print** dialog box opens.

② Select a Printer

Select the printer you want to print to from the **Name** drop-down list in the **Printer** section.

③ Adjust the Properties

If you want to adjust any printer settings, click the **Properties** button. The dialog box that appears when you click **Properties** varies from printer to printer. Click **OK** to close the printer's **Properties** dialog box once you've made any needed changes. If, for example, your printer's properties support multiple pages per sheet, you can select the number of drawing slides you want on each printed page (as opposed to the one slide per page that Draw normally prints).

④ Adjust the Print Options

Click the **Options** button to display the **Printer Options** dialog box. From the **Printer Options** dialog box, you can adjust several print settings, such as whether you want to print in grayscale or black and white (to save color ink or toner), whether you want the date and time printed, and whether you want Draw to scale down your drawing to fit a single printed page if needed.

Click the **OK** button to close the **Printer Options** dialog box.

⑤ Select What to Print

Click to select either **All** or **Pages** to designate whether you want to print the entire drawing (assuming multiple slides reside in the drawing) or only a portion of it. If you clicked **Pages**, type the page number or a range of page numbers (such as **2–5** or **1–10, 15–25**) that you want to print. If a single drawing takes multiple pages, you can control how many of those pages you want to print.

⑥ Determine the Number of Copies to Print

Click the arrow next to the **Number of Copies** option to determine how many copies you want to print.

TIP

If you select **File, Export as PDF**, Draw saves your document in the common PDF format, which you can send to any computer with Adobe Acrobat Reader, allowing the users to view or print your drawing even if they don't have Draw (see ③⑥ **Save a Document as a PDF File** for information on PDF terminology and usage).

NOTE

Unlike Writer and Calc, Draw does not support a print preview feature—and it doesn't need one. What you see in the drawing area (in Slide view) is what your drawing will look like when you print it.

TIP

If you have a fax modem, you can select your fax from the **Name** list to send your drawing to a fax recipient.

NOTE

Although it's called the **Printer Options** dialog box, this dialog box is not printer specific; rather, it controls the way your drawing appears when printed. If, for instance, you want to produce a brochure, you could click to select the **Brochure** option and specify whether you want Draw to print on both the front and back of the paper. For automatic double-sided printing, you need a printer that supports double-sided printing.

7 **Print the Drawing**

Once you've determined how many pages and copies to print, click the **OK** button to print your drawing and close the **Print** dialog box.

15

Improving Your Drawings

IN THIS CHAPTER:

In this chapter, you'll learn how to put the details into your drawings. Starting with a blank drawing area, there is very little you cannot generate with Draw. With the millions of colors available, today's video cards, and high-resolution screens, you have the tools to create fine drawings that can represent any picture you want to produce.

But Draw isn't just for drawings!

Commercial users who create art for logos, slogans, fliers, and other areas will feel at home with Draw's tools. The shapes and alignment tools ensure that your commercial artwork conveys the very message you need it to convey.

110 Draw from Scratch

Before You Begin

✔ **105** Set Draw Options
✔ **106** Create a New Drawing

See Also

→ **111** Place Shapes on the Drawing Area

Freehand drawing is perhaps the first thing most people want to try when they learn a new drawing program. Draw enables you to freeform draw, but on your freeform drawing you can also place all kinds of shapes and graphic images; you can mix it all up on a Draw drawing.

If you're new to Draw, the drawing tools may seem a little awkward at first. When you select a tool and draw with it, as soon as you finish the line or shape, the mouse cursor changes back to its regular pointing cursor, and to use the tool once again, you must select the tool once again. Therefore, if you need to draw several freeform objects, such as birds flying, it might seem as though you must keep selecting the freeform drawing tool each time you add to your drawing. Fortunately, although it may not be fully intuitive, there is a way to keep tools selected that you want to use multiple times, and you learn how to do that here.

1 Select the Freeform Line

Start Draw and go to work! It doesn't matter at this point what you draw if you're new to Draw; you need to get a feel of the basic steps necessary for drawing and placing objects on the drawing area.

The drawing area is enclosed by your paper's outline. You do not have to place objects directly on the paper outline of your drawing area. You can move graphics out of the way by dragging them off the paper temporarily until you're ready to use them and then drag them onto the page.

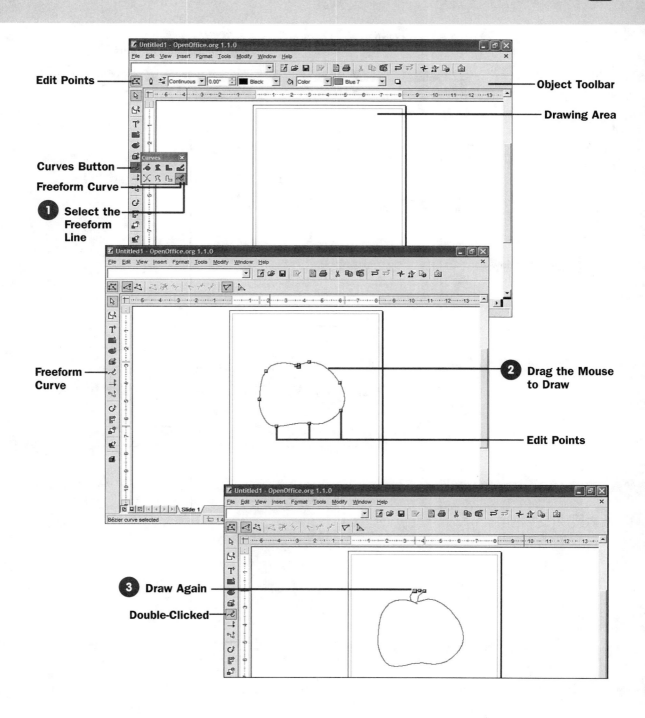

Edit Points

Object Toolbar

Drawing Area

Curves Button

Freeform Curve

1 Select the Freeform Line

Freeform Curve

2 Drag the Mouse to Draw

Edit Points

3 Draw Again

Double-Clicked

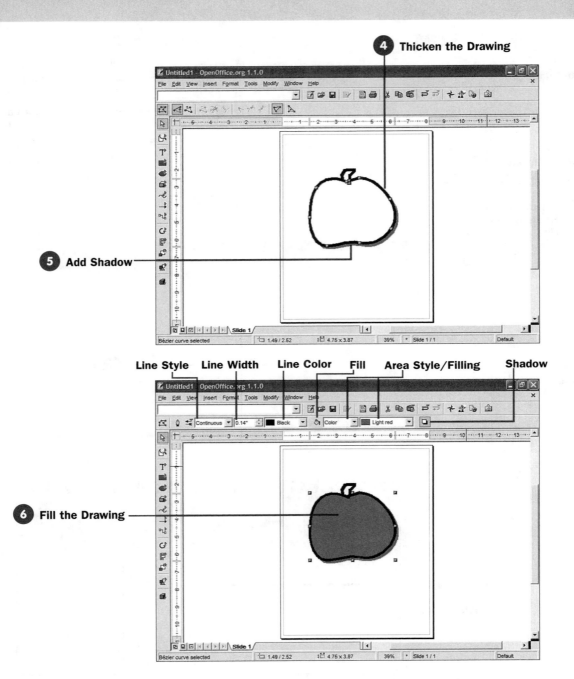

4 Thicken the Drawing

5 Add Shadow

Line Style Line Width Line Color Fill Area Style/Filling Shadow

6 Fill the Drawing

When you're ready to draw, just long-click the **Main** toolbar's **Curve** tool to display the **Curve** toolbar. Click the **Freeform Curve** button. Your mouse cursor changes from the pointer to a crosshair shape with the **Freeform Curve** icon showing next to it.

2 Drag the Mouse to Draw

Drag your mouse (or draw on your computer's drawing tablet if you have one). First click the starting point of the line you're about to draw and hold down your mouse button as you draw a line. The line is freeform because you're using the **Freeform Curve** tool, so you can draw any line, curve, or shape you wish. When you finish, release your mouse button.

Edit points appear throughout your drawing so that you can manipulate those parts of the drawing. These are *not* resizing handles; instead, you can drag an edit point in or out, and only that part of the drawing will move in or out.

If you want to change the size of your drawing, you cannot use the edit points to do so. You must hide the edit points so that you can drag to increase your entire drawing and not just that one section of the drawing. To hide the edit points, click the **Object** toolbar's **Edit Points** button. Now, when and if you click a line in your drawing, resizing handles appear uniformly in a square around your line, and you can then resize the freeform line. Clicking **Edit Points** shows the edit points once more.

3 Draw Again

To draw another freeform line, you must click the **Freeform** button once again to use it again. In other words, each tool that you select by clicking the **Main** toolbar stays active only for one use of that tool. If you're doing a lot of drawing with one of the tools, such as the **Freeform** tool, you won't want to keep selecting the tool after each line you draw. Therefore, Draw lets you double-click any tool to keep that tool active (until you select another).

4 Thicken the Drawing

You can add thickness to your entire drawing by selecting all the lines and thickening them. To select every freeform line in your drawing, press **Ctrl+A**. This **Select All** command displays the edit points for everything on your screen.

NOTE

The **Curve** button changed to the **Freeform Curve** button's icon on your **Main** toolbar. You can click this button to reuse the **Freeform Curve** tool once more without having to long-click the **Curve** button first. You'll only need to long-click the **Curve** button again if you want to select a tool other than the **Freeform** tool on the **Curve** toolbar.

TIP

If you want to draw a closed shape, such as the outline of a face, release your mouse button near the point at which you began drawing.

KEY TERM

Edit points—Also called *data points*. This term refers to points on your drawing, represented by small square boxes, that you drag to modify that part of the shape or freeform line.

NOTE

To delete any part of your drawing, click to select the part you want to delete. (Make sure you can see either the resizing handles or the edit points.) Press the **Del** button to delete that part of your drawing. The **Edit**, **Undo** menu option (**Ctrl+Z**) will replace what you deleted if you delete the wrong piece of the drawing.

NOTE

The **Object** toolbar goes away when you display edit points because displaying the edit points changes the **Object** toolbar so that it shows only edit point-related buttons. Click the **Edit Points** button once again to hide the **Edit Points** buttons and to return to the regular **Object** toolbar.

TIP

You can import graphic images from files onto your drawing area, as you might do for a corporate logo that you want to label a drawing with. Remember that if you've elected to display image placeholders instead of the images themselves, an image anchor will appear as a placeholder for the image. You'll need to select the appropriate **View** option to see the graphic image as it will finally look in your drawing.

With all the points selected, you can easily change the thickness of the lines used. The **Object** toolbar includes several tools you can use to modify your drawing, including a line type and thickness tool. With all your edit points selected, click the up arrow on the **Object** toolbar's **Line Width** control. As you click, your drawing's selected lines will thicken. You can also change the line color by selecting from the **Object** toolbar's **Line Color** control, and you can change the line itself by selecting from the **Line Style** list box.

⑤ Add Shadow

The remaining **Object** toolbar's tools include a **Line** button that enables you to control minute aspects of your drawing's lines, fill buttons that you use to fill the center of enclosed drawing areas with patterns and colors, and a **Shadow** button that adds a shadow effect to your object. Click the **Shadow** button now to add a shadow to your line so you can see the effect.

⑥ Fill the Drawing

If you've drawn an enclosed area, click any place on the line that encloses that area. If the **Edit Points** button is active, click it once more to return to the resizing handles that select the object you want to fill. Select the type of fill pattern you wish to add from the **Area Style/Filling**'s left button (the **Area Style** list box). If you want to fill with a color, select **Color** from the **Area Style/Filling** list box (known as the **Filling** list box, although why the ToolTips don't label these individually is a mystery). The **Area Style** enables you to choose many kinds of fills other than a solid color, such as a hatching or a bitmapped image fill from a graphics file. **115** Fill an Object describes more about filling objects on your drawing area.

111 Place Shapes on the Drawing Area

Although you don't create anything fancy in this task, you do get a tour of Draw's shapes. You must be able to select from and place the various shapes available to you. Draw provides ovals, rectangles, *polygons*, and other shapes, including three-dimensional versions of most of these.

Before getting complicated, you need to master the selection and placement of these shapes on your drawing area. Once you see how to place one shape on the drawing area, the rest are just as simple to do.

The steps in this task walk you through the list of shapes you can place on your drawings.

1 Select a Rectangle Tool

Long-click the **Rectangle** button on your **Main** toolbar. Draw opens a floating toolbar that shows eight rectangles you can draw, from filled and unfilled squares to filled and unfilled rounded rectangles. If you place a filled shape on your drawing, you can always change the fill color before or after you place the shape on your drawing area.

2 Draw the Rectangle Shape

Select one of the rectangles by clicking it once. Your mouse cursor changes to that shape and the **Rectangle** button changes to the shape you selected. Remember that you can only place the shape once on your drawing area before your mouse cursor will return to its normal pointer. To place several occurrences of the same shape on your drawing, double-click that shape's button before drawing.

To place the rectangle on your drawing, click and hold your mouse button where you want to place one corner of the shape and drag your mouse to the opposite corner of the shape you wish to draw. Draw draws the shape as you drag your mouse. When you finish drawing the shape, release your mouse button to anchor the shape into position. You can always resize and change the style of your shape after you've drawn it.

Before You Begin

✔ **106** Create a New Drawing

See Also

→ **113** About Perfecting Shapes

→ **114** Create a New Shape

KEY TERM

Polygons—Multisided shapes. A square and rectangle are four-sided polygons, and a stop sign is an eight-sided polygon. Polygons don't have to be symmetrical.

TIPS

Use the ToolTips feature if you forget what a shape or tool does. For example, let your mouse pointer hover over any button on the **Main** toolbar and Draw pops up a ToolTip box that names the button (for example, the **Lines and Arrows** button).

If you want to change the line style, thickness, or color before you draw a shape, you can do so from the **Object** toolbar. See **110** Draw from Scratch for more information about the **Object** toolbar.

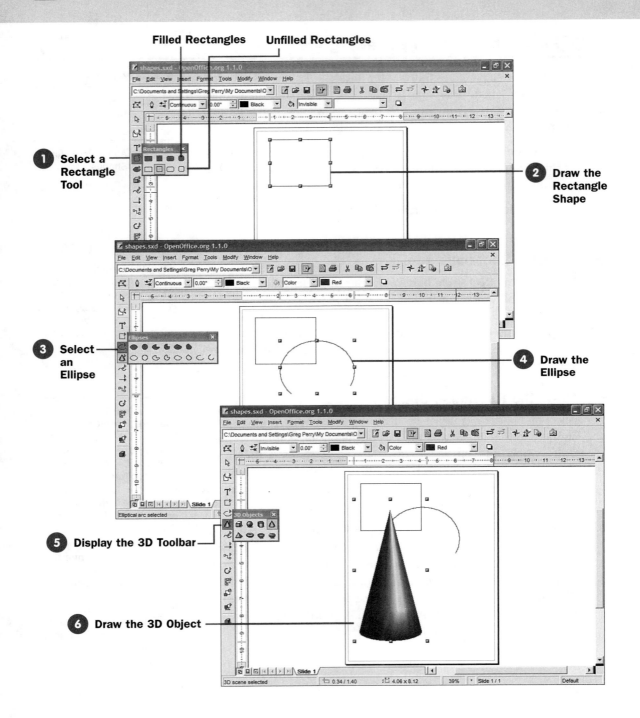

Filled Rectangles   Unfilled Rectangles

1 Select a Rectangle Tool

2 Draw the Rectangle Shape

3 Select an Ellipse

4 Draw the Ellipse

5 Display the 3D Toolbar

6 Draw the 3D Object

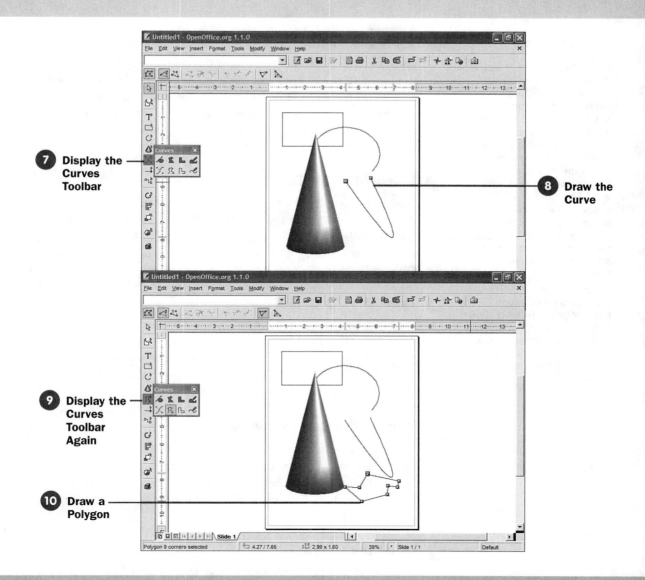

⑦ **Display the Curves Toolbar**

⑧ **Draw the Curve**

⑨ **Display the Curves Toolbar Again**

⑩ **Draw a Polygon**

③ **Select an Ellipse**

Long-click to open the **Ellipse** toolbar. You'll use this toolbar to draw circles, ovals, pie shapes, and partial ovals as well as filled versions of them. (No filled versions exist for either of the two arc tools because an arc is not a closed shape that can hold a fill.)

NOTES

If the **Contour mode** option is checked in your View options (see **105** Set Draw Options), you won't see the 3D shape but only its resizing handles. You must uncheck the **Contour mode** option to see your 3D shape on the screen. (The shape will print either way.) This option is for users who work on slower computers whose screens take far too long to update every time they change a drawing that includes 3D shapes.

In 45-degree polygons, each edge is always a multiple of a 45-degree angle from the previous edge, as is always the case with squares and rectangles.

4 **Draw the Ellipse**

Once you've clicked to select one of the ellipse tools, use that tool to place that shape onto your drawing area. If you draw one of the arcs, Draw first draws the entire circle that would fill the arc. When you release your mouse, a radius line comes out from the center of the circle that you drag left or right, erasing the edge of the circle, until you get the arc you wanted.

5 **Display the 3D Toolbar**

Wait until you get a look at that 3D toolbar! You'll want to start drawing objects just to see their three-dimensional effect. Draw provides cubes, spheres, cylinders, cones, pyramids, and other shapes that come right out at you. Click the **Main** toolbar's **3D Objects** button.

6 **Draw the 3D Object**

Once you've clicked to select one of the 3D tools, use that tool to place that 3D shape onto your drawing area. Depending on the speed of your computer, the 3D shape will take slightly longer to draw than the other shapes due to the more complex computations behind it.

7 **Display the Curves Toolbar**

The **Curves** toolbar, when you click the **Main** toolbar's **Curves** button to open it, produces a toolbar with more tools than just curves. This is the same **Main** toolbar button you clicked earlier to choose the **Freeform** tool. You can draw a curve, a polygon, a 45-degree polygon, and filled versions of each.

8 **Draw the Curve**

To draw a curve, click the **Curves** tool to select it. Click on your drawing area where you want to start the curve. Drag your mouse over the span of the curve and release your mouse button after you've spanned the entire curve length. Your curve initially looks like a straight line, but now the fun begins.

Unlike with most other tools, when you release the mouse button after drawing a curve, you have only designated part of the shape. You must now move your mouse to another location to begin developing the curve; as you move your mouse, the end of the line moves with your mouse, forming a curve to meet your mouse pointer. When the curve is positioned where you want it, double-click your mouse to anchor that end of the curve.

⑨ Display the Curves Toolbar Again

Once again, open the **Curves** toolbar by clicking the **Main** toolbar's **Curves** button. You can now draw a polygon.

⑩ Draw a Polygon

To draw a polygon, click either the **Polygon** or **45-Degree Polygon** tool to select it. Click your drawing area where you want to start the multisided polygon. Drag your mouse in the direction of the polygon's first side. Release your mouse button to anchor that side; then drag your mouse once again to draw the next side. Keep drawing the polygon's sides. To end the polygon, double-click your mouse button. If you want to draw an enclosed polygon, finish as close as you can to the starting point of your polygon before you double-click to anchor the polygon into position.

▲ NOTE

Once you've dragged your mouse to start the curve, don't drag the mouse again. Just move your mouse to adjust the curve as needed; the curve adjusts as you move the mouse.

💡 TIP

Hold the **Shift** key at any point in the polygon where you want a right angle of 45-degrees. For example, if you're drawing a right triangle, you would press **Shift** when you draw the second half of the right angle.

112 Draw Lines

You can easily add lines and arrows to your drawings. In addition to arrows and lines, Draw also supports the use of many kinds of connectors. With lines, arrows, and connectors, you can draw flow diagrams such as organization charts and flowcharts.

Draw gives you the choice of four kinds of connectors:

- Standard connectors with 90-degree angle bends that form a kind of blocked Z pattern

- Line connectors with two halves whose midpoint you can adjust

- Straight connectors that draw one connecting line to another

- Curved connectors that draw curved lines from one object to the next

Before You Begin

✔ 110 Draw from Scratch
✔ 111 Place Shapes on the Drawing Area

See Also

→ 114 Create a New Shape

▲ NOTE

You choose what appears on the ends of connectors, such as an arrow, a small box, or a circle.

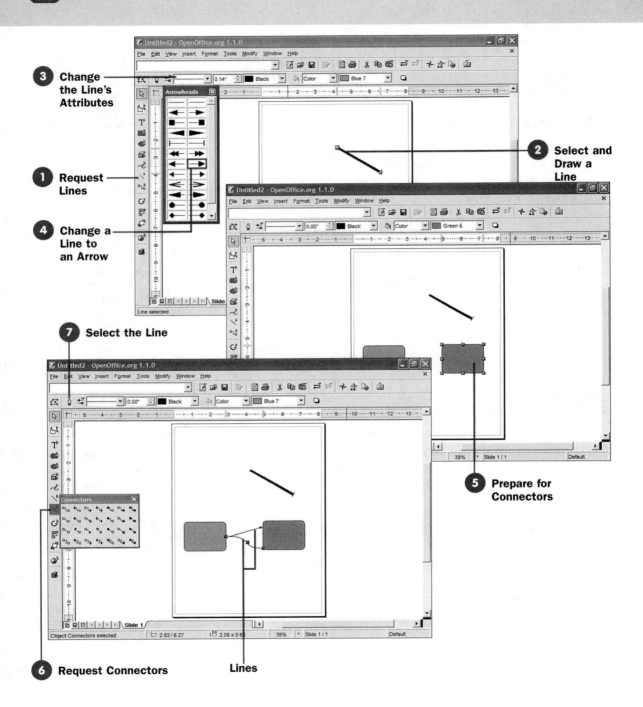

3 Change the Line's Attributes

1 Request Lines

4 Change a Line to an Arrow

2 Select and Draw a Line

7 Select the Line

5 Prepare for Connectors

6 Request Connectors

Lines

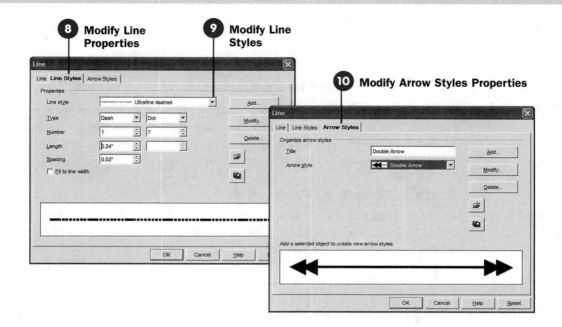

⑧ **Modify Line Properties**

⑨ **Modify Line Styles**

⑩ **Modify Arrow Styles Properties**

You'll want to experiment with the various lines, arrows, and connectors until you see all that Draw has to offer. The **Object** toolbar contains the thickness and color controls you'll need to adjust the attributes of the lines, arrows, and connectors.

❶ Request Lines

Long-click to open the **Lines** toolbar from your **Main** toolbar. You'll see the various lines and arrows. The icon on each of the buttons shows what your selected line or arrow will look like. For example, the *dimension line* is a line with arrows on each end that intersect straight lines.

❷ Select and Draw a Line

Select a line from the lines and arrow tools that you find on the toolbar. As with any shape, you can double-click the tool to keep it active when you want to draw multiple occurrences of that line or arrow. Click the starting point for the line or arrow and drag your

KEY TERM

Dimension line—A line with arrows on each end that intersect perpendicular straight lines used to show a dimension such as the width of a cabinet that you draw.

NOTE

The direction that the arrow points on the **Lines** toolbar determines the direction your drawn arrow will point.

mouse to the ending point. You can draw lines and arrows in any direction, except for the 45-degree line, which you can only draw straight up, straight down, or at a diagonal angle.

3 Change the Line's Attributes

You can select a color and line thickness either before or after you draw the line or arrow. If you want to change an attribute after you draw the line or arrow, you can click to select the line or arrow and then change its thickness and color.

4 Change a Line to an Arrow

You can convert a line to an arrow by first clicking to select the line and then clicking the **Arrow Style** list box from your **Object** toolbar. The **Arrow Style** list box contains more forms of arrows, including double-headed arrows, than is available from the **Lines** toolbar.

5 Prepare for Connectors

Draw two shapes on your drawing area that you will later connect with connectors.

6 Request Connectors

Click to open the **Connectors** toolbar from your **Main** toolbar. Select a connector and click the first object you drew to connect. Drag your mouse to the next object. As you drag your mouse, Draw updates the connecting line according to the style of the connector. You can connect the same two shapes with multiple connectors, so feel free to add another different kind of connecting line to familiarize yourself with the connectors.

7 Select the Line

Draw enables you to adjust lines and connectors with precision from the **Line** dialog box. Select one of the lines or connectors you've drawn and click the **Line** button on your **Object** toolbar.

8 Modify Line Properties

The **Line** dialog box enables you to adjust every detail of the selected line, arrow, or connector. The **Line** page lets you control the line style, color, width, and whether or not the line allows graphics beneath it to show through by the amount of the **Transparency** option. In addition, the **Line** page enables you to change or select from arrow styles, widths, and measurements. A preview at the bottom of the dialog box shows you the result of any change you make to the selected line.

❾ Modify Line Styles

Click to select the **Line Styles** page. Here, you not only select a style but you can help create a new style by specifying the number of dashes or dots that follow one another across the length of your selected line. If you change the line's styles, you will be able to save that style for use later in another drawing.

❿ Modify Arrow Styles Properties

The **Arrow Styles** page enables you to adjust the look of any arrow you select in your drawing. If you change an arrow's style, you will be able to save that style for use later in another drawing. Click **OK** when you want to apply your **Line** dialog box settings to your selected line, connector, or arrow.

113 About Perfecting Shapes

Once you learn how to apply one shape, all the other shapes are simple to add to your drawings. Draw gives you the tools you need to add shapes in a format that suits you best. Surprisingly, a judicious use of your **Shift** and **Alt** keys can dramatically improve your ability to add shapes to your drawings.

When you first learn how to add shapes to your drawings, you'll usually also learn how to adjust their thickness and color. **111** **Place Shapes on the Drawing Area** and **112** **Draw Lines** show examples of how to change these kinds of attributes. Generally, you'll be able to change all the formatting attributes you wish to change from the **Object** toolbar.

In addition to the **Object** toolbar, you have several other ways to change the way your shapes look. **116** **About Manipulating Objects** describes how to use your mouse to adjust a shape's length, size, and skew. As you place shapes on your drawing, however, you can take advantage of some less obvious ways to make the shapes look the way you want them to look.

Before You Begin

✔ **111** Place Shapes on the Drawing Area

✔ **112** Draw Lines

See Also

→ **114** Create a New Shape

NOTE

Using the **45-degree Line** tool is identical to using the regular **Line** tool and holding **Shift**. By using **Shift**, you can also apply 45-degree angles to many more lines and arrows.

For example, if you hold the **Shift** key while drawing certain shapes, some interesting things happen:

- Hold **Shift** while drawing a straight line or arrow, and Draw limits you to 45-degree angles, meaning you can draw the line or arrow straight up and down, left or right, or at 45-degree diagonal intersections, but nowhere else. When you need to draw perfectly horizontal, vertical, or diagonal lines and arrows, remember this trick.

- Hold **Shift** when drawing rectangles, even when not using the **Square** tool, and your rectangles are drawn as perfect squares. If you've selected a **Rectangle** tool instead of one of the **Square** tools by double-clicking it, using **Shift** keeps you from having to select the **Square** tool when you need a square on your drawing.

- Hold **Shift** while drawing polygons, and each line you add with the **Shift** key is limited to 45-degree increments from the previous polygon edge.

- Hold **Shift** when drawing ellipses, even when not using a **Circle** tool, and your ellipses are drawn as perfect circles. **Shift** also keeps your arcs and pies in perfect semicircles instead of letting them become oval.

The **Shift** key has yet another purpose when you move selected items from one place on your drawing to another. Holding **Shift** while you drag an object keeps the movement on a 45-degree plane, making sure you move the object perfectly horizontally, vertically, or at a perfect 45-degree diagonal angle. **116** **About Manipulating Objects** discusses more about selecting, moving, and copying shapes.

Depending on your drawing, it may be easier to draw your shape from its center instead of from one of its corners or edges. For example, suppose you wish to center an oval around some text. Almost always, you'll draw the oval as usual, clicking where its edge is to begin and then dragging the oval down to its other side, enclosing the text as you go.

Once you place the oval on the drawing, you'll then have to drag the resizing handles to align the oval better around the text. Some of the oval, at first, might be overlapping some of the text, whereas other parts of the oval extend too far outside the text area.

Before drawing the oval (or any shape), you can press and hold the **Alt** key to draw that shape from its center. As you drag your mouse, the shape increases in size, moving away from the center where you began drawing. When you release your mouse button, the shape anchors into position. Often, by using the **Alt** key, you keep from having to adjust the shape later because you can better orient the shape around other text and objects on your drawing.

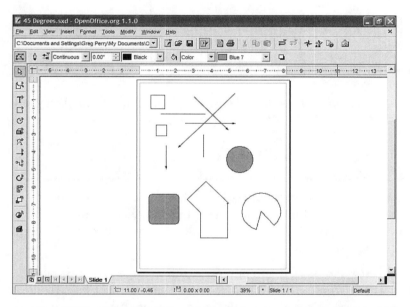

Holding Shift while drawing certain shapes maintains perfect circles, squares, and 45-degree angles.

Started Drawing at Center

Holding Alt draws a shape from its center point outward, enabling you to position the shape better around other objects and text.

114 Create a New Shape

Before You Begin

✔ **111** Place Shapes on the Drawing Area

✔ **113** About Perfecting Shapes

See Also

➜ **117** About Grouping Objects

NOTE

You can only use two or more two-dimensional shapes such as the rectangles and ellipses to create new shapes. Draw does not support the construction of new shapes based on three-dimensional shapes.

You can create your own shapes in Draw. Although you cannot add those shapes to the **Main** toolbar's shape toolbars, you can reuse a shape that you create and resize and modify the shape just as you would resize and format any of Draw's built-in shapes.

To create new shapes from two or more existing shapes, you first place different shapes on the drawing area, overlapping in some way. The first object you place becomes the shape that determines the combined shape's properties. In other words, if the first shape you place on the drawing area is red, your newly created shape (after you place several more objects on that one and merge them) will also be red. You can apply any fill and hatching patterns to your new shape, just as you can apply them to any built-in shape.

❶ Place Two Shapes to Merge

Select and place two shapes on your drawing. They don't have to be the same shape, but make sure they overlap. (You can use more than two shapes to create a new shape if you want to.)

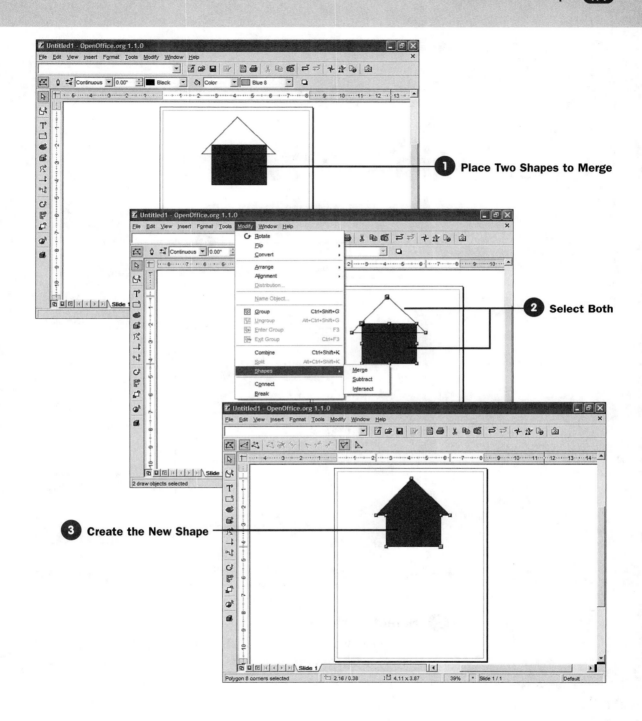

1 Place Two Shapes to Merge

2 Select Both

3 Create the New Shape

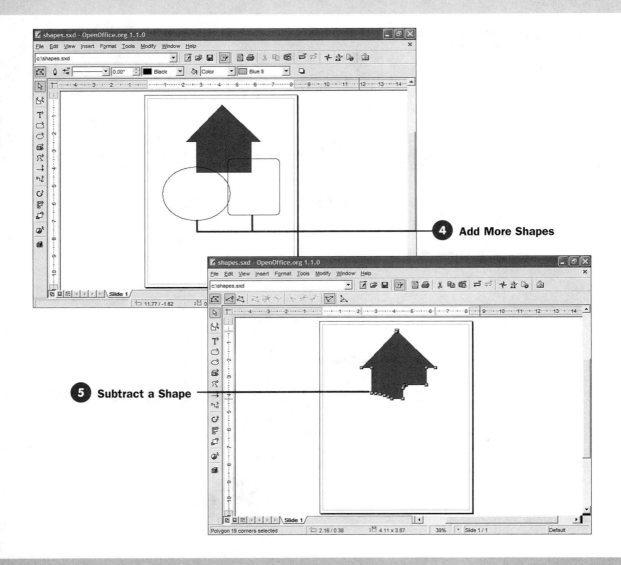

4 Add More Shapes

5 Subtract a Shape

2 Select Both

Hold your **Shift** key and click both objects to select both of them. Select **Modify**, **Shapes** from the menu.

❸ Create the New Shape

Select **Merge** from the **Shapes** menu to create a new shape from the selected shapes. All the selected shapes take on the properties (such as color, line thickness, and so on) of the first shape you placed on the drawing area. If somewhere inside the shape the drawing area shows through, that hole will be left unfilled.

❹ Add More Shapes

Draw also supports the subtraction of certain shapes. To see this in action, add two more shapes to your newly created shape. Keep in mind that your created shape is the earliest of the three shapes you applied to the drawing area, so it takes precedence when you subtract out the other objects.

❺ Subtract a Shape

Press **Ctrl+A** to select all the shapes on your drawing area, including the newly created shape. Select **Modify**, **Shapes**, **Subtract** to remove all shapes that intersect your first shape (in this case, the shape you created). The two new shapes and any overlapping portions of your created shape disappear. You can use the **Subtract** menu command to pick away pieces of a shape or a drawing that you don't wish to show. (If you'd selected the **Modify**, **Shapes**, **Intersect** command instead of the **Modify**, **Shapes**, **Subtract** command, Draw would have kept only those parts of the shapes that overlap each other—that is, the intersecting pieces—and removed the rest.)

NOTE

116 **About Manipulating Objects** describes the selection and grouping of multiple shapes.

TIP

Once you've created the new shape, you can copy, move, and duplicate that shape elsewhere on your drawing without having to re-create it.

---

115 Fill an Object

If you've placed shapes on the drawing area already, you're probably already familiar with the **Object** toolbar's style, width, color, and fill options. (**110** **Draw from Scratch** describes the use of the **Object** toolbar in detail.) Instead of relying solely on the **Object** toolbar, you can use a more complete dialog box, called the **Area** dialog box, that enables you to control every aspect of a shape's fill.

You can choose the colors, gradients, and hatching patterns, and you can even select graphic images to fill up the space inside your shapes. One timesaving feature of the **Area** dialog box is its capability to save

Before You Begin

✔ **111** Place Shapes on the Drawing Area

✔ **114** Create a New Shape

See Also

→ **116** About Manipulating Objects

new fill combinations that you define so that you don't have to select
the same options again when you want to reuse a fill pattern of some
kind.

➊ Draw an Object to Fill

Draw a shape in your drawing area that you can fill.

➋ Request Fill of Area

With the shape selected, select **Format**, **Area** to display the **Area**
dialog box. The first page of the dialog box, **Area**, basically provides the same fill tools as the **Object** toolbar does. You can elect to
use no fill, a color fill, a gradient fill, a hatching pattern fill, or a
bitmap fill (from a graphic image stored on your disk). As you
select the respective **Fill** section options, the **Area** page changes to
reflect the options you've selected. For example, if you click the
Gradient option, the **Area** page offers a long list of gradient patterns you can choose from and enables you to determine how dramatically the gradient moves, in incremental pixels, from one
color to another.

➌ Specify a Shadow

Click to select the **Shadow** page of the **Area** dialog box. Here, you
can apply a shadowing effect to your selected object (including 3D
text you've placed on the drawing). The **Position** option enables
you to determine where the shadow will fall; for example, if you
click the lower-right corner, the shadow will drop from the lower-
right corner of your selected shape when you click **OK** to apply the
shadow.

➍ Select a Transparency

If you elected to add a color fill to the shape, perhaps on the **Area**
page, you can determine how much of the underlying objects show
through the filled area. The **No transparency** option makes the
selected object's fill overwrite anything below it. If you choose the
Transparency option, you can determine, in percentage terms,
how much any objects underneath the fill area show through. If
you choose the **Gradient** option, you determine how the color or
other fill transitions from one edge or corner of the shape to the
opposite edge or corner.

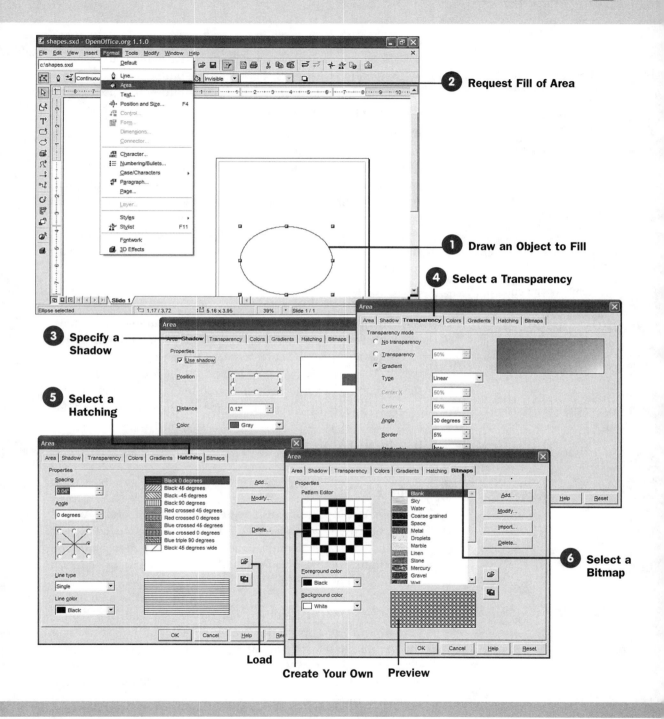

2 Request Fill of Area

1 Draw an Object to Fill

4 Select a Transparency

3 Specify a Shadow

5 Select a Hatching

6 Select a Bitmap

Load

Create Your Own   Preview

Click the **Colors** tab to display the **Colors** page of the **Area** dialog box. Here, you can choose a color or even generate your own color by combining *RGB values*. Click the **Save** button if you generate a color that you might want to reuse in the future. To reuse a saved color, click the **Load** button and select the color you wish to use.

If you click the **Gradients** tab, you are able to specify exact attributes of the gradient you want to fill with. As mentioned earlier in this task, keeping all default gradient values is recommended until you familiarize yourself with their effects. On the **Gradients** page, you can determine the gradient's central location, the angle of the gradient as it moves from one color to another, how much of a border the gradient will have, and the extent of the gradient's "from" and "to" colors. As with the **Colors** page, you can save a specialized gradient that you generate for later use.

⑤ Select a Hatching

Click to select the **Hatching** page. Here, you can select from the available hatching patterns to fill your shape. In addition, you can determine the spacing between hatch marks with the **Spacing** option. You can specify the angle used for the hatching grid lines, the direction of the hatch rotation, and the type and color of lines to use inside the hatching pattern. You can save a specialized gradient that you generate for later use. To reuse a saved hatching pattern, click the **Load** button and select the hatching pattern you wish to use.

⑥ Select a Bitmap

Click the **Bitmaps** tab to display the **Bitmaps** page of the **Area** dialog box. Here, you can select from several bitmapped images to fill your shape. The **Bitmaps** page even enables you to create your own bitmap pattern. If you select **Blank** instead of another bitmap pattern, the **Pattern Editor** activates. Click the boxes in the **Pattern Editor** to fill them in. As you do, the preview area updates to show you what your pattern will look like as a fill. The **Foreground color** option determines the color of the selected boxes (as you click to select them), and the **Background color** option determines the pattern's background. Be sure to save your pattern by clicking the **Save** button if you want to reuse the same bitmap pattern in the future.

116 About Manipulating Objects

Producing accurate drawings often requires more than just an artistic ability; you must be able to keep control of the objects on your screen. Much of the artwork you create will require that you reuse objects you've already drawn, especially in commercial artwork for logos and advertisements.

Copying and pasting of the shapes, text, and all objects you place on your drawing area works differently from copying and pasting in other OpenOffice.org programs. Draw's graphical nature requires special handling when you want to copy and paste objects.

For example, when you want to move an object, you don't really need to cut and paste it. Just click to select the object and drag it to another location. If you want to move multiple objects, select them all before dragging them to another location. If your drawing has multiple objects, you can click to select one of them. Draw moves the selection to each succeeding object (in the order you drew them) each time you press **Tab**.

To make a copy of an object, you can do so without using the **Edit** menu to copy and paste, as you must do in most other Windows programs. Be warned, though, that it takes a little practice to make copies of Draw objects. To copy an object from one drawing location to another, follow these steps:

1. Click to select the object you want to copy. Make sure you click toward the edge of the object so you see the resizing handles and the rectangular outline of the shape instead of the edit points.

2. Before moving your mouse, but after you've clicked the shape's outline, press the **Ctrl** key.

3. While holding **Ctrl**, drag your mouse to the area where you want the copy to appear. Release both the mouse and the **Ctrl** key to place the copy into position.

If you want to copy or paste an object in one drawing to another drawing, you will need to use the Windows Clipboard to do so. Click to select the object, select either **Copy** or **Cut** from the **Edit** menu, then switch to the other drawing and select **Paste** from the **Edit** menu. The shortcut keys **Ctrl+C**, **Ctrl+X**, and **Ctrl+V** all work for the **Copy**, **Cut**, and **Paste** commands, respectively.

Before You Begin

✔ **111** Place Shapes on the Drawing Area

✔ **113** About Perfecting Shapes

See Also

→ **118** Align Objects

 TIP

To select multiple shapes, hold the **Shift** key and click each object you want to select. Select all your drawing's objects by pressing **Ctrl+A**.

Hold Ctrl to Copy from Here...

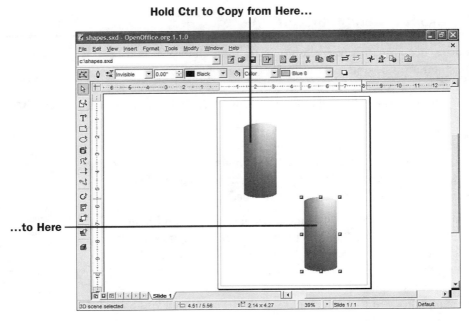

...to Here

Use the Ctrl key to make copies of objects in other areas of your drawing.

TIP

If you have a difficult time showing resizing handles when you want to display edit points, or vice versa, click the object to display either the edit points or the resizing handles. If you want to work with the other, click once on the **Object** toolbar's **Edit Points** button.

NOTE

Technically, the edit points and resizing handles of arcs use different terminology. The two edit points on each end of the arc are called *data points*, and the resizing handles are called *control points*.

After you click a shape to display the shape's resizing handles, you can drag any resizing handle to resize the shape. The shape resizes, increasing or decreasing, as you drag any resizing handle outward or inward, respectively. Draw maintains the shape's scale as you resize the shape if you drag one of the four corner resizing handles. If you drag one of the resizing handles that appear in the middle of any edge, the object skews wider or taller as you drag your mouse.

The edit points enable you to edit and fine-tune the outlines around objects. Different shapes utilize edit points differently. For example, when you draw an arc, the arc has only two edit points: one at the arc's starting point and one at the end. By dragging these edit points (as opposed to dragging resizing handles), you change the completeness of the arc.

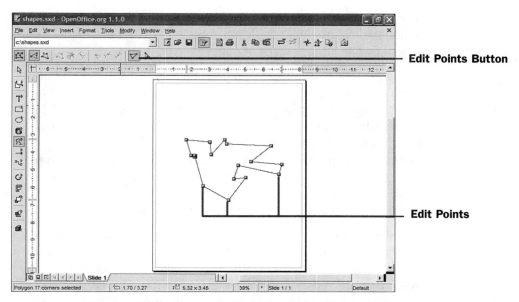

Edit Points Button

Edit Points

To show the eight resizing handles when you only see edit points, click the Edit Points button.

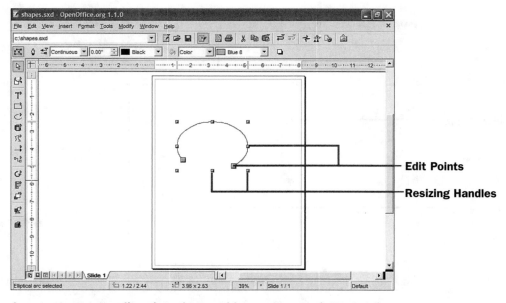

Edit Points

Resizing Handles

Arcs support two edit points that enable you to complete or reduce the arc's shape.

Polygons and other multisided shapes and lines display far more edit points. You can always click an edit point to drag that piece of the shape in or out while all the other edit points keep their locations.

Although many-sided shapes and freeform curved lines often contain many edit points, the edit points don't always fall where you need to adjust a segment of the shape. Once you click the **Object** toolbar's **Edit Points** button to display the edit points, you can move any edit point to a more convenient location by first clicking the **Object** bar's **Move Points** button and then moving one of the edit points to a more appropriate spot on the line. Instead of moving an existing edit point, you can insert a new edit point by clicking the **Insert Points** button and then clicking where you want the new edit point to appear.

The other **Edit Points** buttons behave differently depending on the object. For example, clicking the **Close Bézier** button applies a straight line from any line's starting point to the end point, no matter how crooked and curved the line is. The Bézier line initially adds one control point to your line. As you drag the Bézier line around your drawing, three more control points appear that enable you to expand or contract your drawing based on the length, slope, and direction of the Bézier line.

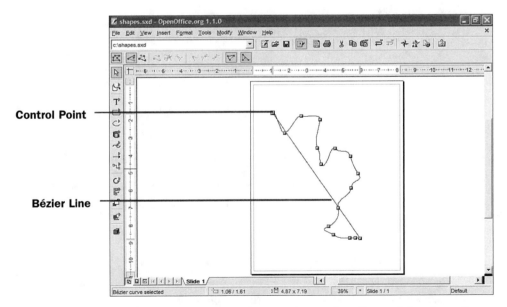

A Bézier line connects the starting and ending points of any line.

117 About Grouping Objects

As you draw objects on your drawing area, Draw keeps track of the order in which you draw them. Draw maintains a logical overlap as you lay one item on top of another. It's obvious, for example, that the rounded square in the middle was the last item placed on the following figure's drawing area and that the rightmost square was the first item placed on the figure because it falls beneath all three of the other objects. Can you tell from the placement which shapes were placed second and third?

Before You Begin

✔ **114** Create a New Shape

✔ **116** About Manipulating Objects

See Also

→ **118** Align Objects

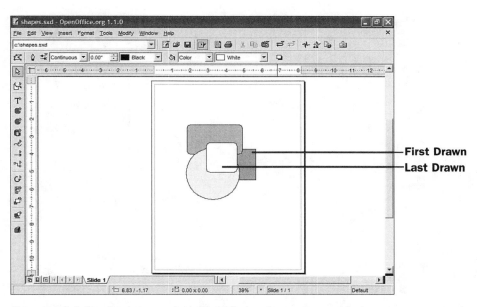

Draw maintains the appropriate stacking order as you add shapes to your drawing.

If you want to move an object down the stack or up the stack, just click to select the item, right-click your mouse to display a menu, select **Arrange** from the menu, and then send the item back into the stack one level at a time, send the item to the very back of the stack, or bring the item forward as much as you wish. The **Arrange** menu options allow any item to be placed anywhere in the stack of objects you wish.

When you press **Ctrl+A** to select all the objects in your drawing, or when you press **Shift** and click multiple objects to select them, you then have a *group* of items.

NOTE

In this figure, the rectangle at the top was drawn second and the circle was drawn third.

KEY TERM

Group—A set of two or more selected objects in Draw.

Blank areas will always appear where the combined objects originally overlapped.

When you work with a group as a whole, such as resizing or moving the group, Draw maintains the separate identities of the objects in that group. You can always click just one item in the group and remove it from the group or bring it forward or backward within the group. If you want to combine the items, you will, in effect, merge the shapes into a single shape. Unlike new shapes you create (see **114** **Create a New Shape**), you can split apart combined shapes.

To combine a selected group of shapes, select **Modify**, **Combine** from the menu. Whatever the properties of the lowermost shape (including color), all the shapes in the combined shape will take on those same properties.

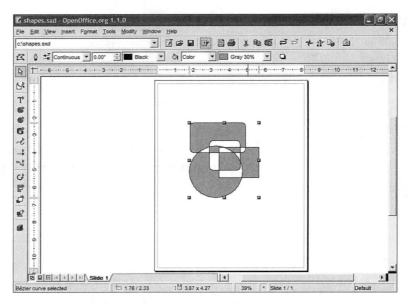

Combined objects take on the appearance of the lowermost object in the stack.

Once the objects are combined, you can resize, copy, and move them as a single object. Instead of keeping these objects combined, however, you can uncombine them. By selecting the overall combined object and then selecting **Modify**, **Split** from the menu, you can separate the objects out once again, although they stay in their combined locations until you click and drag one of the pieces out. In addition, the separate shapes have all the color, line thickness, and other properties of the bottommost shape before you combined them. Any differentiation in color or other attributes they originally had will be gone when you split the shapes.

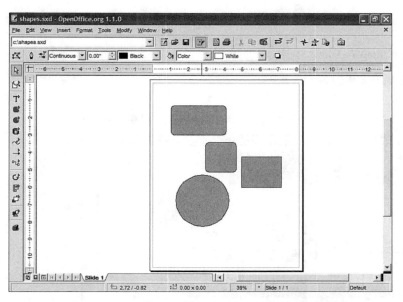

You can split combined shapes but they retain their combined attributes.

118 Align Objects

Draw's snap lines help you ensure that your Draw shapes align properly with one another. Whether you want to display items across or down a page, when you use snap lines, you can make your objects follow those snap lines (also called *snap to* lines) without getting… well, out of line.

Snap lines act as an imaginary grid on your drawing's background. You can control every aspect of your snap lines, from their width, to their direction, to their distance from one another. Be sure to set your **Grid** options category so the **Snap to** option is checked to make use of snap lines. See **105** **Set Draw Options** for more information on setting options.

In addition to snap to lines, you can set snap to points. These points define locations in your drawing that you want all objects close to those points to move to. Perhaps you place objects in a semicircle by temporarily drawing a curve that will form the curved base for your figures. You can add snap to points along the curve. When you delete the curve, the snap to points will remain, and you can add objects to those points later.

Before You Begin

✔ **111** Place Shapes on the Drawing Area

✔ **113** About Perfecting Shapes

See Also

→ **119** Add Text to a Drawing

◢ NOTE

Snap lines are useful for aligning objects, but they do not print when you print your drawing and they don't show during the presentation.

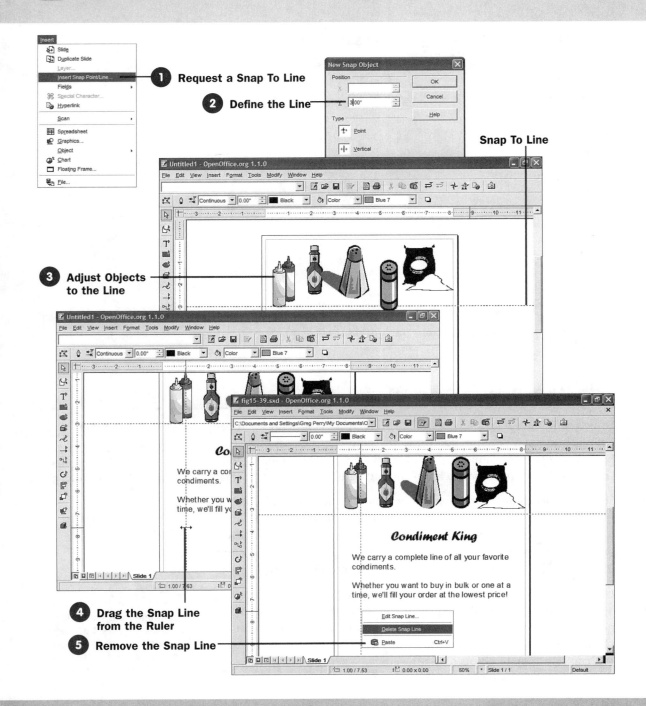

1 Request a Snap To Line

2 Define the Line

Snap To Line

3 Adjust Objects to the Line

4 Drag the Snap Line from the Ruler

5 Remove the Snap Line

1 **Request a Snap To Line**

Select **Snap Point/Line** from the **Insert** menu.

2 **Define the Line**

Define the snap line using the **New Snap Object** dialog box that appears. If you're defining a vertical snap to line, you must set the **X** position (use the ruler as a guide). If you're defining a horizontal snap to line, you must set the **Y** position. Therefore, if you want to align a set of images across the top of your drawing, 3 inches down from the top, you'll create a horizontal snap line with a **Y** setting of **3.00"**.

When creating a snap to point, you must enter both an x-axis and a y-axis value.

Click to select either **Point**, **Vertical**, or **Horizontal** to specify the kind of snap you want. Click **OK** to draw the snap line or snap point.

3 **Adjust the Objects to the Line**

The purpose of the snap line is to act as a magnet for whatever you drag close to it. If you add a snap line to an existing drawing, you can drag the objects you want to snap to that line close to it. When an object's edge gets close to the snap line, Draw immediately pulls that object to the line.

4 **Drag the Snap Line from the Ruler**

Instead of using the **New Snap Object** dialog box to add your snap line, you can more quickly drag from inside either ruler out to your drawing to apply a snap line.

To draw a vertical snap line, click anywhere on the vertical ruler and drag your mouse to the left into your drawing. As you drag your mouse, the snap line appears, and when you release your mouse, the snap line will be anchored into place. To draw a horizontal snap line, click anywhere on the horizontal ruler and drag down into your drawing.

NOTE

Snap lines appear as dashed lines vertically or horizontally across your drawing. A snap point appears as a dashed crosshair showing the point of the snap.

TIP

If you don't like the position of any snap line or point, just click and drag the line or point with your mouse to a new position.

⑤ Remove the Snap Line

Right-click the snap line to produce a menu. From the menu you can edit or delete the line. When you select **Edit Snap Line**, the **Edit Snap Line** dialog box appears, where you can type a new x-axis or y-axis value. If you select **Delete**, you'll erase the snap line.

119 Add Text to a Drawing

Before You Begin

✔ **110** Draw from Scratch

See Also

→ **123** Add 3D Text

TIP

All text is assumed to be horizontal. If you want vertical text, enable the Asian language tools by selecting **Tools**, **Options**, **Language Settings**, **Languages**.

Drawings certainly don't rely only on lines and shapes to make their point. You can easily add text to your drawings. The **Main** toolbar's **Text** button is the launching point for most of the text you'll place on your drawing area.

The **Text** button enables you to place three kinds of text onto your drawing:

- Text inside text boxes.
- Text that fits itself to a frame. This kind of text behaves like a graphic image in that the text resizes when you resize the frame.
- Callouts or legends that describe parts of your drawing, with a line moving from the item being described to the text, not unlike a cartoon's caption above the characters' heads.

① Request Text

Long-click to open the **Text** toolbar. Click the first **Text** button. (If you plan to add more text, double-click the **Text** button to keep it active.)

② Drag to Create a Text Box

Click where you want the starting point of your text's text box to appear. Drag your mouse down and to the right, releasing the mouse after the text box is in place. A text cursor will appear inside the text box, waiting for you to type the text.

③ Type and Format the Text

Rarely will you draw the text box to the exact dimensions you need. That is fine. Go ahead and type your text anyway. If you need to resize the text box, click to display its resizing handles and then drag to resize the text box. You can drag any edge of the resizing outline to move the text box if you need to adjust its position.

Once you've typed the text, all the character-formatting options are available to you, including the alignment buttons that justify the text inside your text box. To change the format of only some of the text, select that text and then select **Format**, **Character** to display the **Character** dialog box, where you can adjust the font, size, and color of the text.

TIP

Once you've displayed a text box's resizing handles, press **F2** to return to the text-editing mode inside the text box.

NOTE

Even though the text resizes with the frame, you can still apply character-formatting commands, such as italics and a different font, to the text.

④ Fit the Text to a Frame

Click the **Main** toolbar's **Text** button once again to display the **Text** toolbar. Click to select the **Fit Text to Frame** button. You'll now drag a frame to the area where you want the text.

Type the text inside the frame. When you do, you'll notice that the text formats itself to fit perfectly inside the frame. If you resize the frame, the text inside the frame resizes.

⑤ Add a Callout

Click the **Main** toolbar's **Text** button once again to display the **Text** toolbar. Click to select the **Callouts** button. You'll now drag a callout frame to the area where you want the callout.

Almost always, the callout is too small to work, so drag the callout's resizing handles to fit it better to your drawing. Type the text for your callout (you may have to press **F2** to type the text if the callout remains selected).

Once you've resized and positioned your callout properly, you may want to drag the single callout line to a place that differs slightly from its current location. Drag the callout's edit point on its callout tail to where you want the callout's line to begin.

① Request Text ② Drag to Create a Text Box ③ Type and Format the Text

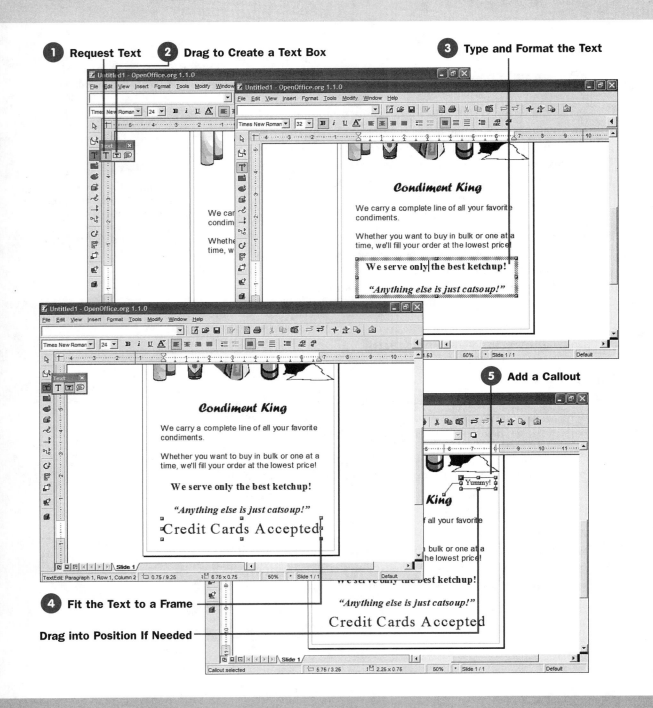

⑤ Add a Callout

④ Fit the Text to a Frame

Drag into Position If Needed

16

Putting on Finishing Touches with Draw

IN THIS CHAPTER:

Themes—A collection of graphic files you save as a group under a theme name. The Gallery comes with several predesigned themes, such as Backgrounds and Bullets.

Draw provides many useful tools that you can use for drawings. You might use Draw for months before discovering how each tool can benefit you, but you'll always feel well-rewarded when you come upon one. For example, Draw's Gallery is a comprehensive collection of graphics, sounds, and other objects, arranged in named *themes*.

This chapter explains how to use the Gallery to improve your images. In addition, you'll learn to take your drawings to the next step by adding three-dimensional text. Finally, the world is available inside your own drawings because Draw supports direct scanning of outside materials directly into your drawings. Once these scanned images are in your drawings, you'll be able to manipulate them just as you can any other graphic images.

120 About the Gallery

Before You Begin

✔ **116** About Manipulating Objects

See Also

→ **121** Insert Gallery Objects

→ **122** Add New Items to Gallery

NOTE

Why sounds in drawings? Actually, all the OpenOffice.org programs support the use of the Gallery. The sounds are especially useful for Impress presentations.

When you first display the Gallery, you'll see the following collection of predesigned themes:

- **3D Effects**—Objects with several three-dimensional aspects, including a collection of three-dimensional numbers you can place as graphics onto your drawings

- **Backgrounds**—A collection of textured patterns such as marble, gravel, cloth, and many more textures with various colors that you can use as your drawings' backgrounds

- **Bullets**—A collection of various items you can use as bullets in your drawings when creating bulleted lists

- **Homepage**—Web-related graphics that you can use to create Web page graphics, including special buttons and navigational tools that are common on Web pages

- **My Theme**—Collections of graphics that you've put together and saved

- **New Theme**—Gallery's area where you add new themes to the Gallery's collection

- **Rulers**—Not the measuring kinds of rulers, but straight colorful edges in multiple designs that you can add to drawings to create borders

- **Sounds**—Sounds you can add to your files

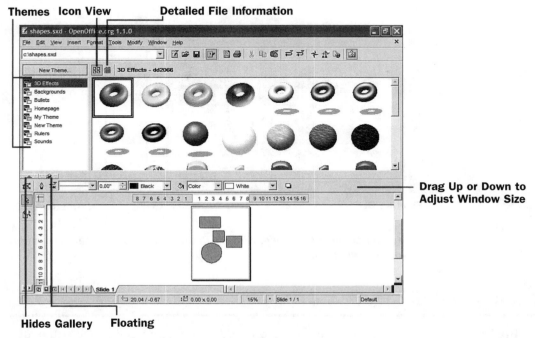

Themes Icon View   Detailed File Information

Drag Up or Down to
Adjust Window Size

Hides Gallery   Floating

Selecting Tools, Gallery opens and displays the Gallery.

The Gallery can consume quite a lot of screen real estate. If you click the Gallery's **Floating** button, the Gallery turns into a floating toolbar window that you can move around your screen. You can then resize the Gallery as a floating toolbar so it occupies a better position on your screen and so your drawing area isn't reduced by the size of the Gallery.

To convert the Gallery to a floating toolbar, click to select the **Floating** button. Then hold **Ctrl** while double-clicking any blank area above the Gallery's preview area. Hold **Ctrl** and double-click the same area to convert the Gallery back into a docked window on your screen.

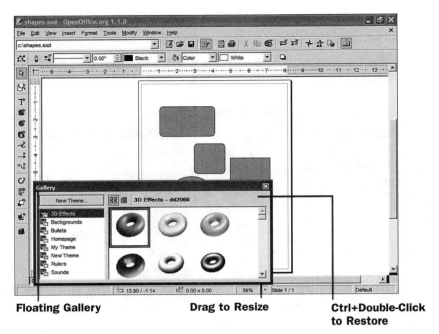

Floating Gallery   **Drag to Resize**   **Ctrl+Double-Click
                                                            to Restore**

*When you convert the Gallery into a floating toolbar, you can see more
of your drawing area.*

121 Insert Gallery Objects

Before You Begin

✔ **120** About the Gallery

See Also

→ **122** Add New Items to
    Gallery

 NOTE

Unless you regularly
change Gallery objects,
you'll find it easiest to
insert Gallery objects as
copies.

Inserting Gallery objects into your drawings requires little more than displaying the Gallery, selecting a theme, selecting the item you want to
insert, and then adjusting the inserted item's size and location once you
place it onto your drawing.

When you insert Gallery objects, you have two choices to make:

- **Insert a copy**—Creates a new copy of the Gallery item and inserts
  it into your drawing.

- **Insert as a link**—If the original Gallery item changes, your drawing's linked object changes as well. If you change a Gallery object
  that's been linked to in a drawing, when you subsequently open
  that drawing for editing or printing, the Gallery object will take on
  its newest appearance.

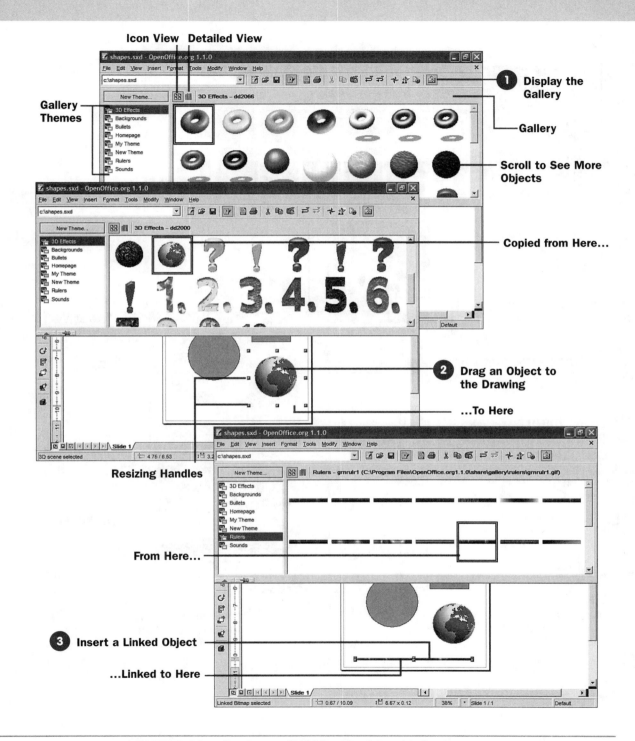

Icon View   Detailed View

Gallery Themes

1 Display the Gallery

Gallery

Scroll to See More Objects

Copied from Here...

2 Drag an Object to the Drawing

...To Here

Resizing Handles

From Here...

3 Insert a Linked Object

...Linked to Here

4 Insert a Background

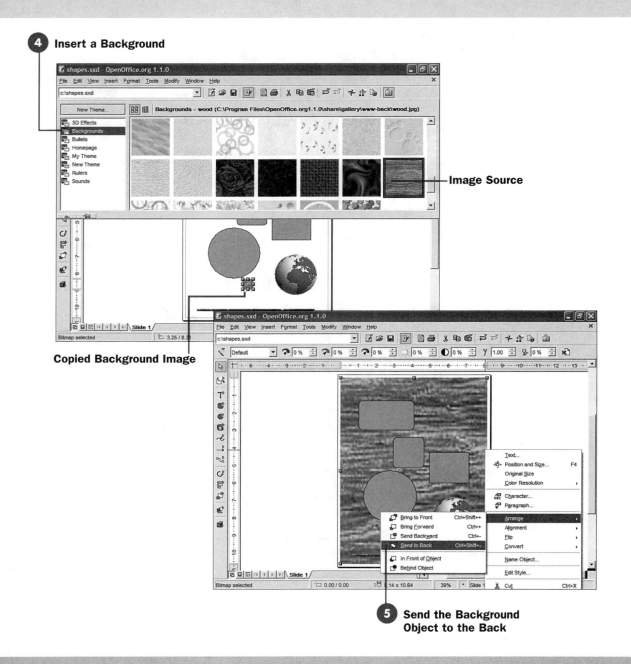

Image Source

Copied Background Image

5 Send the Background Object to the Back

1 Display the Gallery

Select **Tools**, **Gallery** or click the **Function** bar's **Gallery** icon to display the Gallery. Click to select the appropriate theme you wish to choose from. If you need to, scroll the Gallery window down to see more objects.

2 Drag an Object to the Drawing

Click and drag the object you want into your drawing area. When you drag an object, Draw places a copy, not a link, to that item, so a copy is saved with your drawing. Once the image is in your drawing, you can move and resize it.

3 Insert a Linked Object

To insert a linked object instead of copying an object into your drawing, hold the **Shift** and **Ctrl** keys while you drag the object to your drawing.

4 Insert a Background

To add one of the Gallery's background images to your drawing, click to select the **Backgrounds** theme. Actually, any Gallery graphic image can serve as the background, but the ones listed in the **Backgrounds** theme are designed to be background patterns and are not really suitable for standalone images.

Drag the image to your drawing. You must now expand the image to fill your entire drawing area so it consumes the entire background. Drag to resize the image's resizing handles until it fills your screen. Don't worry about overwriting other objects on your drawing.

5 Send the Background Object to the Back

Right-click the background image and select **Arrange**, **Send to Back** to move the background image to the very back of your drawing so that all the other images and text can be seen. Adjust the background if needed to completely fill your drawing area. Be careful that your background is not so busy that it detracts from your drawing's primary elements.

TIP

Click the **Detailed View** button to see the filenames and locations for most of the Gallery's objects.

NOTE

As you can see, linked objects behave just as copied objects when you insert them. Linked objects can change, however, if their original Gallery objects change.

TIP

You may need to close the Gallery to see your entire drawing and adjust the background. Click the **Gallery** button to close it.

122 Add New Items to Gallery

TIP

Resist the temptation to store new images in the theme labeled **My Theme**. Instead, create new themes with specific names that relate to related groups of objects you'll place there.

NOTE

You can also add sound files to a theme, but the sound files do little good in Draw-related themes.

You can add new items to the Gallery's theme categories. In addition, you can create entirely new themes. For example, if you design graphics for a sports-related organization, you'll surely create a theme called **Sports**, and possibly several subthemes, such as **Sports-Football**, **Sports-Baseball**, and **Sports-Hockey**.

The themes exist only so that you can group similar objects together. Once separated into themes, all your related images appear together for you to find quicker than if they were spread across multiple themes or if all your images were included in only one theme.

1 Request a New Theme

Click the Gallery's **New Theme** button. The **Properties** dialog box opens.

2 Name the Theme

Type a name in the **General** page of the dialog box. Give the theme a meaningful name that relates to the objects you'll place in that theme category. You want to be able to locate your images quickly.

3 Add Files to the Theme

Click the dialog box's **Files** tab to add files to the new theme if you have any graphics to add.

First click the **Find Files** button and locate the folder that contains the image or images you wish to add to your theme. Click the **Add** button to display a **Browse** dialog box from which you can select images to add to the theme. Draw displays the filenames from that folder. You can click the **Preview** option to see a preview of any selected files in the list.

If you want to add all the images, click the **Add All** button. If you only want to add one or a few images to the Gallery, click to select these images (hold **Ctrl** and click to select multiple images) and then click the **Add** button. When you finish adding images, click **Close**.

① **Request a New Theme**

② **Name the Theme**

③ **Add Files to the Theme**

④ **Review Your Theme**

⑤ **Add Images Quickly**

...To Here

From Here...

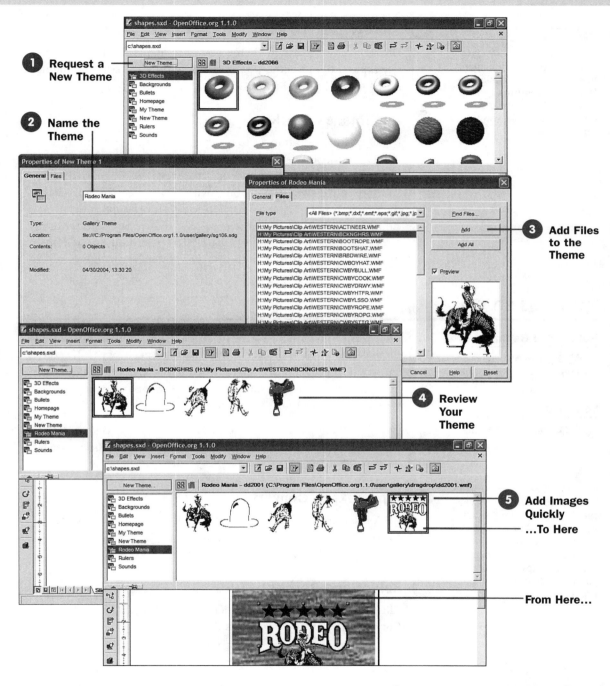

TIP

You can delete an image from any theme by clicking the image and pressing **Del**. Draw confirms that you want to delete the image before removing it from the Gallery.

4 **Review Your Theme**

Draw displays your new theme and its contents. Review the contents and add more images if needed by right-clicking the theme name and selecting **Properties**.

5 **Add Images Quickly**

If you want to add images to an existing theme, you can do so quickly. For instance, perhaps you've added text to an existing image to create a logo or perhaps combined two or more images. You may have even drawn your own. All you need to do is drag the image from your drawing area to an empty spot in the Gallery's theme. When you release your mouse button after dragging the image to the Gallery, the Gallery will maintain a copy of the image so you can insert it into subsequent drawings.

123 Add 3D Text

Before You Begin

✔ **118** Align Objects

✔ **119** Add Text to a Drawing

See Also

→ **124** Convert 2D to 3D

NOTE

You cannot edit the characters inside text itself once you convert that text to three-dimensional text. You can edit the text's image properties, however, just as you can edit any graphic image.

When you want fancier text, convert that plain two-dimensional text to three-dimensional text. You can control several aspects of the 3D conversion, and you'll quickly spruce up your headlines, signs, and banners. Once you convert text to 3D, you can modify some of the three-dimensional effects, such as the rotation of the text.

Converting text is often simpler, but follows a similar process to the conversion of two-dimensional graphic images to three dimensions (see **124** Convert 2D to 3D).

1 **Type Text to Convert**

Click the **Main** toolbar's **Text** tool and type the text you want to convert to 3D. Change the size and font of the text so it's close to the size you wish to make the 3D text.

2 **Select and Request 3D**

Click to select the text. Right-click the selected text and select **Convert**, **To 3D**. Draw converts the text.

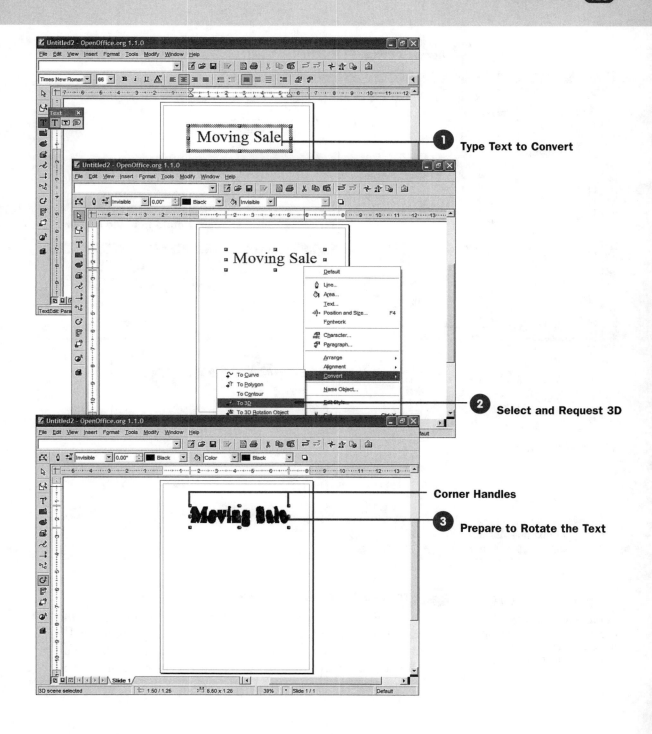

1 Type Text to Convert

2 Select and Request 3D

Corner Handles

3 Prepare to Rotate the Text

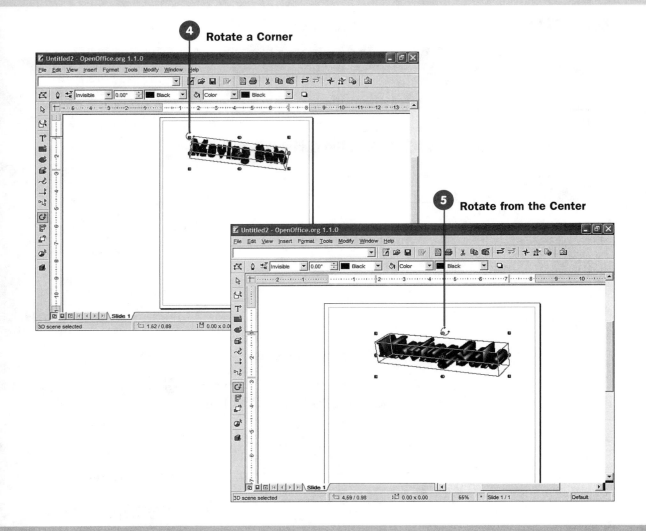

Rotate a Corner

Rotate from the Center

KEY TERM

Corner handles—Red circles that act as 3D resizing handles that you can drag to rotate 3D text.

3 **Prepare to Rotate the Text**

You can rotate the text to change the 3D appearance. To rotate the text, you must click to select the 3D text (resizing handles will appear) and then click the 3D text once again. The resizing handles turn from green squares to red circles. These are the 3D text's *corner handles*.

4 Rotate a Corner

Drag one of the corner handles up or down, and the 3D text will rotate in the direction you drag your mouse. Your mouse pointer changes to a rotate symbol to indicate that the 3D text is ready for rotation.

5 Rotate from the Center

Click and drag one of the center handles. As you do, you'll see that instead of the 3D text rotating up or down, the text will rotate on its side-to-side axis, producing a different rotational effect.

TIP

Once you convert 2D text to 3D, you can apply Draw's 3D effects to the 3D text. See **124** Convert 2D to 3D for more information on Draw's 3D effects.

124 Convert 2D to 3D

Draw can actually convert a two-dimensional, flat drawing to a three-dimensional drawing. During the conversion, you can control many of the resulting 3D attributes, such as lighting and shading. Although the 2D-to-3D conversion is not a perfect one, and although Draw does not contain as many three-dimensional controls as the software Hollywood uses to make its movies, Draw's three-dimensional prowess is quite good. When one considers the price (free), it's about as good of value as you'll get on earth.

1 Add the 2D Image

Add any two-dimensional images to your drawing area that you want to convert to 3D. Click to select an image to convert.

2 Request 3D Effects

Select **Format**, **3D Effects** to begin the conversion. Draw opens the **3D Effects** dialog box, which displays several options from which you can choose to convert your 2D drawing to 3D.

The **Favorites** list offers several 3D shapes in several colors and textures. When you select one of these shapes, you're giving Draw an example of how you wish your 2D image to be converted. Therefore, you'll find the closest-matching 3D image in the **Favorites** list to specify the general nature of the 3D look you want. The **3D Effects** dialog box also contains two buttons. One is

Before You Begin

✔ **116** About Manipulating Objects

✔ **123** Add 3D Text

See Also

→ **125** Import a Graphic Image into Draw

NOTE

Draw can take a while to convert some images to 3D and has been known to freeze when attempting to convert a rather complex 2D image. Generally, you'll have no trouble as long as your 2D images aren't already almost 3D. When working with such graphics, select **File**, **Save** regularly just in case a recent edit causes Draw to freeze and you have to close Draw and start over.

Understanding all the mathematics that produce appropriate 3D effects is fairly advanced. This task just skims the surface. Fortunately, you can always try one of the options, adjust the 3D effect, and then select the **Undo** command to back up and try something else. So fully understanding the mathematics behind 3D images isn't a requirement to producing them with Draw—fortunately!

If your 2D object has a lot of white space inside its area, that space will remain white, and Draw only converts the image's edges to a 3D effect. If your 2D object is colored inside, Draw can apply more of a 3D effect to the sides of the object.

named **3D Attributes Only** (rest your mouse cursor over the buttons to see their purpose). It does the least amount of work in the quickest amount of time to convert your 2D image using only enough attributes from your **Favorites** sample to put your shape into three dimensions. If you instead click the second button, **Assign All Attributes**, Draw will apply all the lighting, colors, and shadows from the **Favorites** item you've selected. The buttons across the top of the **3D Effects** dialog box enable you to specify settings such as the 3D geometry, shading, lighting, texture, and material.

❸ Convert to 3D

Select a **Favorites** item and click the **3D Attributes Only** button. A preview of a sample 3D object that takes on the sample's characteristics will appear. Unfortunately, the preview is a sphere and not a preview of how your actual 2D image will look after being converted. When you click the **Assign** button, Draw converts your 2D image to a 3D image. The **3D Effects** dialog box remains on the screen, where you can continue to select options from it.

❹ Further Refine the 3D Effect

You can click to select from the various buttons atop the **3D Effects** dialog box to apply various settings to your image. For example, if you click the **Illumination** button, you can control the amount and color of the lighting on your object. Click to select the **Material** button to apply a metal-like plating to the object.

❺ Quickly Convert to 3D

Draw supports a quick conversion to 3D, and you can apply this in a similar manner to how you convert 2D text to 3D (see **123** **Add 3D Text**). Click to select a 2D image; then right-click the image to display a menu. Select **Convert, To 3D** from the menu to apply a quick 3D pattern to your item. Once the image is converted, you can click to select the converted image and then click again to display corner handles (see **123** **Add 3D Text** for information on corner handles) that you can use to rotate the object in 3D space so that its orientation suits your needs.

You can also select **Format, 3D Effects** to adjust the 3D attributes, such as the illumination and material used if the image doesn't look the way you want it to look.

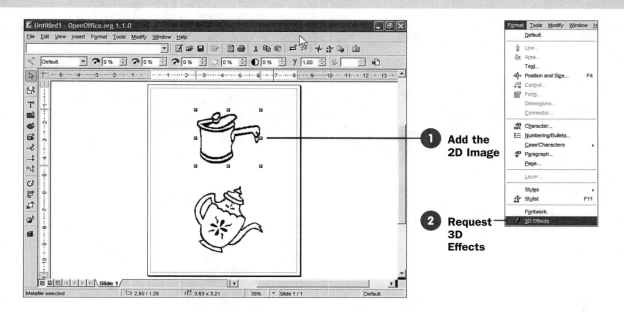

1 Add the 2D Image

2 Request 3D Effects

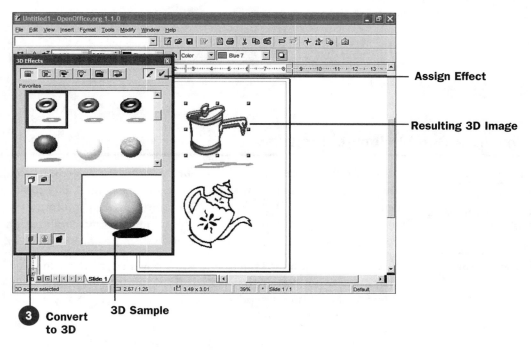

Assign Effect

Resulting 3D Image

3 Convert to 3D

3D Sample

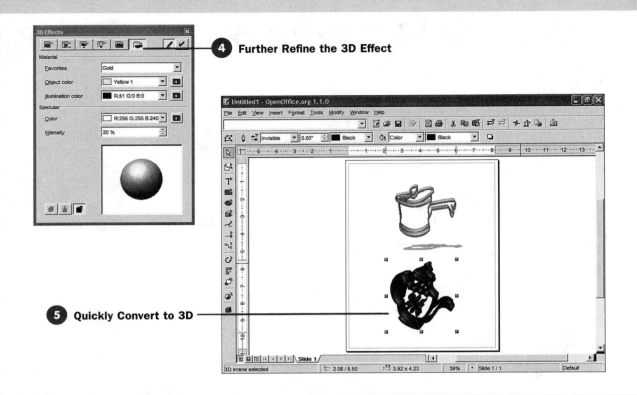

4 Further Refine the 3D Effect

5 Quickly Convert to 3D

125 Import a Graphic Image into Draw

Before You Begin

✔ 110 Draw from Scratch

✔ 116 About Manipulating Objects

See Also

→ 126 Scan a Picture into Draw

Draw certainly doesn't limit you to your own artwork. You can import other people's artwork! Draw supports virtually every kind of graphics file in use today, and you can easily import images into your drawings. Once those images are there, you can resize, move, copy, duplicate, and even convert them to 3D, just as you can do with the objects you draw.

Once you insert graphic images into your drawing, you can edit the images somewhat. When you click to select your inserted image, your **Object** toolbar changes to provide the following aspects that you can change about the inserted image:

- **Graphics mode**—Select the graphics mode from a list of available modes (such as **Watermark**, which places a pale and very light version of your image on the drawing's background).

- **Red, Green, and Blue**—Options that change the amount of these three primary colors in your image. Here, –100% indicates a complete lack of the color, and 100% indicates the heaviest use of the color possible.

- **Brightness**—Enables you to adjust the brightness from –100% (complete darkness) to 100% (completely lit).

- **Contrast**—Specifies the image's contract, from –100% (no contrast) to 100% (full contrast).

- **Gamma**—Specifies the *gamma value*, from 0,10 (lowest gamma) to 10 (highest possible gamma value).

- **Transparency**—Specifies how much transparency, from 0% to 100%, that the image shows.

- **Crop**—Displays a dialog box where you can *crop* the image.

1 Request an Image

Select **Insert**, **Graphics** from the menu to display the **Insert Graphics** dialog box, where you can locate the image you want to insert into your drawing.

2 Select the Image

Browse to the location where your images are on disk (or across a network) by selecting from the **Look in** list box. Locate the file you want to insert and click it. If you also click the **Preview** option, a preview of that image appears so you can be sure you have the correct one.

3 Insert the Image

Click the **Insert Graphics** dialog box's **Open** button to insert your selected image into your drawing. You can resize, move, copy, and apply other Draw editing functions to your inserted image.

4 Edit the Image

Select the image, and the **Object** toolbar changes to reflect the editing functions you can apply to your image.

NOTE

You can copy an image to your drawing or link to an image. Either way, the image appears in your drawing. However, if you link instead of copy the image, your drawing will update if the original image ever changes.

KEY TERMS

Gamma value—The brightness of an image's midtone colors.

Crop—The cutting off of parts of an image or, in the case of Draw images, the scaled shrinking of an image to a smaller size from within the **Crop** dialog box.

NOTE

Click the **Link** option if you want Draw to link to the image instead of making a copy and inserting the copy into your drawing. You can convert a linked image to a copy by selecting **Edit**, **Links** from the menu and selecting **Break Link** from the dialog box that appears.

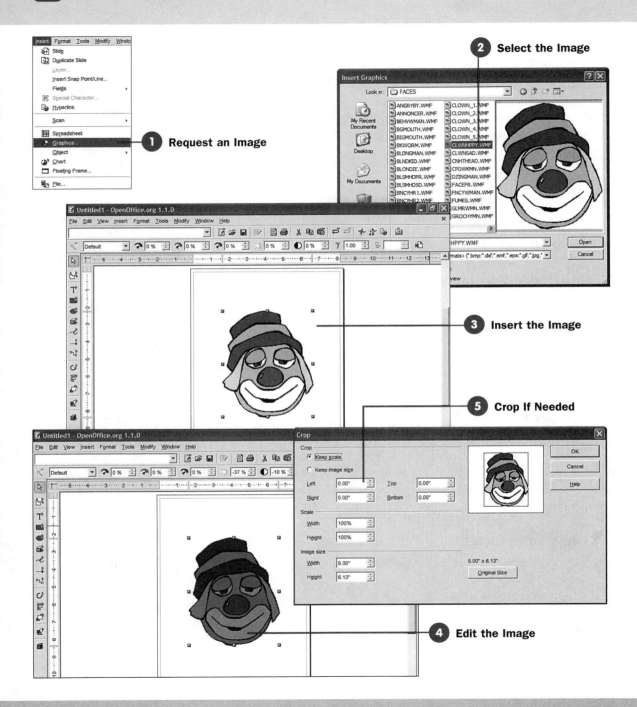

2 Select the Image

1 Request an Image

3 Insert the Image

5 Crop If Needed

4 Edit the Image

5 **Crop If Needed**

Click the **Object** toolbar's **Crop** button to open the **Crop** dialog box. Remember that you can crop down or up the scale of the image (from within the **Scale** section) or crop off portions of the actual image itself. To restore the image if you overcrop, you can click the **Original Size** button to restore the image to its original form. Click **OK** to apply your cropping instructions.

126 Scan a Picture into Draw

If you want to insert a picture into your drawing but the picture resides on paper, or perhaps in a magazine or book, you can scan the image directly into your drawing. As long as you use a TWAIN-compliant scanner, as most are, Draw can accept your scanned image. (See **27** **Insert Graphics in a Document** for information on TWAIN devices.)

When your scanner is TWAIN compliant, your scanner will often scan using its own scanning routines. So the exact steps for scanning images into Draw varies depending on the scanner and its supplied driver software. Nevertheless, the general step-by-step procedure for inserting scanned images remains the same no matter what kind of scanner you use.

1 **Prepare the Document for a Scanned Image**

Create a new drawing and add any elements that might help you better position your scan.

2 **Request the Scan**

Select **Insert, Scan, Select Source.**

3 **Control the Scan**

Depending on your scanner's software, you will be given the chance to scan a preview first, adjust resolution and colors, and modify other aspects of the scan. When your software allows it, accept the scanned preview (if you requested a preview), and Draw inserts the scanned image into your drawing.

Before You Begin

✔ **116** About Manipulating Objects

✔ **118** Align Objects

NOTE

You can scan a picture and save it as a graphic image and then insert that image into your drawing. By scanning directly into your drawing, you save the extra step.

 TIP

Scanned images can be huge. Decrease your scanned image size if possible from within your scanner's software if you want to send your drawing to others over email.

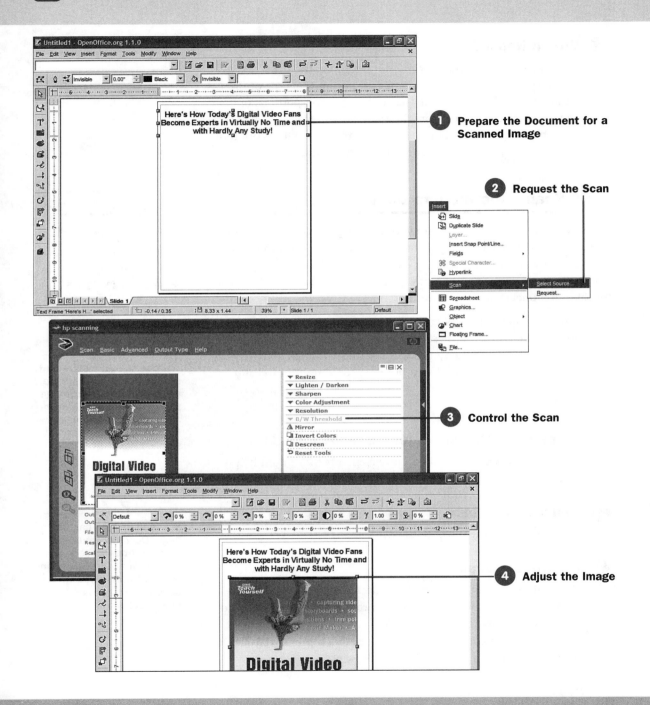

① Prepare the Document for a Scanned Image

② Request the Scan

③ Control the Scan

④ Adjust the Image

PART IV: Drawing on Your Inner Artist with Draw

4 Adjust the Image

Your scanned image will rarely come into your drawing at the exact placement and size you wish to see. Once your scanned image appears inside your drawing, you'll need to adjust the image's placement and size by dragging the resizing handles and moving the image to where you want it to go.

PART V

Enhancing Your Work with OpenOffice.org's Other Features

IN THIS PART:

17

Enhancing Your Work with More OpenOffice.org Features

IN THIS CHAPTER:

Master documents—A repository of documents, called *subdocuments*, each of which might be a chapter or document worked on by several people, as you might find in corporate reports submitted by multiple departments.

This chapter concludes the jam-packed, task-heavy OpenOffice.org book you have in your hands. By mastering most of the tasks in this book, you not only have a great overview of OpenOffice.org's features, you truly know the ins and outs of OpenOffice.org and can create outstanding documents, spreadsheets, presentations, and drawings.

In this final chapter, you'll get a taste of some of OpenOffice.org's more advanced features, such as the automation of certain OpenOffice.org tasks. If you find yourself repeating the same series of keystrokes or menu selections over and over, you can automate those steps to speed the work in the future. In addition, you'll learn how to manage more extensive Writer documents, such as you'll use when writing complete books with Writer. Maintaining chapters and all the elements that go into such a large, multipart document is not a chore when you learn how to leverage the concept of *master documents*.

The integration of OpenOffice.org's programs is crucial to OpenOffice.org's success and use. Being able to insert Calc spreadsheets into Writer documents and being able to insert Draw's drawings into your Impress presentations means that you can complete all your work within OpenOffice.org's consistent interface, and you have to learn far fewer commands and menus than you'd have to learn if you needed additional programs to do your job.

Of course, to be honest, OpenOffice.org's true integrated power shines in its support for loading and saving Microsoft Office documents, spreadsheets, and presentations. You can load, edit, and save virtually all Microsoft Office files within OpenOffice.org. You can set up OpenOffice.org to work even more closely with Microsoft Office documents, such as changing your program links to make Writer open any document you select that has Word's .doc filename extension. Many OpenOffice.org users *are* users because they did not want to pay what they perceived to be a very high upgrade cost to upgrade once again to Microsoft Office. These users are thrilled that OpenOffice.org opens, edits, and saves all the work they previously created with Microsoft Office.

127 About OpenOffice.org Macros

Two ways exist to automate work with OpenOffice.org:

- *Macros* record keystrokes that enable you to automate certain routine tasks that you want to repeat later.

- OpenOffice.org's *Applications Programming Interface* enables you to write complex, command-driven applications that run beneath the surface as you or your clients and fellow workers use OpenOffice.org documents, spreadsheets, presentations, and drawings. For example, you could use the API to create a general ledger program that uses a series of automated Calc spreadsheets that form the basis of your company's complete general ledger program. The programs written with the API might control which data is requested and when, print reports, and consolidate and close the general ledger accounts at the end of each period. Such automation requires extensive programming, but OpenOffice.org's API allows for such extensive programming.

This task and **128** **Create and Use a Macro** discuss macros, the simpler of the two automation tools available to OpenOffice.org users. Not only is the API extremely complex, it requires the use of programming logic as well as a separate software program called the *Software Development Kit* (SDK), which the standard version of OpenOffice.org doesn't come with because most OpenOffice.org users will never need the SDK.

Creating macros is simple. OpenOffice.org learns by example! As **128** **Create and Use a Macro** shows, when you're ready to create a macro, you only need to tell whatever OpenOffice.org program you're in at the time to begin recording your next few keystrokes. When you tell the program to stop recording the keystrokes, you save them in a named macro.

To run a macro, you assign some kind of trigger action to the macro. For example, you can place a special field inside a Calc spreadsheet that, when you click that field's area, automatically executes the macro and carries out the keystrokes you saved in the macro.

See Also

→ **128** Create and Use a Macro

KEY TERMS

Macros—A series of keystrokes, menu selections, dialog box selections, and other keyboard-related activities that you save as recorded steps to be rerun later. Macros save time because you don't have to repeat the same series of steps every time you perform a repetitive task.

Applications Programming Interface—The *API*, as it is known, is a programming language and interface that manipulates OpenOffice.org data and programs, enabling you to create complex applications.

Software Development Kit—The *SDK*, as it is known, is an add-on that adds the program engine to your OpenOffice.org installation to support API programming.

 TIP

For more information on the API and SDK, see the Web site http://api.openoffice.org/.

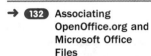 Create and Use a Macro

Before You Begin

✔ **127** About
OpenOffice.org
Macros

See Also

➜ **132** Associating
OpenOffice.org and
Microsoft Office
Files

NOTE

This list is not exhaustive;
OpenOffice.org supports
several additional—but
more advanced—methods
of macro execution.

When you find yourself performing the same series of keystrokes over
and over, perhaps in a series of menu selections or dialog box selections,
you should store those keystrokes in a macro. Once the keystrokes are
recorded in a macro, you can easily repeat them simply by requesting
the macro.

You can request that an OpenOffice.org program run a macro by setting
up a graphic image or by specifying that the macro run when you point
to an object with your mouse. Actually, OpenOffice.org supports several
ways to trigger the execution of a recorded macro, including the
following:

- Pressing a key combination that you assign to the macro
- Clicking an object such as a graphic image
- Moving the mouse over or away from an object
- Clicking a hyperlink you've assigned to a macro
- Loading of a graphic image
- Typing of certain text
- Selecting a macro to run from the Macro dialog box
- Resizing or moving a frame around an object

① **Start Recording a Macro**

Once you've determined that you want to automate mouse clicks,
mouse movements, or keystrokes to store as a macro, select **Tools**,
Macros, **Record Macro** to start recording the macro. The small
Record Macro dialog box appears with a single button on it,
labeled **Stop Recording**. You now must walk through the actions
that you want OpenOffice.org to record. Once you've finished the
final keystroke, click the **Stop Recording** button and save the
macro before specifying how it is to be executed.

1 Start Recording a Macro

Stops Macro Recording

2 Perform Keystrokes in the Macro

3 Name and Save the Macro

Other Ways to Trigger Macros

Selecting the Special Bullet Symbol

4 Assign the Macro to an Event

Newly Assigned Keystroke

Locate Your Macro

5 Test Your Macro

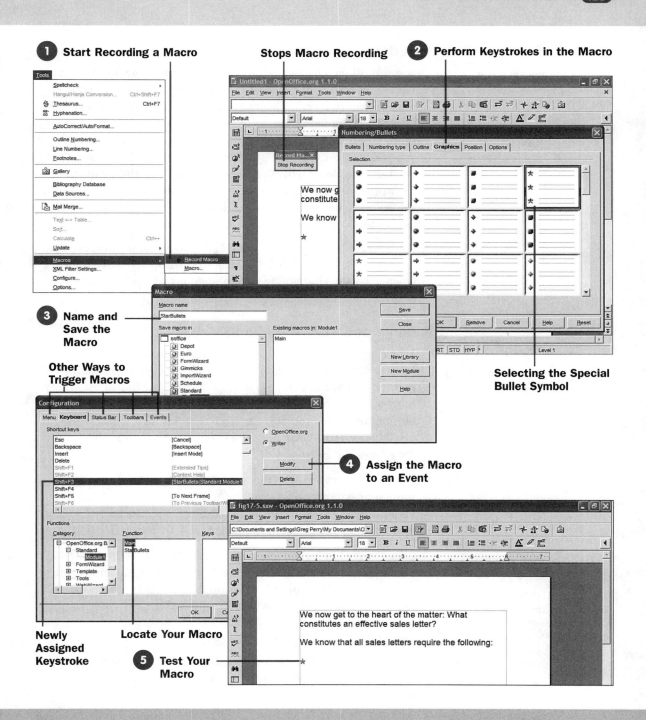

2 **Perform Keystrokes in the Macro**

Perform all the keystrokes that you want in this macro. For example, if you have to use special bullets in some reports, you can create a macro that not only begins a bulleted list but also selects the appropriate bullet symbol to use (as opposed to the default bullet symbol that normally appears). Such a macro would require that you click the **Bullets On** button on the **Object** toolbar, select the **Format**, **Numbering/Bullets** menu option, click the **Graphics** tab to display the **Graphics** page, click the symbol you wish to use for the bulleted list, and finally click the **OK** button to close the dialog box.

Once you've finished with all the keystrokes, menu traversal, and dialog box selections, click the **Stop Recording** button to inform OpenOffice.org that you're through adding keystrokes to the macro. The **Macro** dialog box appears.

3 **Name and Save the Macro**

Type a name for your macro in the **Macro name** text box. You can select a different location to store the macro from the default location, named **Standard**, but for most macros, the **Standard** library is an appropriate place to store your macro. You can create new libraries of related macros. Click the **New Library** button to add a new library to the collection. Click **Save** to store your macro under the name you assigned to it.

You now can execute the macro without having to repeat those same series of keystrokes ever again. Your macro will be listed in the library where you saved it. In addition, the **Macro** dialog box now contains additional buttons.

Click the **Assign** button to open the **Configuration** dialog box, where you can determine how the macro is to be triggered in the future. Click the **Keyboard** tab to display the **Keyboard** page. Here, you can assign a *shortcut key* that will trigger your macro.

4 **Assign the Macro to an Event**

Perhaps the most straightforward way to execute a macro's keystroke instructions is to assign the macro to a shortcut key combination that you don't use for other commands. For example,

Shift+F3 isn't used throughout all of OpenOffice.org, so you could assign that keystroke to your macro.

Before selecting a shortcut key for your macro, first locate the macro in the **Category** and **Function** sections of the **Configuration** dialog box. Scroll the **Category** list until you see your macro's category, which in this and most cases (unless you stored your macro in a different library in step 3) will be inside the **OpenOffice.org BASIC Macros** section. Click the plus sign to expand the libraries shown in the **OpenOffice.org BASIC Macros** library section and then click to expand the **Standard** library collection. Click the **Module1** library, and your macro (possibly along with others) will appear in the **Function** section to the right. Click to select your macro, and now you will assign a shortcut keystroke to that macro.

In the upper-right corner of the **Keyboard** page, you can select either the **OpenOffice.org** option or the application you've just created the macro in (such as Writer), and the list of shortcut keys shown in the **Shortcut keys** list changes. You can scroll through the list to see which keys are already assigned and which are not. By selecting either the **OpenOffice.org** option or your specific application, you inform OpenOffice.org that you're assigning this macro to a keystroke either globally across all OpenOffice.org programs or only in your current program (such as Writer).

Now that you've located and selected your macro, scroll the **Shortcut keys** list until you locate a shortcut key that is either not assigned or one you want to reassign to your macro. When you click the **Modify** button, OpenOffice.org assigns your macro to that shortcut keystroke.

The other tabs on the **Configuration** dialog box control other macro triggers. For example, the **Menu** page enables you to assign macros to menu commands that already exist or even to new menu commands that you want to add yourself. The **Status Bar** page determines what you want to appear on the status bar, such as the current date and time if you wish (although it's slightly odd that OpenOffice.org's designers would have put this page among these other commands). The **Toolbars** page determines which toolbars appear, and you can click the **Customize** button to change the buttons on the toolbars and to assign your own macros to the

NOTES

If you had not first located your macro, OpenOffice.org could not have known you were assigning the macro you just created to a shortcut key. An argument can be made that because you just created the macro, OpenOffice.org should already have that macro selected for you when you get to the **Keyboard** page of this dialog box.

You can reassign some of the shortcut keys already defined by OpenOffice.org. For example, you can reassign the **Ctrl+A** (Select All) keystroke so your macro executes in place of the shortcut key's original intent. If the **Keyboard** page's **Modify** button is active when you select a shortcut key from the list, you can assign that keystroke to your macro.

buttons. The **Events** page is where you can assign macros to specific events, such as moving and clicking your mouse over images and other triggers. For example, if you want a macro to run every time you create a new Writer document, click the **Writer** option, locate your macro from the **Macros** libraries, and select **Create Document** from the list of events at the top of the dialog box. When you click **Assign**, your macro will run every time you create a new Writer document.

If you click **Save**, OpenOffice.org displays the **Save Keyboard Configuration** dialog box, where you can save the current collection of keystrokes. The **Load** button loads previously saved keystrokes. If you share OpenOffice.org with other workers, you might want to develop your own macros and keyboard combinations. You aren't limited to macros for new shortcut key assignments; you can, for example, scroll through the **Category** and **Function** sections to locate virtually any menu or keystroke action available inside OpenOffice.org, such as the boldface formatting command, and assign that action to another shortcut key. However, once you begin reassigning several keystrokes, others that use OpenOffice.org can very well be confused when their regular keys stop working as expected! So you'll want to save and load your collection of keystrokes and macros before you use OpenOffice.org and then click **Reset** to reassign everything back to its original, default state once you've finished working. You can click **OK** to close the **Keyboard** page and the **Configuration** dialog box.

⑤ Test Your Macro

Never assume your macro works until you've tested it, preferably several times in several different situations. Depending on what is selected at the time you start your macro, you may find that your macro overwrites data. For example, if you've written a macro to start a bulleted list using a special graphic bullet symbol, when you select text right before you run your macro, the bullet may very well overwrite that selected text. If so, you may want to rerecord the macro so that the first keystroke you press is the **Esc** key, just to ensure that any previously selected text is unselected before the macro runs. Some macros, however, you create to work on selected text or to work after you select menu options, so you won't always want to start them with the **Esc** keystroke. Test your macro in all possible situations where you might use it to help ensure that you've written the most accurate macro possible that does exactly what you want done.

129 About Master Documents

Master documents are to Writer what spreadsheets are to Calc; a master document is a collection, or *repository*, of individual Writer documents, just as a spreadsheet is a repository of individual Calc sheets. Master documents enable you to manage large documents, as you might for a book with several chapters in it. If several people work in a group and wish to share the workload by editing pieces of a large document, a master document can help them better manage that task.

Inside a master document are *subdocuments*. In reality, a master document does not truly hold the subdocuments but merely acts as a master linker to those subdocuments. The master document maintains the links to the subdocuments so that they print, organize, and are indexed as though they are one huge, single document, but you still edit and save the documents individually.

Consider an author who uses Writer to write her book. She can create an overall master document for the book. Inside the master document, she can link to several subdocuments for the book's introduction, chapters, and appendix documents. By utilizing the master document's organization of these subdocuments (which are really just separate Writer documents), she can treat all the subdocuments as though they were part of a single document.

The benefit here is that page numbering, footnotes, figure captions, indexes, and table of contents all number properly in the context of the overall master document. Therefore, if the introduction's subdocument contains one footnote numbered 1, Chapter 1's subdocument contains a footnote that continues that numbering at 2, and so on. If the author removes a footnote from the middle of the book, all subsequent chapters' footnotes renumber accordingly because they all fall within the single master document context. Without the master document, footnotes begin with 1 in each new document the author creates.

Before You Begin

✔ **21** Create a Table of Contents

✔ **22** Create an Index

✔ **35** Add a Footnote or Endnote

See Also

➜ **130** Create a Master Document

KEY TERM

Subdocuments— Documents held and organized inside a master document.

TIP

You can add styles to the master document's template and apply those styles to all subdocuments contained by that master document. Therefore, you don't have to add each style individually to each subdocument.

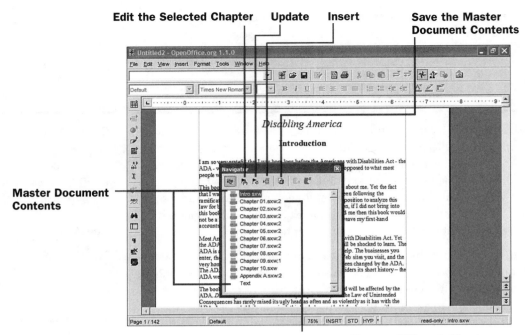

Edit the Selected Chapter   Update   Insert   Save the Master Document Contents

Master Document Contents

Select to Move to Different Chapter

The Navigator window is your key to maneuvering throughout your master document and its subdocuments.

When you print a master document, all subdocuments that the master document contains print in their proper order. Writer's Navigator window is one of the best ways to maneuver through your master document's subdocuments.

130 Create a Master Document

Before You Begin

✔ **129** About Master Documents

As **129** About Master Documents explains, the Navigator window is the key to using master documents effectively. Through the Navigator window, you can do the following:

- Add existing subdocuments to your master document
- Create new subdocuments
- Rearrange the order of the subdocuments

- Remove subdocuments from the master document

- Quickly edit a subdocument

- Update the master document when a subdocument changes

① Create a New Master Document

Select **File**, **New**, **Master Document** from Writer's menu. Writer creates a new, blank master document that looks just like any regular document. In addition, Writer automatically opens the **Navigator** window from where you'll add and manage the subdocuments.

② Add Files to the Master Document

You now must add files to the master document. These files will be Writer documents and may be standalone documents, but when you add them as subdocuments to the master document, these files become linked. Each subdocument's footnotes, table of contents entries, index entries, and caption numbers will interrelate and become dependent on the rest of the subdocuments.

Navigator's first entry is always **Text**, and you should double-click this entry and type some introductory text or some message for your master document (you can later move this text to the end of the master document where it's out of the way). You only need a short note, such as **This is my master document for my book**. This text acts like a global placeholder for all the subdocument styles. It's as though the master document needs to have its own text, even a single line or word of text, that belongs solely to it. The master document then can maintain styles that it links to its text and then can make available to all the other subdocuments when needed.

You now should add the subdocuments. To add a document, click and hold the **Navigator** window's **Insert** button to display a menu. Select **File** from the menu, and the **Insert** dialog box opens. Locate the folder where your files are stored by selecting from the **Look in** list box and then click the document or documents you wish to add to the master document.

 TIP

Hold **Ctrl** while you click to select document names to select multiple documents at once.

Blank Area Shows the Master Document

Navigator Window

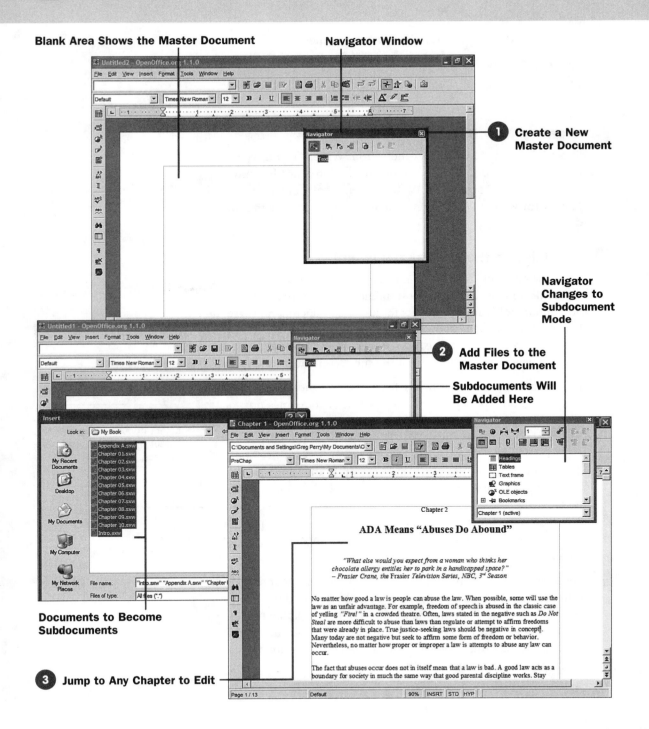

1 Create a New Master Document

Navigator Changes to Subdocument Mode

2 Add Files to the Master Document

Subdocuments Will Be Added Here

Documents to Become Subdocuments

3 Jump to Any Chapter to Edit

Update

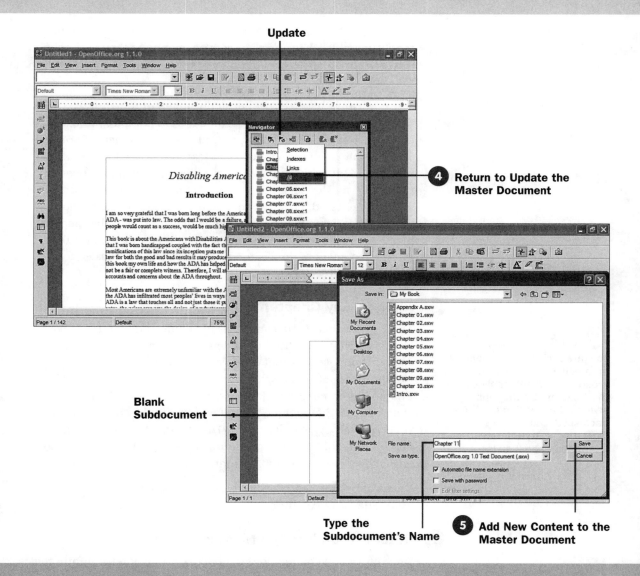

④ Return to Update the Master Document

Blank Subdocument

Type the Subdocument's Name

⑤ Add New Content to the Master Document

Once you've selected the documents to add to your master document, click the **Insert** button. All the subdocuments will become linked to the master document. You will be able to scroll through your entire book by scrolling through the master document. If a subdocument doesn't appear in the order you wish inside the master document, click to select the subdocument and then click the **Move Up** or **Move Down** button to reposition the subdocument in the list.

You now can work with the master document and treat it as though it were a single, huge document. For example, you can print the master document to print all the subdocuments in order. The one thing you cannot do is edit text in any subdocument. To make changes to any subdocument—thereby making changes to the overall master document—you must navigate to the created subdocument and make changes there. You change the formatting, add text, and perform any other edits needed in the subdocument. After editing the subdocument, you then must inform the master document of those changes by updating the master document, as you'll see next.

3 Jump to Any Chapter to Edit

 TIP

To start each subdocument on a new page within the master document, apply the **Heading 1** paragraph style to the first line in each subdocument. See **17** Use a Style for more information about styles.

Think of your master document as the launch pad for any subdocument within your master document. For example, to edit Chapter 2, simply double-click that chapter in the master document's **Navigator** window to display Chapter 2. (You can also highlight Chapter 2's name and click the **Navigator** window's **Edit** button to open Chapter 2 for editing.) You now can edit the chapter just as you would any Writer document. The **Navigator** window turns into a normal document's **Navigator** window, without any of the master document's special **Navigator** window properties.

Once you've finished the edits, save the subdocument with the usual **File**, **Save** command.

4 Return to Update the Master Document

Since you made changes to the subdocument, you must inform the master document of those changes. Open Writer's **Window** menu and select the master document (you can use the **Alt+Tab** keystroke to jump to the master document window as well) to view it. Long-click the **Update** button and choose **All** if you want Writer to update every subdocument's content inside the master document. (If you changed only the selected chapter, choose **Selection**, and if you changed only links, such as footnotes or index entries, select either **Indexes** or **Links**.)

Writer reloads every subdocument in the master document, updates any links, such as footnote and index entries, to maintain their order, and finally updates the master document that you see in the master document's editing area. Any changes you made to a chapter will now appear in the master document, which you can see if you scroll down the master document. Those changes would not have been there before you updated the master document.

5 Add New Content to the Master Document

You aren't required to add pre-existing documents to your master document. You can create new documents that immediately become subdocuments. Long-click the **Navigator** window's **Insert** button and select **New Document** to create a blank, new subdocument. As soon as the subdocument's editing area appears, Writer displays the **Save As** dialog box so you can assign a name to your subdocument. As you type the new subdocument's contents, any index, footnote, caption number, or other master document reference can be updated (with the master document's **Update** button) once you complete the subdocument and return to the master document.

Save the master document when you finish your editing session to ensure that it and the subdocuments are saved and linked properly for your next editing session.

TIP
Save your master document as a PDF file to create an entire eBook readable on many different kinds of computers.

131 About Sharing OpenOffice.org Files with Other Applications

OpenOffice.org plays well with others! Specifically, and most important, OpenOffice.org reads and writes Microsoft Office files with ease. When saving your work in Writer, Calc, or Impress, the **Save As** dialog box always provides you with both OpenOffice.org-based file types as well as Microsoft Office file types. In addition, OpenOffice.org saves files in the StarOffice format, if you elect to do that, although the sheer number of Microsoft Office users around the world makes the sharing of Office data most critical.

See Also

→ **132** Associating OpenOffice.org and Microsoft Office Files

→ **133** Upgrade OpenOffice.org to a New Version

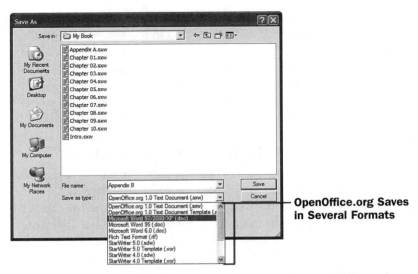

OpenOffice.org Saves in Several Formats

When you save a Writer, Calc, or Impress file, you can elect to save that file in a non-OpenOffice.org format to be read and edited in other programs.

In reality, it is Microsoft Office that is not compatible with OpenOffice.org! Microsoft Office offers no way to save files in OpenOffice.org's native file format. To convert an Office file to OpenOffice.org format, you must first open the Office file and then save the file after selecting an OpenOffice.org format from the **Save as type** list.

NOTE

Microsoft Office provides no native support for PDF files.

Another powerful OpenOffice.org feature is its capability to export documents directly into Adobe's PDF format. Your files are then available to be read on many different systems from all across the Internet. See **36** **Save a Document as a PDF File** for information on the PDF format.

When loading Microsoft Office documents, spreadsheets, and presentations into OpenOffice.org's programs, you may run into conversion problems.

For Microsoft Word documents, these features will not always convert in OpenOffice.org:

- AutoShapes

- Revision marks

- OLE objects

- Some form fields

- Indexes

- Tables, frames, and multicolumn formatting

- Hyperlinks and bookmarks

- WordArt graphics

- Animated characters and text

For Microsoft Excel worksheets, these features will not always convert in OpenOffice.org:

- AutoShapes

- OLE objects

- Some form fields

- Pivot tables

- New chart types

- Conditional formatting

- Some esoteric functions and formulas

For Microsoft PowerPoint presentations, these features will not always convert in OpenOffice.org:

- AutoShapes

- Tab, line, and paragraph spacing

- Master background graphics

- Grouped objects

- Macros

- Some multimedia effects

NOTE

Not every feature in this list is always a problem. For example, many Writer users import Word multicolumn newsletters without any trouble. You cannot rely on 100%-accurate conversions in every case, however.

You can assign file types to certain applications. If you have both Microsoft Office and OpenOffice.org installed on the same computer, you probably want to use one more than the other but still keep both installed. **132 Associating OpenOffice.org and Microsoft Office Files** explains how to select which program opens files related to it. For

KEY TERM

Visual Basic for Applications—Abbreviated as *VBA* and refers to the programming language used to write advanced applications with Microsoft Office.

example, do you want Impress or PowerPoint to be the Windows default program that opens presentation files ending in the .ppt filename extension?

In addition to these features, OpenOffice.org does not support *Visual Basic for Applications*. Some programming macros and codes work, and some do not. Expect a rather extensive conversion effort if you need to convert between VBA and OpenOffice.org's API.

132 Associating OpenOffice.org and Microsoft Office Files

Before You Begin

✔ **131** About Sharing OpenOffice.org Files with Other Applications

See Also

→ **133** Upgrade OpenOffice.org to a New Version

NOTE

To perform Office and OpenOffice.org file associations, you must use OpenOffice.org's Quickstarter program. QuickStarter is a program you must run from your operating system. This task begins by starting Quickstarter from Windows so that you then have access to OpenOffice.org file associations.

If you routinely work with both OpenOffice.org and Microsoft Office files, as you might when you share work with other users, you need a way to associate your files to one program or the other. For example, if you prefer OpenOffice.org but you must regularly edit Microsoft Word documents, you might want to be able to click a Word document, which ends with the .doc filename extension, and have Writer start and load the document automatically. If you have both Office and OpenOffice.org installed, your current file associations might make Word open the file instead.

OpenOffice.org includes a utility program you can run to associate documents, spreadsheets, and presentations to OpenOffice.org instead of to their default Office programs.

 Locate and Run OpenOffice.org Setup

Exit OpenOffice.org if you're currently using one of the OpenOffice.org programs. From the Windows desktop, press **Windows+R** (press your **Windows** key and keep it held while you press **R**, then let up on both) to open the **Run** dialog box. You must install Quickstarter from this Windows **Run** dialog box.

Once the **Run** dialog box appears, click **Browse** to locate your OpenOffice.org installation. Usually, OpenOffice.org resides at C:\Program Files\OpenOffice.org1.1.2, but on your computer you may have installed OpenOffice.org in a different location.

Click to select the file named Setup.lnk and click the **Run** dialog box's **OK** button to start the OpenOffice.org setup program.

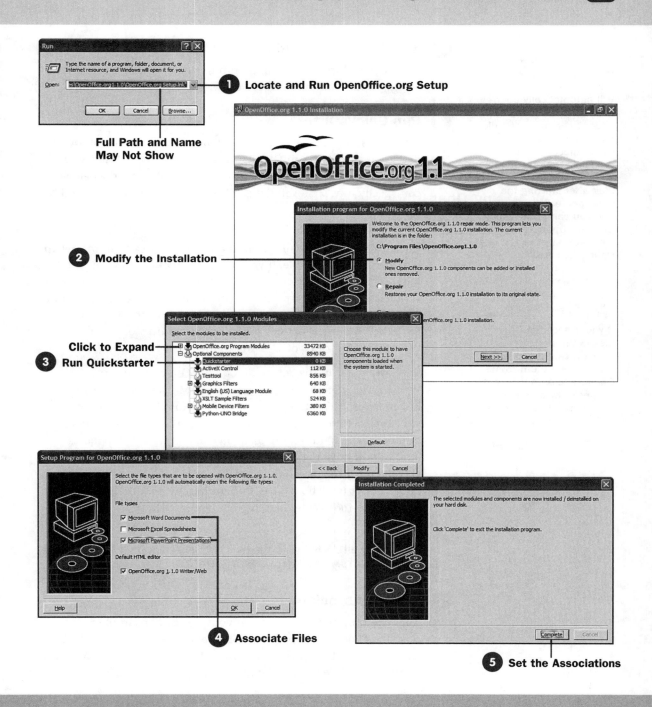

1 Locate and Run OpenOffice.org Setup

Full Path and Name May Not Show

2 Modify the Installation

Click to Expand

3 Run Quickstarter

4 Associate Files

5 Set the Associations

② Modify the Installation

Once OpenOffice.org's Setup program begins, click to select the **Modify** option and then click **Next** to continue with the setup.

③ Run Quickstarter

Click to expand the **Optional Components** entry in the **Modules** dialog box. Click to run **Quickstarter** and then click **Modify** to change Quickstarter settings. A dialog box will appear, where you can specify any Microsoft Office file associations you wish to add.

④ Associate Files

Click any or all of the files from the **File types** section of the **Setup** dialog box. For example, if you want OpenOffice.org to open all Microsoft Word documents and all PowerPoint presentations using Writer and Impress, respectively, you would click the first and third options. Leaving any option unchecked, such as the **Microsoft Excel Spreadsheets** option, means that the Microsoft program will still open those kinds of files automatically.

The last option in the **Setup** dialog box, **OpenOffice.org 1.1.2 Writer/Web**, determines your default HTML Web editor. If you have Microsoft FrontPage installed, for example, when you click your Internet browser's **Edit** button, FrontPage probably starts automatically. With FrontPage, you can edit that Web page as long as you have proper access to do so. The dialog box's **Default HTML editor** section enables you to change to OpenOffice.org's HTML editor (which is Writer's program that handles HTML formatting) so that Writer begins when you click your Web browser's **Edit** button.

Once you've selected your file associations, click **OK** to move to the final dialog box.

⑤ Set the Associations

Click the **Complete** button to set your associations in place and to close the Quickstarter program. The next time you click a Word, Excel, or PowerPoint file in Windows, the appropriate program will automatically start with that file loaded for you to view and edit.

133 Upgrade OpenOffice.org to a New Version

Keep OpenOffice.org up to date, and OpenOffice.org will always perform as well as possible. The authors of OpenOffice.org continually update the programs to add features, correct bugs, and update the help documentation. You should routinely go to the OpenOffice.org Web site to check for updates and add-on programs for OpenOffice.org.

Upgrading OpenOffice.org typically requires that you check your current version and see if a newer one is available on the Web site. If so, you'll download the new version and install it.

1 Check Your Version

From any OpenOffice.org program, select **Help**, **About OpenOffice.org** to see the current version number. Don't go by the graphic logo; check the exact version number you have installed by reading the first line of text in the **About OpenOffice.org** dialog box. Click **OK** to close the **About** dialog box.

2 Check the Latest Online Version

Start your Web browser and traverse to http://OpenOffice.org/ and look for the latest version number. The latest version is usually the very first number on the Web page's main display area. If the version number is greater than the one you've installed, you should upgrade your system to the newer version.

3 Locate the Upgrade

Click the OpenOffice.org Web page's **Download** tab to display the **Download Central** page. The new version to which you'll upgrade will most likely be the first item in the list.

4 Specify Your System

Select your language, operating system, and your closest download site location to begin the download. The **File Download** dialog box will appear. Specify a location and click **Save** to start the transfer of the upgraded version from OpenOffice.org's servers to your computer.

Before You Begin

✔ **131** About Sharing OpenOffice.org Files with Other Applications

✔ **132** Associating OpenOffice.org and Microsoft Office Files

NOTE

Any and all data files you've created in previous versions of OpenOffice.org remain on your disk unchanged when you upgrade.

TIP

With the **About** dialog box still open, you can press **Ctrl+S+D+T** to view a scrolling list of the names of the developers who created OpenOffice.org.

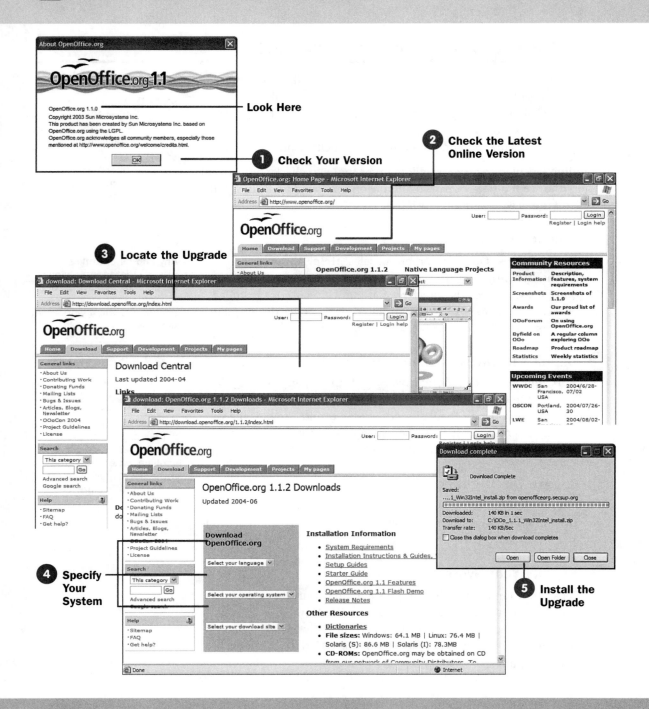

Look Here

OpenOffice.org 1.1.0

1 Check Your Version

2 Check the Latest Online Version

3 Locate the Upgrade

4 Specify Your System

5 Install the Upgrade

⑤ Install the Upgrade

Click **Open** to start the upgrade of your OpenOffice.org installation. The upgrade will act like a new installation, but your current option settings will be retained when possible. You may have to restart your computer when the upgrade finishes to reset everything properly and to start your new version of OpenOffice.org.

Index

Symbols

A

arcs, 127

area charts (Calc), 258

Area command (Draw Format menu), 414

Area dialog box, 413-416

arguments (Calc), 205

arrows

    line conversions, 406

    styles, 407

ascending, 284

asterisks (*)

    bulleted lists, 98

    wildcard searches, 58

AutoCAD Interchange Format (.dxf), 384

AutoComplete (Writer), 142

AutoCorrect (Writer), 143

    adding entries, 146

    deleting entries, 144

    dialog box, 144

    exceptions, 144-147

    mistakes, correcting, 143

    options, 146

    quotes, 146

    replacements, viewing, 144

    undoing, 143

    word completion, 147

AutoCorrect dialog box (Writer), 144

AutoCorrect/AutoFormat command (Writer Tools menu), 144

AutoFilter (Calc), 285

AutoFormat

    Calc, 224, 227-229

    Writer, 143

AutoFormat Chart dialog box, 258

AutoFormat command (Format menu)

    Calc, 229

    Writer, 119

AutoFormat dialog box, 116

    Calc, 229

    tables (Writer), 119

autoformatting tables, 115, 119

AutoLayout (Impress), 302

automatic help (Writer), 142-143

automating

    API, 455

    slide shows, 359, 363

    tasks. *See* macros

AutoPilot

    functions, 210-213

    Impress, 300

    Writer, 36

AutoPilot Letter dialog box, 36

AutoPilot Presentation dialog box, 300

AutoSpellCheck (Writer), 142

Average() function, 206-207

B

backgrounds

    Gallery, 430

    Impress, 297

    presentations, 334-335

    spreadsheets, 234, 239

    Writer, 86

basic fonts options (Writer), 30

bitmap patterns, 416

Bitmaps page (Area dialog box), 416

.bmp (Windows Bitmap) file format, 384

C

How can we make this index more useful? Email us at indexes@samspublishing.com

481

How can we make this index more useful? Email us at indexes@samspublishing.com

483

D

How can we make this index more useful? Email us at indexes@samspublishing.com

485

How can we make this index more useful? Email us at indexes@samspublishing.com

487

How can we make this index more useful? Email us at indexes@samspublishing.com

489

How can we make this index more useful? Email us at indexes@samspublishing.com

491

expressions (mathematical), 138

details, 141

Math object, 140

selecting, 141

symbols, adding, 141

extended tips (help), 22

extensions (files)

Calc, 161

Microsoft Office, 14

F

faxes, 33

fields

databases, 277

Writer, 148

Fields, Page Number command (Writer Insert menu), 151

File menu commands

Calc

Export, 272

Export as PDF, 272

New, Templates and Documents, 247

Open, 161, 168

Page Preview, 189

Print, 189, 274

Save, 161

Templates, Organize, 251

Draw

New, Drawing, 384

Open, 385

Print, 390

Save, 384

Impress

Export, 370

Open, 305

Print, 308

Open, 14

Writer

Export to PDF, 155

New, Master Document, 463

New, Templates and Documents, 94

New, Text Document, 35

Open, 39

Page Preview, 65

Print, 65

Save, 39

Templates, Save, 96

files

compatibilities

Adobe Acrobat, 468

Microsoft Excel, 469

Microsoft Office, 468-472

Microsoft PowerPoint, 469

Microsoft Word, 468

drawing formats, 384

extensions, 14, 161

Microsoft Office, 14

PDFs, 154-156

sharing, 467-470

VBA support, 470

fills

Calc data, 201, 204-205

drawings, 398

handles, 204

shapes, 413-416

Filter, AutoFilter command (Calc Data menu), 287

How can we make this index more useful? Email us at indexes@samspublishing.com

495

H

How can we make this index more useful? Email us at indexes@samspublishing.com

497

J – K

L

M

How can we make this index more useful? Email us at indexes@samspublishing.com

499

N

New, Templates and Documents command (File menu)

    Calc, 247

    Writer, 94

New, Text Document command (Writer File menu), 35

New Snap Object dialog box, 425

New Theme button (Gallery), 436

New Theme (Gallery), 430

newspaper-style documents, 86, 89

nonbreaking spaces, 43

nonprinting characters, 48, 72

Nonprinting Characters button (Main toolbar), 48

Note command (Calc Insert menu), 240

notes

    cells (Calc), 240-242

    presentations, 308

        adding, 363, 366

        presentations, 365

Notes View button, 363

Notes view (Impress), 316, 363

Now() function, 218

numbered lists, 101, 104

Numbering type tab (Numbering/Bullets dialog box), 104

Numbering/Bullets command (Writer Format menu), 101

Numbering/Bullets dialog box

    Bullets tab, 101

    Numbering type tab, 104

numbers (Calc)

    entering, 174

    formatting, 232

O

Object Linking and Embedding (OLE), 344

Object toolbar, 18-19, 398

objects

    3D, 441-442

    aligning, 423, 426

    bitmap patterns, 416

    connections, 378

    copying, 417

    edit points, 418-420

    filling, 398, 413-416

    Gallery, 432, 436-438

    gradients, 416

    grouping, 421-422

    hatching, 416

    Math, 140

    moving, 417

    resizing, 418

    selecting, 417

    transparency, 414

    ungrouping, 422

OLE (Object Linking and Embedding), 344

Open command (File menu), 14

    Calc, 161, 168

    Draw, 385

    Impress, 305

    Writer, 39

Open dialog box

    Draw, 385

    Writer, 39

Open Document command (OpenOffice.org menu), 13

opening

    documents, 37-39

    drawings, 384-386

How can we make this index more useful? Email us at indexes@samspublishing.com

501

P

How can we make this index more useful? Email us at indexes@samspublishing.com

503

Q

R

S

How can we make this index more useful? Email us at indexes@samspublishing.com

505

T

How can we make this index more useful? Email us at indexes@samspublishing.com

509

W

How can we make this index more useful? Email us at indexes@samspublishing.com

513

X – Z

How can we make this index more useful? Email us at indexes@samspublishing.com

515

License Agreement

By opening this package, you are also agreeing to be bound by the following agreement:

You may not copy or redistribute the entire CD-ROM as a whole. Copying and redistribution of individual software programs on the CD-ROM is governed by terms set by individual copyright holders.

The installer and code from the author(s) are copyrighted by the publisher and the author(s). Individual programs and other items on the CD-ROM are copyrighted or are under an Open Source license by their various authors or other copyright holders.

This software is sold as-is without warranty of any kind, either expressed or implied, including but not limited to the implied warranties of merchantability and fitness for a particular purpose. Neither the publisher nor its dealers or distributors assumes any liability for any alleged or actual damages arising from the use of this program. (Some states do not allow for the exclusion of implied warranties, so the exclusion may not apply to you.)

What's on the CD-ROM

The companion CD-ROM contains OpenOffice.org 1.1.2 for Linux, Mac OS X, Solaris (Intel and SPARC), and Windows.

Windows Installation Instructions

1. Insert the disc into your CD-ROM drive and double-click on the My Computer icon.

2. Double-click on the icon representing your CD-ROM drive.

3. Double-click on `start.exe` Follow the on-screen prompts to finish the installation.

Mac OS X Installation Instructions

1. Insert the disc into your CD-ROM drive.

2. Double-click on the CD-ROM icon.

3. Double-click on `Start`. Follow the on-screen prompts to finish the installation.

Linux and Unix Installation Instructions

These installation instructions assume that you have a passing familiarity with UNIX commands and the basic setup of your machine. As UNIX has many flavors, only generic commands are used. If you have any problems with the commands, please consult the appropriate man page or your system administrator.

Insert CD-ROM in CD drive. If you have a volume manager, mounting of the CD-ROM will be automatic. If you don't have a volume manager, you can mount the CD-ROM by typing:

```
mount  -tiso9660  /dev/cdrom  /mnt/cdrom
```

`/mnt/cdrom` is just a mount point, but it must exist when you issue the mount command. You may also use any empty directory for a mount point if you don't want to use `/mnt/cdrom`.

Open the `readme.htm` file for descriptions and installation instructions.

Key Terms

Don't let unfamiliar terms discourage you from learning all you can about OpenOffice.org. If you don't completely understand what one of these words means, flip to the indicated page, read the full definition there, and find techniques related to that term.

Absolute reference *A cell reference that does not change if you copy the formula elsewhere.*   **Page 180**

Anchor *A Writer placeholder that shows itself as an icon of a boat anchor.*   **122**

Anchor point *One corner of a range of cells; typically, the upper-left cell in a range is considered the anchor point.*   **198**

Arc *Half an ellipse, such as a half-moon.*   **127**

Arguments *Values appearing inside a function's parentheses that the function uses in some way to produce its result.*   **205**

Ascending *The sort method where lower values are sorted early in the list and higher values fall at the end of the list.*   **284**

AutoCorrect *The ability of OpenOffice.org programs to analyze what you just typed and replace with a corrected version if needed.*   **143**

AutoFilter *A Calc database filter where you select from a list of values to filter by and view.*   **285**

AutoFit *The ability of AutoFormat to keep the original widths and heights of the cells that AutoFormat formats.*   **229**

AutoFormat *The process that Calc uses to format spreadsheets from a collection of predetermined styles.*   **224**

AutoLayout *A predesigned slide layout for Impress presentation slides.*   **302**

AutoPilot *Preformatted guides that help you create personal and business letters and forms more easily than if you began with a blank page.*   **33**

Cell *A row and column intersection in a Writer or Calc table or spreadsheet.*   **111**

Cell reference *The name of the cell, composed of its column and row intersection, such as G14. This is also called the cell address.*   **162**

Conditional formatting *The process of formatting Calc cells automatically, based on the data they contain.*   **243**

Crop *The cutting off of parts of an image or, in the case of Draw images, the scaled shrinking of an image to a smaller size from within the Crop dialog box.*   **445**

Custom sort list *A predefined list of values (such as month names and the days of the week), or a list you define from the Tools, Options, Spreadsheet, Custom Lists option, that determines a special sorting rank that differs from the normal alphabetic or numerical sorts.*   **Page 285**

Data range *A range you define that specifies exactly which rows and columns comprise the records and fields of your database.*   **280**

Data series *A single, contiguous group of data that you might select from a column or row to chart.*   **258**

Data validity *A check to determine whether data entered into a cell is valid, defined by a set of criteria that you set up.*   **267**

Database *A collection of data that is often organized in rows and columns to make searching and sorting easy to do.*   **276**

Edit points *This term refers to points on your drawing, represented by small square boxes, that you drag to modify that part of the shape or freeform line.*   **397**

Endnotes *A note at the end of a document referenced by number somewhere in the document.*   **152**

Fill handle *A small black box, at the bottom-right corner of a selected cell or range, that you drag to the right (or down or up) to fill the range of data with values related to the selected range.*   **204**

Footer *Text that appears at the bottom of every page in a section or document.*   **148**

Footnotes *A note at the bottom of a page referenced by a number somewhere on the page.*   **152**

Formulas *Equations composed of numeric values and often cell addresses and range names that produce a mathematical result.*   **177**

Functions *Built-in mathematical and logical routines that perform common calculations.*   **194**

Group *A set of two or more selected objects in Draw.*   **421**

Header *Text that appears at the top of every page in a section or document.*   **148**

Hyperlinks *Text that's usually underlined in help screens (and Web pages too) that you can click to navigate to other areas.*   **20**

Insert mode *The state of Writer where new text you type is inserted before existing text. It is indicated by the INSRT message on the status bar.*   **43**